*HAVE A BALL! Love Dad*

# Fodor's 95 London

*by Kate Sekules*

D0451925

PRAISE FOR FODOR'S GUIDES

*"Fodor's guides . . . are an admirable blend of the cultural and the practical."*
—The Washington Post

*"Researched by people chosen because they lived or have lived in the country, well-written, and with good historical sections . . . Obligatory reading for millions of tourists."*
—The Independent, *London*

*"Usable, sophisticated restaurant coverage, with an emphasis on good value."*
—Andy Birsh, Gourmet restaurant columnist, quoted by Gannett News Service

*"Packed with dependable information."*
—Atlanta Journal Constitution

*"Fodor's always delivers high quality . . . thoughtfully presented . . . thorough."*
—Houston Post

*"Valuable because of their comprehensiveness."*
—Minneapolis Star-Tribune

Fodor's Travel Publications, Inc.
New York • Toronto • London • Sydney • Auckland

## Copyright © 1994 by Fodor's Travel Publications, Inc.

ISBN 0–679–02731–9

### Fodor's London

**Editor:** Craig Seligman
**Editorial Contributors:** Robert Blake, John Elsom, Janet Foley, Echo Garrett, Bevin McLaughlin, Ann Saunders, Mary Ellen Schultz, Nancy van Itallie
**Creative Director:** Fabrizio La Rocca
**Cartographer:** David Lindroth
**Illustrator:** Karl Tanner
**Cover Photograph:** Rob Atkins/Image Bank
**Design:** Vignelli Associates

### About the Author

A native Londoner, Kate Sekules writes about travel, food, and fitness for many magazines, including *Vogue*, *BBC Holidays*, and *Health & Fitness*, and for the *Time Out Guide to Eating and Drinking in London*. She also writes fiction and is a longtime Fodor's contributor.

### Special Sales

# Contents

## Maps

# Foreword

While every care has been taken to ensure the accuracy of the information in this guide, the passage of time will always bring change, and consequently, the publisher cannot accept responsibility for errors that may occur.

All prices and opening times quoted here are based on information supplied to us at press time. Hours and admission fees may change, however, and the prudent traveler will avoid inconvenience by calling ahead.

Fodor's wants to hear about your travel experiences, both pleasant and unpleasant. When a hotel or restaurant fails to live up to its billing, let us know and we will investigate the complaint and revise our entries where the facts warrant it.

Send your letters to the editors of Fodor's Travel Publications, 201 E. 50th Street, New York, NY 10022.

# Highlights '95 and Fodor's Choice

# Highlights '95

Sound the trumpets! The 1995 **Festival of Arts and Culture** celebrates the United Kingdom's ample supply of these commodities in what the British Tourist Authority's chairman calls "simply the biggest worldwide celebration ever planned." Still in the embryo stage as we go to press, much of the festival centers on London, especially the parts that coincide with various anniversaries—viz., four centenaries, one bi-, and one tercentenary. The London-based institutions celebrating their 100th birthday are the **Proms,** the egalitarian Albert Hall summer concert series, which culminates in a televised, flag-waving, mass "Land of Hope and Glory" sing-along; the **National Trust,** savior—some say embalmer—of the stately homes of England; **Westminster Cathedral** (not the Abbey); and **Cinema.** The bicentenary is of Hampstead resident **John Keats'**s birth, and the tercentenary is of the great British composer **Henry Purcell'**s death. Festivities include an early summer Keats week and a party on his Halloween birthday, a "National Anthems" program of Purcell choral evensong in a cathedral near you, and a 10-day South Bank Centre Purcell fest in March. They culminate in the September (1995) **London Thames Festival**—three weeks of partying along greater London's 22-mile stretch of the river.

A smaller, simpler scheme to promote London's arts was inaugurated in 1994 and looks set to be repeated this year, although nobody was committing to anything at press time. Whether or not there's a second **London Arts Season** in February and March 1995, one welcome legacy of the first is now here to stay. **The White Card** allows as many visits to the 13 participating museums and galleries as its holder can squeeze in, all for a flat fee of £15 for three days or £30 for a week (these rates are tentative, and may be lower). The Season itself brings the city's major performances and exhibitions together in easy-to-use packages, with a single booking hot line (last year the number was 071/396–4567) and an Information Centre to simplify arts access, and an additional discount docket, the London Arts Card, available free to all. Visit the British Travel Centre at 12 Regent Street for the latest information.

The Thames is seeing all kinds of action this year. Most important, the slightly tired **South Bank Centre**—that cluster of elephant-colored Brutalist blocks across Waterloo Bridge, which contain the core of the capital's arts—is having a total rethink. The Parisian-scale redevelopment, which includes a new 450-seat performance venue, aims to rejuvenate the underexploited Bankside area into a total downtown art city, just in time for the millennium. At press time, 10 architects had got their plans through to the finals; the actual designer of London's biggest development since Canary Wharf (and one that, this time, Londoners may actually use) will have been selected by the time you read this. The money's on the safe options—Richard Rogers (the Lloyds building, Paris's Pompidou Center) or Norman Foster (everything else modernist)—to win the title of Master Planner in charge of turning what the Environment Secretary called "one of London's great wasted assets" into one of its greatest assets.

Also on the South Bank of the Thames, James Bond's successors at **MI6,** Britain's secret service, have just moved into their new riverside eyeblot next to Vauxhall Bridge, designed by the postmodernists' darling, Terry Farrell. This white hulk of a pseudo-Deco aircraft hangar may well make London's spies nostalgic for the days when nobody knew in which building they skulked. You can see it from the **Tate Gallery,** itself expanding somewhere along the river fairly soon, though the decision on whether it will decant part of itself into the former **Bankside Power Station** opposite St. Paul's, into Jubilee Gardens by the Festival Hall, or next to the spies at Vauxhall was on the point of being made at press time. Whatever the Tate decides to do with its outsize collections, *something* notable should be happening soon to Bankside, Giles Gilbert Scott's (he also designed the red telephone box) monumental central-towered brick-built "Temple of Power"—a claim we cannot make for London's other disused power station, poor old **Battersea,** which is still crumbling and empty after seeing many plans bite the dust.

Near Bankside Power Station, the **Shakespeare Globe Theatre,** ambitious dream scheme of the late lamented American movie director and entrepreneur Sam Wanamaker, is slated to open in April 1995, although funds are still needed. You can purchase a permanent London home for your name by donating £300 to the project, for which you will be thanked with an inscribed flagstone in the surrounding piazza. Shakespeare gets celebrated earlier than that, though, at the **Barbican Shakespeare Festival** in October–November 1994—the "largest multi-disciplined Shakespeare festival ever mounted in London," no less.

Back on the Thames, yet more riverfront excitement is imminent on the South Bank, east of Westminster Bridge, at **County Hall,** the former home of the much missed Greater London Council. The structure is now halfway through its conversion into something London needs desperately—a grand hotel on the Thames. Not only will the giant 570-bedroom hotel have the finest views in town—overlooking Westminster Bridge and the Houses of Parliament (with which even the Savoy's beautiful-but-pricey Riverview Suites cannot compete)—but the developers, Shirayama and Virgin Atlantic, are proposing a bargain £90/night rack rate, for which you get a health club with pool, a children's center, conference facilities, and no fewer than six restaurants thrown in. The opening is slated for 1996, by which time **Westminster Bridge** should be about halfway through its £8 million restoration. The construction, of course, will play havoc with one of London's favorite sights, not to mention its traffic flow. The latter problem will be exacerbated by the repairs scheduled for eight other London bridges, some of which will be in progress by the time you read this. In fact, the only bridge guaranteed to be fully operational is the newest: Tower Bridge, which just celebrated its 100th birthday in June 1994, and has already been spruced up, complete with a wonderful new museum inside.

Other hotel news is sparse. All that's really happened, apart from the customary renovations and maintenance, is that Britain's purveyors of the Holiday Camp experience, Butlin's, has opened its first central London camp, or **Butlin's Grand Hotel,** as they insist on calling it. You will notice its absence from our Lodging chapter, and here's why: Although its rack rates are tiny (starting at £99 for a three-night weekend, breakfast and dinner included), Butlin's is a cultural phenomenon so arcane that even most Brits have trouble coping. Imagine a summer camp where parents stay with their kids, enter Knobbly Knee, Glamorous Granny, and Amateur Talent Nite contests, and live on a diet of fries, and you get close. That picture is not entirely fair to an operation as successful as the opening of this enormous Bayswater hotel implies, but Butlin's usefulness is limited to those who want their vacations directed by smiley entertainment police called Redcoats. If the notion appeals, contact Butlin's Grand Hotel (42 Princes Sq., W2 4NJ, tel. 0171/229–1292, fax 0171/221–1176).

The restaurant scene is more lively, and London's new-found foodiness goes from strength to strength. Though only negligible details were available at press time, **Sir Terence Conran** was planning to follow his triumphs at Bibendum, Le Pont de la Tour, and—most recently and enormously—Quaglino's with yet another total dining experience. This one, to be housed in the old Marquee Club in Soho's Wardour Street (famous for showcasing the early Stones, among others), will be roughly the size of Luxembourg, with about twice the covers of Quaglino's and the title of Europe's Largest Restaurant already in the bag. Additional dining notes: Taking orders by the time you read this should be cost-conscious outposts from Big Chefs **Marco Pierre White** (of The Restaurant at the Hyde Park Hotel, and The Canteen), **Bruno Loubet** (of Bistrot Bruno, ex-Four Seasons), and probably **Gary Rhodes** (of the Greenhouse). Marco's is at his old place, Harvey's, in far-off Wandsworth; Bruno's is at a West End brasserie called L'Odeon.

The British political scene—a thing that outsiders often find difficult to penetrate—cheered everyone up during the dreary winter days of '94 with a string of hilarious sex scandals, culminating in the (actually very sad) case of the MP who met his end indulging in an autoerotic fantasy apparently well-known among public schoolboys. The various adulterous affairs, alleged homosexual dalliances, and romantic entanglements with nubile House of Commons research assistants which had led up to this climax had played such havoc with the Tory public image that a Labour Government looked set to succeed for the first time in 15 years. "Labour is the best friend London has," said that party's then leader, John Smith, capitalizing on said Tory weakness, while promising to address London's problems of housing, unemployment, health care, and crime. As we go to press, a new Labour leader is on the point of being elected after Smith's tragically early death. So things have changed again.

Finally, England's capital has been having a fine old time, culturally speaking, with the smell of change in the air as we count down the years to the millennium. Whichever political party leads London into the next century, it will have its purse tied with new strings. The United Kingdom's **National Lottery** kicks off in 1995 and is slated to raise at least £375 million a year, to be distributed among five agencies: the Arts Councils, the National Heritage Memorial Fund, the Sports Councils, the Charities Board, and something mysterious called the **Millennium Fund,** whose only mandate is that it support at least one major project in each country of the United Kingdom. What this £75 million a year until 2001 will contribute to London, nobody yet knows, but possibilities include a national dance house (the Royal Opera House currently serves double duty), a giant-screen movie palace under the aegis of the British Film Institute, and—most enticing of all—a scheme dubbed **Albertopolis,** which would realize Queen Victoria's arts-mad consort's dream of a "cultural high street" around the great South Kensington museums. Albert started the ball rolling in his lifetime, but—as anyone attempting a day out in the Albert Hall environs can verify—the project didn't get very far. Sir Norman Foster (inevitably) already has the plans, so watch this space.

# Fodor's Choice

No two people will agree on what makes a perfect vacation, but it's fun and helpful to know what others think. We hope you'll have a chance to experience some of Fodor's Choices yourself while visiting London. For detailed information about each entry, refer to the appropriate chapters within this guidebook.

## Views

From Waterloo Bridge at dusk, across to St. Paul's

The city seen from Parliament Hill Fields on a bright day

Down the Mall to Buckingham Palace, from underneath Admiralty Arch

The towers of Whitehall seen from St. James's Park, especially when lit up on a summer's night

Greenwich Royal Naval Hospital, viewed from Island Gardens, across the Thames

The Houses of Parliament at sunset, seen across the river from St. Thomas's Hospital

Tower Bridge, floodlit, which confronts you as you come out of the Design Museum on a winter's night

## Walks

Across Kensington Gardens, Hyde Park, and St. James's Park —from Kensington Palace to the Horse Guards

Across Regent's Park at sunset, east (Cumberland Terrace) to west (the Mosque), pausing in summer to watch (or play) softball

Along the South Bank of the Thames, from Lambeth Palace to Blackfriars Bridge

Downriver from Chiswick Mall to Hammersmith Bridge

Across Hampstead Heath, from Hampstead Village to Kenwood

## Parks and Gardens

Chelsea Physic Garden on an uncrowded Wednesday afternoon

Holland Park, dusk, late May, when the rhododendrons are out and there's opera at the theater

Queen Mary's Rose Garden, Regent's Park, in early summer

The Knot Garden at Hampton Court, and the spring tulips in the main gardens there

The Chelsea Flower Show, Royal Hospital, in May

## Monuments

The Duke of Wellington's funeral car in St. Paul's

Admiral Lord Nelson atop his 165-foot Corinthian Column in Trafalgar Square—of course

Wren's Monument to the Great Fire of London

The aluminum Eros (actually the Angel of Christian Charity), Piccadilly Circus

The statue of Winston Churchill in Parliament Square

Karl Marx's outsize black stone head, on his grave at Highgate Cemetery

## Museums

The Wallace Collection, Manchester Square

Sir John Soane's Museum, Lincoln's Inn Fields

The National Portrait Gallery

The Horniman Museum, Dulwich

The British Museum, with plenty of time on your hands

The Natural History Museum, with or without a child

## Times to Treasure

The first day of the Wimbledon Lawn Tennis Championships —then you know it's summer

Tea at Fortnum and Mason's Fountain Restaurant or Browns Hotel

The trip down the Thames to Greenwich

The Oxford and Cambridge Boat Race from the towpath, end of March

Sidewalk dining, Charlotte Street, or a pint of bitter in the garden of the Spaniards Inn, Hampstead

The first night of a new production at the Royal National Theatre

## Shopping

Saturday in the Portobello Road Market

The January sale at Harrods

Wandering round the Covent Garden area

The Burlington Arcade on a wet day

Secondhand book trawling on Charing Cross Road

## Hotels

$$$$ Blakes
The Dorchester
The Savoy
$$$ The Beaufort
Dorset Square
The Gore
Hazlitt's
$$ Basil Street
The Portobello
$ The Vicarage

## Restaurants

$$$$ Bibendum
$$$ The Ivy
Kensington Place
Orso
$$ Bertorelli's
Bistrot Bruno
Fung Shing
Joe Allen's
Wódka
$ Geales
Wagamama

## Pubs

Black Friar
Dove Inn
The Lamb
Prospect of Whitby
Spaniards Inn

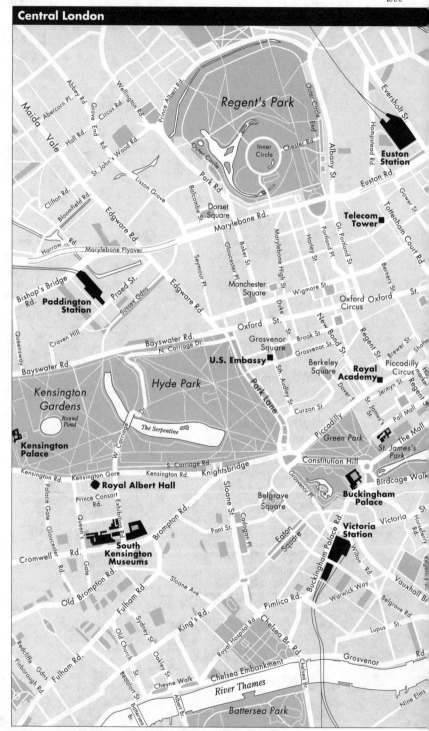

# Central London

Regent's Park

Outer Circle

Inner Circle

Outer Circle

Chester Rd.

Albany St.

Eversholt St.

Hampstead Rd.

**Euston Station**

Maida Vale

Abercorn Pl.

Abbey Rd.

Grove End Rd.

Hall Rd.

Circus Rd.

Wellington Rd.

Prince Albert Rd.

St. John's Wood Rd.

Lisson Grove

Clifton Rd.

Bloomfield Rd.

Harrow Rd.

Edgware Rd.

Marylebone Flyover

Park Rd.

Balcombe St.

Dorset Square

Marylebone Rd.

Gloucester Pl.

Baker St.

Marylebone High St.

Harley St.

Portland Pl.

Gt. Portland St.

Euston Rd.

Gower St.

Tottenham Court Rd.

**Telecom Tower**

Bishop's Bridge Rd.

**Paddington Station**

Praed St.

Sussex Gdns.

Edgware Rd.

Seymour Pl.

Manchester Square

Wigmore St.

Oxford Oxford Circus

Berners St.

St.

Queensway

Craven Hill

Bayswater Rd.

N. Carriage Dr.

Bayswater Rd.

Oxford St.

Duke St.

New Bond St.

Brook St.

**Grosvenor Square**

Grosvenor St.

Regent St.

Brewer St.

Shafte

market

**U.S. Embassy**

Sth. Audley St.

Berkeley Square

Dover St.

**Royal Academy**

Piccadilly Circus

Jermyn St.

Regent St.

**Kensington Gardens**

Round Pond

The Serpentine

**Hyde Park**

W. Carriage Dr.

Park Lane

Curzon St.

Piccadilly

St. James's St.

Pall Mall

The Mall

**Kensington Palace**

Palace Gate

Gloucester Rd.

Queen's Gate

Kensington Rd.

Kensington Gore

S. Carriage Rd.

Kensington Rd.

Knightsbridge

**Green Park**

St. James's Park

Constitution Hill

Birdcage Walk

Prince Consort Rd.

Exhibition Rd.

**Royal Albert Hall**

Brompton Rd.

Sloane St.

Belgrave Square

Grosvenor Pl.

**Buckingham Palace**

Victoria

Horseferry Rd.

Regency St.

Cromwell Rd.

**South Kensington Museums**

Pont St.

Cadogan Pl.

Eaton Square

Buckingham Palace Rd.

**Victoria Station**

Wilton Rd.

Vauxhall Br.

Old Brompton Rd.

Redcliffe Gdns.

Finborough Rd.

Fulham Rd.

Sloane Ave.

Sydney St.

Old Church St.

King's Rd.

Royal Hospital Rd.

Pimlico Rd.

Chelsea Br. Rd.

Warwick Way

Belgrave Rd.

Lupus St.

Beaufort St.

Oakley St.

Cheyne Walk

Chelsea Embankment

Albert Br.

Battersea Br.

Chelsea Br.

**River Thames**

Grosvenor

Rd.

Nine Elms

**Battersea Park**

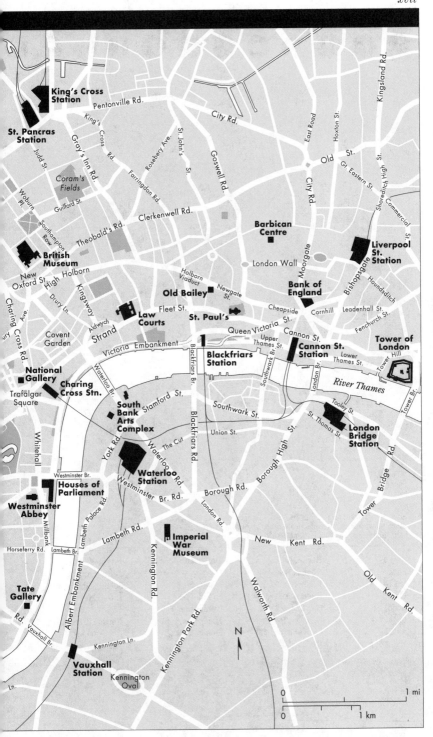

# World Time Zones

Numbers below vertical bands relate each zone to Greenwich Mean Time (0 hrs.).
Local times frequently differ from these general indications,
as indicated by light-face numbers on map.

| | | | |
|---|---|---|---|
| Algiers, **29** | Berlin, **34** | Delhi, **48** | Istanbul, **40** |
| Anchorage, **3** | Bogotá, **19** | Denver, **8** | Jerusalem, **42** |
| Athens, **41** | Budapest, **37** | Djakarta, **53** | Johannesburg, **44** |
| Auckland, **1** | Buenos Aires, **24** | Dublin, **26** | Lima, **20** |
| Baghdad, **46** | Caracas, **22** | Edmonton, **7** | Lisbon, **28** |
| Bangkok, **50** | Chicago, **9** | Hong Kong, **56** | London (Greenwich), **27** |
| Beijing, **54** | Copenhagen, **33** | Honolulu, **2** | Los Angeles, **6** |
| | Dallas, **10** | | Madrid, **38** |
| | | | Manila, **57** |

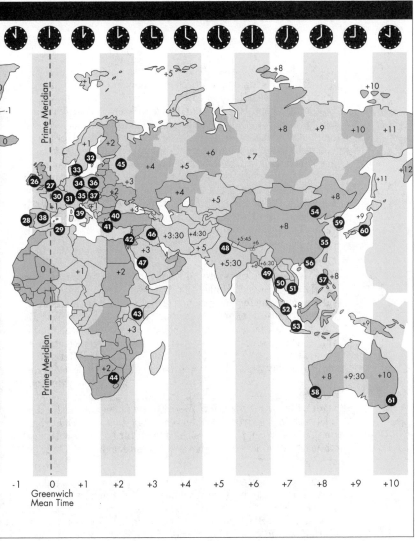

# Introduction

Londoned is an enormous city—600 square miles—on a tiny island, hosting about 7 million Londoners, ⅛ of the entire population of England, Scotland, and Wales; but it has never felt big to me. It is fashioned on a different scale from other capital cities, as if, given the English penchant for modesty and understatement, it felt embarrassed by its size. Each of the 32 boroughs that comprise the whole has its own attitude, and most are subdivided into yet smaller enclaves exhibiting yet more particular behaviors, so that there is really no such person as a generic Londoner. Stay here long enough, and Professor Higgins's feat of deducing Eliza Dolittle's very street of birth from the shape of her vowels will seem like nothing special. It's a cliché, but London really is a city of villages.

I have lived in several of these, and am, through long practice, fluent in the language of a few others, but "my" village, Holland Park, is the one I know best, and it illustrates as well as any how London is changing. Holland Park is small—just a few streets surrounding the former grounds of Holland House, a Jacobean mansion whose remains (it was bombed during World War II) now house a restaurant, a gallery, an open-air theater, and a youth hostel. North of the park, Holland Park Avenue metamorphoses into the windy local high street, Notting Hill Gate, then into bleak Bayswater Road, abutted on its right by Kensington Gardens and Hyde Park before breaking, where the main London gallows once stood, into irritating, commercial Oxford Street. But here, for a few West Eleven moments (postal-district terminology you'd do well to master, to help with navigation), it is a broad, plane tree–lined boulevard, strung with vast white-stuccoed late-Victorian houses and looking an awful lot like Paris.

In our sophisticated age, the European ambience of Holland Park Avenue has been seized upon by niche-marketeers, and we now have two French patisseries, three international newsstands, a BMW showroom, and a candlelit Provencale restaurant within a couple of blocks. The history racket is doing similar things all over town, history being what London has to sell now that it no longer cuts much ice in the world economy. It would be sentimental to prefer the avenue's old hardware store and late-night family grocer (open till 9!) to the fancy Continental shops that have replaced them—London's got to move with the times, after all.

Both good and bad come with the new territory. The Pakistani family who used to take turns minding the grocery store bought the block a decade later. Those Patels are now a well-known London dynasty, with most of the capital's newsstands in their empire—a satisfying reversal of roles from the British Raj days. Meanwhile, homeless Londoners (the number is about 100,000, and rising) work the overpriced yuppie supermarket threshold selling their magazine, *The Big Issue*, for a profit of 25p per guilty conscience. As one of the many villages built during Victoria's reign, Holland Park is a neighborhood unaccustomed to urban blight. But much of London has weathered several centuries of coping with the indigent population.

That's one of the best things about the city: Everything has been seen before, and history is forever poking its nose in. Whatever you're doing, you're doing it on top of a past layered like striated rock. You can see the cross sections clearly sometimes, as in the City, where lumps of Roman wall nest in the postmodern blocks of the street helpfully named London Wall. Walk toward the Thames to Cheapside, which you can tell was the medieval marketplace if you know the meaning of "ceap" ("to barter"), and there's the little Norman church of St. Mary-le-Bow, rebuilt by Wren and then again after the Blitz, but still ringing the Bow Bells. Then look to your right, and you'll be gobsmacked by the dome of St. Paul's. Of course, all you really wanted was to find a place for lunch—which is nearly impossible on a weekend in this office wasteland.

Instead of going weak-kneed at the sights, Londoners are apt to complain about such privations, while pretending simultaneously that no other city in the United Kingdom exists. Edinburghers and Liverpudlians can complain till Big Ben tolls 13, but Londoners continue to pull rank with a complacency that amuses and infuriates visitors in about equal measure. London definitely *used* to be important. The vein of water running through its center has always linked the city with the sea, and it once gave British mariners a head start in the race to mine the world's riches and bring them home. The river proved convenient for building not only palaces (at Westminster, Whitehall, Hampton Court, Richmond, Greenwich) but an empire, too.

The empire dissolved, but the first Thames bridge is still there, in almost the same spot that the emperor Claudius picked in AD 43, and although the current drab concrete incarnation dates only from 1972, it's still called London Bridge. The Tudor one was much better—something I learned before I was 10 from visits to the Museum of London, which used to live nearby in Kensington Palace. I liked the old bridge because of the row of decapitated heads stuck on poles above the gatehouse, which you could see on the model. It added a frisson to history, which more recent exhibitions, like the amazingly popular London Dungeon, have rather cynically packaged.

The old London Bridge lasted 600 years. Lined with shops and houses, it presided over a string of fairs *on* the Thames, when winters were colder and the water froze thick. Nowadays we're lucky to see a single snowfall come winter—and the operative word *is* "lucky." We are genuinely obsessed by the weather, because we have so much of it, though most of it is damp. Snow varies the scenery, stops any tube train with an overground route, makes kids of everyone with a makeshift toboggan and access to a park (which is 99% of the population), and fosters a community spirit normally proscribed by the city's geography and its citizens' cool. Winters were colder as recently as the '60s, when waiting for the crust to thicken enough to skate on the Round Pond in Kensington Gardens—now good only for model-boat sailors and duck feeders—was only a matter of time.

The corollary to our temperate winter, though, is a fresh confidence in summer sufficient to support herds of sidewalk tables. Holland Park Avenue no longer has the monopoly on Parisian ambience. All over town, an epidemic of Continental-style café chains serving croissants and *salade frisée* has devoured the traditional tobacco-stained pubs serving warm bitter and bags of pork scratchings. Most of the remaining pubs have turned into faux-Edwardian parlors with coffee machines and etchings. The change has been going on for about a decade, and it suits London, as does its yet more recent (and momentous) discovery that restaurants are allowed to serve good food in smart surroundings and not charge the earth.

London is increasingly a European city, as if England were no longer stranded alone in the sea. In fact, ever since airplanes superseded ships, this island race has been undergoing an identity crisis, which reached its apogee in the '70s when Prime Minister Edward Heath sailed us irrevocably into the Common Market. Occasionally Britain still holds out against some European Community legislation or other, attempting to reassert differences that are following executions at the Tower and British Colonial supremacy into history. But however much the social climate changes, London is built on a firm foundation. Until the ravens desert the Tower of London—which is when, they say, the kingdom will fall—we have Westminster Abbey, and St. Paul's and the Houses of Parliament, the Georgian squares and grand Victorian houses, the green miles of parks, the river, the museums and galleries and theaters, and 32 boroughs of villages to keep us going.

# 1 Essential Information

# Before You Go

## Government Tourist Offices

Contact the **British Tourist Authority** for information.

**In the United States** 551 5th Ave., Suite 701, New York, NY 10176, tel. 212/986–2200 or 800/462–2748; Suite 1510, 625 N. Michigan Ave., Chicago, IL 60611, tel. 312/787–0490; World Trade Center, 350 S. Figueroa St., Suite 450, Los Angeles, CA 90071, tel. 213/628–3525; 2580 Cumberland Pkwy., Suite 470, Atlanta, GA 30339, tel. 404/432–9635.

**In Canada** 111 Avenue Rd., 4th Floor, Toronto, Ont. M5R 3J8, tel. 416/925–6326.

**In the United Kingdom** Victoria Station Forecourt, London SWIV 1JT, in person only. For phone information, *see* Tourist Information in Staying in London, *below.*

**U.S. Government Travel Briefings** The U.S. Department of State's **Overseas Citizens Emergency Center** (Room 4811, Washington, DC 20520; enclose S.A.S.E.) issues Consular Information Sheets, which cover crime, security, political climate, and health risks as well as embassy locations, entry requirements, currency regulations, and other routine matters. For the latest information, stop in at any U.S. passport office, consulate, or embassy; call the interactive hot line (tel. 202/647–5225; fax 202/647-3000); or, with your PC's modem, tap into the Bureau of Consular Affairs' computer bulletin board (tel. 202/647–9225).

## Tours and Packages

Should you buy your travel arrangements to London packaged or do it yourself? There are advantages either way. Buying packaged arrangements saves you money, particularly if you can find a program that includes exactly the features you want. You also get a pretty good idea of what your trip will cost from the outset. You have two options: fully escorted tours and independent packages. Escorted tours mean having limited free time and traveling with strangers. Escorted tours are most often via motorcoach, with a tour director in charge. Your baggage is handled, your time rigorously scheduled, and most meals planned. Escorted tours can therefore be the most hassle-free way to see London, as well as usually the least expensive. Independent packages allow plenty of flexibility. They generally include airline travel and hotels, with certain options available, such as sightseeing, car rental, and excursions. Independent packages are usually more expensive than escorted tours, but your time is your own.

While you can book directly through tour operators, you will pay no more to go through a travel agent, who will be able to tell you about tours and packages from a number of operators. Whatever program you ultimately choose, be sure to find out exactly what is included: taxes, tips, transfers, meals, baggage handling, ground transportation, entertainment, excursions, sports or recreation (and rental equipment if necessary). Ask about the level of hotel used, its location, the size of its rooms, the kind of beds, and its amenities, such as pool, room service, or programs for children, if they're important to you. Find out the operator's cancellation penalties. Nearly everyone charges them, and the only way to avoid them is to buy trip-cancellation insurance (*see* Insurance, *below*). Also ask about the single supplement, a surcharge assessed to solo travelers. Some operators do not make you pay it if you agree to be matched up with a roommate of the same sex, even if one is not found by departure time. Remember that a program that has features you won't use may not be the most cost-wise choice.

**Fully Escorted Tours**
Escorted tours are usually sold in three categories: deluxe, first-class, and tourist or budget class. The most important differences are the price and the level of accommodations. Some operators specialize in one category, while others offer a range. Many escorted tour operators allow you to purchase additional nights in London either before or after your tour. Most also offer theater tickets. So, technically, part of your trip is actually "independent." Look into **Certified Vacations** (Box 1525, Ft. Lauderdale, FL 33302, tel. 305/522–1414 or 800/233–7260); **Globus** (5301 S. Federal Circle, Littleton, CO 80123, tel. 303/797–2800 or 800/221–0090); **Trafalgar Tours** (21 E. 26th St., New York, NY 10010, tel. 212/689–8977 or 800/854–0103); **Olson-Travelworld** (970 W. 190th St., Suite 425, Torrance, CA 90502, tel. 310/546–8400, 800/421–5785, or 800/421–2255 from CA); and **V E Tours** (7270 N.W. 12th St., Suite 210, Miami, FL 33126, tel. 800/222–8383). Budget offerings include programs by **AESU Travel** (2 Hamill Rd., Suite 248, Baltimore, MD 21210, tel. 410/323–4416 or 800/638–7640), **Cosmos Tourama,** a sister company of **Globus** (*see above*), and the "Cost Savers" of **Trafalgar Tours** (*see above*).

Most itineraries are jam-packed with sightseeing, so you see a lot in a short amount of time (usually one place per day). To judge just how fast-paced the tour is, review the itinerary carefully. If you are in a different hotel each night, you will be getting up early each day to head out, travel to your next destination, do some sightseeing, have dinner, and go to bed, then you'll start all over again. If you want some free time, make sure it's mentioned in the tour brochure; if you want to be escorted to every meal, confirm that any tour you consider does that. Also, when comparing programs, be sure to find out if the motorcoach is air-conditioned and has a rest room on board. Make your selection based on price and stops on the itinerary.

**Independent Packages**
Independent packages, which travel agents call FITs (for foreign independent travel), are offered by airlines, tour operators who may also do escorted programs, and any number of other companies from large, established firms to small, new entrepreneurs. Their programs come in a wide range of prices based on levels of luxury and options—in addition to hotel and airfare, sightseeing, car rental, transfers, admission to local attractions, and other extras.

**European Holidays** (137 S. Pugh St., State College, PA 16801, tel. 814/238–3557 or 800/752–9578) has a "London Stay Put" package with city tours and countryside excursions. **Trafalgar Tours** (*see above*) does a London theater week that includes airfare, hotel, Continental breakfast daily, and theater tickets. Other independent packages are offered by **Abercrombie & Kent** (1520 Kensington Rd., Oak Brook, IL 60521, tel. 708/954–2944 or 800/323–7308); **American Airlines Fly AAway Vacations** (tel. 800/321–2121); **British Airways** (tel. 800/AIR–WAYS); **CIE Tours** (108 Ridgedale Ave., Morristown, NJ 07960, tel. 201/292–3438 or 800/CIE–TOUR); **Continental Airlines' Grand Destinations** (tel. 800/634–5555); **DER Tours** (11933 Wilshire Blvd., Los Angeles, CA 90025, tel. 310/479–4140 or 800/782–2424); **TWA Getaway Vacations** (tel. 800/438–2929); and **United Airlines' Vacation Planning Center** (tel. 800/328–6877).

Note that when pricing different packages, it sometimes pays to purchase the same arrangements separately, as when a rock-bottom promotional airfare is being offered, for example. Again, base your choice on what's available at your budget for the destinations you want to visit.

**Special-Interest Travel**  Many of London's special-interest tours focus on annual events like the Chelsea Flower Show and Wimbledon. Special-interest programs may be fully escorted or independent. Some require a certain amount of expertise, but most are for the average traveler with an interest and are usually hosted by experts in the subject matter. When the program is escorted, it enjoys the advantages and disadvantages of all escorted programs; because your fellow travelers are apt to be passionate or knowledgeable about the subject, they can prove as enjoyable a part of your travel experience as the destination itself. The price range is wide, but the cost is usually higher—sometimes a lot higher—than for ordinary escorted tours and packages, because of the expert guiding and special activities.

*Culture*  **Polly Stewart Fritch** (1 Scott La., Greenwich, CT 06831, tel. 203/661–7742) offers "cross-culinary" tours with cooking demonstrations and behind-the-scenes visits to unique markets.

*Flower Shows*  **Trafalgar Tours** (*see above*) does a program in May to the Chelsea Flower Show. **Coopersmith's England** (6441 Valley View Rd., Oakland, CA 94611, tel. 510/339–2499) combines admission to the Chelsea Flower Show with visits to stately homes and gardens in the region.

*Music and Theater*  **Dailey-Thorp Travel** (330 W. 58th St., New York, NY 10019, tel. 212/307–1555; book through travel agents), which specializes in music and opera, has a London Theater Week; **Keith Prowse & Co.** (234 W. 44th St., Suite 1000, New York, NY 10036, tel. 212/398–1430 or 800/669–7469) also offers theater packages and tours. Other agents who sell tickets to London theater, music festivals, or concerts include: **Edwards & Edwards** (tel. 212/944–0290 or 800/366–4845), **European Tours** (tel. 401/272–5005), **London Stages** (tel. 818/881–8433 or 800/729–8432), **London Theatre & More** (tel. 214/369–1962 or 800/683–0799), **Showline** (tel. 201/962–9246 or 800/962–9246), and **Sterling Tours** (tel. 619/299–3010) or 800/727–4359).

*Singles and Young Couples*  **AESU Travel** (*see above*), **Contiki** (tel. 714/740–0808 or 800/266–8454), and **Trafalgar Tours** (*see above*) have programs designed for travelers ages 35 and under, with some free time.

*Sports*  **Steve Furgal's International Tennis Tours** (11828 Rancho Bernardo Rd., Suite 123-305, San Diego, CA 92128, tel. 619/487–7777 or 800/258–3664) does tours to Wimbledon. **Keith Prowse & Co.** (*see above*) has packages to Wimbledon, the British Open, and Royal Ascot. **Sportsworld Travel** (1730 Northeast Expressway, Atlanta, GA 30329, tel. 800/278–6738) also handles packages to Wimbledon. **Trafalgar Tours** (*see above*) also does a special package to the Grand National horse show that includes not only tickets but also admission to a catered, private tent.

## When to Go

The heaviest tourist season in Britain runs from mid-April to mid-October, with a small peak around Christmas—though the tide never really ebbs away. The spring is the time to see the countryside and the London gardens at their freshest; early summer to catch the roses and full garden splendor; the fall for near-ideal exploring conditions. The British take their vacations mainly in July and August, and the resorts are crowded. London in summer, however, though full of visitors, is also full of interesting things to see and do. But be warned: Air-conditioning is *very* rare in London, and in a hot summer you'll swelter. The winter can be rather dismal and is frequently wet and usually cold, but all the theaters, concerts, and exhibitions are going full speed.

**Climate** London's weather has always been contrary, and in recent years it has become positively erratic, with hot summers and mild winters proving the greenhouse effect is running rampant over Britain. It is virtually impossible to forecast what the pattern might be, but you can be fairly certain that it will not be what you expect! The main feature of the British weather is that it is generally mild—with some savage exceptions, especially in summer. It is also fairly damp—though even that has been changing in recent years with recurring periods of drought.

What follows are the average daily maximum and minimum temperatures for London.

| Jan. | 43F | 6C | May | 62F | 17C | Sept. | 65F | 19C |
|------|-----|-----|------|-----|-----|-------|-----|-----|
| | 36 | 2 | | 47 | 8 | | 52 | 11 |
| Feb. | 44F | 7C | June | 69F | 20C | Oct. | 58F | 14C |
| | 36 | 2 | | 53 | 12 | | 46 | 8 |
| Mar. | 50F | 10C | July | 71F | 22C | Nov. | 50F | 10C |
| | 38 | 3 | | 56 | 14 | | 42 | 5 |
| Apr. | 56F | 13C | Aug. | 71F | 21C | Dec. | 45F | 7C |
| | 42 | 6 | | 56 | 13 | | 38 | 4 |

*Information* For current weather conditions and forecasts for cities in the United
*Sources* States and abroad, plus the local time and helpful travel tips, call the **Weather Channel Connection** (tel. 900/932–8437; 95¢ per minute) from a touch-tone phone.

## Festivals and Seasonal Events

Top seasonal events in and around London include the Chelsea Flower Show in May, the queen's official birthday parade in June, Derby Day at Epsom Racecourse in June, and Wimbledon Lawn Tennis Championships and Henley Regatta in June. Tickets for the prestigious sporting events must be obtained months in advance. There is a complete list of ticket agencies in *Britain Events*, available from the **British Travel Centre** (12 Regent St., London SW17 4PQ, in person only).

**Jan. 5–15: London International Boat Show,** the largest boat show in Europe. Earl's Court Exhibition Centre, Warwick Rd., London SW5 9TA, tel. 01784/473–377.

**Mar. 7–18 and Sept. 12–23: Chelsea Antiques Fair,** a twice-yearly fair with wide range of pre-1830 pieces for sale. Old Town Hall, King's Rd., Chelsea SW3 4PW, tel. 01444/482–514.

**Mar. 16–Apr. 9: Daily Mail Ideal Home Exhibition,** consumer show of new products and ideas for the home. Earl's Court Exhibition Centre, Warwick Rd., London SW5 9TA, tel. 01895/677–677.

**During Mar.: Camden Jazz Festival** is 10 days of concerts sponsored by the Borough of Camden. For information, call 0171/860–5866.

**Mid-Apr.: London Marathon,** a New York–style marathon through London's streets. Information from Box 262, Richmond, Surrey TW10 5JB, tel. 0181/948–7935.

**May 3–9: British Antique Dealers' Association Fair,** the newest of the major fairs: large and prestigious, with many affordable pieces. Information from BADA, Oriel House, 26 The Quadrant, Richmond, Surrey TW9 1DL, tel. 0181/948–9802.

**May 10–14: Royal Windsor Horse Show,** a major show-jumping event attended by some members of the Royal Family. Show Box Office, 4 Grove Parade, Buxton, Derbyshire SK17 6AJ, tel. 01298/72272.

**May 23–26: Chelsea Flower Show,** Britain's major flower show, covers 22 acres. Royal Hospital Rd., Chelsea SW3, tel. 0171/630–7422.

**Late May–Late Aug.: Glyndebourne Festival Opera** is a unique opportunity to see international stars in a bucolic setting, with a newly refurbished theater. Tickets go fast and early. Glyndebourne Festival Opera, Lewes, Sussex BN8 5UU, tel. 01273/812–321.

**Early June: Beating Retreat by the Guards Massed Bands,** when more than 500 musicians parade at Horse Guards, Whitehall. Tickets from Household Division Fund, Block 8, Wellington Barracks, Birdcage Walk, London SW1E 6HQ, tel. 0171/414–3253.

**June 7: Derby Day** is the best-known event in the horse-racing calendar. This year, it may change from Wednesday to Saturday the 3rd or 10th, so call to check. Information from United Racecourses Ltd., Racecourse Paddock, Epsom, Surrey KT18 5NJ, tel. 013727/26311.

**June 4: Trooping the Colour,** Queen Elizabeth's colorful official birthday parade, is held at Horse Guards, Whitehall. Write for tickets *only* between January 1 and February 28, enclosing a self-addressed stamped envelope: Ticket Office, Headquarters, Household Division, Chelsea Barracks, London SW1H 8RF, tel. 0171/414–2497.

**June 15–24: The Grosvenor House Antiques Fair** is one of the most prestigious antiques fairs in Britain. Grosvenor House Hotel, Park La., London W1A 3AA, tel. 0171/499–6363.

**June 20–July 3: Wimbledon Lawn Tennis Championships,** held at the All England Lawn Tennis and Croquet Club in Wimbledon. Write early to enter the lottery for tickets for Centre and Number One courts; tickets for outside courts available daily at the gate. Church Rd., Wimbledon, London SW19 5AE, tel. 0181/946–2244.

**June 28–July 2: Henley Royal Regatta,** an international rowing event and top social occasion, at Henley-upon-Thames, Oxfordshire. For information, call 01491/572–153.

**Mid-July–mid-Sept.: Henry Wood Promenade Concerts,** a marvelous series of concerts at the Royal Albert Hall. Box Office, Royal Albert Hall, Kensington Gore SW7 2AP, tel. 0171/589–8212.

**July 9–26: City of London Festival** is an arts festival held throughout the City. For information, call 0171/377–0540.

**July 18–29: The Royal Tournament** features military displays and pageantry by the Royal Navy, the Royal Marines, the Army, and the Royal Air Force. Earl's Court Exhibition Centre, Warwick Rd., London SW5 9TA, tel. 0171/370–8226.

**Oct. 3–8: The Horse of the Year Show** has the world's top show jumpers at the Wembley Arena. At press time, Sept. 26–Oct. 1 were possible alternative dates. Show Box Office, 4 Grove Parade, Buxton, Derbyshire SK17 6AJ, tel. 01298/72272.

**Nov. 5: London to Brighton Veteran Car Run,** a run from Hyde Park in London to Brighton in East Sussex. No tickets required. For information, call 01753/681–736.

**Mid-Nov.: Lord Mayor's Procession and Show.** At the lord mayor's inauguration, a procession takes place from the Guildhall in the City to the Royal Courts of Justice. No tickets required. For information, call 0171/606–3030.

**Dec. 14–18: Olympia International Show Jumping Championships,** international equestrian competition in Olympia's Grand Hall. For information, call 0171/370–8209.

**What to Pack**

Clothing   You'll need an overcoat for winter and a light coat or warm jacket for summer, and there's rarely a time of year when a raincoat or an umbrella won't come in handy. As in any American city, jackets and ties are appropriate for expensive restaurants and night spots; casual clothes are fine elsewhere. Jeans are as popular in Great Britain as they are at home and are perfectly acceptable for sightseeing and informal dining. Tweeds and nonmatching jackets are popular here with men. For women, ordinary street dress is acceptable everywhere.

Miscellaneous   Bring an extra pair of eyeglasses or contact lenses in your carry-on luggage. If you have a health problem that may require you to purchase a prescription drug, take enough to last the duration of the trip or have your doctor write a prescription using the drug's generic name, as brand names vary from country to country. Always carry prescription drugs in their original packaging to avoid problems with customs officials. Don't pack them in luggage that you plan to check in case your bags go astray. If you plan to stay in budget hotels, take your own soap. Don't forget to pack a list of the addresses of offices that supply refunds for lost or stolen traveler's checks.

Electricity   The electrical current in London is 220 volts, 50 cycles alternating current (AC); the United States runs on 110-volt, 60-cycle AC current. Unlike wall outlets in the United States, which accept plugs with two flat prongs, outlets in London take plugs with three prongs.

*Adapters,*   To use U.S.-made electrical appliances abroad, you'll need an adapt-
*Converters,*   er plug. Unless the appliance is dual-voltage and made for travel,
*Transformers*   you'll also need a converter. Hotels sometimes have 110-volt outlets for low-wattage appliances marked "For Shavers Only" near the sink; don't use them for a high-wattage appliance like a blow-dryer. If you're traveling with an older laptop computer, carry a transformer. New laptop computers are auto-sensing, operating equally well on 110 and 220 volts, so you need only the appropriate adapter plug. For a copy of the free brochure "Foreign Electricity Is No Deep Dark Secret," send a self-addressed, stamped envelope to adapter-converter manufacturer Franzus Company (Customer Service, Dept. B50, Murtha Industrial Park, Box 142, Beacon Falls, CT 06403, tel. 203/723–6664).

Luggage   Free airline baggage allowances depend on the airline, the route,
*Regulations*   and the class of your ticket; ask in advance. In general, on domestic flights and on international flights between the United States and foreign destinations, you are entitled to check two bags—neither exceeding 62 inches, or 158 centimeters (length + width + height), or weighing more than 70 pounds (32 kilograms). A third piece may be brought aboard as a carryon; its total dimensions are generally limited to less than 45 inches (114 centimeters), so it will fit easily under the seat in front of you or in the overhead compartment. In the United States the Federal Aviation Administration (FAA) gives airlines broad latitude to limit carry-on allowances and tailor them to different aircraft and operational conditions. Charges for excess, oversize, or overweight pieces vary, so inquire before you pack.

If you are flying between two foreign destinations, note that baggage allowances may be determined not by the piece method but by the weight method, which generally allows 88 pounds (40 kilograms) of luggage in first class, 66 pounds (30 kilograms) in business class, and 44 pounds (20 kilograms) in economy. If your flight between two cities abroad *connects* with your transatlantic or transpacific flight, the piece method still applies.

*Safeguarding Your Luggage* Before leaving home, itemize your bags' contents and their worth in case they go astray. To minimize that risk, tag them inside and out with your name, address, and phone number. (If you use your home address, cover it so that potential thieves can't see it.) Put a copy of your itinerary inside each bag so that you can easily be tracked. At check-in, make sure that the tag attached by baggage handlers bears the correct three-letter code for your destination. If your bags do not arrive with you, or if you detect damage, immediately file a written report with the airline before you leave the airport.

## Taking Money Abroad

Traveler's Checks Traveler's checks are preferable in metropolitan centers, although you'll need cash in rural areas and small towns. The most widely recognized are **American Express, Citicorp, Diners Club, Thomas Cook,** and **Visa,** which are sold by major commercial banks. Both American Express and Thomas Cook issue checks that can be countersigned and used by you or your traveling companion. Typically the issuing company or the bank at which you make your purchase charges 1% to 3% of the checks' face value as a fee. Some foreign banks charge as much as 20% of the face value as the fee for cashing traveler's checks in a foreign currency. Buy a few checks in small denominations to cash toward the end of your trip, so you won't be left with excess foreign currency. Record the numbers of checks as you spend them, and keep this list separate from the checks.

Currency Exchange Banks offer the most favorable exchange rates. If you use currency exchange booths at airports, rail and bus stations, hotels, stores, and privately run exchange firms, you'll typically get less favorable rates, but you may find the hours more convenient.

You can get good rates and avoid long lines at airport currency-exchange booths by getting a small amount of currency at **Thomas Cook Currency Services** (630 5th Ave., New York, NY 10111, tel. 212/757–6915 or 800/223–7373 for locations in major metropolitan areas throughout the United States) or **Ruesch International** (tel. 800/424–2923 for locations) before you depart. Check with your travel agent to be sure that the currency of the country you will be visiting can be imported.

## Getting Money from Home

Cash Machines Many automated teller machines (ATMs) are tied to international networks such as **Cirrus** and **Plus.** You can use your bank card at ATMs away from home to withdraw money from your checking account and get cash advances on a credit-card account if your card has been programmed with a personal identification number, or PIN. Check in advance on limits on withdrawals and cash advances within specified periods. If you know your PIN number as a word, learn the numerical equivalent: Keypads on many British ATMs show no letters, only numbers. Ask whether your bank-card or credit-card PIN will need to be reprogrammed for use in the area you'll be visiting. Four digits are commonly used overseas. Note that Discover is accepted only in the United States. On cash advances you are charged interest from the day you receive the money from ATMs as well as from tellers. Although transaction fees for ATM withdrawals abroad may be higher than fees for withdrawals at home, Cirrus and

Plus exchange rates are excellent, because they are based on whole-sale rates only offered by major banks.

Be sure to plan ahead: Obtain ATM locations and the names of affiliated cash-machine networks before departure. For specific foreign Cirrus locations, call 800/424–7787; for foreign Plus locations, consult the Plus directory at your local bank.

**Wiring Money**  You don't have to be a cardholder to send or receive a **MoneyGram from American Express** for up to $10,000. Go to a MoneyGram agent in retail and convenience stores and American Express travel offices, pay up to $1,000 with a credit card and anything over that in cash. You are allowed a free long-distance call to give the transaction code to your intended recipient, who needs only present identification and the reference number to the nearest MoneyGram agent to pick up the cash. MoneyGram agents are in more than 70 countries (call 800/926–9400 for locations). Fees range from 3% to 10%, depending on the amount and how you pay.

You can also use **Western Union.** To wire money, take either cash or a cashier's check to the nearest office or call and use your MasterCard or Visa. Money sent from the United States or Canada will be available for pick up at agent locations in Great Britain within minutes. Once the money is in the system it can be picked up at *any* one of 22,000 locations (call 800/325–6000 for the one nearest you).

## British Currency

The units of currency in Great Britain are pound sterling (£) and pence (p): £50, £20, £10, and £5 bills; £1 (100p), 50p, 20p, 10p, 5p, 2p, and 1p coins. At press time, the exchange rate was about $1.50 U.S. dollars, or $2 Canadian dollars, to the British pound.

## What It Will Cost

London *can* be an expensive city to visit, but, with care, you need not find it so. The dollar-sterling exchange rate has finally turned in the dollar's favor, so if you haven't visited in a few years, you may be pleasantly surprised. You should still watch where you cash your traveler's checks, since rates and service charges vary considerably.

The main item on your budget will be your hotel. London hotels are expensive relative to those in other European countries, and the service that they offer is not always commensurate with the amount they charge. The better-value hotels often lie outside the central area of the city, which means adding transportation costs to the hotel rate, and so reducing the benefit.

The situation with restaurants is very different. London is bursting with eating places of every price and cuisine; finding somewhere to match both your palate and your pocketbook will be no problem at all. (For price ranges for hotels and restaurants *see* Chapter 5, Lodging, and Chapter 6, Dining.)

Getting around town can be expensive, but the Underground (subway) and bus systems run on a simple area system, with plenty of special tickets on offer for visitors. The cost will depend on the length of your stay and the amount of use you want to make of the facilities—the more you use the travel cards, the greater the savings. (*See* Getting Around London in Staying in London, *below*.)

**Sample Costs** A movie in the West End costs £5–£9.50 (less on Mondays and at matinees); a theater seat, from £6 to about £20, more for hit shows; admission to a museum or gallery, around £3 (though many are free); coffee, around £1; a pint of light (lager) beer in a pub, £1.70; whiskey, gin, vodka, and so forth, by the glass in a pub, £1.50 and up (the measure is smaller than in the United States); house wine by the glass in a pub or wine bar, around £1.50, in a restaurant, £3.50; a Coke, around 80p; a ham sandwich from a sandwich bar in the West End, £1.80; a one-mile taxi ride, £4; an average Underground or bus ride, £1.20, a longer one, £2.10.

## Long-Distance Calling

AT&T, MCI, and Sprint have several services that make calling home or the office more affordable and convenient when you're on the road. Use one of them to avoid pricey hotel surcharges. **AT&T** Calling Card (tel. 800/225–5288) and the AT&T Universal Card (tel. 800/662–7759) give you access to the service. With AT&T's USADirect (tel. 800/874–4000 for codes in the countries you'll be visiting) you can reach an AT&T operator with a local or toll-free call. **MCI**'s Call USA (MCI Customer Service, tel. 800/444–4444) allows that service from 85 countries or from country to country via MCI WorldReach. **Sprint** Express (tel. 800/877–4646) has a toll-free number travelers abroad can dial to reach a Sprint operator in the United States.

## Passports and Visas

If your passport is lost or stolen abroad, report it immediately to the nearest embassy or consulate and to the local police. If you can provide the consular officer with the information contained in the passport, he or she will usually be able to issue you a new passport. For this reason, it is a good idea to keep a photocopy of the data page of your passport separate from your money and traveler's checks. Also leave a photocopy with a relative or friend at home.

**U.S. Citizens** All U.S. citizens, even infants, need a valid passport to enter Great Britain for stays of up to six months.

You can pick up new and renewal application forms at any of the 13 U.S. Passport Agency offices and at some post offices and courthouses. Although passports are usually mailed within four weeks of your application's receipt, allow five weeks or more from April through summer. Call the Department of State Office of Passport Services' information line (tel. 202/647–0518) for fees, documentation requirements, and other details.

**Canadian Citizens** Canadian citizens need a valid passport to enter Great Britain for stays of up to six months.

Application forms are available at 23 regional passport offices as well as at post offices and travel agencies. Whether applying for a first or subsequent passport, you must apply in person. Children under 16 may be included on a parent's passport but must have their own passport to travel alone. Passports are valid for five years and are usually mailed within two weeks of an application's receipt. For more information in English or French, call the passport office (tel. 514/283–2152 or 800/567–6868).

## Customs and Duties

**On Arrival** There are two levels of duty-free allowance for travelers entering Great Britain: one for goods bought outside the EC, the other for goods bought in the EC (Belgium, Greece, the Netherlands, Denmark, Italy, Portugal, France, the Irish Republic, Spain, Germany, or Luxembourg).

In the first category, you may import duty-free: 200 cigarettes or 100 cigarillos or 50 cigars or 250 grams of tobacco; two liters of table wine and, in addition, (a) one liter of alcohol over 22% by volume (most spirits), (b) two liters of alcohol under 22% by volume (fortified or sparkling wine), or (c) two more liters of table wine; 50 milliliters of perfume; ¼ liter of toilet water; and other goods up to a value of £36, but not more than 50 liters of beer or 25 cigarette lighters.

In the second category, the EC has set guidelines for the import of certain goods. Following side trips entirely within the EC, you no longer need to go through Customs on your return to the United Kingdom; however, if you exceed the guideline amounts, you may be required to prove that the goods are for your personal use only ("personal use" includes gifts). The guideline levels are: 800 cigarettes, 400 cigarillos, 200 cigars, and 1 kilogram of smoking tobacco, plus 10 liters of spirits, 20 liters of fortified wine, 90 liters of wine, and 110 liters of beer. No animals or pets of any kind can be brought into the United Kingdom without a lengthy quarantine. The penalties are severe and strictly enforced. Similarly, fresh meats, plants and vegetables, controlled drugs, and firearms and ammunition may not be brought into Great Britain.

You will face no customs formalities if you enter Scotland or Wales from any other part of the United Kingdom, though anyone coming from Northern Ireland should expect a security check.

**Returning Home** **U.S. Customs** If you've been out of the country for at least 48 hours and haven't already used the exemption, or any part of it, in the past 30 days, you may bring home $400 worth of foreign goods duty-free. So can each member of your family, regardless of age; and your exemptions may be pooled, so one of you can bring in more if another brings in less. A flat 10% duty applies to the next $1,000 of goods; above $1,400, the rate varies with the merchandise. (If the 48-hour or 30-day limits apply, your duty-free allowance drops to $25, which may not be pooled.) Please note that these are the *general* rules, applicable to most countries, including Great Britain.

Travelers 21 or older may bring back one liter of alcohol duty-free, provided the beverage laws of the state through which they reenter the United States allow it. In addition, 100 non-Cuban cigars and 200 cigarettes are allowed, regardless of your age. Antiques and works of art more than 100 years old are duty-free.

Gifts valued at less than $50 may be mailed to the United States duty-free, with a limit of one package per day per addressee, and do not count as part of your exemption (do not send alcohol or tobacco products or perfume valued at more than $5); mark the package "Unsolicited Gift" and write the nature of the gift and its retail value on the outside. Most reputable stores will handle the mailing for you.

For a copy of "Know Before You Go," a free brochure detailing what you may and may not bring back to the United States, rates of duty, and other pointers, contact the U.S. Customs Service (Box 7407, Washington, DC 20044, tel. 202/927–6724).

*Canadian* Once per calendar year, when you've been out of Canada for at least
*Customs* seven days, you may bring in C$300 worth of goods duty-free. If
you've been away less than seven days but more than 48 hours, the
duty-free exemption drops to C$100 but can be claimed any number
of times (as can a C$20 duty-free exemption for absences of 24 hours
or more). You cannot combine the yearly and 48-hour exemptions,
use the C$300 exemption only partially (to save the balance for a lat-
er trip), or pool exemptions with family members. Goods claimed
under the C$300 exemption may follow you by mail; those claimed
under the lesser exemptions must accompany you on your return.

Alcohol and tobacco products may be included in the yearly and 48-
hour exemptions but not in the 24-hour exemption. If you meet the
age requirements of the province through which you reenter Canada, you may bring in, duty-free, 1.14 liters (40 imperial ounces) of
wine or liquor *or* two dozen 12-ounce cans or bottles of beer or ale. If
you are 16 or older, you may bring in, duty-free, 200 cigarettes, 50
cigars or cigarillos, and 400 tobacco sticks or 400 grams of manufac-
tured tobacco. Alcohol and tobacco must accompany you on your return.

An unlimited number of gifts valued up to C$60 each may be mailed
to Canada duty-free. These do not count as part of your exemption.
Label the package "Unsolicited Gift—Value under $60." Alcohol
and tobacco are excluded.

For more information, including details of duties on items that exceed your duty-free limit, ask the Revenue Canada Customs and Excise Department (2265 St. Laurent Blvd. S, Ottawa, Ont. K1G 4K3,
tel. 613/957–0275) for a copy of the free brochure "I Declare/Je Dé-
clare."

## Traveling with Cameras, Camcorders, and Laptops

**About Film** If your camera is new or if you haven't used it for a while, shoot and
**and Cameras** develop a few rolls of film before leaving home. Store film in a cool,
dry place—never in the car's glove compartment or on the shelf un-
der the rear window.

Airport security X-rays generally aren't harmful to film with ISO
below 400. To protect your film, carry it with you in a clear plastic
bag and ask for a hand inspection. Such requests are honored at U.S.
airports, up to the inspector abroad. Don't depend on a lead-lined
bag to protect film in checked luggage—the airline may increase the
radiation to see what's inside. Call the Kodak Information Center
(tel. 800/242–2424) for details.

**About** Before your trip, put camcorders through their paces, invest in a
**Camcorders** skylight filter to protect the lens, and check all the batteries. Most
newer camcorders are equipped with batteries that can be re-
charged with a universal or worldwide AC adapter charger (or
multivoltage converter) usable whether the voltage is 110 or 220. All
that's needed is the appropriate plug.

**About** Videotape is not damaged by X-rays, but it may be harmed by the
**Videotape** magnetic field of a walk-through metal detector, so ask for a hand-
check. Airport security personnel may ask you to turn on the
camcorder to prove that it's what it appears to be, so make sure the
battery is charged. Note that rather than the National Television
System Committee video standard (NTSC) used in the United
States and Canada, Great Britain uses SECAM technology. You will
not be able to view your tapes through the local TV set or view mov-

ies bought there in your home VCR. Blank tapes bought in Great Britain can be used for NTSC camcorder taping, but they are pricey.

**About Laptops** Security X-rays do not harm hard-disk or floppy-disk storage, but you may request a hand-check, at which point you may be asked to turn on the computer to prove that it is what it appears to be. (Check your battery before departure.) Most airlines allow you to use your laptop aloft except during takeoff and landing (so as not to interfere with navigation equipment). For international travel, register your foreign-made laptop with U.S. Customs as you leave the country. If your laptop is U.S.-made, call the consulate of the country you'll be visiting to find out whether it should be registered with customs upon arrival. Before departure, find out about repair facilities at your destination, and don't forget any transformer or adapter plug you may need (*see* Electricity, *above*).

## Insurance

Most tour operators, travel agents, and insurance agents sell specialized health-and-accident, flight, trip-cancellation, and luggage insurance as well as comprehensive policies with some or all of these features. But before you make any purchase, review your existing health and homeowner policies to find out whether they cover expenses incurred while traveling.

**Health-and-Accident Insurance** Specific policy provisions of supplemental health-and-accident insurance for travelers include reimbursement for from $1,000 to $150,000 worth of medical and/or dental expenses caused by an accident or illness during a trip. The personal-accident, or death-and-dismemberment, provision pays a lump sum to your beneficiaries if you die or to you if you lose one or more limbs or your eyesight; the lump sum awarded can range from $15,000 to $500,000. The medical-assistance provision may reimburse you for the cost of referrals, evacuation, or repatriation and other services, or it may automatically enroll you as a member of a particular medical-assistance company.

**Flight Insurance** Often bought as a last-minute impulse at the airport, flight insurance pays a lump sum when a plane crashes either to a beneficiary if the insured dies or sometimes to a surviving passenger who loses eyesight or a limb. Like most impulse buys, flight insurance is expensive and basically unnecessary. It supplements the airlines' coverage described in the limits-of-liability paragraphs on your ticket. Charging an airline ticket to a major credit card often automatically entitles you to coverage and may also embrace travel by bus, train, and ship.

**Baggage Insurance** In the event of loss, damage, or theft on international flights, airlines' liability is $20 per kilogram for checked baggage (roughly about $640 per 70-pound bag) and $400 per passenger for unchecked baggage. On domestic flights, the ceiling is $1,250 per passenger. Excess-valuation insurance can be bought directly from the airline at check-in for about $10 per $1,000 worth of coverage. However, you cannot buy it at any price for the rather extensive list of excluded items shown on your airline ticket.

**Trip Insurance** **Trip-cancellation-and-interruption insurance** protects you in the event you are unable to undertake or finish your trip, especially if your airline ticket, cruise, or package tour does not allow changes or cancellations. The amount of coverage you purchase should equal the cost of your trip should you, a traveling companion, or a family member fall ill, forcing you to stay home, plus the nondiscounted one-way airline ticket you would need to buy if you had to return home early. Read the fine print carefully, especially sections defining "family member" and "preexisting medical conditions." **Default or bankruptcy insurance** protects you against a supplier's failure to deliver. Such policies often do not cover default by a travel agency, tour operator, airline, or cruise line if you bought your tour and the coverage directly from the firm in question. Tours packaged by one of the 33 members of the United States Tour Operators Association (USTOA, 211 E. 51 St., Suite 12B, New York, NY 10022, tel. 212/750–7371), which requires members to maintain $1 million each in an account to reimburse clients in case of default, are likely to present the fewest difficulties. Even better, pay for travel arrangements with a major credit card, so that you can refuse to pay the bill if services have not been rendered—and let the card company fight your battles.

**Comprehensive Policies**  Companies supplying comprehensive policies with some or all of the above features include **Access America, Inc.** (Box 90315, Richmond, VA 23230, tel. 800/284–8300); **Carefree Travel Insurance** (Box 310, 120 Mineola Blvd., Mineola, NY 11501, tel. 516/294–0220 or 800/323–3149); **Tele-Trip** (Mutual of Omaha Plaza, Box 31762, Omaha, NE 68131, tel. 800/228–9792); **The Travelers Companies** (1 Tower Sq., Hartford, CT 06183, tel. 203/277–0111 or 800/243–3174); **Travel Guard International** (1145 Clark St., Stevens Point, WI 54481, tel. 715/345–0505 or 800/782–5151); and **Wallach and Company, Inc.** (107 W. Federal St., Box 480, Middleburg, VA 22117, tel. 703/687–3166 or 800/237–6615).

## Car Rentals

When considering a rental car, it's worth noting that unless you are going to be traveling a lot outside London, a car in the city will often be more of a liability than an asset.

All major car-rental companies are represented in London, including **Alamo** (tel. 800/327–9633); **Avis** (tel. 800/331–1212 or 800/879–2847 in Canada); **Budget** (tel. 800/527–0700); **Eurodollar Rent A Car Ltd.** (tel. 800/800–6000); **Hertz** (tel. 800/654–3131 or 800/263-0600 in Canada); and **National** (tel. 800/227–7368), known internationally as InterRent and Europcar (tel. 800/227–7368). Typically, unlimited-mileage rates range from $120 per day for an economy car to $160 for a large car; weekly unlimited-mileage rates range from $150 to $300. This does not include VAT tax, which in London is 17% on car rentals.

**Requirements**  Your own driver's license is acceptable. An International Driver's Permit, available from the American or Canadian Automobile Association, is a good idea.

**Extra Charges**  Picking up the car in one city or country and leaving it in another may entail substantial drop-off charges or one-way service fees. Some rental agencies will charge you extra if you return the car *before* the time specified on your contract. Ask before making unscheduled drop-offs. Fill the tank when you turn in the vehicle to avoid being charged for refueling at what you'll swear is the most expensive pump in town. The cost of a collision or loss-damage waiver (*see below*) can be high, also. Automatic transmissions and air-conditioning are not universally available abroad; ask for them when you book if you want them, and check the cost before you commit yourself to the rental.

**Cutting Costs** If you know you will want a car for more than a day or two, you can save by planning ahead. Major international companies have programs that discount their standard rates by 15%–30% if you make the reservation before departure (anywhere from 24 hours to 14 days), rent for a minimum number of days (typically three or four), and prepay the rental. Ask about these advance-purchase schemes when you call for information. More economical rentals may come as part of fly/drive or other packages, even bare-bones deals that combine only the rental plus an airline ticket (*see* Tours and Packages, *above*).

Several companies operate as wholesalers—they do not own their own fleets but rent in bulk from those that do and offer advantageous rates to their customers. Rentals through such companies must be arranged and paid for before you leave the United States. Among them are **Auto Europe** (Box 1097, Camden, ME 04843, tel. 207/236–8235, 800/223–5555, or 800/458–9503 in Canada); **Europe by Car** (mailing address, 1 Rockefeller Plaza, New York, NY 10020; walk-in address, 14 W. 49th St., New York, NY 10020, tel. 212/581–3040 or 212/245–1713; 9000 Sunset Blvd., Los Angeles, CA 90069, tel. 213/252–9401 or 800/223–1516 in CA); **Foremost Euro-Car** (5430 Van Nuys Blvd., Suite 306, Van Nuys, CA 91401, tel. 818/786–1960 or 800/272–3299); **The Kemwel Group** (106 Calvert St., Harrison, NY 10528, tel. 914/835–5555 or 800/678–0678). You won't see these wholesalers' deals advertised; they're even better in summer, when business travel is down. Always ask whether the prices are guaranteed in U.S. dollars or foreign currency and if unlimited mileage is available. Find out about any required deposits, cancellation penalties, and drop-off charges, and confirm the cost of any required insurance coverage.

**Insurance and Collision Damage Waiver** Before you rent a car, find out exactly what coverage, if any, is provided by your personal auto insurer and the rental company. Don't assume that you are covered. If you do want insurance from the rental company, secondary coverage may be the only type offered. You may already have secondary coverage if you charge the rental to a credit card.

In general, if you have an accident, you are responsible for the automobile. Car rental companies may offer a collision damage waiver (CDW), which ranges in cost from $4 to $14 a day. You should decline the CDW only if you are certain you are covered through your personal insurer or credit card company.

## Rail Passes

If you plan to travel a lot in Britain, you might consider purchasing a **BritRail Pass,** which gives unlimited travel over the entire British Rail network.

A variety of passes is offered. The adult first-class pass costs $299 for eight days, $489 for 15 days, $615 for 22 days, and $715 for one month. The adult second-class pass costs $219 for eight days, $339 for 15 days, $425 for 22 days, and $495 for one month. Senior citizens can obtain a **Senior Citizen Pass,** which entitles the bearer to unlimited first-class travel. It costs $279 for eight days, $455 for 15 days, $555 for 22 days, and $655 for one month. The senior citizen second-class pass costs $199 for eight days, $305 for 15 days, $379 for 22 days, and $445 for one month. Young people (aged 16–25) can purchase the **BritRail Youthpass,** which allows unlimited second-class travel. It costs $179 for eight days, $269 for 15 days, $339 for 22 days, and $395 for one month.

If you plan to move around, but also to stop in different regions to explore, the **Flexipass** offers a certain amount of travel within its one-month period of validity; with a four-day pass, for example, you get four days' unlimited rail travel. The adult standard pass costs $189 for four days, $269 for eight days, and $395 for 15 days. First-class costs $249 for four days, $389 for eight days, and $575 for 15 days. Senior citizens and 16- to 25-year-olds get reduced rates. There's also a two-month Youth Flexipass offering 15 days' travel for $309.

You *must* purchase the **BritRail Pass** before you leave home. It is available from most travel agents throughout the world, or from BritRail Travel International offices (1500 Broadway, New York, NY 10036, tel. 212/575–2667; 94 Cumberland St., Toronto, Ont. M5R 1A3, tel. 416/482–1777).

## Student and Youth Travel

**Travel Agencies**  **Council Travel Services (CTS),** a subsidiary of the nonprofit Council on International Educational Exchange, specializes in low-cost travel arrangements abroad for students and is the exclusive U.S. agent for several discount cards. Also newly available from CTS are domestic air passes for bargain travel within the United States. CIEE's twice-yearly *Student Travels* magazine is available at the CTS office at CIEE headquarters (205 E. 42nd St., 16th Floor, New York, NY 10017, tel. 212/661–1450) and in Boston (tel. 617/266–1926), Miami (tel. 305/670–9261), Los Angeles (tel. 310/208–3551) and at 43 branches in college towns nationwide (free in person, $1 by mail). **Campus Connections** (1100 E. Marlton Pike, Cherry Hill, NJ 08034, tel. 800/428–3235) specializes in discounted accommodations and airline fares for students. The **Educational Travel Centre** (438 N. Frances St., Madison, WI 53703, tel. 608/256–5551) offers low-cost domestic and international airline tickets, mostly for flights departing from Chicago, and rail passes. Other travel agencies catering to students include **TMI Student Travel** (1146 Pleasant St., Watertown, MA 02172, tel. 617/661–8187 or 800/245–3672) and **Travel Cuts** (187 College St., Toronto, Ont. M5T 1P7, tel. 416/979–2406).

**Discount Cards**  For discounts on transportation and on museum and attractions admissions, buy the **International Student Identity Card** (ISIC) if you're a bona fide student, or the **International Youth Card** (IYC) if you're under 26. In the United States the ISIC and IYC cards cost $16 each and include basic travel accident and sickness coverage. Apply to **CIEE** (*see* address *above*, tel. 212/661–1414; the application is in *Student Travels*). In Canada the cards are available for $15 each from **Travel Cuts** (*see above*). In the United Kingdom they cost £5 and £4 respectively at student unions and student travel companies, including Council Travel's London office (28A Poland St., London W1V 3DB, tel. 071/437–7767).

**Hosteling**  A **Hostelling International** (HI) membership card is the key to more than 6,000 hostels in 70 countries; the sex-segregated, dormitory-style sleeping quarters, including some for families, go for $7 to $20 a night per person. Membership is available in the United States through **Hostelling International/American Youth Hostels** (HI/AYH, 733 15th St. NW, Washington, DC 20005, tel. 202/783–6161), the American link in the worldwide chain, and costs $25 for adults 18–54, $10 for those under 18, $15 for those 55 and over, and $35 for families. Volume 1 of the two-volume *Guide to Budget Accommodation* lists hostels in Europe and the Mediterranean ($13.95, including postage). IYHF membership is available in Canada through **Hostel-**

ling International-Canada (205 Catherine St., Suite 400, Ottawa, Ont. K2P 1C3, tel. 613/748–5638) for $26.75.

## Traveling with Children

**Publications**  The *Children's Guide to London,* by Christopher Pick (Cadogan
*Local Guides*  Books, 16 Lower Marsh, London SE1 7RJ; £3.50), and *Kids' London,* by Elizabeth Holt and Molly Perham (St. Martin's Press, 175 5th Ave., New York, NY 10010; $5.95), cover the subject. Up-to-date information is available in *Capital Radio's London for Kids* magazine, available at newsstands (£1.50).

The booklet *Children's London* (available free from the London Tourist Board, Tourist Information Centre, Victoria Station Fore-court, London SW1V 1JT, tel. 0171/730–3488) gives a complete story.

*Newsletter*  *Family Travel Times,* published 10 times a year by **Travel With Your Children** (TWYCH, 45 W. 18th St., 7th Floor Tower, New York, NY 10011, tel. 212/206–0688; annual subscription $55), covers destinations, types of vacations, and modes of travel.

*Books*  *Traveling with Children—And Enjoying It,* by Arlene K. Butler ($11.95 plus $3 shipping; Globe Pequot Press, Box 833, Old Saybrook, CT 06475, tel. 800/243–0495 or 800/962–0973 in CT) helps you plan your trip with children, from toddlers to teens. *Innocents Abroad: Traveling with Kids in Europe,* by Valerie Wolf Deutsch and Laura Sutherland ($15.95 or $4.95 paperback, Penguin USA, 120 Woodbine St., Bergenfield, NJ 07621, tel. 800/253–6476), covers child- and teen-friendly activities, food, and transportation.

**Tour**  **American Institute for Foreign Study** (AIFS, 102 Greenwich Ave.,
**Operators**  Greenwich, CT 06830, tel. 203/869–9090) offers a family vacation program in London and England specifically designed for parents and children. **Grandtravel** (6900 Wisconsin Ave., Suite 706, Chevy Chase, MD 20815, tel. 301/986–0790 or 800/247–7651) offers international and domestic tours for people traveling with their grandchildren. The catalogue, as charmingly written and illustrated as a children's book, positively invites armchair traveling with lap-sitters aboard. **Families Welcome!** (21 W. Colony Pl., Suite 140, Durham, NC 27705, tel. 919/489–2555 or 800/326–0724) packages and sells family tours to Europe.

**Getting There**  On international flights, the fare for infants under age 2 not occupy-
*Airfares*  ing a seat is generally either free or 10% of the accompanying adult's fare; children ages 2–11 usually pay half to two-thirds of the adult fare. On domestic flights, children under 2 not occupying a seat travel free, and older children currently travel on the "lowest applicable" adult fare.

*Baggage*  In general, infants paying 10% of the adult fare are allowed one carry-on bag, not to exceed 70 pounds or 45 inches (length + width + height), and a collapsible stroller; check with the airline before departure, because you may be allowed less if the flight is full. The adult baggage allowance applies for children paying half or more of the adult fare.

*Safety Seats*  The FAA recommends the use of safety seats aloft and details approved models in the free leaflet "Child/Infant Safety Seats Recommended for Use in Aircraft" (available from the Federal Aviation Administration, APA–200, 800 Independence Ave. SW, Washington, DC 20591, tel. 202/267–3479). Airline policy varies. U.S. carriers allow FAA-approved models bearing a sticker declaring their

FAA approval. Because these seats are strapped into a regular passenger seat, they may require that parents buy a ticket even for an infant under 2 who would otherwise ride free. Foreign carriers may not allow infant seats, may charge the child's rather than the infant's fare for their use, or may require you to hold your baby during take-off and landing, thus defeating the seat's purpose.

*Facilities Aloft* Some airlines provide other services for children, such as children's meals and freestanding bassinets (only to those with seats at the bulkhead, where there's enough legroom). Make your request when reserving. The annual February/March issue of *Family Travel Times* gives details of the children's services of dozens of airlines (*see above*). "Kids and Teens in Flight" (free from the U.S. Department of Transportation, tel. 202/366–2220) offers tips for children flying alone.

Hotels **Forte Hotels** have special Babycare Kits and children's menus; children under 5 are free and ages 6–13 in parents' room enjoy reduced rates. **Basil Street Hotel** (Basil St., Knightsbridge, London SW3 1AH, tel. 0171/581–3311) is notably friendly and offers moderately priced two-room suites connected by a bath, while the **Edward Lear** (28 Seymour St., London W1H 5WD, tel. 0171/402–5401) has inexpensive family rooms. (Keep in mind that in Great Britain, hotels will often allow only three people in a room.)

Baby-sitting First check with the hotel desk for recommended child-care ar-
Services rangements. Local agencies: **Nanny Service** (9 Paddington St., London W1M 3LA, tel. 0171/935–3515), **The Nanny Co. Ltd.** (168 Sloane St., London SW1X 9QF, tel. 0171/581–5454), **Universal Aunts** (19 The Chase, London SW4 ONP, tel. 0171/738–8937).

Pen Pals For addresses of children in London to whom your children can write before your trip, send a self-addressed, stamped envelope to **International Friendship League** (55 Mt. Vernon St., Boston, MA 02108, tel. 617/523–4273).

Hot Line For information and advice when in London call **Kidsline** (tel. 0171/ 222–8070).

---

### Hints for Travelers with Disabilities

Local **Stationlink,** a wheelchair-accessible "midibus" service, connects
Information nine BritRail stations and Victoria Coach Station. Contact London
Sources Transport's Unit for Disabled Passengers (55 Broadway, London SW1H OBD, tel. 0171/222–5600, Minicom 0171/918–3051) for details on this as well as other access information. **Artsline** (tel. 0171/388–2227) provides information on accessibility of arts events, while **Holiday Care Service** (2 Old Bank Chambers, Station Rd., Horley, Surrey RH6 9HW, tel. 01293/774535) can tell you about accommodations.

Also contact the **Royal Association for Disability and Rehabilitation** (RADAR, 12 City Forum, 250 City Rd., London EC14 8AF, tel. 0171/250–3222), which publishes travel information for the disabled in Britain, and **Mobility International** (228 Borough High St., London SE1 1JX, tel. 0171/403–5688), the headquarters of an international membership organization that serves as a clearinghouse of travel information for people with disabilities.

Organizations Several organizations provide travel information for people with disabilities. Among them are the **Information Center for Individuals with Disabilities** (Fort Point Pl., 27–43 Wormwood St., Boston, MA 02210, tel. 617/727–5540 or 800/462–5015 in MA between 11 and 4, or leave message; TDD tel. 617/345–9743); **Mobility International USA** (Box 10767, Eugene, OR 97440, tel. and TDD 503/343–1284, fax 503/343–6812), the U.S. branch of an international organization based in Britain and present in 30 countries (*see above*); **MossRehab Hospital Travel Information Service** (1200 W. Tabor Rd., Philadelphia, PA 19141, tel. 215/456–9603, TDD 215/456–9602); **Travel Industry and Disabled Exchange** (TIDE, 5435 Donna Ave., Tarzana, CA 91356, tel. 818/368–5648, fax 818/344–0078); and **Travelin' Talk** (Box 3534, Clarksville, TN 37043, tel. 615/552–6670, fax 615/552–1182).

**Travel Agencies** **Flying Wheels Travel** (143 W. Bridge St., Box 382, Owatonna, MN 55060, tel. 507/451–5005 or 800/535–6790) is a travel agency specializing in domestic and worldwide cruises, tours, and independent travel itineraries for people with mobility impairments.

**Publications** Two free publications are available from the Consumer Information Center (Pueblo, CO 81009): "New Horizons for the Air Traveler with a Disability," a U.S. Department of Transportation booklet describing changes resulting from the 1986 Air Carrier Access Act and those still to come from the 1990 Americans with Disabilities Act (include Department 608Y in the address), and the Airport Operators Council's *Access Travel: Airports* (Dept. 5804), which describes facilities and services for the disabled at more than 500 airports worldwide.

*Travelin' Talk Directory* (*see* Organizations, *above*) was published in 1993. This 500-page resource book ($35) is packed with information for travelers with disabilities. Twin Peaks Press (Box 129, Vancouver, WA 98666, tel. 206/694–2462 or 800/637–2256) publishes the *Directory of Travel Agencies for the Disabled* ($19.95), listing more than 370 agencies worldwide, and *Wheelchair Vagabond* ($14.95), a collection of personal travel tips. Add $2 per book for shipping.

## Hints for Older Travelers

**Organizations** The **American Association of Retired Persons** (AARP, 601 E St. NW, Washington, DC 20049, tel. 202/434–2277) provides independent travelers who are members of the AARP (open to those age 50 or older; $8 per person or couple annually) with the Purchase Privilege Program, which offers discounts on hotels, car rentals, and sightseeing. AARP also arranges group tours, cruises, and apartment living through AARP Travel Experience from American Express (400 Pinnacle Way, Suite 450, Norcross, GA 30071, tel. 800/927–0111 or 800/745–4567).

Two other organizations offer discounts on lodgings, car rentals, and other travel products, along with such nontravel perks as magazines and newsletters: the **National Council of Senior Citizens** (1331 F St. NW, Washington, DC 20004, tel. 202/347–8800; membership $12 annually) and **Mature Outlook** (6001 N. Clark St., Chicago, IL 60660, tel. 800/336–6330; $9.95 annually).

Note: Mention your senior-citizen identification card when booking hotel reservations for reduced rates, not when checking out. At restaurants, show your card before you're seated; discounts may be limited to certain menus, days, or hours. If you are renting a car, ask about promotional rates that might improve on your senior-citizen discount.

**Tour Operators** The following tour operators specialize in older travelers: **Evergreen Travel Service** (4114 198th St. SW, Suite 3, Lynnwood, WA 98036, tel. 206/776–1184 or 800/548–7245), has introduced the "Lazy Bones" tours for those who like a slower pace. If you want to take your grandchildren, look into **Grandtravel** (*see* Traveling with Children, *above*); **Saga International Holidays** (222 Berkeley St., Boston, MA 02116, tel. 800/343–0273), caters to those over age 60 who like to travel in groups.

**Publications**  *The 50+ Traveler's Guidebook: Where to Go, Where to Stay, What to Do* by Anita Williams and Merrimac Dillon ($12.95; St. Martin's Press, 175 5th Ave., New York, NY 10010) is available in bookstores and offers many useful tips. "The Mature Traveler" (Box 50820, Reno, NV 89513, tel. 702/786–7419; $29.95), a monthly newsletter, contains many travel deals for older travelers.

### Hints for Gay and Lesbian Travelers

Also *see* The Gay Scene in Chapter 8, The Arts and Nightlife.

**Organizations**  The **International Gay Travel Association** (Box 4974, Key West, FL 33041, tel. 305/292–0217 or 800/448-8550), which has 700 members, will provide you with names of travel agents and tour operators who specialize in gay travel. The **Gay & Lesbian Visitors Center of New York Inc.** (135 W. 20th St., 3rd Floor, New York, NY 10011, tel. 212/463–9030; $100 annually) mails a monthly newsletter, valuable coupons, and more to its members.

**Tour Operators and Travel Agencies**  The dominant travel agency in the market is **Above and Beyond** (3568 Sacramento St., San Francisco, CA 94118, tel. 415/922–2683 or 800/397–2681). Tour operator **Olympus Vacations** (8424 Santa Monica Blvd., Suite 721, West Hollywood, CA 90069; tel. 310/657–2220) offers all-gay-and-lesbian resort holidays. **Skylink Women's Travel** (746 Ashland Ave., Santa Monica, CA 90405, tel. 310/452–0506 or 800/225–5759) handles individual travel for lesbians all over the world and conducts two international and five domestic group trips annually.

**Publications**  The premiere international travel magazine for gays and lesbians is *Our World* (1104 N. Nova Rd., Suite 251, Daytona Beach, FL 32117, tel. 904/441–5367; $35 for 10 issues). "Out & About" (tel. 203/789–8518 or 800/929–2268; $49 for 10 issues) is a 16-page monthly newsletter with extensive information on resorts, hotels, and airlines that are gay-friendly.

# Arriving and Departing

### From North America by Plane

Since the air routes between North America and London are heavily traveled, you have many airlines and fares to choose from. But fares change with stunning rapidity, so consult your travel agent on which bargains are currently available.

Flights are either nonstop, direct, or connecting. A **nonstop** flight requires no change of plane and makes no stops. A **direct** flight stops at least once and can involve a change of plane, although the flight number remains the same; if the first leg is late, the second waits. This is not the case with a **connecting** flight, which involves a different plane and a different flight number.

**Airlines**  U.S. airlines serving London include **Continental** (tel. 800/231–0856); **Delta** (tel. 800/241–4141); **TWA** (tel. 800/892–4141); **United** (tel. 800/241–6522); **USAir** (tel. 800/428–4322); **American Airlines,** which also serves Manchester, England (tel. 800/433–7300); and **Northwest Airlines,** which also serves Glasgow, Scotland (tel. 800/

447–4747). U.K. airlines with offices in the United States include **British Airways** (tel. 800/247–9297) and **Virgin Atlantic** (tel. 800/862–8621).

**Flying Time to London** From New York: 6½ hours. From Chicago: 7½ hours. From Los Angeles: 10 hours.

**Cutting Flight Costs** The Sunday travel section of most newspapers is a good source of deals. When booking, particularly through an unfamiliar company, call the Better Business Bureau and your local or state Consumer Protection Bureau to find out whether any complaints have been registered against the company, pay with a credit card if you can, and consider trip-cancellation and default insurance (*see* Insurance, *above*).

*Promotional Airfares* Less expensive fares, called promotional or discount fares, are round-trip and involve restrictions, which vary according to the route and season. You must usually buy the ticket—commonly called an APEX (advance purchase excursion) when it's for international travel—in advance (seven, 14, or 21 days is usual), although some of the major airlines have added no-frills, cheap flights to compete with new bargain airlines on certain routes.

With the major airlines the cheaper fares generally require minimum and maximum stays (for instance, over a Saturday night or at least seven and no more than 30 days). Airlines generally allow some return date changes for a $25-to-$50 fee, but most low-fare tickets are nonrefundable. Only a death in the family would prompt the airline to return any of your money if you cancel a nonrefundable ticket. However, you can apply an unused nonrefundable ticket toward a new ticket, again with a small fee. The lowest fare is subject to availability, and only a small percentage of the plane's total seats will be sold at that price. Contact the U.S. Department of Transportation's Office of Consumer Affairs (I–25, Washington, DC 20590, tel. 202/366–2220) for a copy of "Fly-Rights: A Guide to Air Travel in the U.S." *The Official Frequent Flyer Guidebook* by Randy Petersen ($14.99 plus $3 shipping; 4715-C Town Center Dr., Colorado Springs, CO 80916, tel. 719/597–8899 or 800/487–8893) yields valuable hints on getting the most for your air travel dollars.

*Consolidators* Consolidators or bulk-fare operators—"bucket shops"—buy blocks of seats on scheduled flights that airlines anticipate they won't be able to sell. They pay wholesale prices, add a markup, and resell the seats to travel agents or directly to the public at prices that still undercut the airline's promotional or discount fares (higher than a charter ticket but lower than an APEX ticket, and usually without the advance-purchase restriction). Moreover, some consolidators sometimes give you your money back. Carefully read the fine print detailing penalties for changes and cancellations. If you doubt the reliability of a company, call the airline once you've made your booking and confirm that you do, indeed, have a reservation on the flight.

The biggest U.S. consolidator, C. L. Thomson Express, sells only to travel agents. Well-established consolidators selling to the public include **UniTravel** (Box 12485, St. Louis, MO 63132, tel. 314/569–0900 or 800/325–2222), **Council Charter** (205 E. 42nd St., New York, NY 10017, tel. 212/661–0311 or 800/800–8222), and **Travac** (989 6th Ave., New York, NY 10018, tel. 212/563–3303 or 800/872–8800).

*Charter Flights* Charters usually have the lowest fares and the most restrictions. Departures are limited and seldom on time, and you can lose all or most of your money if you cancel. (The closer to departure you cancel, the more you lose, although sometimes you will be charged only a small fee if you supply a substitute passenger.) The charterer, on the other hand, may legally cancel the flight for any reason up to 10 days before departure; within 10 days of departure, the flight may be canceled only if it becomes physically impossible to operate it. The charterer may also revise the itinerary or increase the price after you have bought the ticket, but if the new arrangement constitutes a "major change," you have the right to a refund. Before buying a charter ticket, read the fine print for the company's refund policy and details on major changes. Money for charter flights is usually paid into a bank escrow account, the name of which should be on the contract. If you don't pay by credit card, make your check payable to the escrow account (unless you're dealing with a travel agent, in which case, his or her check should be payable to the escrow account). The U.S. Department of Transportation's Office of Consumer Affairs (I–25, Washington, DC 20590, tel. 202/366–2220) can answer questions on charters and send you its "Plane Talk: Public Charter Flights" information sheet.

Charter operators may offer flights alone or with ground arrangements that constitute a charter package. You typically must book charters through your travel agent. One good source is **Charterlink** (988 Sing Sing Rd., Horseheads, NY 14845, tel. 607/739–7148 or 800/221–1802), a no-fee charter broker that operates 24 hours a day.

*Discount Travel Clubs* Travel clubs offer members unsold space on airplanes, cruise ships, and package tours at as much as 50% below regular prices. Membership may include a regular bulletin or access to a toll-free hot line giving details of available trips departing from three or four days to several months in the future. Most also offer 50% discounts off hotel rack rates, but double-check with the hotel to make sure it isn't offering a better promotional rate independent of the club. Clubs include **Discount Travel International** (114 Forrest Ave., Suite 203, Narberth, PA 19072, tel. 215/668–7184; $45 annually, single or family), **Entertainment Travel Editions** (Box 1068, Trumbull, CT 06611, tel. 800/445–4137; $28–$48 annually), **Great American Traveler** (Box 27965, Salt Lake City, UT 84127, tel. 800/548–2812; $29.95 annually), **Moment's Notice Discount Travel Club** (425 Madison Ave., New York, NY 10017, tel. 212/486–0503; $45 annually, single or family), **Privilege Card** (3391 Peachtree Rd. NE, Suite 110, Atlanta, GA 30326, tel. 404/262–0222 or 800/236–9732; domestic annual membership $49.95, international $74.95), **Travelers Advantage** (CUC Travel Service, 49 Music Sq. W, Nashville, TN 37203, tel. 800/548–1116; $49 annually, single or family), and **Worldwide Discount Travel Club** (1674 Meridian Ave., Miami Beach, FL 33139, tel. 305/534–2082; $50 annually for family, $40 single).

**Enjoying the Flight** Fly at night if you're able to sleep on a plane. Because the air aloft is dry, drink plenty of beverages while on board; remember that drinking alcohol contributes to jet lag, as do heavy meals. Sleepers usually prefer window seats to curl up against; restless passengers ask to be on the aisle. Bulkhead seats, in the front row of each cabin, have more legroom, but since there's no seat ahead, trays attach awkwardly to the arms of your seat, and you must stow all possessions overhead. Bulkhead seats are usually reserved for people with disabilities, the elderly, and people traveling with babies.

**Smoking** Since February 1990, smoking has been banned on all domestic flights of less than six hours' duration; the ban also applies to domestic segments of international flights aboard U.S. and foreign carriers. On U.S. carriers flying overseas, a seat in a no-smoking section must be provided for every passenger who requests one, and the section must be enlarged to accommodate such passengers if necessary as long as they have complied with the airline's deadline for check-in and seat assignment. If smoking bothers you, request a seat far from the smoking section.

Foreign airlines are exempt from these rules but do provide no-smoking sections, and some nations, including Canada as of July 1, 1993, have gone as far as to ban smoking on all domestic flights; other countries may ban smoking on flights of less than a specified duration. The International Civil Aviation Organization has set July 1, 1996, as the date to ban smoking aboard airlines worldwide, but the body has no power to enforce its decisions.

## The Channel Tunnel

The **Channel Tunnel** opened in May 1994, providing the fastest route across the Channel—35 minutes from Folkestone to Calais, or 60 minutes from motorway to motorway. It consists of two large 50-kilometer (31-mile) long tunnels for trains, one in each direction, linked by a smaller service tunnel running between them. **Le Shuttle** (tel. 0345/353535 in Great Britain, 800/388–3876 in the United States), a special car, bus, and truck train, which was scheduled to begin service in 1994, operates a continuous loop, with trains departing every 15 minutes at peak times and at least once an hour through the night. No reservations are necessary, although tickets may be purchased in advance from travel agents. Most passengers travel in their own car, staying with the vehicle throughout the "crossing," with progress updates via radio and display screens. Motorcyclists park their bikes in a separate section with its own passenger compartment, while foot passengers must book passage by coach (*see* Getting Around Great Britain by Train, *below*).

The Tunnel is reached from exit 11a of the M20/A20. Drivers purchase tickets from tollbooths, then pass through frontier control before loading onto the next available service. Unloading at Calais takes eight minutes. Ticket prices start at £130 for a low-season five-day round-trip in a small car and are based on the number of passengers. Peak season fares are not always competitive with ferry prices.

**Eurostar** (for information, tel. 0171/922–4486 in the U.K., 800/942–4866 in the U.S.) high-speed train service was scheduled to begin in 1994, with passenger-only trains whisking riders between new stations in Pairs (Gare du Nord) and London (Waterloo) in three hours and between London and Brussels (Midi) in 3¼ hours. The service of five trains daily each way was scheduled to increase in 1995 to 15 trains daily in each direction. At press time, ticket prices had not been set. Tickets are available in the United Kingdom through **Intercity Europe,** the international wing of BritRail (London/Victoria Station, tel. 0171/834–2345 or 0171/828–8092 for credit-card bookings), and in the United States through **Rail Europe** (tel. 800/942–4866) and **BritRail Travel** (1500 Broadway, New York, NY 10036, tel. 800/677–8585).

## Getting Around Great Britain

**By Train** London is served by no fewer than 15 railroad stations, so be absolutely certain of the station for your departure or arrival. All have Underground (subway) stations either in the train station or within a few minutes' walk, and most are served by several bus routes. Railtrack owns all track and stations, while British Rail still controls all major railroad services, though it is in the process of splitting into

# London Underground

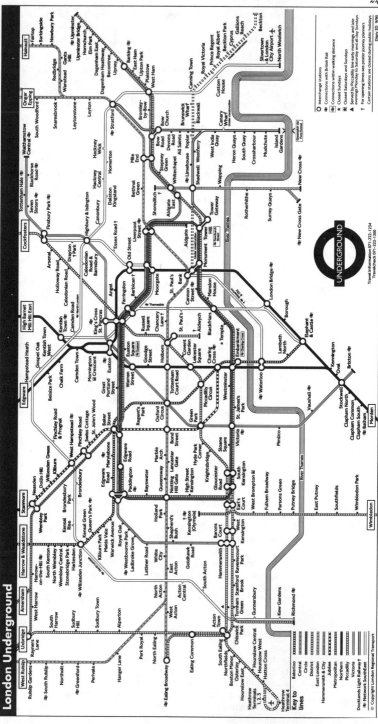

seven divisions that are to be sold to private operators. The only section sold so far is the Gatwick Express line. The principal routes that connect London to other major towns and cities are on an Inter-City network; unlike its European counterparts, British Rail makes no extra charge for the use of this express-service network.

*Seat Reservations* Seats cannot be reserved by phone. You should apply in person to any British Rail Travel Centre or directly to the station from which you depart.

*Major Stations* **Charing Cross** (tel. 0171/928–5100) serves southeast England, including Canterbury, Margate, and Dover/Folkestone. **Euston/St. Pancras** (tel. 0171/387–7070) serves East Anglia, Essex, the northeast, the northwest, and northern Wales, including Coventry, Stratford-upon-Avon, Birmingham, Manchester, Liverpool, Windermere, Glasgow, and Inverness. **King's Cross** (tel. 0171/278–2477) serves the east Midlands, the northeast including York, Leeds, Newcastle, and north and east Scotland including Edinburgh and Aberdeen. **Liverpool Street** (tel. 0171/928–5100) serves Essex and East Anglia. **Paddington** (tel. 0171/262–6767) serves the south Midlands, west and south Wales, and the west country, including Reading, Bath, Bristol, Oxford, Cardiff, Swansea, Exeter, Plymouth, and Penzance. **Victoria** (tel. 0171/928–5100) serves southern England, including Gatwick Airport, Brighton, Dover/Folkestone, and the south coast. **Waterloo** (tel. 0171/928–5100) serves the southwest, including Salisbury, Bournemouth, Portsmouth, Southampton, and the isles of Wight, Jersey, and Guernsey.

*Fares* Generally speaking, it is less expensive to buy a return (round-trip) ticket, especially for day trips not far from London; always inquire at the information office to find out what discount fares are available for your route. Buying a ticket on the train is the most expensive way to go, since you must pay the full one-way fare. You can hear a recorded summary of timetable and fare information to many Inter-City destinations by dialing the appropriate "dial and listen" numbers listed under British Rail in the telephone book.

**By Bus** "Bus" in Britain generally refers to local buses, "coach" to long-distance buses similar to Greyhound in the United States.

The **National Express** coach service has routes to more than 1,000 major towns and cities in Britain. It's considerably cheaper than the train, although the trips will usually take longer. National Express offers two types of service: an ordinary service that makes frequent stops for refreshment breaks, and a *Rapide* service, which has hostess and refreshment facilities on board. Day returns are available on both, but reservation is advised on the *Rapide* service. National Express coaches leave Victoria Coach Station (Buckingham Palace Rd.) at regular intervals, depending on destination. For travel information, call 0171/730–0202.

In addition to National Express, **Green Line** operates bus services within a 30- to 40-mile radius of London. A *Golden Rover* ticket is available for either one or three days. For more information, call 0181/668–7261.

**By Car** London bristles with approach routes; the major ones are designated as either "motorways" (six-lane superhighways; look for an "M" followed by a number) or "A" roads (the letter "A" followed by a number); the latter may be either "dual carriageways" (four-lane divided highways) or two-lane highways. The speed limit on motorways and dual carriageways is 70 mph, and on all other highways it is 60 mph.

Because of their greater number of lanes, motorways are usually a faster option for getting in or out of town than A roads, and many motorways merge back into A roads some distance out of London. However, during weekday rush hour you can easily spend a half-hour or more stuck in traffic jams; stay tuned to radio stations for regular traffic updates.

The often-congested M25 encircles Greater London—an option if you're staying in the suburbs and want a getaway route.

**From Downtown to the Airports**

**To Heathrow** The Piccadilly Line of the Underground connects with Heathrow (all terminals). Trains run every four to eight minutes; journey time is roughly 50 minutes; price is £3 one-way. London Transport's *Airbus* service also runs to Heathrow; two routes stop at many central locations, including most major hotels. The A1 leaves every 30 minutes from Victoria Station, daily 6:40 AM–8:15 PM; travel time is about an hour. The A2 leaves Russell Square, near Euston Station, with the same frequency as the A1, daily 6 AM–8:25 PM; travel time is about an hour and 20 minutes. Price for each route is £5 one-way.

An alternative to the Airbus, serving Heathrow, is the 390 bus, which departs Stand 8, Buckingham Palace Road, weekdays at 7:35, 9:35, 11:05 AM and 1:05, 3:45, 5:20, 6:35, and 9:15 PM (times vary slightly on weekends), stopping at Hyde Park Corner and Kensington High Street. Journey time is about an hour, and the fare is £4 one-way.

By car, the most direct route from central London is via the M4. By taxi, the fare from downtown should be about £25 plus tip, though this and the journey time will depend on the traffic.

**To Gatwick** Fast nonstop trains leave Victoria Station every 15 minutes, 5:30 AM–10 PM; five times an hour, 10–midnight; and hourly, midnight–5 AM. Journey time varies from 30 to 39 minutes. Price is £8.60 one-way. Regular bus services are provided by *Green Line Coaches* (tel. 0181/668–7261), including the Flightline 777, which leaves Victoria Coach Station hourly, 5:30 AM–11:25 PM. A one-way ticket costs £6. Travel time: about 70 minutes.

By car, take the A23 and then the M23 from central London. Taxis from the city to Gatwick are prohibitively expensive—you may find that it is much more reasonable to take the train.

**To Stansted** London's third airport opened in March 1991. It serves mainly European destinations. The terminal is now linked to Liverpool Street via the Stansted Express. Trains run half-hourly and cost £9.80 one-way.

# Staying in London

## Important Addresses and Numbers

**Tourist Information** The main **London Tourist Information Centre** at Victoria Station Forecourt provides details about London and the rest of Britain, including general information, tickets for tube and bus, hotel reservations, theater, concert, and tour reservations, and various other services. It's open weekdays and Saturday 8–7, Sunday 8–5. Other information centers are at *Heathrow Airport* (Terminals 1, 2, and 3) and *Gatwick Airport* (International Arrivals Concourse), and, open during store hours only, in *Harrods* (Brompton Rd., SW1 7XL) and *Selfridges* (Oxford St., W1A 2LR).

The **London Travel Service** (Bridge House, Ware, Hertfordshire SG12 9DE, tel. 01920/469755) offers travel, hotel, and tour reservations for London (weekdays 9–5:30, Sat. 9–5).

The **British Travel Centre** (12 Regent St., SW1Y 4PQ, in person only) offers travel, hotel, and entertainment information for the whole of Britain (weekdays 9–6:30, Sat. 10–4).

The London Tourist Board's **Visitorcall** phone guide to London gives information about events, theater, museums, transport, shopping, restaurants, etc., all on different numbers. Phone 01839/123456 for a "menu." A three-month events calendar (tel. 01839/401279), or annual version (tel. 01839/401278), is available by fax (set fax machine to polling mode, or press start/receive after the tone). Visitorcall charges a premium rate of 48p per minute or a 36p-per-minute cheap rate.

**Embassies and Consulates**
**U.S. Embassy** (24 Grosvenor Sq., W1A 1AE, tel. 0171/499–9000). Located inside the embassy is the American Aid Society, a charity set up to help Americans in distress. Dial the embassy number and ask for extension 570 or 571.

**Canadian High Commission** (Canada House, Trafalgar Sq., London SW1Y 5BJ, tel. 0171/629–9492).

**Emergencies**
For police, fire department, or ambulance, dial 999.

The following hospitals have 24-hour emergency wards: **Charing Cross** (Fulham Palace Rd., Hammersmith W6, tel. 0181/846–1234); **Guys** (St. Thomas St., SE1, tel. 0171/407–7600); **Royal Free** (Pond St., Hampstead, NW3, tel. 0171/794–0500); **St. Bartholomew's** (West Smithfield, EC1, tel. 0171/600–9000); **St. Thomas's** (Lambeth Palace Rd., SE1, tel. 0171/928–9292); **Westminster** (Dean Ryle St., Horseferry Rd., SW1, tel. 0171/828–9811).

**Pharmacies**
Chemists (drugstores) with late opening hours include **Bliss Chemist** (50–56 Willesden La., NW6, tel. 0171/624–8000; 5 Marble Arch, W1, tel. 0171/723–6116), open daily 9 AM–midnight, and **Boots** (439 Oxford St., W1, tel. 0171/409–2857), open Thursday 8:30–7.

**Travel Agencies**
**American Express** (6 Haymarket, SW1, tel. 0171/930–4411; 89 Mount St., W1, tel. 0171/499–4436), **Thomas Cook** (4 Henrietta St., WC2, tel. 0171/240–4872; 1 Marble Arch, W1, tel. 0171/706–4188; and other branches).

**Credit Cards**
Here are the numbers to call for assistance should your credit cards be lost or stolen: **Access (MasterCard)** (tel. 01702/352255); **American Express** (tel. 0171/222–9633 for credit cards or 01800/521313 for traveler's checks); **Barclaycard (Visa)** (tel. 01604/230230); **Diners Club** (tel. 01252/516261).

## Telephones

**Local Calls**
There are four types of phones: BT (British Telecom) ones that accept (a) only coins, (b) only BT phonecards, or (c) BT phonecards and credit cards; and (d) Mercury phones that accept Mercury phonecards and credit cards.

The coin-operated phones are of the push-button variety; most take all but 1p coins. Insert the coins *before* dialing (minimum charge is 10p). If you hear a repeated single tone after dialing, the line is busy; a continuous tone means the number is unobtainable (or that you have dialed the wrong—or no—prefix). The indicator panel shows you how much money is left; add more whenever you like. If there is no answer, replace the receiver and your money will be returned.

Both BT and Mercury card phones operate with special cards that you can buy from post offices or newsstands. They are ideal for longer calls, are composed of units of 10p, and come in values of £2, £4, and £10. To use, lift the receiver, insert your card, and dial the number. An indicator panel shows the number of units used. At the end of your call the card will be returned. Where credit cards are taken, slide the card through, as indicated.

For long-distance calls within Britain, dial the area code (which begins with a zero), followed by the number.

London numbers are prefixed by 0171 for inner London or 0181 for outer London. You do not need to dial either if calling from inside the same zone, but you will have to dial 0181 from an 0171 number, and 0171 from an 0181 number. Drop the zero from the prefix and dial only 171 or 181 when calling London from overseas.

All calls are charged according to the time of day. Standard rate is weekdays 8 AM–6 PM; cheap rate is weekdays 6 PM–8 AM and all day on weekends.

**International Calls** These are usually cheaper when made weekdays between 8 PM and 8 AM, and at any time on weekends. For direct dialing, dial 010 (or 00 after April 16, 1995), then the country code, area code, and number. For the international operator, credit card, or collect calls, dial 155. For directory inquiries (information) in most countries, dial 153. Bear in mind that hotels usually levy a hefty surcharge on calls made from hotel rooms; it's better to use the pay phones located in most hotel foyers.

**Operators and Information** To call the operator, dial 100; directory inquiries (information) for London numbers only, 142; information for the rest of Britain, 192. A charge is made for directory inquiries.

## Mail

The **London Chief Post Office** (King Edward St., EC1A 1AA, tel. 0171/239–5047) is open weekdays 8:30–6. The **Trafalgar Square Post Office** (24–28 William IV St., WC2N 4DL, tel. 0171/930–9580) is open Monday–Saturday 8–8. Most other post offices are open weekdays 9–5:30, Saturday 9–12:30 or 1. Stamps may be bought from main or subpost offices (the latter are located in stores), from stamp machines outside post offices, and from many newsagents stores and newsstands. Mailboxes are known as post or letter boxes and are painted bright red; large tubular ones are set on the edge of sidewalks, while smaller boxes are set into post office walls.

**Rates** Postal rates are: airmail letters up to 10 grams to North America, 41p; postcards 35p, aerogrammes 36p. Letters within Britain are 25p for first class, 19p for second class. Always check rates in advance, however, as they are subject to change.

**Receiving Mail** If you're uncertain where you'll be staying, you can have mail sent to you c/o Poste Restante, **London Chief Post Office** (King Edward St., EC1A 1AA). The service is free and may be used for three months. You'll need your passport or some other form of identification to claim your mail. Alternatively, **American Express** (6 Haymarket, SW1Y 4BS, tel. 0171/930–4411, or any other branch) will accept letters free of charge on behalf of its customers; noncustomers pay 60p per visit to the mailroom.

## Getting Around London

**By Underground**
Known colloquially as "the tube," London's extensive Underground system is by far the most widely used form of city transport. Trains run both beneath and above ground out into the suburbs, and all stations are clearly marked with the London Underground circular symbol. (In Britain, the word "subway" means "pedestrian underpass.") Trains are all one class; smoking is *not* allowed on board or in the stations.

There are 10 basic lines—all named—plus the East London line, which runs from Shoreditch and Whitechapel across the Thames and south to New Cross, and the Docklands Light Railway, which runs from Stratford in east London to Greenwich, with an extension to the Royal Docks that should be completed by the time you read this. The Central, District, Northern, Metropolitan, and Piccadilly lines all have branches, so be sure to note which branch is needed for your particular destination. Electronic platform signs tell you the final stop and route of the next train, and some signs also indicate how many minutes you'll have to wait for the train to arrive.

*Hours*
From Monday to Saturday, trains begin running just after 5 AM; the last services leave central London between midnight and 12:30 AM. On Sundays, trains start two hours later and finish about an hour earlier. Frequency of trains depends on the route and the time of day, but normally you should not have to wait more than 10 minutes in central areas.

*Fares*
For both buses and tube fares, London is divided into six concentric zones; the fare goes up the farther out you travel. Ask at Underground ticket counters for the London Transport booklets that give details of all the various ticket options for the tube; after some experimenting, you'll soon know which ticket best serves your particular needs. Here is a brief summary of the major ticket categories:

**Singles and Returns.** For one trip between any two stations, you can buy an ordinary single (one-way ticket) for travel anytime on the day of issue; if you're coming back on the same route the same day, then an ordinary return (round-trip ticket) costs twice the single fare. Singles vary in price from 90p to £3—not a good option for the sightseer who wants to make several journeys in a day.

**One Day Travelcard.** Allows unrestricted travel on both bus and tube; valid weekdays after 9:30 AM, weekends, and all national holidays. Cost: £2.70–£3.70; children £1.40.

**LT Card.** The same as above, but without the time restrictions; it costs £3.90–£6.30, children £1.90–£2.70.

**Weekly and Monthly Travelcards.** These bus-and-tube bargains vary in cost according to the number of zones covered. They have no time restrictions on weekday use and can be bought from some newsdealers, as well as from Underground and railroad stations (a photo is required; there are booths in the stations).

**Visitor's Travelcard.** May be bought in the United States and Canada for three, four, and seven days; the same as the LT Card, but with a booklet of discount vouchers to London attractions. In the United States they cost $25, $32, and $49 respectively ($11, $13, and $21 for children); in Canada, C$29, C$36, and C$55 respectively (C$13, C$15, and C$25 for children). Apply to travel agents or, in the United States, to BritRail Travel International (1500 Broadway, New York, NY 10036, tel. 212/382–3737).

*Information* A pocket map of the entire tube network is available free from most Underground ticket counters. There is a large map on the wall of each platform.

There are LT (London Transport) Travel Information Centres at the following tube stations: Heathrow, daily, varying times at each terminal; Victoria, daily 8:15 AM–9:30 PM; Piccadilly Circus, daily 8:15–6; Oxford Circus, Monday–Saturday 8:15–6; Euston, Monday–Thursday and Saturday 7:15–6, Friday 7:15 AM–7:30 PM, Sunday 8:15–6; and King's Cross, Monday–Thursday 8:15–6, Friday 7:15 AM–7:30 PM, Saturday 7:15–6. For information on all London bus and tube times, fares, etc., call 0171/222–1234; the line is operated 24 hours.

**By Bus** London's bus system consists of bright red double- and single-deckers, plus other buses of various colors. Destinations are displayed on the front and back, with the bus number on the front, back, and side. Not all buses run the full length of their route at all times, so always check the termination point before boarding, preferably with the conductor or driver. Some buses still have a conductor whom you pay after finding a seat, but there are a lot of "one-man" buses on the road, in which you pay the driver upon boarding.

Buses stop only at clearly indicated stops. Main stops—at which the bus *should* stop automatically—have a plain white background with a red LT symbol on it. There are also request stops with red signs, a white symbol, and the word "Request" added; at these you must hail the bus to make it stop. Smoking is not allowed on any bus. Although you can see much of the town from a bus, *don't* take one if you want to get anywhere in a hurry; traffic often slows to a crawl, and during rush hour you may find yourself waiting 40 minutes for a bus and then not being able to get on it once it arrives. If you do go by bus, ask at a Travel Information Centre for a free London Bus Map.

*Fares* One-way fares start at 90p in the central zone. As previously mentioned, Travelcards are good for both tube and bus.

**By Taxi** Those big black taxicabs are as much a part of the London streetscape as the red double-decker buses, yet many have been replaced by the new boxy, sharp-edged model, while the beauty of others is marred by the advertising they carry on their sides. Hotels and main tourist areas have cab stands (just take the first in line), but you can also flag one down from the roadside. If the yellow "for hire" sign on the top is lit, then the taxi is available. Many cab drivers often cruise at night with their "for hire" signs unlit; this is to enable them to choose their passengers and avoid those they think might cause trouble. If you see an unlit, passengerless cab, hail it: You might be lucky.

*Fares* Fares start at £1 for the first 582 yards and increase by units of 20p per 291 yards or 60 seconds. A 40p surcharge is added on weekday nights 8–midnight and Saturday up to 8 PM. The surcharge rises to 60p on Saturday night, Sunday, and national holidays—except over Christmas and New Year's Eve when it rises to £2. Fares are usually raised in June of each year.

**By Car** The best advice about driving in London is: don't. Because the capital grew up as a series of villages, there never was a central plan for London's streets, and the result is a winding mass of chaos, aggravated by a passion for one-way streets.

If you must risk life and limb, however, note that the speed limit is 30 mph in the royal parks, as well as (theoretically) in all streets—unless you see the large 40 mph signs (and small repeater signs attached to lampposts) found only in the suburbs. Other basic rules:

Pedestrians have right-of-way on "zebra" crossings (those black-and-white stripes that stretch across the street between two Belisha beacons—orange-flashing globe lights on posts). The curb on each side of the zebra crossing has zigzag markings. It is illegal to park within the zigzag area, or to pass another vehicle at a zebra crossing. On other crossings pedestrians must yield to traffic, but they do have right-of-way over traffic turning left at controlled crossings—if they have the nerve.

Traffic lights sometimes have arrow-style lights directing left or right turns; it is therefore important not to get into the turn lane if you mean to go straight ahead, so try to catch a glimpse of the road markings in time. The use of horns is prohibited between 11:30 PM and 7 AM.

You can park at night in 30-mph zones, provided you are within 25 yards of a lit street lamp, but not within 15 yards of a road junction. To park on a bus route, you must show side (parking) lights, but you'll probably get a ticket anyway. On "Red Routes"—busy stretches with red lines painted in the gutter—you may not even stop to let out a passenger. During the day—and probably at all times—it is safest to believe that you can park nowhere except at a meter, in a garage, or where you are sure there are no lines or signs; otherwise, you run the risk of a tow-away cost of about £100, or a wheel clamp, which costs £38 to have removed, plus £20–£40 for the parking ticket you will also have earned. Note that it is illegal to park on the sidewalk in London.

**London Districts** Greater London is divided into 32 boroughs—33, counting the City of London, which has all the powers of a London borough. More useful for finding your way around, however, are the subdivisions of London into various postal districts. Throughout the guide we've listed the full postal code for places you're likely to be contacting by mail, although you'll find the first half of the code more important. The first one or two letters give the location: N=north, NW=northwest, etc. Don't expect the numbering to be logical, however. You won't, for example, find W2 next to W3.

## Guided Tours

**Orientation Tours**
**By Bus** **London Transport**'s **London Plus** guided sightseeing tours (tel. 0171/828–6449) offer passengers a good introduction to the city from double-decker buses, which are open-topped in summer. Tours run daily every half-hour, or more during summer, 10–5, from Marble Arch, Victoria, Piccadilly, Harrods, Trafalgar Square, and some 30 more places of interest. You may board or alight at any stop to view the sights, and then get back on the next bus. Tickets (£12 adults, £6 children) may be bought from the driver. Other agencies offering half- and full-day bus tours include **Evan Evans** (tel. 0171/930–2377), **Frames Rickards** (tel. 0171/837–3111), **Travellers Check-In** (tel. 0171/580–8284), and **The Big Bus Company** (tel. 0181/944–7810). These tours include stops at places such as St. Paul's Cathedral and Westminster Abbey. Prices and pickup points vary according to the sights visited, but many pickup points are at major hotels.

**By River** From April to October, boats cruise the Thames, offering a different view of the London skyline. Most leave from Westminster Pier (tel. 0171/930–4097), Charing Cross Pier (Victoria Embankment, tel. 0171/839–3312), and Tower Pier (tel. 0171/488–0344). Downstream routes go to the Tower of London, Greenwich, and the Thames Barrier; upstream destinations include Kew, Richmond, and Hampton Court. Most of the launches seat between 100 and 250 passengers, have a public address system, and provide a running

# London Postal Districts

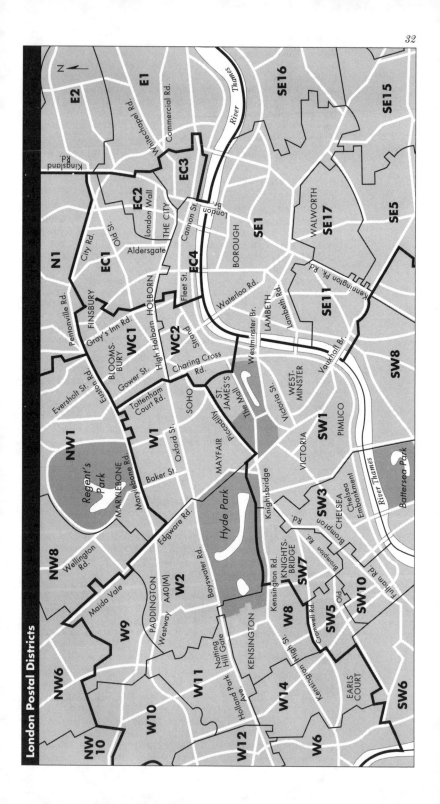

commentary on passing points of interest. Depending upon destination, river trips may last from one to four hours. For more information, call **Catamaran Cruisers** (tel. 0171/839–3572), **Tidal Cruises** (tel. 0171/928–9009), or **Westminster Passenger Services Association** (tel. 0171/930–4097).

*By Canal* During summer, narrow boats and barges cruise London's two canals, the Grand Union and Regent's Canal; most vessels (they seat about 60) operate on the latter, which runs between Little Venice in the west (nearest tube: Warwick Avenue on the Bakerloo Line) and Camden Lock (about 200 yards north of Camden Town tube station). **Jason's Trip** (tel. 0171/286–3428) operates one-way and round-trip narrow-boat cruises on this route. During April, May, and September, there are two cruises per day; from June to August, there are four. Trips last 1½ hours and cost £3.75 for adults, £2.50 for children and senior citizens round-trip.

**London Waterbus Co.** (tel. 0171/482–2550) offers the Zoo Waterbus service daily from March to September, on weekends in winter. A round-trip canal cruise, London Zoo–Camden Lock, costs £3.20 adults, £1.90 children. Combined zoo entrance–waterbus tickets are also available.

**Canal Cruises** (tel. 0171/485–4433) also offers cruises from March to October on the *Jenny Wren* (£3.90 adults, £1.80 children and senior citizens), and all year on the floating restaurant *My Fair Lady* (Tues.–Sat. dinner, £24.95; Sun. lunch, £16.95).

**Walking Tours** One of the best ways to get to know London is on foot, and there are many guided walking tours from which to choose. **The Original London Walks** (tel. 0171/624–3978) has a very wide selection and takes justifiable pride in the infectious enthusiasm of its guides. **City Walks** (tel. 0171/700–6931), **Streets of London** (tel. 0181/346–9255), and **Citisights** (tel. 0181/806–4325) are some of the other better-known firms, but you can investigate more tours at the London Tourist Information Centre at Victoria Station. The lengths of walks vary (usually one to three hours), and you can generally find one to suit even the most specific of interests—Shakespeare's London, say, or a Jack the Ripper tour. Prices range around £4 for adults.

For those who would rather explore on their own, the City of London Corporation has laid out a **Heritage Walk** leading through Bank, Leadenhall, and Monument streets; follow the trail by the directional stars set into the sidewalks. A map of this walk may be found in *A Visitor's Guide to the City of London*, available from the City Information Centre across from St. Paul's Cathedral. Another option is to follow the **Silver Jubilee Walkway**, created in 1977 in honor of the 25th anniversary of the accession of the present queen. The entire route covers 10 miles and is marked by a series of silver crowns set into the sidewalks; Parliament Square makes a good starting point. Books available from the British Travel Centre (12 Regent St., W1) list other London Regional Transport walks.

**Excursions** **LT, Evan Evans, Frames Rickards,** and **Travellers Check-In** (*see* Orientation Tours, *above*) all offer day excursions by bus (some combine bus and boat) to places of interest within easy reach of London, such as Windsor, Hampton Court, Oxford, Stratford-upon-Avon, and Bath. Prices vary and may include lunch and admission or admission only.

**Personal Guides** **Autofleet** (The Old Exchange, 2 Tudor Rd., Hampton Mssx., tel. 0181/941–5288) has a fleet of classy autos—Rolls-Royce, Phantom,

Jaguar, Mercedes—and arrange chauffeur-driven tours around London and out of town. Prices range from £90 for three hours to £180 for a full day. Details on similar private operators may be found in brochures at the London Tourist Information Centre in Victoria Station or at the British Travel Centre.

## Opening and Closing Times

**Banks** are normally open weekdays 9:30–3:30, but some branches are now open later and provide services on Saturday. Banks at major airports and train stations also have extended hours. **Museums** are usually open Monday–Saturday 10–5 or 10–6, Sunday 2–5 or 2–6, including most national holidays, but not major ones like Christmas Day, Boxing Day (Dec. 26), and New Year's Day. Check individual listings for definite opening hours. **Pubs,** since mid-1988, are generally open Monday–Saturday 11 AM–11 PM, Sunday noon–3 and 7–10 or 10:30, though these hours vary. **Stores** typically stay open Monday–Saturday 9–5:30 or 9–6. Some have late opening hours on Wednesday or Thursday until 7 or 7:30 PM, and in spite of the blue laws, many are open on Sunday.

**National Holidays** In England and Wales, they're January 1; April 14 (Good Friday); April 17 (Easter Monday); May 1 (Mayday Holiday); May 29 (Spring Bank Holiday); August 28 (Summer Bank Holiday); December 25 and 26 (Christmas Day and Boxing Day).

## Tipping

Many restaurants and large hotels (particularly those belonging to chains) will automatically add a 10%–15% service charge to your bill, so always check in advance before you hand out any extra money. You are, of course, welcome to tip on top of that for exceptional service. If you are dissatisfied with the service, however, refuse to pay the service charge, stating your reasons for doing so; you will be within your rights legally.

Do not tip movie or theater ushers, elevator operators, or bar staff in pubs—although you may buy them a drink if you're feeling generous. Washroom attendants may display a saucer, in which it's reasonable to leave 20p or so.

Here's a guide for other tipping situations: **Restaurants:** 10%–15% of the check for full meals if service is not already included; a small token if you're just having coffee or tea. **Taxis:** 10%–15%, or perhaps a little more for a short ride. **Porters:** 50p–£1 per bag. **Doormen:** £1 for hailing taxis or for carrying bags to check-in desk. **Bellhops:** £1 for carrying bags to rooms, £1 for room service. **Hairdressers:** 10%–15% of the bill, plus £1–£2 for the hair-washer.

## Credit Cards

The following credit-card abbreviations are used: AE, American Express; DC, Diner's Club; MC, MasterCard; V, Visa.

# 2 Portraits of London

# London at a Glance: A Chronology

This date table parallels events in London's history with events in the world at large, especially in the Americas, to give a sense of perspective to the chronology of London. The dates of British kings and queens are those of their reigns, not of their lives.

c. 400 BC  Early Iron Age hamlet built at Heathrow (now London airport)

54 BC  Julius Caesar arrives with short-lived expedition

AD 43  Romans conquer Britain, led by the Emperor Claudius

60  Boudicca, queen of Iceni, razes the first Roman Londinium to the ground

c. 100  The Romans make Londinium center of their British activities, though not the capital

410  Romans withdraw from Britain

410–500  Anglo-Saxon invasion and settlement

700s  Viking invasion and settlement begins

856  Alfred the Great (871–99), King of the West Saxons, "restored London and made it habitable"

1042  Edward the Confessor (1042–66) moves his court to Westminster and begins the reconstruction of the Abbey and its monastic buildings

1066  William the Conqueror (1066–87), Duke of Normandy, wins the battle of Hastings

1067  William grants London a charter confirming its rights and privileges

1078  The Tower of London begins with the building of the White Tower

1097  Westminster Hall completed under William II, Rufus (1087–1100)

1123  St. Bartholomew's Hospital founded by Rahere

1132  Charter of Liberties granted by Henry I (1100–35), giving London the right to choose its own sheriffs

1136  Fire destroys London Bridge (new one built 1176–1209)

1185  Knights Templar build the New Temple by the Thames

1191  First mayor of London elected

1265  First parliament held in Westminster Abbey Chapter House

1314  Old St. Paul's Cathedral completed

1327  Incorporation of first trade guilds (which govern the City for centuries)

1348–58  The Black Death in London; one third of the population dies

1382  The Peasants' Revolt destroys part of the city

1411  The Guildhall (already centuries on the same site) rebuilt

**1476** William Caxton (1422–91) introduces printing to England in Westminster

**c. 1483** London's population estimated at around 75,000

**1515** Henry VII's tomb in Westminster Abbey completed

**1529** Hampton Court given by Cardinal Wolsey to Henry VIII; it becomes a favorite royal residence

**1568** Royal Exchange founded

**1588** Preparations at Tilbury to repel the Spanish invasion; the Armada defeated in the Channel

**1599** Shakespeare's Globe Theatre built on the South Bank

**1603** Population of London over 200,000

**1605** Unsuccessful Gunpowder Plot to blow up the Houses of Parliament

**1619–22** Banqueting House built

**1640s** New fortifications for the defense of the capital built at the start of the Civil War between the Crown and Parliament forces

**1649** Charles I (1625–49) beheaded outside the Banqueting House on Whitehall

**1658** Oliver Cromwell (Lord Protector) dies

**1660** Charles II (1649–85) restored to the throne (the Restoration) after exile in Europe

**1665** The Great Plague; deaths probably reach 100,000 (official figure for one week alone was 8,297)

**1666** The Great Fire burns for three days; 89 churches, 13,200 houses destroyed over an area of 400 streets

**1675** Sir Christopher Wren (1632–1723) begins work on the new St. Paul's Cathedral

**1682–92** Main work on the Royal Hospital Chelsea

**1688** William III (1689–1702) transfers royal residence from Whitehall Palace to Kensington Palace

**1694** The Bank of England founded

**1698** Whitehall Palace destroyed by fire

**1732** Number 10 Downing Street becomes the prime minister's official residence

**1739–53** Mansion House built

**1755** Trooping the Colour first performed for George II

**1762** George III (1760–1820) makes Buckingham Palace the royal residence

**1773** Stock Exchange founded in Threadneedle Street

**1792** Bank of England built

**1801** Population just under 1,000,000 (first census)

**1802** First gaslights on the London streets

**1805** Spectacular funeral of Horatio Nelson (1758–1805), who was killed at the battle of Trafalgar

**1812** Regent's Park laid out

1817 First Waterloo Bridge built

1827 Marble Arch erected (in 1851 moved to the northeast corner of Hyde Park)

1829–41 Trafalgar Square laid out

1834 The Houses of Parliament gutted by fire; 1840–52 the present Westminster Palace built

1835 Madame Tussaud settles in Baker Street

1836 London's first railway begins operation, London Bridge to Deptford

1837 Victoria (1837–1901) comes to the throne

1838 National Gallery opens in Trafalgar Square

1845 British Museum completed

1851 The Great Exhibition, Prince Albert's brainchild, held in the Crystal Palace, Hyde Park

1863 Arrival of the Underground (the tube), first train on the Metropolitan Line

1869 Albert Embankment completed, first stage in containing the Thames floodwaters

1870 The Albert Hall opens

1878 First electric street lights

1894 Tower Bridge constructed

1897 Queen Victoria celebrates her Diamond Jubilee

1901 Victoria dies, marking the end of an era; London's population reaches around 4,500,000

1914–18 World War I—London bombed (1915) by German zeppelins; (355 incendiaries, 567 explosives; 670 killed, 1,962 injured)

1926 General Strike; London is partly paralyzed

1935 London County Council establishes a Green Belt to preserve the city's outer open spaces

1939–45 World War II—air raids, between Sept. '40 and July '41 45,000–50,000 bombs (including incendiaries) are dropped on London; '44 Flying Bomb (Doodlebug) raids; '45 V2 raids; during the lat-ter two series of raids 8,938 killed, 24,504 injured. Total casualties for the whole war, about 30,000 killed, more than 50,000 injured

1946 Heathrow Airport opens

1951 The Festival of Britain spurs postwar uplift

1953 Coronation of Queen Elizabeth II (born 1926)

1956 Clean Air Act abolishes open fires and makes London's mists and fogs a romantic memory

1965 Sir Winston Churchill's funeral, a great public pageant; the Post Office Tower—now the Telecom Tower—one of Britain's tallest buildings, opens

1973 New Stock Exchange opens

1974 Covent Garden fruit and vegetable market moves across the Thames; the original area is remodeled

1976 National Theatre opens on the South Bank

1977  Queen Elizabeth celebrates her Silver Jubilee

1979  Margaret Thatcher elected Prime Minister

1981  National Westminster Tower, Britain's tallest building, opens in the City; Prince Charles marries Lady Diana Spencer in St. Paul's Cathedral

1982  The Barbican Centre opens

1983  The first woman lord mayor takes office

1984  The Thames Barrier, designed to prevent flooding in central London, is inaugurated

1986  The Greater London Council (the city's centralized municipal government) is abolished by Parliament; London's population now stands at approximately 6,696,000

1990  Margaret Thatcher resigns as Prime Minister

1991  Cesar Pelli's Tower—One Canada Square—opens at Canary Wharf and becomes Britain's tallest building

1994  The Channel Tunnel opens a direct rail link between Britain and Europe

# Wren and the Great Fire of London

*By Ann Saunders*

*Author of Art and Architecture of London, Dr. Saunders lectures to visiting American students on London history and costume. She is a leading figure in the London Topographical Society.*

Since England as a whole is so rich in medieval churches, the perceptive visitor to the City of London may wonder why there are none around. Except for five on the northern edge of the City, there seems to be nothing earlier than the late 17th century. The answer lies in the four terrible days and nights, between September 2 and 5, 1666, when fire destroyed five-sixths of the mainly timber-built, medieval city. Those four days did three to four times as much damage as did Hitler's bombs and rockets in the six years of World War II. This was how it happened.

On the night of Saturday, September 2, 1666, the king's own baker, Master Robert Farynor, put out the oven fire in his bakehouse in Pudding Lane near the north end of London Bridge and went to bed. He was quite certain that he had extinguished his stove, but in the small hours of the morning his manservant was awakened by smoke and, realizing that the house was on fire, roused the household, whose members crept to safety across the roof to the house next door, with the exception of a maid who, scared of heights, died in the flames.

For the next four days, the fire raged. A steady wind blew from the northeast, the Essex side, of the city, driving the flames through the narrow streets of timber-framed houses. The flames were carried toward Thames Street, the riverside area, where stocks of oil, coal, hay, timber, and hemp lay piled on the quayside; the fire could not have been given a surer foothold. At first, the severity of the danger was not realized; Samuel Pepys, civil servant and diarist, roused by his servant who was working late, looked out of the window "but being unused to such fires as followed, I thought it far enough off, and so went to bed again and to sleep." At about the same time, some wary citizens had called the Lord Mayor, Sir Thomas Bludworth, from his bed. He dismissed the danger. "Pish! a woman might piss it out," he was reported as having said; and the opportunity to control the fire was lost. Before morning, St. Magnus Church was destroyed and the Thames water house on the north end of the bridge, which could throw a jet of water over the steeple of the church, was gone, too. People began, desperately, to evacuate their goods; some threw their treasures into the Thames in the hope that they might be washed back on a later tide. Samuel Pepys dug a hole in his back garden to bury state papers—his home served as the Admiralty's office—and his much valued Parmesan cheese.

The fire began to work its way into the heart of the City; it destroyed the Royal Exchange, took the medieval Guildhall, whose oak timbers were so stout that for hours they glowed "in a bright, shining coale, as it had been a palace of gold or a great building of burnished brass." At last the fire reached St. Paul's Cathedral, crowning the western hill of the City. The o'd cathedral had been one of the great wonders of medieval Europe. The City booksellers, convinced that the sanctity of the cathedral and the thickness of its stone walls would be proof even against this fire, had filled the crypt with their books. Their faith was ill-founded for the flames took hold of St. Paul's and gutted it. The lead of the roof flowed in volcanic torrents down Ludgate Hill.

The king, Charles II, and his brother, the duke of York, alerted by Pepys, organized fire-fighting teams from among the panic-stricken citizens; houses were blown up to create firebreaks, thatched roofs torn down to prevent sparks from igniting them. But it was not till Wednesday night that the wind dropped, and a light fall of rain, early on Thursday morning, made it possible to gain some sort of control over the disaster. In those four days, the fire had swept from close to the eastern boundary of the City, near to London Tower, as far westward as Fleet Street, to within a hundred yards of the Temple church. Some 400 streets containing 13,200 houses were wiped out; London lost St. Paul's Cathedral, 87 churches, the Guildhall, the Royal Exchange, the Custom House, the Leadenhall, and 44 City Company Halls. All that remained was a paring around the northeastern and northern edges. Five medieval churches remained unscathed, as did St. Bartholomew-the-Great further north. Samuel Pepys's house was safe, too.

The person who best kept his head was the king himself. On September 13, he issued a proclamation declaring that London would be rebuilt of stouter, less combustible materials, that the streets must be wider, that a proper survey should be made so that no man should lose what was rightly his, that he himself would be responsible for the rebuilding of the Custom House, and that those who rebuilt in an approved manner would be rebated the hearth tax (domestic rates) for seven years. Others reacted to the king's lead with equal speed and efficiency; within a week of the fire's ending, the king received a plan from a young mathematician, Dr. Christopher Wren of Oxford University, demonstrating how the city might be newly laid out in an ideal, geometric manner. Within the following week, four more such plans reached the monarch. Charles, who had spent his years of exile during and after the Civil War as a poor relation at the magnificent court of Louis XIV, wanted to seize this chance to emulate France. But he was a realistic man. A commission was set up—six men, three chosen by the king and three by the City, two of whom had already put forward plans of their own. Wren was one of the king's team. Commendably prompt, the Commission announced their finding on October 24. London must be rebuilt on the old street plan, with such road widenings and improvements as could be made without causing too much disturbance. Speed in rebuilding and the restoration of trade were imperative.

It is fashionable to lament the rejection of Wren's plan as London's great lost opportunity. I myself doubt this. A great city evolves gradually; its streets and buildings represent the needs, concerns, ambitions, and dreams of its citizens. Overall plannings or redevelopments, whether they be the product of one man's vision or a committee's consensus, are apt to disregard the human needs of those who are going to live there. London may well have been wise to retain its medieval street plan.

I n this emergency, 17th-century society—the king, the City authorities, Parliament—moved with a speed almost unbelievable in the 20th century. By February 1667, a series of bills had been drafted, debated, and passed to become the Fire Acts. They laid down that houses of standard types were to be built of noncombustible materials with flat, uniform frontages. The picturesque timber-framed, lathe-and-plaster dwellings, one floor jutting out above another, possibly with a thatched roof as crown, were banished from the City. A special Fire Court was set up to resolve disputes about land and tenure, the judges and lawyers volunteering to work without fees in this unparalleled emergency; it sat for six years and gave judgment in some 1,500 cases which, considering that 13,200 houses had been destroyed, many of them held in multiple tenancies, suggests that most parties exercised common sense and restraint in building claims. When all was settled, the City authorities, by way of thanks and recognition of services, commissioned full-length portraits of the 22 judges, which are still in the possession of the Guildhall.

The homeless citizens were instructed to pay half a mark (37½p) for a hastily sworn-in surveyor to stake out the limits of their former houses so that the land could be cleared and rebuilding begin. The great shortages were of money, men, and materials. But a tax to be levied on coal entering the Port of London was authorized to pay for the reconstruction of St. Paul's, the churches, and public buildings; the City authorities and the Livery Companies dug into their resources and, in days when prudent people kept a good part of their substance in gold pieces in a money-chest under their own roofs, neighbor lent to neighbor and the great rebuilding began. The new houses were built from London's own earth; the clay of the Thames basin, once fired, made excellent bricks. The Guild laws, restricting labor to local residents, were relaxed so that help could come in from all over the country. By 1671, within five years, more than 7,000 houses—95% of what was to be rebuilt—were completed or well under way; the new Custom House was finished, and the Royal Exchange enlarged and reopened. In that year, Lord Mayor's Day was once again celebrated with ceremony and pageantry.

The coal tax came in slowly at first and this, coupled with lack of stone, meant that the cathedral and city churches remained unbuilt, though sites were cleared and men worshipped in temporary "tabernacles." Eighty-seven churches had been destroyed, 51 were rebuilt, many parishes being amalgamated. For all of these, Wren provided the designs, though inevitably the detailed working-out was undertaken by other hands, and site supervision was necessarily the responsibility of others. Fourteen churches were begun in 1670; between the mid-1670s and the early 1680s, there were some 30 under construction. By 1685, the main structures of most were completed; towers and spires were added or finished in the early 1700s, after half a generation's breathing space. In creating these churches, Wren—the son of a dean, the nephew of a bishop—had to decide what an Anglican church should look like. The great medieval Catholic tradition of church building had fallen into abeyance with the Reformation; then, the emphasis had been on the altar, and an impenetrable screen often separated the priest from his flock. Now, communion was to be celebrated in the sight of all, since all would participate, and a greater importance would be given to the sermon, which would have to be audible—in short, the need was for a church for *congregational* worship. Wren advanced no single solution but, in almost all his churches, he placed the emphasis on the body of the nave and brought the chancel well within the church.

**W**ren was, in most cases, working on cramped and irregularly shaped sites and, at the beginning, it was still uncertain how large and how steady an income would be produced by the coal tax. The exteriors of Wren's churches are very plain; sometimes, in London's busy streets, it is possible to walk past and, unless you are observant, to miss the entrance—St. Peter, Cornhill, is a good example. But one feature stands out, even today: To each church, Wren gave a distinctive tower, spire, or steeple, and by them you can still pilot your way around the City's streets. Inside the church the provision of fittings was the responsibility of the parish and so, from examining the altar, the pulpit, the organ, the font, and the woodwork in general, we can deduce a good deal about the wealth and taste of each 17th-century parish.

Of those 51 churches, time, chance, the developer, and wartime damage have taken their toll. Between 1781 and 1939, 19 of Wren's churches were destroyed; another seven were lost to the bombs and were not restored after the war. Of those that remain, most are in excellent condition, well looked-after, and well-loved. Some remain as parish churches; others, owing to dwindling congregations, have become Guild churches with special weekday responsibilities toward London's daytime, working population, or toward particular religious or social needs. Many of them depend upon voluntary help with supervision, and so are not open all the time. But they are still there, playing their part in the religious, social, and ceremonial life of the City.

All the time that he was planning or supervising the City churches, Wren was thinking about St. Paul's. Even before the fire, he had been called in by the Dean and Chapter to advise on how the cathedral should be restored after the damage and decay of the Civil War and the Commonwealth years. After the disaster, when it proved impossible to improvise a temporary church because of the calcined condition of the remaining fabric,

Dean Sancroft, later Archbishop of Canterbury, wrote to Wren, "You are so absolutely and indispensably necessary to us that we can do nothing, resolve on nothing, without you." After several rejected plans, Wren undertook the Great Model, which can still be seen in the crypt of St. Paul's. It is over 18 feet long, cost over £500 to make—a first-class house on a main street could then be had for £400. It was to be a single-story building in the shape of a Greek cross with arms of equal length, with a giant portico, and a dome 120 feet wide—eight feet wider than the present dome and only 17 feet smaller than St. Peter's in Rome. But the design was too revolutionary, too great a departure from the traditional Latin cross of the old cathedral, and the clergy rejected it. Their reaction was not all prejudice; there was a practical need to choose a building that could be completed a part at a time. Wren resolved to "make no more models, or publicly to expose his Drawings" but, patient as always, produced a compromise design, Latin cross in shape with a cupola surmounted with a spire. Nine years of deliberation and argument had slipped by since the fire; it was time for work to begin. The king gave his Warrant to this hybrid plan in May 1675, authorizing Wren, whom he had knighted two years before and who had been Surveyor-General since 1669, to make "variations, rather ornamental than essential, as from time to time he should see proper." Wren took advantage of this liberty to return much closer to his preferred design, and to give us the masterpiece which is St. Paul's.

**W**hen the site was cleared and they began to set out the foundations, Wren told a workman to find a sizable piece of stone to use as a marker. The man brought, at random and by chance, a piece of an old gravestone with one word upon it: RESURGAM—the Latin for "I shall rise again." Everyone took this to be a good omen. And rise the cathedral did—520 feet long and 365 feet in height, from the crown of the lantern over the dome to the ground—and all in a comparatively short space of time, the first service being held in the choir on December 2, 1697. Even so, there were criticisms and disagreements: At one stage, hoping to speed matters, Parliament tried to hold back half of each of Wren's annual payments of £200 until the work was completed. There were also agitations for the dome to be clad in copper rather than in somber and dignified lead. Despite everything, Wren and his team of craftsmen and skilled laborers worked on steadily. His son, the younger Christopher, placed the last stone on the lantern late in October 1708, watched by old Edward Strong the mason, whose brother Thomas had laid the foundation stone in June 1675. It had taken 120 years and 13 architects to build St. Peter's in Rome; St. Paul's was the work of one man, completed in half a lifetime.

Wren lies buried in the crypt, with the proudest epitaph that any architect could ever have: *Lector, si monumentum requiris, circumspice*—Reader, if you seek his monument, look around you.

# London's Theaters

By John Elsom

President of the International Association of Theater Critics, John Elsom is also a professor at the City University, London.

**L**ondon is famous for its theaters and there are a lot of them, more than in Paris, New York, or Moscow. They are comparatively easy to find, which is helpful for the visitor, and they come in all shapes and sizes, from stately opera houses and national theaters to tiny "black box" studios. There are historic theaters, and ones that opened last week, and ones maybe that should not have opened at all. I have to admit that, having been a theater critic in London for over 20 years, I still sometimes feel like a child let loose in a candy store. What did I do right, God, that I should be so lucky?

But there is one embarrassing problem. When friends come to London for a few days, they often ask me what shows they should see, and this is rarely an easy question to answer. It is not just a matter of remembering what productions are actually playing in some 60 theaters during the days in question, but of guessing at their tastes. If I recommend a boring play to somebody whom I suspect of being a rather boring person, then I quickly discover that he or she is not boring at all, but sharp, sophisticated, and very indignant; the opposite, of course, can also happen. Due to some quirk of temperament—although there may be a loftier explanation—I never feel satisfied with the safe choices, the ones that any travel company would recommend.

Most people, for example, like musicals; and over the past 10 years, London has taken over from New York as the world's center for spectacular musicals. The Broadway hits, *Cats, Les Misérables*, and *The Phantom of the Opera*, all originated in London (where they are still playing), as did *Miss Saigon, Aspects of Love*, and *Jesus Christ, Superstar!* As if in some transatlantic pact, several musical hits, *Anything Goes, Into the Woods*, and *42nd Street*, came from Broadway in recent years. At one time it was said that British theater could not produce musicals. It had neither the talent nor the resources. All that has changed.

There are other obvious recommendations. Shakespeare is alive and well and usually being performed by one of our two national companies: the Royal Shakespeare Company and the Royal National Theatre Company. For opera and ballet lovers, and for those who enjoy grand settings, there is the Royal Opera House, Covent Garden, or its often more adventurous rival, the English National Opera at the Coliseum. For tired businessmen, there are glamor revues in Soho; for families, there are West End comedies and whodunits; and for those who like to contribute to *The Guinness Book of Records*, Agatha Christie's *The Mousetrap* has been playing continuously in London since 1952, the longest unbroken run of any play anywhere in the world.

But no self-respecting critic would ever recommend *The Mousetrap*, not even to an enemy—suggestions like that can be left to the London Tourist Board. This is not just intellectual snobbery. Plays by Christie and Noël Coward, not to mention Shakespeare, Shaw, Wilde, and Maugham, are performed all over the world. To millions of people, they represent the international face of British theater—slick, efficient, and often profound entertainment. But there is a private face as well, more anxious, cautious, and human, and when friends visit London, I want to introduce them to the distinctive quality of our theaters rather than to the postcard images.

When I try to explain, however, what is so special about them, I start stammeringly to use phrases like "living history" and "a sense of continuity." The theater in London has evolved over three centuries, and at no time has the weight of the past squeezed the life from the present. Nor have traditions been ignored to pursue the latest fashion. Even in Sir Henry Irving's day (the late 19th century), or David Garrick's (the mid-18th century), a delicate balance was maintained between the old, the new, and the futuristic.

In practical terms, this means that British actors are usually trained to speak Shakespeare, as well as Samuel Beckett, that our directors have a strong grounding in classical theater, and that our writers use skills in phraseology and dramatic construction that owe a considerable debt to the past. Christopher Hampton and Tom Stoppard can write epigrams to match those of Oscar Wilde. But nowhere is this blend of past and present more vividly illustrated than in the architecture and geography of London's theaterland.

London is often described as a collection of villages, built at different times and reflecting the priorities of the ages that brought them into being. The same might be said of its theaters. The theaters on the South Bank, for example, near Waterloo Station, were all built or renovated during the 1960s and 1970s, at a time when civic and national idealism conspired to provide culture for the people. The National Theatre, one example of this altruism, is a bold concrete construction, with defiant flytowers, likened by one of its less enthusiastic supporters to a bunker, presumably with hidden guns either trained upon or defending the Houses of Parliament across the river.

The Barbican, near St. Paul's, is another example of post-war reconstruction, which now provides a London home for the Royal Shakespeare Company. A forbidding and sometimes confusing mass of apartment buildings and high-rises, the Barbican is the largest arts center in Europe, with two theaters, an art gallery, a concert hall, a motionpicture theater, a library, and the Guildhall School of Music and Drama. However formidable the Barbican and the National Theatre may seem from a distance, their foyers and auditoriums are spacious and welcoming, with bookstores, cafés, restaurants, and spaces for small musical ensembles and poetry readings. No commercial impresario could afford to be so lavish with space, or would want to pay the heating bills. These were theaters designed for an age of public subsidy, and their programs reflect this high-mindedness.

**T**he West End theaters, on the other hand, were mainly built at the turn of the century, for openly commercial reasons, as part of an attempt to turn Piccadilly and Shaftesbury Avenue into a dignified playground for the newly rich Victorian and Edwardian middle classes. Piccadilly has since become the center for the British entertainment industry, which now embraces much more than the theater itself to include films, records, videos, television, and fashion as well. In the dozens of restaurants around Shaftesbury Avenue, half of British show business seems to take its lunch; the air is full of stage gossip and the smells of exotic cooking. The other half dines in the trendier brasseries of Covent Garden.

Piccadilly Circus itself is a poor reflection of what it once was, when the neon lights first lit up the exuberant facades of its Victorian mansions. Nowadays, afflicted by schemes for its improvement, it feels unloved and unfinished. But there are gems, among them the delightful Criterion Theatre, first built in 1873 and rebuilt in 1884, and recently restored to its original soft, muted colors, painted ceilings, and eccentric tiling. It was the first British theater to be placed below street level. The lessons learned from the failures in its air-conditioning system were later applied to ventilating the Underground.

Since Piccadilly Circus itself was developed in 1885, the Criterion Theatre is one of its original buildings, clearly expressing a Victorian middle-class wish for intimate, comfortable theaters, far removed from the big, vulgar music halls (vaudeville theaters). Since it was intended for that purpose, the stage and the auditorium are most suited to comfortable plays, comedies, and dramas with small casts and no complicated scenery.

Fanning out from Piccadilly Circus are three famous theater streets: Haymarket, Coventry Street (leading to Leicester Square), and Shaftesbury Avenue. Leicester Square now has only one theater, the modern Prince of Wales designed to house musicals and spectacular revues. The other Leicester Square theaters have been transformed into movies and nightclubs, but in the Square itself, there is a half-price ticket booth offering discounted seats for many productions on the day of the performance only.

In 1721, a summer theater opened on Haymarket, known as the Little Theatre in the Hay. It had to battle against government restrictions, but it eventually received a royal patent to become the Theatre Royal, Haymarket. The existing theater, which opened in 1821, is notable, apart from its classical columns and portico, for being the first theater anywhere to have what is now known as a "picture frame" stage. In the 1880s it became famous for elegant, drawing room plays ("society drama"), and some of that high style has persisted today.

On the other side of the road there is another historic theater, Her Majesty's, built in 1896–97 by the actor-manager, Sir Herbert Beerbohm Tree. As an actor, Tree is best remembered as Svengali in *Trilby*, while as a director, he was noted for his scenic effects—real rabbits hopping around an ethereal glade in *A Midsummer Night's Dream*. He would thoroughly have approved of the current production at Her Majesty's, *The Phantom of the Opera*. He would have wanted to play both the Phantom and the falling chandelier. It is a very appropriate musical for this theater, with its gilt and marbled-plaster auditorium in a style derived, as Tree proudly but inaccurately boasted, from the court of the French Sun King himself, Louis XIV.

**S**haftesbury Avenue was built in the 1890s and early 1900s to be a show business boulevard. The Edwardian theaters line up, side by side, sumptuously dressed like *demimondaines* and as virtuous: The Apollo, the Lyric, the Queen's, the Globe, and, at Cambridge Circus, where the avenue intersects Charing Cross Road, the massive Palace Theatre, a center for musicals. These were the theaters which, in the 1930s, saw the triumphs of Noël Coward and John Gielgud, the young Laurence Olivier and Gertie Lawrence; and they survived the war to everybody's surprise with their pride merely ruffled. Only the deplorable modern facade to the Queen's Theatre shows what damage might have been done.

These are theaters primarily designed for civilized, social gatherings, intimate but not too small, elaborate but not grandiose. Partly because of such theaters, Britain has developed a tradition of intelligent, middlebrow comedy writing, of which Coward and Somerset Maugham were exponents in the 1930s, just as Alan Ayckbourn, Simon Gray, Michael Frayn, Peter Shaffer, and Tom Stoppard are today. As if to suggest that such witty sophistication is skin-deep, Soho lurks beyond the Shaftesbury Avenue stage doors, a maze of narrow streets and alleys, where London swung in the 1960s.

Many felt that Soho swung too far in the wrong direction and it certainly acquired a sleazy reputation. But the area has once more become a cosmopolitan center for the entertainment industry. There are jazz clubs (including Ronnie Scott's) and the London headquarters of movie, record, and television companies. There are several theaters too, including the London Palladium, the last and most prestigious vaudeville house in London, the Piccadilly, and what was once known as the Windmill Theatre—named after the Moulin Rouge, which used to offer London versions of the opulent sex revues of Paris.

The old Windmill, apart from offering statuesque nudes and drafty fan dancers, had a remarkable reputation for discovering comics, who had to be funny to raise a smile from the dirty old men. Peter Sellers was just one of the comics who served their apprenticeships at the Windmill. Now, Raymond's Revuebar has taken over from the Windmill as a glamour theater and has a little studio attached, the Boulevard, which stages a changing program of musicals, new plays, and comedy.

Shaftesbury Avenue crosses over Charing Cross Road and continues up toward Holborn, ending in the large punctuation mark of the Shaftesbury Theatre. But on the other side of Cambridge

Circus, the character of theaterland changes. The bustle and raffishness of Soho has gone, and the feeling is of being in an Edwardian penny arcade. There are Edwardian theaters in Charing Cross Road itself and in St. Martin's Lane, but this is, in fact, an older district of London, more Regency and early Victorian than Edwardian, the district of which the West End was originally deemed to be "west."

This is Covent Garden, where Eliza Doolittle once sold flowers in a supposedly incurable Cockney accent, before (in Shaw's *Pygmalion* and *My Fair Lady)* Professor Higgins redeemed her from the gutter. The old market has been similarly transformed into a smart and cheerful piazza, with bright, trendy stores and some lively street theater, including on occasions the best tap dancing in town. The Theatre Museum now occupies one former warehouse in the market, both appropriate and a little superfluous, for the whole area is steeped in British theatrical history.

Backing the marketplace on one side is the Royal Opera House, built in six months, from December 1857 to May 1858, which achieved a small miracle of clear design, elegant elaboration, and spaciousness. In another street near the piazza is the Theatre Royal, Drury Lane, completed in 1812, the finest example of Georgian classical theater architecture in Britain. These two theaters, both built on sites occupied by theaters since the early 18th century, were for a hundred years in deadly rivalry. They were the "Patent Houses," the only ones allowed to perform straight, nonmusical plays. Until their exclusive rights were revoked in 1843, the various actor-managers that ran them, and many of the writers who created the successes that they staged, waged endless struggles for supremacy.

But the history of Covent Garden does not end with the patent houses, for in a side street near Drury Lane is the old Lyceum Theatre, where Sir Henry Irving strutted the boards in the last decades of the 1800s and terrified audiences in *The Bells.* Irving, the most eminent British actor since Garrick a hundred years before, and the first to be knighted, did much to restore and popularize the plays of Shakespeare. In his Beefsteak Club, in rooms above his theater, he entertained members of the royal family.

To the south of Covent Garden, in the Strand, is the Savoy Theatre. Built by the impresario D'Oyly Carte in 1881, it immediately became the home of the Savoyard operas by Gilbert and Sullivan. The Savoy was the first public building in the world to be lit entirely by electric light, made possible "by the incandescent lamps of Mr. J. W. Swan of Newcastle-upon-Tyne," much to the annoyance of Irving, who preferred the grainy, foggy texture of gas lamps. It was damaged by a fire in January 1990 and is currently being reconstructed.

In 1905, the Aldwych and the Strand Theatres opened as part of a development scheme housing the Waldorf Hotel. The Aldwych was famous in the 1930s for its farces, written by Ben Travers for a redoubtable comedy team; but it became even better known in the 1960s as the temporary London home of the Royal Shakespeare Company. Another Covent Garden theater, formerly the New and now the Albery (to the west of the area on St. Martin's Lane), housed the Old Vic company during the latter years of World War II. Those seasons are still remembered as providing the most exciting classical productions ever seen in Britain, one answer to the "doodlebugs"—the rocket bombs fired against London.

**A**ll these theaters (and there are many more) are within easy walking distance of one another. Despite its diversity, the heart of London's theaterland is remarkably compact. But if you talk to ardent drama students, or to high-minded enthusiasts with no professional ambitions at all, they might tell you about the theater without even mentioning the West End. This is because, for the past 50 years, the most exciting productions in town have started in theaters away from the center. Before 1939, the Old Vic near Waterloo Station provided the best productions of Shakespeare, usually staged with very little money; while Sadlers Wells in Islington (which was a sister theater to the Old Vic) pioneered British opera and ballet.

During the 1950s, the revival of postwar British theater was spearheaded by two companies led by two charismatic directors, George Devine and Joan Littlewood. The Royal Court in Sloane Square was taken over in 1955 by the English Stage Company, with Devine as its artistic director and with the declared policy of encouraging new playwrights. The results were immediate and dramatic. John Osborne's *Look Back in Anger* in 1956 caught the postwar mood of iconoclasm and doubt; and in the wake of that success came other young dramatists, including Arnold Wesker, Edward Bond, and Howard Brenton. Devine died in 1966, but the tradition that he established has continued, and the Royal Court is still one of the leading avant-garde theaters in London, along with Islington's Almeida and several fellow West London theaters: the Gate in Notting Hill, Riverside Studios in Hammersmith, and the Bush Theatre in Shepherds Bush.

Littlewood was less of an intellectual. She wanted to create a working-class theater movement, left-wing and serious in intent, but popular in means. She harnessed the old techniques of vaudeville and pantomime to themes that ranged from nuclear disarmament to the history of World War I (in *Oh, What a Lovely War!*, 1963). Although she long ago retired, the Theatre Workshop in Stratford, East London, has become a model for other theaters and their directors, not only in Britain. It even kicked off the '90s with a huge hit, *Five Guys Named Moe*, still playing at the Lyric Shaftsbury Avenue and, since March '92, on Broadway.

There was, in fact, a remarkable group of directors, writers, and actors in Britain during the 1950s and 1960s, who collectively transformed the theater. One of their main targets was the commercialism and, as they saw it, the complacency of the West

End; values they sought to challenge. The success of this post-war theater movement can be illustrated most obviously by the establishment of the two national companies. There had been steady demands for a national theater for more than a hundred years: In the 1960s, Britain established two, both working in old theaters (the Aldwych and the Old Vic) until new ones could be built for them. They developed different reputations. The National Theatre, led by Olivier, was considered to be an "actors' theater," with the performances of Olivier himself leading the way. The Royal Shakespeare Company was a "directors' theater," where the emphasis among the actors was on teamwork. The National Theatre tackled a wider range of drama, world classics, and major new plays as well as revivals of famous British plays. The Royal Shakespeare Company, led by Peter Hall, had as its house dramatist Shakespeare; and, in Stratford-upon-Avon, its main theater was committed to the work of the Elizabethan and Jacobean playwrights. In London, and in its various studios, the RSC could, and did, introduce new and European plays into its repertoire. Its company style evolved during the 1980s toward major musicals *(Les Misérables)* and such epics as its dramatization of Charles Dickens's *Nicholas Nickleby*.

The differences between the two companies became blurred when Hall succeeded Olivier at the National Theatre in 1973, and was followed at the Royal Shakespeare Company by Trevor Nunn (then Terry Hands and now Adrian Noble). The national companies also expanded with time; currently the RSC runs five theaters, three in Stratford and two at the Barbican, with additional RSC productions playing in the West End and touring extensively throughout the country. The NT has its three contrasting theaters on the South Bank, the Olivier, the Lyttelton, and the Cottesloe, and also regularly transfers productions to the West End.

There were, however, other results from the postwar British theater revival, such as the establishment of suburban and regional repertory theaters, of which the Lyric, Hammersmith, and Greenwich theaters are the best examples. Another effect, dating from the late 1960s and early 1970s, was the growth of fringe theater clubs, which now can be found all round London. The standards are variable, but they can be very high, particularly at the Gate, the Bush, the Hampstead Theatre in Swiss Cottage, and the Almeida.

And so, to return to the original questions: What shows should visitors see in London? What are the leading theaters? I usually try to suggest a package, which includes one West End comedy, one major new play, one musical, a classical production at one of the national companies, and some talent-spotting, checking the listings in *Time Out* (the weekly "What's On" magazine) to find out what is playing in the fringe theaters or at the Royal Court. Within each of these choices, I recommend mainly on the quality of the production, but also try to bear in mind the nature of the theater, particularly its history and architecture.

Having thus solemnly deliberated, and presented a well-balanced program, I can sit back, confident that most of my friends will ignore it anyway and see *Cats*, *The Mousetrap*, and the Tower of London, before flopping with exhaustion on the floor of Harrods Food Hall. Never mind. I tried.

# 3 Exploring London

London grew from a wooden bridge built over the Thames in the year 43 to its current 7 million souls and 600 square miles in haphazard fashion, meandering from its two official centers: Westminster, seat of government and royalty, and the City, site of finance and commerce. Many a tourist meanders the same way, and below are comprehensive sections on the famous parts of **Westminster and Royal London** and the **City.**

However, London's *un*official centers multiply and mutate year after year, and it would be a shame to stop at the postcard views. Life is not lived in monuments, as the patrician patrons of the great Georgian architects understood when they commissioned the elegant squares and town houses of **St. James's** and **Mayfair** for newly rich merchants. Thanks to World War II bombs and today's newly rich merchants, the West End's elegance is patchy now. On its border, the once-seedy **Soho** is still pleasuring the flesh (gastronomically these days); and Westminster Abbey's original vegetable patch (or convent garden), which became the site of London's first square, **Covent Garden,** is now an unmissable stop on any agenda.

If the great, green parks (*see* Hyde Park, Kensington Gardens, and Notting Hill and Regent's Park and Hampstead, *below*) are, as in Lord Chatham's phrase, "the lungs of London," then the River Thames is its backbone. The river underlay the commercial success that made London great, and along its banks stand reminders from every century. Though there was traffic as far east as the **Docklands** from Roman times, they had their first boom in the Victorian era; today they are undergoing a peculiar stop-start renaissance. It's said that only cockneys "born within the sound of Bow Bells" in the adjacent **East End** are authentic Londoners, and so our tour around one of London's most diverse and least known areas may be the quintessential local experience.

Back on the river, the **South Bank** section absorbs the Southwark stews of Shakespeare's day, the concert hall from the '50s Festival of Britain, the arts complex from the '70s, and—farther downstream—the gorgeous 17th- and 18th-century symmetry of **Greenwich,** where the world's time is measured.

## Highlights for First-time Visitors

**British Museum** (*see* Bloomsbury and Legal London)
**Houses of Parliament** (*see* Westminster and Royal London)
**Hyde Park** (*see* Hyde Park and Kensington Gardens)
**National Gallery** (*see* Westminster and Royal London)
**Piccadilly Circus** (*see* St. James's and Mayfair)
**St. Paul's Cathedral** (*see* The City)
**Tower Bridge** (*see* The City)
**Tower of London** (*see* The City)
**Victoria and Albert Museum** (*see* Knightsbridge, Kensington, and Holland Park)
**Westminster Abbey** (*see* Westminster and Royal London)

# Westminster and Royal London

*Numbers in the margin correspond to points of interest on the West-minster and Royal London map.*

This tour is London For Beginners. If you went no farther than these few acres, you would have seen many of the famous sights, from the Houses of Parliament, Big Ben, Westminster Abbey, and Bucking-ham Palace, to two of the world's greatest art collections, the National and the Tate Galleries. It might be possible to do it all in a day, but picking a highlight or two is a better idea. The galleries alone deserve a day apiece, and if you're going to the Abbey in summer, queuing up will consume most of your stamina. This is concentrated sightseeing, so pace yourself.

Westminster is by far the younger of the capital's two centers, post-dating the City by some 1,000 years. Edward the Confessor put it on the map when he packed up his court from its cramped City quarters and went west a couple of miles, founding the abbey church of West-minster—the minster west of the City—in 1050. Subsequent kings continued to hold court there until Henry VIII decamped to White-hall Palace in 1512, leaving Westminster to the politicians. And there they still are, not in the palace, which was burned almost to the ground in 1834, but in the Victorian mock-Gothic Houses of Par-liament, whose 320-foot Clock Tower is as much a symbol of London as the Eiffel Tower is of Paris.

## Trafalgar Square and the National Gallery

**Trafalgar Square** is the obvious place to start for several reasons. It is the center of London, by dint of a plaque on the corner of the Strand and Charing Cross Road from which distances on U.K. sign-posts are measured. It is the home of the National Gallery and of one of London's most distinctive landmarks, Nelson's Column; also of many a political demonstration, a raucous New Year's party, and the highest concentration of bus stops and pigeons in the capital. In short, it is London's most famous square.

Long ago the site housed the Royal Mews, where Edward I (1239–1307) kept his royal hawks and lodged his falconers. (Not the num-berless Edward the Confessor of Westminster Abbey fame, who died in 1066, this one was known as "Longshanks" and died of dysen-tery in 1307.) Later, all the kings' horses were stabled here, in in-creasingly smart quarters, until 1830, when John Nash had the buildings torn down as part of his Charing Cross Improvement Scheme—which he did not live to complete. The baton was passed to Sir Charles Barry, architect of the Houses of Parliament, and in 1840 the Square was paved, with the fountains added five years lat-er. (Sir Edwin Lutyens remodeled them in 1939, and they were fur-ther enhanced with cavorting sea creatures after World War II.)

Keeping watch from his 145-foot granite perch is E. H. Baily's 1843 statue of Admiral Lord Horatio Nelson, one of England's favorite heroes. Around the foot of **Nelson's Column,** three bas-reliefs depict his victories at Cape St. Vincent, the Battle of the Nile, and Copen-hagen, and a fourth his death at Trafalgar itself in 1805; all four were cast from cannon he captured. The four majestic lions, designed by the Victorian painter Sir Edwin Landseer, were added in 1867. The calling cards of generations of picturesque pigeons have been a cor-

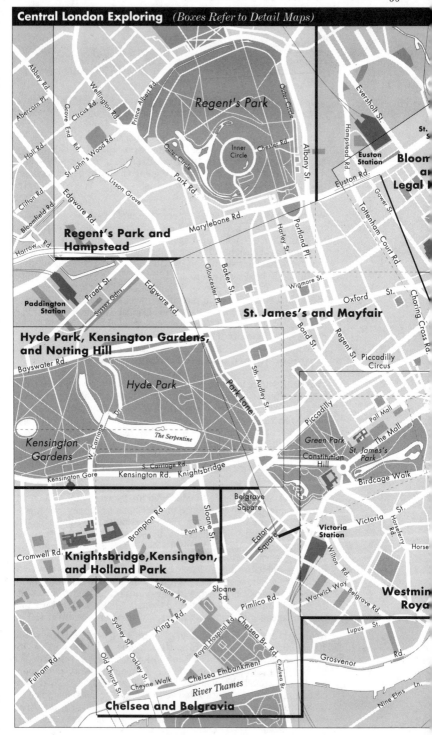

**Central London Exploring** *(Boxes Refer to Detail Maps)*

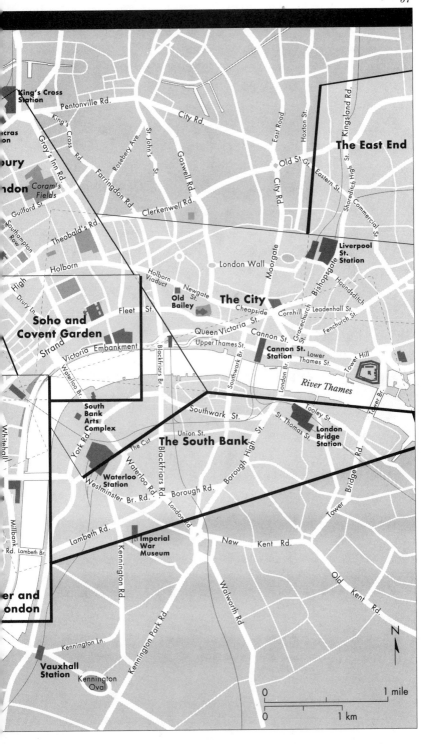

# Westminster and Royal London

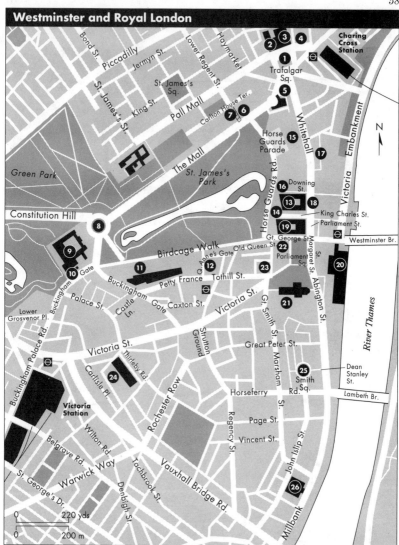

rosive problem for the statue, but it may have been finally solved by a 150th-birthday present of a pigeon-proof gel coating. You can read about the area on a plaque marking the anniversary. Street performers have been licensed for the first time, and they should enhance the square's intermittent atmosphere of celebration. This is strongest in December, first when the lights on the gigantic Christmas tree (an annual gift from Norway to thank the British for harboring their royal family during World War II) are turned on, and then when thousands see in the New Year. (Be careful, though: In 1986, five people were crushed to death by the New Year's crowds.)

The north side of the square is filled by the low, gray, colonnaded neo-classical facade of the **National Gallery.** The institution was founded in 1824, when George IV and a connoisseur named Sir George Beaumont persuaded a reluctant government to spend £57,000 on part of the recently deceased philanthropist John Julius Angerstein's collection. These 38 paintings, including works by Raphael, Rembrandt, Titian, and Rubens, were augmented by 16 of Sir George's own and exhibited in Angerstein's Pall Mall residence until 1838, when William Wilkin's building was completed. By the end of the century, enthusiastic directors and generous patrons had turned the National Gallery into one of the world's foremost collections, with works from painters of the Italian Renaissance and earlier, from the Flemish and Dutch masters, the Spanish school, and of course the English tradition, including Hogarth, Gainsborough, Stubbs, and Constable.

In 1991, following years of wrangling and the rehanging of the entire collection, the Sainsbury Wing was opened. It had been financed by the eponymous British grocery dynasty to house the early Renaissance collection, and designed—eventually—by the American architect Robert Venturi after previous plans were abandoned. (Prince Charles hadn't liked them. "A monstrous carbuncle on the face of a much-loved friend" was his infamous comment.)

The collection is really too overwhelming to absorb in a single viewing. It is wise to acquaint yourself with the layout—easy to negotiate compared with other European galleries—and plot a route in advance. The **Micro Gallery,** a computer information center in the Sainsbury Wing, might be the place to start. You can access in-depth information on any work here, choose your favorites, and print out a free personal tour map that marks the paintings you most want to see. Careful, though—you could spend hours in here scrolling through the colorful potted history of art.

Among the 2,200-odd paintings, most of them on permanent display, many are instantly recognizable. Since we lack the space for a comprehensive overview, what follows is a list of 10 of the most familiar to jog your memory, whet your appetite, and offer a starting point for your own exploration. The first five are in the Sainsbury Wing. In chronological order:

**van Eyck** (c. 1395–1441), *The Arnolfini Marriage.* A solemn couple hold hands, the fish-eye mirror behind them mysteriously illuminating what can't be seen from the front.
**Uccello** (1397–1475), *The Battle of San Romano.* In a work commissioned by the Medici family, the Florentine commander on a rearing white warhorse leads armored knights to battle with the Sienese.
**Bellini** (c.1430–1516), *The Doge Leonardo Loredan.* The artist captured the Venetian doge's beatific expression (and snail-shell "buttons") at the beginning of his 20 years in office.
**Botticelli** (1445–1510), *Venus and Mars.* Mars sleeps, exhausted by

the love goddess, oblivious to the lance wielded by mischievous putti and the buzzing of wasps (*vespe* = the Vespucci family for whom Botticelli worked?).

**Leonardo da Vinci** (1452–1519), *The Virgin and Child*. This haunting black chalk cartoon is partly famous for having been attacked at gunpoint, and now gets extra protection behind glass and screens.

**Caravaggio** (1573–1610), *The Supper at Emmaus*. A cinematically lit, freshly resurrected Christ blesses bread in an astonishingly domestic vision from the master of chiaroscuro.

**Velasquez** (1599–1660), *The Toilet of Venus*. "The Rokeby Venus," named for her previous home in Yorkshire, has the most famously beautiful back in any gallery. She's the only surviving female nude by Velasquez.

**Constable** (1776–1837), *The Hay Wain*. Rendered overfamiliar by too many birthday cards, this is the definitive version of rural England.

**Turner** (1775–1851), *The Fighting Téméraire*. Most of the collection's other Turners were moved to the Tate Gallery; the final voyage of the great French battleship into a livid, hazy sunset stayed here.

**Seurat** (1859–1891), *Bathers at Asnières*. This static summer day's idyll is the pointillist extraordinaire's best-known work.

Glaring omissions from the above include Titian, Holbein, Bosch, Brueghel, Rembrandt, Vermeer, Rubens, Canaletto, Claude, Rembrandt, Teipolo, Gainsborough, Ingres, Monet, Renoir, Van Gogh . . . you get the picture. *Trafalgar Sq., tel. 0171/839–3321; 0171/839–3526 (recorded general information); 0171/389–1773 (recorded exhibition information). Admission free; admission charge for special exhibitions. Free 1-hr guided tours start at the Sainsbury Wing weekdays at 11:30 and 2:30, Sat. 2 and 3:30. Open Mon.–Sat. 10–6, Sun. 2–6; June–Aug., also Wed. until 8; closed Good Friday, May Day, Dec. 24–26, Jan. 1.*

---

**Time Out**    **The Brasserie** in the Sainsbury Wing of the National Gallery offers a fashionable lunch—mussels, gravadlax, charcuterie, salads, a hot dish—plus baguette sandwiches, pastries, tea, coffee, and wine, in a sophisticated, spacious room on the second floor.

---

Once you're done exploring the gallery's contents, stop a moment on the steps in front and admire the view over Trafalgar Square toward Admiralty Arch, with Canada House on the west side and South Africa House on the east. On the sloping lawn in front is Grinling Gibbons's statue of James II, who failed to return Britain to Catholicism during his short reign (1685–8). Gibbons, "Master Carver in Wood to the Crown," was much in vogue at the end of the 17th century (see his choir-stall carvings at St Paul's). At the other end of the lawn is a bronze of George Washington presented to the British by the Commonwealth of Virginia in 1921.

❸ The **National Portrait Gallery** just around the corner is a much smaller affair, an idiosyncratic collection that presents a potted history of Britain through its residents, past and present. As an art collection it is eccentric, since the subject, not the artist, is the point, and there are notable works (a Holbein portrait of Henry VIII, Stubbs and Hockney self-portraits) mixed up with photographs, busts, caricatures, and amateur paintings. (The miniature of Jane Austen by her sister Cassandra, for instance, is the only likeness we have of the great novelist). Many of the faces are obscure and will be just as unknown to English visitors, since the portraits outlasted their sitters' fame. But the annotation is comprehensive, and there is a new, sepa-

rate research center for those who get hooked on particular personages—part of an expansion that has cleaned up the layout (still chronological, with the oldest at the top) and added a photography
gallery.

Across the street, east of the National Gallery, is the much-loved
**❹** church of **St. Martin-in-the-Fields,** completed in 1726. James Gibbs's
classical-temple-with-spire design, unusual at the time, has become
familiar as the pattern for churches in early colonial America.
Though it seems dwarfed by the surrounding structures, the spire is
actually slightly taller than Nelson's Column. It is a welcome sight
for the homeless, who have sought soup and shelter here since 1914.
The church is also a haven for music lovers, since the internationally
known Academy of St. Martin-in-the-Fields was founded here, and a
popular program of free lunchtime and evening concerts continues
today. St Martin's is often called the royal parish church, partly because Charles II was christened here—not because his mistress,
Nell Gwyn, lies under the stones, alongside William Hogarth,
Thomas Chippendale (the cabinet maker), and Jack Sheppard, the
notorious highwayman. Also in the crypt is the **London Brass-Rubbing Centre,** where you can make your own souvenir knight from
replica tomb brasses, with metallic waxes, paper, and instructions
provided. For professionally made souvenirs, there is a crafts market in the courtyard behind the church. *St. Martin-in-the-Fields,
Trafalgar Sq., tel. 0171/437–6023. Rubbing fee from £1 according to
size of brass selected. Open Mon.–Sat. 10–6, Sun. noon–6; closed
Good Friday, Dec. 24–26, Jan. 1.*

There's a pathetic history attached to the **equestrian statue of
Charles I** that stands near Whitehall on the southern slope of Trafalgar Square (on a pedestal *possibly* designed by Sir Christopher
Wren and *possibly* carved by Grinling Gibbons). After Charles's
High Treasurer ordered it (from Hubert le Sueur), the Puritan Oliver Cromwell tumbled Charles from the throne and commissioned a
scrap dealer with the appropriate name of Rivett to melt the king
down. Rivett made a fortune peddling knickknacks wrought, he
claimed, from its metal, only to produce the statue miraculously unscathed after the restoration of the monarchy—and to make more
cash reselling it to the authorities. In 1767 Charles II had it placed
where it stands today, near the spot where his father was executed
in 1649.

## St. James's Park and the Mall

Leave Trafalgar Square from its southwest corner through
**❺** **Admiralty Arch,** designed in 1910 by Sir Aston Webb as part of a ceremonial route to Buckingham Palace and named after the adjacent
Royal Navy headquarters. As you pass under the enormous triple
archway—though not through the central arch, which is opened
only for state occasions—the atmosphere changes along with the
color of the road, for you are exiting frenetic Trafalgar Square and
entering **The Mall** (rhymes with "gal"), which has nothing to do with
shopping.

The original Mall was laid out around 1660 for the game that gave
Pall Mall (*see below*) its name, and quickly became the place to be
seen. Samuel Pepys, Jonathan Swift, and Alexander Pope all wrote
about it, and it continued as the *beau monde*'s social playground into
the early 19th century, long after the game of pall mall had gone out
of vogue. Something of the former style survives on those summer
days when the queen is throwing a Buckingham Palace garden par-

ty: The Mall is thronged with hundreds of her subjects, from the grand and titled to the humble and hardworking, all of whom have donned hat and frock to take afternoon tea with her—or somewhere near her—on the lawns of Buck House (as Londoners quippingly call the palace). The old Mall still runs alongside the graceful pink 115-foot-wide avenue that replaced it in 1904 for just such occasions.

**St. James's Park,** along the south side of the Mall, is London's smallest, most ornamental park, and the oldest of its royal ones. Henry VIII drained a marsh that festered here next to the lepers' hospital that St. James's Palace replaced, and bred his deer on the newly dry land. Later kings tinkered with it further, James I installing aviary and zoo (complete with crocodiles); Charles I laying formal gardens, which he then had to cross to his execution in 1649; and Charles II employing André Lenôtre, Louis XIV's Versailles landscaper, to remodel it completely with avenues, fruit orchards, and a canal. Its present shape more or less reflects what John Nash designed under George IV, turning the canal into a graceful lake (which was cemented in at a depth of four feet in 1855, so don't even think of swimming) and generally naturalizing the gardens.

More than 30 species of birds—including flamingos, pelicans, geese, ducks, and swans (which belong to the queen)—now congregate on Duck Island at the east end of the lake, attracting ornithologists at dawn. Later on summer days the deck chairs (which you must pay for) are crammed with office lunchers being serenaded by music from the bandstands. The best time to stroll the leafy walkways, though, is after dark, with Westminster Abbey and the Houses of Parliament rising above the floodlit lake, and peace reigning.

Back on the Mall, look to the other (north) side for a more solid example of John Nash's genius, **Carlton House Terrace.** Between 1812 and 1830, under the patronage of George IV (Prince Regent until George III's death in 1820), Nash was responsible for a series of West End developments, of which these white-stucco facades and massive Corinthian columns may be the most imposing. It was a smart address, needless to say, and one that prime ministers Gladstone (1856) and Palmerston (1857–75) enjoyed. Today Carlton House Terrace is home to the Royal College of Pathologists, the ❻ Royal Society, the Turf Club, and, at No. 12, the **Institute of Contemporary Arts,** better known as the **ICA.** Behind its incongruous facade, the ICA has provided a stage for the avant-garde in performance, theater, dance, visual art, and music since it was established in 1947. There are two cinemas, an underused library of video artists' works, a recently expanded bookshop, a café and a bar, and a team of adventurous curators. *The Mall, tel. 0171/930–3647. 1-day membership: £1.50 adults, children under 14 free. An additional charge is made for entry to specific events. Open daily noon– 9:30, later for some events; closed Dec. 24–27, Jan. 1.*

**Time Out** The **ICAfé** is windowless but brightly spotlit, with a self-service counter offering good hot dishes, salads, quiches, and desserts. The bar upstairs, which serves baguette sandwiches, has a picture window overlooking the Mall. Both are packed before popular performances, and are subject to the £1.50 one-day membership fee.

❼ Bisecting Carlton House Terrace are the **Duke of York Steps,** surmounted by the 124-foot Duke of York's Column, from which an 1834 bronze of George III's second son, Frederick, gazes toward the Whitehall War Office. The Duke was popular among his troops until each man in the army had one day's pay extracted to fund this

£25,000 tribute, which was perched so high, said the wits, to keep him away from creditors. He owed £2 million at his death.

## Buckingham Palace to Parliament Square

Facing the palace from the traffic island at the west end of the Mall is the white marble **Queen Victoria Memorial.** The monument was conceived by Sir Aston Webb as the nucleus of his ceremonial Mall route and executed by the sculptor Thomas Brock, who was knighted on the spot when it was revealed to the world in 1911. Many wonder why he was, since the thing is Victoriana incarnate: The frumpy queen glares down the Mall, with golden-winged Victory overhead and her siblings Truth, Justice, and Charity, plus Manufacture, Progress-and-Peace, War-and-Shipbuilding, and so on—in Osbert Sitwell's words, "tons of allegorical females . . . with whole litters of their cretinous children"—surrounding her. Climbing it is not encouraged, even though it's the best vantage point for viewing the daily **Changing of the Guard,** which, with all the pomp and ceremony monarchists and children adore, remains one of London's best free shows. *Guard leaves Wellington Barracks 11 AM, arrives Buckingham Palace 11:30. Daily Apr.–July; alternate days Aug.–March.*

**Buckingham Palace** tops the must-see lists, although the building itself is no masterpiece and has housed the monarch only since Victoria moved here from Kensington Palace at her accession in 1837. At that time the place was a mess. George IV, at *his* accession in 1820, had fancied the idea of moving to Buckingham House, his parents' former home, and had employed John Nash, as usual, to remodel it. The government authorized only "repair and improvement"; Nash, who had other ideas, overspent his budget by about half a million pounds. George died, Nash was dismissed, and Edward Blore finished the building, adding the now familiar east front (facing the Mall). Victoria arrived to faulty drains and sticky doors and windows nevertheless, but they did not mar her affection for the place, nor that of her son, Edward VII. The Portland stone facade dates only from 1913 (it, too, was part of the Aston Webb scheme), and the interior was renovated and redecorated only after World War II bomb damage.

The palace contains some 600 rooms, including the State Ballroom and, of course, the Throne Room. The royal apartments are in the north wing; when the queen is in, the royal standard flies at the masthead. Until recently all were off limits to the public, but a 1992 fire at Windsor Castle created an urgent need for cash. And so the state rooms are now on show—on something of an experimental basis through 1997—for eight weeks in August and September, when the royal family is away. Without an invitation to one of the queen's garden parties, however, you won't see much of the magnificent 45-acre grounds. *Buckingham Palace Rd., tel. 0171/799–2331. Admission: £8 adults, £5.50 senior citizens, £3.50 children under 17. Call for hours, which had not been set at press time.*

The former chapel at the south side, on the other hand, has been open to visitors since 1962 as the **Queen's Gallery.** On display here are paintings from her majesty's collection—the country's largest—including works by Vermeer, Leonardo, Rubens, Rembrandt, Canaletto . . . and Queen Victoria. Sign-of-the-times note: Now that she is a taxpayer, HRH's artworks, along with all her other possessions (for example, Buckingham Palace), are officially part of a business known as "Royal Collection Enterprises." *Buckingham Palace Rd., tel. 0171/799–2331. Admission: £2.50 adults, £1.80 sen-*

*ior citizens, £1.20 children. Open Tues.–Sat. 10–5, Sun. 2–5; closed Dec. 24–Mar. 4, Good Friday.*

Nearly next door stand the Nash-designed **Royal Mews.** Mews were originally falcons' quarters (the name comes from their "mewing," or feather shedding), but horses gradually eclipsed birds of prey. Now some of the magnificent royal beasts live here alongside the fabulous bejeweled, glass, and golden coaches they draw on state occasions. The place is unmissable children's entertainment. *Buckingham Palace Rd., tel. 0171/799–2331. Admission: £2.50 adults, £1.80 senior citizens, £1.20 children. Combined ticket for Queen's Gallery and Royal Mews: £4.50 adults, £3.10 senior citizens, £1.90 children. Open Oct.–Mar., Wed. noon–4; Apr.–Oct., Tues.–Thurs. noon–4; closed Mar. 25–29, Oct. 1–5, Dec. 23–Jan. 5.*

⓫ Turn back along Buckingham Palace Road, continue down Birdcage Walk, and on the right you'll soon see the **Wellington Barracks,** the headquarters of the Guards Division. Five regiments of elite foot guards (Grenadier, Coldstream, Scots, Irish, and Welsh) protect the sovereign and patrol the palace dressed in tunics of gold-purled scarlet and tall fur "busby" helmets of Canadian brown bearskin. (The two items cost more than £4,000 the set.) If you want to learn more about the guards, you can visit the **Guards Museum**; the entrance is next to the Guards Chapel. *Wellington Barracks, Birdcage Walk, tel. 0171/930–4466, ext. 3430. Admission: £2 adults, £1 children under 16 and senior citizens. Open Sat.–Thurs. 10–4; closed national holidays.*

⓬ Past the barracks on the right is the entrance to **Queen Anne's Gate,** two pretty 18th-century closes, once separate but now linked by a statue of the last Stuart monarch. (Another statue of Anne, beside St. Paul's, inspired the doggerel "Brandy Nan, Brandy Nan, you're left in the lurch,/ Your face to the gin shop, your back to the church,"—proving that her attempts to disguise her habitual tipple in a teapot fooled nobody.)

Have a look at the Henry Moore bronze *Mother and Child*, then follow Dartmouth Street out of Queen Anne's Gate. Great George Street, at the end, leads into Parliament Square. But turn left at Storey's Gate for a detour down Horse Guard's Road past the ⓭ **Foreign Office,** built in the 1860s by Sir Giles Gilbert Scott, who was better known for such fantastical Gothic Revival buildings as the House of Commons (*see below*).

Make a right before the Foreign Office into King Charles Street to ⓮ find the **Cabinet War Rooms**—an essential visit for World War II buffs. During air raids the War Cabinet met in this warren of 17 bomb-proof chambers. The Cabinet Room is still arranged as if a meeting were about to convene; in the Map Room, the Allied campaign is charted; the Prime Minister's Room holds the desk from which Churchill made his morale-boosting broadcasts; and the Telephone Room has his hot line to FDR. *Clive Steps, King Charles St., tel. 0171/930–6961. Admission: £3.80 adults, £2.80 senior citizens, £1.90 children under 16. Open daily 10–5:15; closed Good Friday, May Day, Dec. 24–26, Jan. 1.*

Farther along Horse Guards Road, opposite St. James's Park, ⓯ stands **Horse Guards Parade.** Once the tilt-yard of Whitehall Palace, where jousting tournaments were held, it is now notable mainly for the annual Trooping the Colour ceremony, in which the queen takes the Royal Salute, her official birthday gift, on the second Saturday in June. (Like Paddington Bear, the queen has two birthdays; her real one is on April 21.) There is pageantry galore, with marching bands and the occasional guardsman fainting clean away in his bus-by, and throngs of people. The ceremony is televised and also broadcast on Radio 4. You can also attend the queenless rehearsals on the preceding two Saturdays.

The quiet street barred by iron gates that you passed on your right before coming to Horse Guards Parade is **Downing Street,** which con-
tains London's modest version of the White House at **10 Downing Street.** Only three houses remain of the terrace built circa 1680 by Sir George Downing, who spent enough of his youth in America to graduate from Harvard—the second man ever to do so. No. 11 is the residence of the chancellor of the exchequer (secretary of the treasury), No. 12 the party whips' office. No. 10 has officially housed the prime minister since 1732. (The gates were Margaret Thatcher's brainwave.)

At the other end of Downing Street (though, of course, you can't walk through—you have to go all the way around via King Charles Street) is the wide street called Whitehall. Bang in the middle is the other facade of Horse Guards, where two mounted sentries known as the Queen's Life Guard provide what may be London's most frequently taken up photo opportunity. They change, quietly, at 11 AM Monday–Saturday, 10 on Sunday. On a site reaching from here to the Thames and from Trafalgar to Parliament squares once stood Whitehall Palace, established by Henry VIII, who married two of his six wives (Anne Boleyn and Jane Seymour) and breathed his last there. The sheer scale of this 2,000-room labyrinth in red Tudor brick must have been breathtaking, but we won't dwell on it, since it burned to the ground in 1698, thanks to a fire started by a Dutch laundress whose name has not made it to posterity.

All that remains today is **Banqueting House,** but if the rest was like this, we should weep for its loss. Actually, we know that it was quite different. (One foreign visitor accused the palace of being "ill-built, and nothing but a heap of houses.") James I had commissioned Inigo Jones to do a grand remodeling of the palace, and Banqueting House is the only part that got completed. Jones (1573–1652), one of England's great architects and designers, had been influenced by Andrea Palladio's work during a sojourn in Tuscany and had brought that sophistication and purity back with him to London. The graceful and disciplined classical style of Banqueting House must have stunned its early occupants. James I's son, Charles I, enhanced the interior by employing the Flemish painter Peter Paul Rubens to glorify his father all over the ceiling. As it turned out, these allegorical paintings, depicting a wise monarch being received into heaven, were the last thing Charles saw before he was beheaded by Cromwell's Parliamentarians on a scaffold outside in 1649. But his son, Charles II, was able to celebrate the restoration of the monarchy here 20 years later. *Whitehall, tel. 0171/930-4179. Admission: £2.25 adults, £1.79 senior citizens, £1.50 children under 15. Open Mon.–Sat. 10–5; closed Good Friday, Dec. 24–26, Jan. 1, and at short notice for banquets, so call first.*

Walk south on Whitehall toward Parliament Square, and in the middle of the street you'll see the **Cenotaph,** a stark white monolith designed in 1920 by Edward Lutyens to commemorate the 1918 armistice. On Remembrance Day (the Sunday nearest November 11) it is strewn with blood-red poppies to honor the dead of both world wars, with the first wreath laid by the queen. (Wherever you are on that day, you'll be inveigled to drop pennies for veterans' charities into tins for your own plastic poppy.)

**The Houses of Parliament**

Continue down Whitehall (which becomes Parliament Street beside
**19** Gilbert Scott's Foreign Office), pass the **Home Office** on the right,
bear left, and you will soon be confronted with London's most fa-
**20** mous and photogenic sight: the **Houses of Parliament,** with the Clock
Tower, which everyone mistakenly calls Big Ben, looming largest,
and Westminster Abbey ahead of you across Parliament Square.

The Palace of Westminster, as the complex is still properly called,
was established by Edward the Confessor in the 11th century, when
he moved his court from the City, and has been the seat of English
administrative power ever since. In 1512, Henry VIII abandoned it
for Whitehall (*see above*). It ceased to be an official royal residence
after 1547: At the Reformation, the Royal Chapel was secularized
and became the first meeting place of the Commons. The Lords settled in the White Chamber.

These, along with everything but the **Jewel Tower** and **Westminster
Hall,** were destroyed in 1834 when "the sticks"—the arcane abacus
beneath the Lords' Chamber on which the court had kept its ac-
counts until 1826—were incinerated and the fire got out of hand.
The same cellar had seen an earlier attempt to raze the palace: the
infamous Gunpowder Plot of November 5, 1605, perpetrated by the
Catholic convert Guy Fawkes and his fellow conspirators. If you are
in London in late October or early November, you may see children
with dressed-up teddy bears demanding a "penny for the guy!"
They do it because, to this day, November 5 is Guy Fawkes Day
(a.k.a. Bonfire Night), when fireworks bought with the pennies accompany pyres of these makeshift effigies of Guy Fawkes, and anyone who still knows it recites: "Remember, remember/The 5th of
November,/The Gunpowder Treason and plot./There isn't a reason/
Why gunpowder treason/Should ever be forgot."

After the 1834 fire, architects were invited to submit plans for new
Houses of Parliament in the grandiose "Gothic or Elizabethan
style." Charles Barry's were selected from among 97 entries, partly
because Barry had invited the architect and designer Augustus
Pugin to add the requisite neo-Gothic curlicues to his own Renais-
sance-influenced style. As you can see, it was a happy collaboration,
with Barry's classical proportions offset by Pugin's ornamental
flourishes—although the latter were toned down by Gilbert Scott
when he rebuilt the bomb-damaged House of Commons after World
War II.

The two towers were Pugin's work. The **Clock Tower,** now virtually
the symbol of London, was completed in 1858 after long delays due
to clock bickering. (Barry designed the faces himself in the end.) It
contains the 13-ton bell that chimes the hour (and the quarter)
known as Big Ben. Some say Ben was "Big Ben" Caunt, heavy-
weight champ; others, Sir Benjamin Hall, the far-from-slim Westminster building works commissioner. At press time, the 336-foot-
high **Victoria Tower,** which contains the 3-million-document parliamentary archives, having undergone one of the largest stone restoration and cleaning operations in Europe, had just emerged from its
scaffolding. The rest of the complex was scrubbed down some years
ago; the revelation of the honey stone under the dowdy, smog-black-
ened facades, which seemed almost symbolic at the time, cheered
London up no end.

There are two Houses, the Lords and the Commons. The former consists of over 1,000 peers (nowadays there are more "life peers," with

recently bestowed titles, than aristocrats; there are also 26 Anglican bishops who are "spiritual peers"), the latter of 650 elect~d Members of Parliament (MPs). The party with the most MPs forms the government, its leader becoming Prime Minister; other parties form the Opposition. Since 1642, when Charles I tried to have five MPs arrested, no monarch has been allowed into the House of Commons. The State Opening of Parliament in November consequently takes place in the House of Lords, after a ritual inspection of the cellars in case a modern Guy Fawkes lurks.

Visitors aren't allowed many places in the Houses of Parliament, though the Visitors' Galleries of the House of Commons do afford a fine view of the surprisingly cramped debating chambers. The opposing banks of green leather benches seat only 346 MPs—not that this is much of a problem, since absentees far outnumber the diligent. When MPs vote, they exit by the "Aye" or the "No" corridor, counted by the party "whips" (yes, it is a foxhunting term); when they speak, it is not directly to each other but through the Speaker, who also decides who will get the floor each day. Elaborate procedures notwithstanding, debate is often drowned out by the amazingly immature jeers and insults familiar to TV viewers since 1989, when cameras were first allowed into the House of Commons.

The House of Lords was televised first, perhaps because its procedures are more palatably dignified, with the Lord Chancellor, or Chief Justice, presiding from his official seat, the Woolsack (England's economy was once dependent on this commodity) over a few gently slumbering peers. Or perhaps the Lords were first because of their telegenic gold and scarlet chamber, Pugin's masterpiece. The Upper House remains the highest court of appeal in the land, though its parliamentary powers are restricted to delaying or suspending passage of a bill. It is separated from the Lower House by the octagonal **Central Lobby,** which is where constituents wait for their MPs and also where the press is received—hence the term "lobby correspondent" for a domestic political reporter. Other public areas of the 1,100-room labyrinth are rather magnificently got up in high neo-Gothic style and punctuated with stirring frescoes commissioned by Prince Albert. You pass these en route to the Visitors Galleries—if, that is, you are patient enough to wait in line for hours (the Lords line is shorter) or have applied in advance through your embassy. *St. Stephen's Entrance, St. Margaret St., SW1, tel. 0171/ 219–3000. Admission free. Commons open Mon.–Thurs. 2:30–10, Fri. 9:30–3; Lords open Mon.–Thurs. 2:30–10. Closed Easter week, May bank holiday, July–Oct., 3 weeks at Christmas.*

As you cross Parliament Square, have a look at the statues dotted around: Lord Palmerston and Benjamin Disraeli, prime ministers under Victoria; Sir Robert Peel, who formed the first Metropolitan Police Force (hence the nickname "bobbies"); a hulking, hunched Churchill in a 1973 bronze; Richard the Lionheart; Oliver Cromwell; and, on the far side (as if over the pond), Abraham Lincoln.

## Westminster Abbey

Off the south side of Parliament Square, announced by the teeming human contents of herds of tour buses, stands **Westminster Abbey.** Nearly all of England's monarchs were crowned here, amid vast pomp and circumstance, and most are buried here, too. The place is crammed with spectacular medieval architecture and impressive and moving monuments. It is worth pointing out, though, that the Abbey is still a place of worship, and while attending a service is not

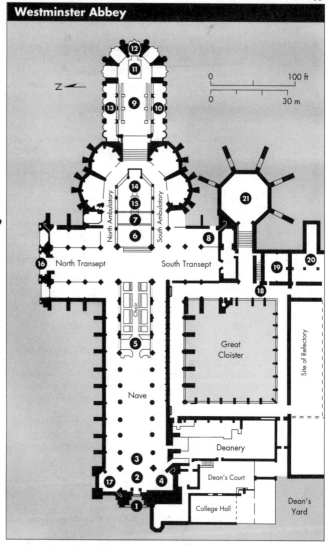

**Westminster Abbey**

something to undertake purely for sightseeing reasons, it provides a glimpse of the Abbey in its full majesty, accompanied by music from the Westminster choristers and the organ that Henry Purcell once played. Some parts are closed on Sunday except to worshipers.

The origins of Westminster Abbey are uncertain. The first church on the site may have been built as early as the 7th century by the Saxon King Sebert (who may be buried here, alongside his queen and sister); a Benedictine abbey was established in the 10th century. There were certainly pre-existing foundations when Edward the Confessor was crowned in 1040, moved his palace to Westminster, and began building a church. Only traces have been found of that incarnation, which was consecrated eight days before Edward's death in 1065. (It appears in the Bayeaux Tapestry.) Edward's canonization in 1139 gave a succession of kings added incentive to shower the Abbey with attention and improvements. Henry III, full of ideas from his travels in France, pulled it down and started again with Amiens and Rheims in mind. In fact it was the master mason Henry de Reyns ("of Rheims") who, between 1245 and 1254, put up the transepts, north front, and rose windows, as well as part of the cloisters and Chapter House; and it was his master plan that, funded by Richard II, was resumed 100 years later. Henry V (reigned 1413–1422) and Henry VII (1485–1509) were the chief succeeding benefactors. The Abbey was eventually completed in 1532. After that, Sir Christopher Wren had a hand in shaping the place; his West Towers were completed in 1745, 22 years after his death. The most riotous elements of the interior were, similarly, much later affairs.

The **Nave** is your first sight on entering; you need to look up to gain a perspective on the awe-inspiring scale of the church, since the eye-level view is obscured by the 19th- (and part 13th-) century choir screen, past which point admission is charged. Before paying, look at the poignant **Tomb of the Unknown Warrior,** an anonymous World War I martyr who lies buried here in memory of the soldiers fallen in both world wars. Nearby is one of the very few tributes to a foreigner, a plaque to Franklin D. Roosevelt.

There is only one way around the Abbey, and as there will almost certainly be a crocodile of shuffling visitors at your heels, you'll need to be alert to catch the highlights. Pass through the **Choir,** with its mid-19th-century choir stalls, into the **North Transept.** Look up to your right to see the painted-glass **Rose Window,** the largest of its kind; left for the first of the extravagant 18th-century monuments in the North Transept chapels. You then proceed into the **Henry VII Chapel,** passing the huge white marble tomb of Elizabeth I, buried with her half sister, "Bloody" Mary I; then the tomb of Henry VII with his queen, Elizabeth of York, by the Renaissance master Torrigiano (otherwise known for having been banished from Florence after breaking Michelangelo's nose). All around are magnificent sculptures of saints, philosophers, and kings, with wild mermaids and monsters carved on the choir stall misericords (undersides), and exquisite fan vaulting above—one of the miracles of Western architecture.

Next you enter the **Chapel of Edward the Confessor,** where beside the royal saint's shrine stands the **Coronation Chair,** which has been briefly graced by nearly every regal posterior. Edward I ordered it around 1300, and it shelters the Stone of Scone (pronounced *skoon*), a brown sandstone block upon which Scottish kings had been crowned since time began, and which Edward I symbolically stole in 1296. Scottish Nationalists borrowed it back for about six months in 1950; otherwise, only Oliver Cromwell (who took it to Westminster Hall to "crown" himself Lord Protector) and wartime caution have removed it from here.

The tombs and monuments for which Westminster Abbey is probably best loved appeared at an accelerated rate starting in the 18th century. One earlier occupant, though, was Geoffrey Chaucer, who in 1400 became the first poet to be buried in **Poets' Corner.** Most of the other honored writers have only their memorials here, not their bones: William Shakespeare and William Blake (who both had a long wait before the dean deemed them holy enough to be here at all), John Milton, Jane Austen, Samuel Taylor Coleridge, William Wordsworth, Charles Dickens. All of Ben Jonson is here, though—buried upright in accord with his modest demand for a two-foot-by-two-foot grave. ("O rare Ben Jonson," reads his epitaph, in a modest pun on the Latin *orare,* "to pray for.") Sir Isaac Newton, James Watt, and Michael Faraday are among the scientists with memorials. There is only one painter: Godfrey Kneller, whose dying words were "By God, I will not be buried in Westminster."

After the elbow battle you are guaranteed in Poets' Corner, you exit the Abbey by a door from the South Transept. *Broad Sanctuary, tel. 0171/222–5152. Admission to nave free, to Royal Chapels and Poets' Corner £3 adults, £1.50 students and senior citizens, £1 children under 16. Open Mon., Tues., Thurs., and Fri. 9–4; Wed. 9–7:45; Sat. 9–2 and 3:45–5; Sun. all day for services only; closed weekdays to visitors during services.*

Outside the west front is an archway into the quiet green **Dean's Yard** and the entrance to the **Cloisters,** where the monks strolled in contemplation. You may do the same, and catch a fine view of the massive flying buttresses above in the process. You may also, for a modest fee, take an impression from one of the tomb brasses in the **Brass-Rubbing Centre** (tel. 0171/222–2085). Also here is the entrance to **Westminster School,** formerly a monastic college, now one of Britain's finest public (which means the exact opposite) schools; Christopher Wren and Ben Jonson number among the old boys.

Also here are the Chapter House and the Norman Undercroft below. The **Chapter House,** a stunning octagonal room supported by a central column and adorned with 14th-century frescoes, is where the King's Council and, after that, an early version of the Commons met between 1257 and 1547. (The monks complained about the noise.) In the **Undercroft,** which survives from Edward the Confessor's original church, note the deliciously macabre effigies made from the death masks and actual clothing of Elizabeth I, Charles II, and Admiral Lord Nelson (complete with eye patch), among others. Finally, the **Pyx Chamber** next door contains the Abbey's treasure, just as it used to when it became the royal strongroom in the 13th century. *Undercroft, Pyx Chamber, and Treasury, tel. 0171/222–5152. Joint admission: £2 adults, £1.60 senior citizens, £1 children under 16. Chapter House, tel. 0171/222–5897. Admission: £1 adults, 80p senior citizens and students, 50p children. All open daily 10:30–4; closed Good Friday, Dec. 24–26.*

**㉒** Dwarfed by the Abbey is its northern neighbor, the church of **St. Margaret's,** founded in the 12th century and rebuilt between 1486 and 1523. It is the parish church of the Houses of Parliament and much sought after for weddings; Samuel Pepys married here in 1655, Winston Churchill in 1908. The east Crucifixion window celebrates another union, the marriage of Prince Arthur and Catherine of Aragon. Unfortunately, it arrived so late that Arthur was dead and Catherine had married his brother, Henry VIII. Sir Walter Raleigh is among the notables buried here, only without his head, which had been removed at Old Palace Yard, Westminster, and kept by his wife, who would ask visitors, "Have you met Sir Walter?" and produce it from a velvet bag.

**㉓** Across the road from the Abbey's west front is **Central Hall,** headquarters of the Methodist Church in Britain. The building, now used mostly for concerts and meetings, was the site of the first General Assembly of the United Nations in 1948. Next door is the 1986 **Queen Elizabeth Conference Centre,** which hosts both official and commercial functions.

## Westminster Cathedral and the Tate Gallery

From Parliament Square, you have a choice between more religion or modern art, with Westminster Cathedral to the southwest and the Tate Gallery along the Thames to the south.

Taking the shorter—and, frankly, less interesting—route to church first, turn your back on the Abbey and exit Parliament Square down **Victoria Street,** the unlovely road to Victoria Station. Though it dates from the early 1860s, most of its Victorian and Edwardian buildings have been replaced by depressing concrete. On the right, note the three-sided steel sign that announces **New Scotland Yard,** which in 1967 replaced the granite-faced, turreted 1890 Thameside edifice (now called the Norman Shaw Building) that Sherlock Holmes knew so well.

㉔ You can't miss **Westminster Cathedral**—once you are almost upon it, that is. It's set back from the left side of the street in a 21-year-old paved square that has fallen on hard times. Westminster Council, the local authority, would like to turn it into the Piazza San Marco of London, but until funding is found, it remains the windy haunt of homeless people and pigeons.

The cathedral is the seat of the Cardinal of Westminster, head of the Roman Catholic Church in Britain; consequently it is London's principal Roman Catholic church. The asymmetrical redbrick Byzantine hulk, dating only from 1903, is banded with stripes of Portland stone and abutted by a 273-foot campanile at the northwest corner, which you can scale by elevator. Faced with the daunting proximity of the heavenly Abbey, the architect, John Francis Bentley, flew in the face of fashion by rejecting neo-Gothic in favor of the Byzantine idiom, which still provides maximum contrast today—not only with the great church, but with just about all of London.

The interior is partly unfinished but worth seeing for its atmosphere of broody mystery; for its walls, covered in mosaic of a hundred different marbles from all over the world; and for a majestic nave—the widest in England—distinguished by a series of Eric Gill reliefs depicting the Stations of the Cross. *Ashley Pl., tel. 0171/834–7452. Admission to tower: £2 adults, £1 senior citizens and children. Cathedral open daily, tower open daily Apr.–Sept.*

Retracing your steps east along Victoria Street, take a right in front of the Abbey into Great Smith Street, then the second left into Great Peter Street, and a right off there for a detour into **Smith Square.** This elegant enclave of perfectly preserved early 18th-century town houses still looks like the London of Dr. Johnson. The address is much sought-after by MPs, especially of the Tory persuasion, since No. 32 is the Conservative Party Headquarters. The Baroque ㉕ church of **St. John's, Smith Square,** completed around 1720, dominates charmingly. It is well known to Londoners as a chamber-music venue; its popular lunchtime concerts are often broadcast on Radio 3.

---

**Time Out**   In the crypt of St. John's is **The Footstool**—about the only place to find refreshment around here. It has an interesting and reasonably priced lunchtime menu and also serves evening meals on concert nights.

---

Leave Smith Square by Dean Stanley Street, which brings you to traffic-laden Millbank along the river; turn right for a 10-minute ㉖ walk to London's *other* world-class art museum, the **Tate Gallery.**

The Tate Gallery of Modern British Art, to give it its full title, opened in 1897, funded by the sugar magnate Sir Henry Tate. "Modern" is slightly misleading, since one of the three collections here consists of British art from 1545 to the present, including works by William Hogarth, Thomas Gainsborough, Sir Joshua Reynolds, and George Stubbs from the 18th century, and by John Constable, William Blake (a mind-blowing collection of his visionary works), and the pre-Raphaelite painters from the 19th. Also from the 19th century is the second of the Tate's collections, the Turner Bequest, consisting of J. M. W. Turner's personal collection; he left it to the nation on condition that the works be displayed together. The James Stirling–designed **Clore Gallery** (to the right of the main gallery) has fulfilled his wish since 1987, and should not be missed.

The Tate's modern collection is international and so vast that it's never all on display at once. The current director, Nicholas Serota, instigated the strategy of cyclical rehanging, which goes some way toward solving the dilemma of the gallery's embarrassment of riches, but also means that a favorite work may not be on view. Nobody knows how long the current search for a second site will take; in the meantime, the most famous and popular works are on permanent display. Just about every artist of the late 19th and 20th centuries you have ever heard of is represented, and a good deal more besides. Your tour will deal you multiple shocks of recognition (Rodin's *The Kiss*, Lichtenstein's *Whaam!*). Here's a short list of names: Matisse, Picasso, Braque, Léger, Kandinsky, Mondrian, Dali, Bacon, de Kooning, Pollock, Rothko, Moore, Hepworth, Warhol, Freud, Hockney. *Millbank, tel. 0171/821–1313 or 0171/ 821–7128 (recorded information). Admission free; admission charged for special exhibitions. Open Mon.–Sat. 10–5:50, Sun. 2– 5:50; closed Good Friday, May Day, Dec. 24–26, Jan. 1.*

**Time Out** The Tate's coffee bar serves superior snacks. The restaurant is expensive, with a long, ambitious wine list and a menu that changes monthly and veers from experiments in Modern British cooking to traditional roast beef and Yorkshire pudding. Always book the restaurant (tel. 0171/887–8877).

# St. James's and Mayfair

*Numbers in the margin correspond to points of interest on the St. James's and Mayfair map.*

These neighboring areas (together with part of the following section, Soho and Covent Garden) make up the West End, which is the real center of London nowadays. Here is the highest concentration of grand hotels, department stores, exclusive shops, glamorous restaurants, commercial art galleries, auction houses, swanky offices—all the accoutrements of a capital city.

The western boundaries of St. James's have already been grazed in the previous section, and you may have gotten the picture: This has been a fashionable part of town from the first, largely by dint of the eponymous palace, St. James's, which was a royal residence—if not *the* palace—from the time of Henry VIII until the beginning of the Victorian era. Mayfair, though it is younger than St. James's, is just as expensively patrician, from leafy squares on the grand scale to the jewels on display at Asprey's. Our jumping-off point is the familiar landmark of Trafalgar Square.

## St. James's

A late-17th-century ghost in the streets of contemporary St. James's would not need to bother walking through walls, since practically none have moved since he knew them. Its boundaries, clockwise from the north, are Piccadilly, Haymarket, The Mall, and Green Park: a neat rectangle, with a protruding spur satisfyingly located at Cockspur Street. The rectangle used to describe "gentlemen's London," where Sir was outfitted head and foot (but not in between, since the tailors were, and still are, north of Piccadilly in Savile Row) before repairing to his club.

❶ Starting in **Trafalgar Square,** you'll find Cockspur Street on the left of Canada House; follow it into St. James's. At the foot of
❷ **Haymarket**—which got its name from the horse fodder sold there until the 1830s—you'll find yourself facing streams of oncoming traffic. At the top is Piccadilly Circus; in between are two stray (from theaterland) theaters, the Haymarket and Her Majesty's, where Lloyd-Webber's *Phantom* has taken up residence. The **Design Centre** at No. 28 is a showcase for British design, from interior to industrial, complete with a research library, gift shop, and café. The American Express office is also here, as are a couple of movie theaters—one very mall-like and hawking every known Yankee snack. Back at the foot of Haymarket, turn right into Pall Mall. Immediately on your right, after the high-rise New Zealand House, is London's
❸ earliest shopping arcade, the splendid Regency **Royal Opera Arcade,** which John Nash finished in 1818.

Pall Mall, like its near-namesake, *the* Mall, rhymes with "shall" and derives its name from the cross between croquet and golf that the Italians, who invented it, called *pallo a maglio,* and the French, who made it chic, called *palle-maille.* In England it was taken up with enthusiasm by James I, who called it "pell mell" and passed it down the royal line, until Charles II had a new road laid out for it in 1661. Needless to say, Catherine Street, as Pall Mall was officially named (after Charles's queen, Catherine of Braganza), was *very* fashionable. No. 79 must have been one of its livelier addresses, since Charles's gregarious mistress, Nell Gwyn, lived there. The king gave her the house when she complained about being a mere leaseholder, protesting that she had "always conveyed free under the Crown" (as it were); it remains, to this day, the only privately owned bit of Pall Mall's south side.

Stroll slowly down Pall Mall, the better to appreciate the creamy facades and perfect proportions along this showcase of 18th- and 19th-
❹ century British architecture. You'll soon hit **Waterloo Place** on your left, a long rectangle punctuated by the **Duke of York memorial** column over the **Duke of York Steps,** which you may have seen from the other (Mall) side on the previous exploring tour. Waterloo Place is littered with statues, among them Florence Nightingale, the "Lady with the Lamp" nurse-heroine of the Crimean War; Captain R. F. Scott, who led a disastrous Antarctic expedition in 1911–12 and is here frozen in a bronze by his wife; Edward VII, mounted; George VI; and, as usual, Victoria, here in terra-cotta.

Flanking Waterloo Place looking onto Pall Mall are two of the gentlemen's clubs for which St. James's came to be known as
❺ Clubland: the **Athenaeum** and the former United Service Club, now the **Institute of Directors.** The latter was built by John Nash in 1827–8 but was given a face-lift by Decimus Burton 30 years later to match it up with the Athenaeum, which he had designed across the way. It's fitting that you gaze on the Athenaeum first, since it was—

# St. James's and Mayfair

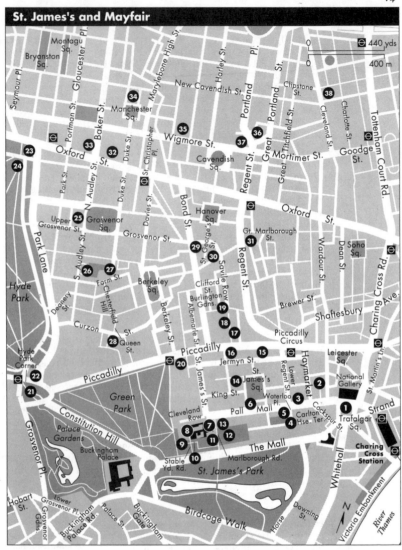

All Souls Church, **36**

Apsley House, **22**

Athenaeum, **5**

British Telecom
Tower, **38**

Burlington Arcade, **18**

Burlington House, **17**

Church of the
Immaculate
Conception, **27**

Clarence House, **10**

Fortnum and
Mason, **16**

Friary Court, **11**

Grosvenor Chapel, **26**

Grosvenor Square, **25**

Haymarket, **2**

Lancaster House, **9**

Langham Hotel, **37**

Liberty, **31**

London Library, **14**

Marble Arch, **23**

Marks and Spencer, **33**

Marlborough
House, **12**

Museum of
Mankind, **19**

Queen's Chapel, **13**

Reform Club, **6**

The Ritz, **20**

Royal Opera Arcade, **3**

St. George's Church, **30**

St. James's Church, **15**

St. James's Palace, **7**

Selfridges, **32**

Shepherd Market, **28**

Sotheby's, **29**

Speakers' Corner, **24**

Trafalgar Square, **1**

Wallace Collection, **34**

Waterloo Place, **4**

Wellington Arch, **21**

Wigmore Hall, **35**

York House, **8**

and is—the most elite of all the societies. (It called itself "The Society" until 1830 just to rub it in.) Most prime ministers and cabinet ministers, archbishops, and bishops have belonged; the founder, John Wilson Croker (the first to call the British right-wingers "Conservatives"), decreed it the club for artists and writers, and so literary types have graced its lists, too (Sir Arthur Conan Doyle, Rudyard Kipling, J. M. Barrie—the posh ones). Women are barred. Most clubs will tolerate female guests these days, but few admit women members, and anyway, even if your anatomy is correct it's almost impossible to become a member unless you have the connections—which, of course, is the whole point.

Next door are two James Barry–designed buildings, the **Travellers' Club** and the **Reform.** The latter is the most famous club of all, thanks partly to Jules Verne's Phineas Fogg, who accepted the around-the-world-in-80-days bet in its smoking room, and was thus soon qualified to join the former. And—hallelujah—women can join the Reform. The **RAC Club** (for Royal Automobile Club, but it's never known as that), with its marble swimming pool, and the **Oxford and Cambridge Club** complete the Pall Mall quota; there are other, even older, establishments—Brooks's, the Carlton, Boodles, and White's (founded in 1736, and the oldest of all)—in St. James's Street around the corner, alongside *the* gentlemen's bespoke (custom) shoemaker, Lobb's, and *the* hatter, James Lock.

Instead of turning right into St. James's Street, stay on Pall Mall until you are arrested by the surprisingly small Tudor brick **St. James's Palace,** with its solitary sentry posted at the gate. Matters to ponder as you look (you can't go in): It was named after a hospital for women lepers, which stood here in the 11th century; Henry VIII had it built; foreign ambassadors to Britain are still accredited to the Court of St. James's even though it has rarely been a primary royal residence; the present queen made her first speech here.

Continue along Cleveland Row by the side of the palace to spy on a pair of current royal residences and a former one. First on the left is **York House,** home of the duke and duchess of Kent. A left turn into Stable Yard Road brings you to **Lancaster House,** built for the Duke of York in the 1820s but more notable recently as the venue for the 1978 conference that led to the end of white rule in Rhodesia/Zimbabwe. On the other side of Stable Yard is **Clarence House,** home to England's best-loved royal (and practically the only scandal-free one), the Queen Mother. It was designed by Nash and built in 1825 for the Duke of Clarence, who became William IV.

Now you come to the Mall. Look left to see the other facade of St. James's Palace, which was designed by Wren in the 17th century. Then turn left up Marlborough Road and you'll see the palace's open-sided **Friary Court.** Turn around, and there is **Marlborough House,** designed by Wren in 1709 for the duchess of Marlborough, who asked for something "strong plain and convenient" bearing no similarity to Blenheim Palace. Judge for yourself, but she must have been pleased with it, because she remained there until she died in 1744. In front of the house is the **Queen's Chapel,** designed by Inigo Jones for the Infanta of Castille when she was betrothed to Charles I in 1623. This was actually the first classical church in England, and attending a service is the only way you can get to delight in it. *Sun. services Easter–July: Holy Communion 8:30 AM, sung Eucharist or morning prayer 11:15.*

Turn left, then right into St. James's Street, and right again into King Street to penetrate to the heart of St. James's and do a spot of shopping. You'd best stick to browsing at 8 King Street, though, which is **Christie's,** the fine-art auctioneers who got £25 million for Van Gogh's *Sunflowers*; ditto No. 7, **Spink & Son,** best known for selling money (coins, banknotes, medals) but with an English and Asian art gallery worth perusing. Coming up on the left, Duke Street harbors further exclusive little art salons; but keep going straight for now, into **St. James's Square,** one of London's oldest and leafiest. It was the most snobbish address of all when it was laid out around 1670, with 14 resident dukes and earls installed by 1720. Since 1841, No. 14—one of the several 18th-century residences spared by World War II bombs—has housed the **London Library,** which with its million or so volumes is the best private humanities library in the land. You can go in and read the famous authors' complaints in the comments book—but not the famous authors' books, unless you join, for £100 a year.

Leave the square via Duke of York Street to reach **Jermyn Street,** where the gentleman purchases his masculine paraphernalia. He buys his shaving sundries and hip flask from Geo. F. Trumper, briar pipe from Astley's, scent from Floris (for women too—both the Prince of Wales and his mother smell of Floris) or Czech & Speake, shirts from Turnbull & Asser, deerstalker and panama from Bates the Hatter, and his cheeses from Paxton & Whitfield (founded in 1740 and a legend among dairies). Shop your way east along Jermyn Street, and you're practically in Piccadilly Circus, ready for the next leg of our tour.

## Piccadilly

In the early 17th century, a humble tailor on the Strand called Robert Baker sold an awful lot of picadils—a collar ruff all the rage in courtly circles—and built a house with the proceeds. Snobs dubbed his new-money mansion Piccadilly Hall, and the name stuck. As for the "Circus" of **Piccadilly Circus,** that refers not to the menagerie of backpackers and camera clickers clustered around the steps of **Eros,** but to the circular junction of five major roads.

Eros, London's favorite statue and symbol of the *Evening Standard* newspaper, is not in fact the Greek god of erotic love at all but the angel of Christian charity, commissioned in 1893 from the young sculptor Alfred Gilbert as a memorial to the philanthropic Earl of Shaftesbury. It cost Gilbert £7,000 to cast the statue he called his "missile of kindness" in the novel medium of aluminum, and since he was paid only £3,000, he promptly went bankrupt and fled the country. (Don't worry—he was knighted in the end.) Eros has lately done his best to bankrupt Westminster Council, too, owing to some urgent leg surgery and a new coat of protective micro-crystalline synthetic wax.

Outside of Eros, there's not much to see in this sometime hub of London beyond a bank of neon advertisements, a very large branch of Tower Records, the tawdry Trocadero Centre (video arcades, food courts, chain stores, the Guinness World of Records), and a perpetual traffic jam. Look up to the east, though, for a glimpse of the curve of Regent Street, to which we'll return in due course.

South of Regent Street, opposite the neon, is the wide, straight road called **Piccadilly.** Walk west along it and you'll soon reach **St. James's Church,** recessed from the street behind a courtyard filled, most days, with a crafts market. Completed in 1684, it was the last of Sir Christopher Wren's London churches, and his own favorite. It also contains one of Grinling Gibbons's finest works, an ornate limewood reredos (the screen behind the altar). A 1940 bomb scored a direct hit here, but the church was completely restored, albeit with a fiberglass spire. It's a lively place, offering all manner of lecture series—many on incongruously New Age themes—and concerts, mostly Baroque, as well as a brass-rubbing center.

**Time Out** **The Wren at St. James's,** attached to the church, has not the faintest whiff of godliness, as the cake display proves. Hot dishes at lunchtime are vegetarian, very good, and very inexpensive. There are tables outside in spring and summer.

Stay on the south side of Piccadilly and you'll pass a succession of English emporia: **Simpson,** the gentlemen's outfitters (behind a disturbingly reflectionless window); **Swaine, Adeney & Brigg & Sons** for "umbrellas and whips"; **Hatchard's,** the booksellers, with an 18th-century front; and **Fortnum and Mason,** the exclusive department store that supplies the queen's groceries. Legend has it that Fortnum's stocks chocolate-coated red ants alongside the glorious teas, marmalades, preserves, and tins of truffles and turtle soup. Try to pass by at the stroke of the hour so you can see the candy-colored automata of Mr. Fortnum and Mr. Mason bowing to a tinkly carillon above the main entrance.

Opposite Fortnum and Mason is **Burlington House,** built in the Palladian style for the Earl of Burlington around 1720, and one of the few surviving mansions from that period. It is home to the **Royal Academy of Arts,** which mounts major art exhibitions, usually years in the planning. The permanent collection (not all on show) includes at least one work by every academician past and present, including Gainsborough, Turner, and Constable, but its prize is, without doubt, a tondo (a sculpted disk) by Michelangelo of the Madonna and Child. It's up the glass staircase in the Sackler Galleries (opened in 1991 and designed by another academician, Sir Norman Foster), where temporary exhibitions are held. Every June, the RA mounts the **Summer Exhibition,** a mishmash of sculpture and painting, both amateur and professional, from abstract expressionist to photo-realist (bias is toward the latter), with about 1,000 things crammed into every cranny—it's an institution. Art-weary now? Try the shop—it's one of the best museum stores in town. *Burlington House, Piccadilly, tel. 0171/439-7438 or 0171/439-4996 (recorded information). Admission varies according to exhibition. Open daily 10–6; closed Good Friday, Dec. 24–26, Jan. 1.*

The two sides of the Burlington House courtyard are occupied by several other learned societies: the Geological Society, Chemistry Society, Linnean Society (naturalists), Society of Antiquaries, and the Royal Astronomical Society. Turning right as you exit, you'll find the entrance to one of Mayfair's enchanting covered shopping alleys, the **Burlington Arcade.** This one, built in 1819, is the second-oldest in London. It's still patrolled by top-hatted beadles, who prevent you from singing, running, or carrying open umbrellas or large parcels (to say nothing of lifting English fancy goods from the mahogany-fronted shops).

At the other end of the arcade, in an extension at the back of Burlington House, is a place you will often—who knows why?—have practically to yourself, the **Museum of Mankind.** This overspill from the British Museum contains the best bits of the ethnographic collection, with amazing artifacts from Aztec, Mayan, African, and other unwestern civilizations beautifully displayed in miles of space. Long-running, imaginatively curated exhibitions are held on the first floor. When the long-awaited new British Library is up and running, the Department of Ethnography will be kicked back to the British Museum, so take advantage now. *6 Burlington Gdns., tel. 0171/437–2224. Admission free. Open Mon.–Sat. 10–5, Sun. 2:30–6; closed Good Friday, May Day, Dec. 23–26, Jan. 1.*

**Time Out**    The suitably themed **Café de Colombia** is usually as peaceful as the Museum of Mankind it inhabits—unless you collide with a school visit. Salads and pastries, Colombian coffee, and wine and beer are on the lunch menu.

Retrace your steps to Piccadilly, turn right, then turn right into Albermarle Street to travel back to the middle of the last century when electricity was young. In the basement of the Royal Institution is the **Faraday Museum,** a reconstruction of the laboratory where the physicist Michael Faraday discovered electromagnetic induction in 1831—with echoes of Frankenstein. *21 Albermarle St., tel. 0171/409–2992. Admission: £1 adults, 50p children. Open Mon.–Fri. 1–4; closed public holidays.*

Cross the road on Piccadilly, turn right, and soon you'll be walking past the long, colonnaded front of the **Ritz** hotel, built in 1909, and meant to remind you of Paris. Beyond it is the 53-acre isosceles triangle of **Green Park,** the Mayfair hotel guests' jogging track. As with St. James's, Charles II made a public garden of the former royal hunting ground, and it too became fashionable—not least among duellists, highwaymen, and, the following century, hot-air balloonists. Nowadays you can see a tacky display of art on the railings, and a nice one of daffodils in spring.

The extreme west end of Piccadilly features the roaring traffic of **Hyde Park Corner,** the cyclist's nightmare. To cross here, you need to descend the pedestrian underpasses, following the signs to the **Wellington Arch** marooned on its central island. This 1828 Decimus Burton triumphal gateway almost wound up at the back door of Buckingham Palace, but here it stands instead, empty now of London's smallest police station, which occupied its cramped insides until 1992. A statue of Wellington also moved on, replaced by Adrian Jones's *Quadriga* in 1912.

Near the park, on the north side of Hyde Park Corner, is **Apsley House**—built by Robert Adam in the 1770s and later refaced and extended—where Wellington lived from the 1820s until his death in 1852. As the **Wellington Museum,** it has been kept as the Iron Duke liked it, his uniforms and weapons, his porcelain and plate, and his extensive art collection, partially looted during military campaigns, displayed heroically. Unmissable, in every sense, is the gigantic Canova statue of a nude (but fig-leafed) Napoléon Bonaparte, Wellington's archenemy. Apsley House got iron shutters in 1830 after rioters, protesting the Duke's opposition to the Reform Bill (he was briefly prime minister), broke the windows. Yes, the British loved him for defeating Napoléon, but mocked him with the name "Iron Duke"—it referred not to his military prowess, but to those shutters. *149 Piccadilly, tel. 0171/499–5676. The museum was closed for renovation at press time; phone for opening times and admission prices.*

## Mayfair

**Mayfair,** like St. James's and Soho, is precisely delineated—a trapezoid contained by Oxford Street and Piccadilly on the north and south, Regent Street and Park Lane on the east and west. Within its boundaries are streets broad and narrow, but mostly unusually straight and grid-like for London, making it fairly easy to negotiate. Real estate here is exorbitant, so this is embassy country and the site of luxury shops and swank hotels.

Starting where we just left off, at Hyde Park Corner, head north along the boundary of Hyde Park, and risk your life crossing wide **Park Lane,** where drivers like to break the speed limit. You'll pass a succession of grand hotels: first the modern blocks of the Inter-Continental and the Hilton, then the triangular Art Deco Dorchester, followed by the "old lady of Park Lane," the Grosvenor House Hotel, on the site of the Earl of Grosvenor's 18th-century palace. After that, between Upper Grosvenor and Green streets, Nos. 93 to 99 plus No. 100, **Dudley House,** with their bow fronts and wrought-iron balconies, are the only survivors of Park Lane's early 19th-century glory days.

**㉓** You have reached **Marble Arch,** the name of both the traffic whirlpool where Bayswater Road segues into Oxford Street and John Nash's 1827 arch, which moved here from Buckingham Palace in 1851. Search the sidewalk by the arch to find the stone plaque that marks (roughly) the place where the Tyburn Tree stood for four centuries, until 1783. This was London's central gallows, a huge wooden structure with hanging space for 21. Hanging days were holidays, the spectacle supposedly functioning as a crime deterrent to the hoi polloi. It didn't work, though. Oranges, gingerbread, and gin were sold, alongside ballads and "personal favors," to vast, rowdy crowds, and the condemned, dressed in finery for his special moment, was treated more as hero than as villain.

Cross over (or under—there are signs to help in the labyrinth) to the **㉔** northeastern corner of Hyde Park, where **Speakers' Corner** harbors a late-20th-century public spectacle. Here, on Sunday afternoons, anyone is welcome to mount a soapbox and declaim upon any topic. It's an irresistible showcase of eccentricity, though sadly diminished since the death in 1994 of the "Protein Man," who thought meat, cheese, and peanuts led to uncontrollable acts of passion that would destroy western civilization. The pamphlets he sold for four decades down Oxford Street are now collector's items.

Ignoring Oxford Street for now, retrace your steps south along Park **㉕** Lane and follow Upper Brook Street to **Grosvenor Square** (pronounced "Grove-na"), laid out 1725–31 and as desirable an address today as it was then. Americans certainly thought so—from John Adams, the second president, who as ambassador lived at No. 38, to Dwight D. Eisenhower, whose wartime headquarters was at No. 20. Now the ugly '50s block of the **U.S. Embassy** occupies the entire west side, and a British memorial to Franklin D. Roosevelt stands in the center. The little brick chapel used by Eisenhower's men during **㉖** World War II, the 1730 **Grosvenor Chapel,** stands a couple of blocks south of the square on South Audley Street, with the entrance to pretty **St. George's Gardens** to its left. Across the gardens is the **㉗** headquarters of the English Jesuits, the mid-19th-century **Church of the Immaculate Conception,** known as Farm Street because that is the name of the street on which it stands.

Continuing south toward Piccadilly, take Chesterfield Hill, then Queen Street, and cross Curzon Street to enter, via the covered **㉘** walkway at No. 47, **Shepherd Market.** This quaint and villagey tangle of streetlets was anything *but* quaint when Edward Shepherd laid it out in 1735 on the site of the orgiastic, fortnight-long May Fair (which gave the whole district its name). Now there are sandwich bars, pubs and restaurants, boutiques and nightclubs, and a (fading) red-light reputation in the narrow lanes.

**Time Out**  **L'Artiste Musclé** (1 Shepherd Market, tel. 0171/493–6150) is a popular wine bar and restaurant with rustic French food, low prices, and a few sidewalk tables that are sought-after at lunch on a sunny day.

Hit Curzon Street again and follow it east, taking Fitzmaurice Place left into **Berkeley Square** (pronounced to rhyme with "starkly"). Not many of its original mid-18th-century houses are left, but look at Nos. 42–46 (especially No. 44, which the architectural historian Sir Nikolaus Pevsner thought London's finest terraced house) and Nos. 49–52 to get some idea of why it was once London's top address—not that it's in the least humble now. The 200-year-old plane trees, which now dignify ugly showrooms and offices, presumably inspired that sentimental ballad about a nightingale singing here.

Leave via Bruton Street on the east side and continue on to **Bond Street,** divided into northern "New" (1710) and southern "Old" (1690) halves. The stretch of New Bond Street you have entered

㉙ boasts **Sotheby's,** the world-famous auction house, at No. 35, but there are other opportunities to flirt with financial ruin on Old Bond Street: the mirror-lined Chanel store, the vainglorious marble acres of Gianni Versace and the boutique of his more sophisticated compatriots Gucci, plus Tiffany's British outpost and art dealers Colnaghi, Léger, Thos. Agnew, and Marlborough Fine Arts. **Cork Street,** which parallels the top half of Old Bond Street, is where London's top dealers in contemporary art have their galleries—you're welcome to browse, but be dressed well. Royal personages buy baubles from Asprey & Co. at the beginning of New Bond Street, with many designers' shops (plus the more affordable fashion store, Fenwicks) continuing all the way up.

Before you reach Oxford Street, turn right into Brook Street (the composer Handel lived at No. 25), which leads to Hanover Square. Turning right down St. George Street brings you to the porticos of

㉚ **St. George's Church,** where Percy Shelley and George Eliot, among others, had their weddings. A right turn after the church down Mill Street brings you into the tailors' mecca of **Savile Row,** the fashionable spot for the bespoke suit since the mid-19th century.

## Regent and Oxford Streets

John Nash and his patron, the Prince Regent—the future George IV—had grand plans for **Regent Street,** which was conceived as a kind of ultra-catwalk from the prince's palace, Carlton House, to Regent's Park (then called Marylebone Park). The section between Piccadilly and Oxford Street was to be called the Quadrant and lined with colonnaded purveyors of "articles of fashion and taste," in a big P.R. exercise to improve London's image as the provincial cousin of smarter European capitals. The scheme was never fully implemented, and what there was fell into such disrepair that, early this century, Aston Webb (of the Mall route) collaborated on the redesign you see today.

It is still a major shopping street, but one with a peculiar dearth of goods one wants to buy. Exceptions exist: **Hamleys,** the gigantic toy

㉛ emporium, is fun; and since 1875 there has been **Liberty,** which originally imported silks from the East, then diversified to other Asian goods, and is now best for its "Liberty print" cottons, its jewelry department, and—still—its high-class Asian imports. The stained-glass–lit mock-Tudor interior, with beams made from battleships, is worth a look.

Shopping continues to dominate as you reach **Oxford Circus** toward the north end of Regent Street. Turn left into **Oxford Street.** The reasons for this thoroughfare's reputation as London's main shopping drag may well elude you as you inch through the crowds (they're marshalled by police at Christmastime) and pass signs reading BANKRUPT! EVERYTHING MUST GO! and DESIGNER BARGAINS (don't bother—they're not). But two reasons to shop Oxford Street remain, and **③② ③③** they are called **Selfridges** and **Marks and Spencer.**

Harry Gordon Selfridge came to London from Chicago in 1906 and opened his store, with its row of massive Ionic columns, in 1909. Now British-run, Selfridges rivals Harrods in size and stock, but its image of lesser glamour has been tenacious. It stands toward the Marble Arch end of the street, close by the flagship branch of everyone's favorite chain store, Marks and Spencer (usually known by its pet names M&S or Marks & Sparks)—supplier of England's underwear, purveyor of woollies (sweaters, that is), producer of dishes passed off as homemade at dinner parties. This place has by far the highest turnover of any shop in the land, so expect crowds at all times. Nearer Oxford Circus, **John Lewis,** another flagship of another major chain of department stores, is known for its dressmaking fabrics and notions and its slogan "Never Knowingly Undersold." Off Oxford Street near Bond Street tube station, to the south and north respectively, are **South Molton Street** and **St. Christopher's Place,** two little pedestrians-only streets that yield further goodies. (*See* Chapter 4, Shopping.)

Take care not to exhaust yourself with consumer activities, because something far more edifying awaits you round the corner, off Duke Street (to the right of Selfridges) in Manchester Square. The **③④** **Wallace Collection,** assembled by four generations of Marquesses of Hertford and given to the nation by the widow of Sir Richard Wallace, bastard son of the fourth, is important, exciting, undervisited—and free. As at the Frick Collection in New York, the setting here, Hertford House, is part of the show. The fine late-18th-century mansion, built for the Duke of Manchester, was completely renovated in the late 1970s, so that treading its deep carpets and ascending its glorious white marble sweep of stairs transports you far, far from the shoe stores and branches of the Gap that you recently left behind.

The first marquess was a patron of Sir Joshua Reynolds, the second bought Hertford House, the third—a flamboyant socialite—favored Sèvres porcelain and 17th-century Dutch painting; but it was the eccentric fourth marquess who, from his self-imposed exile in Paris, really built the collection, snapping up Bouchers, Fragonards, Watteaus, and Lancrets for a song (the French Revolution having rendered them dangerously unfashionable), augmenting these with furniture and sculpture, and sending his son Richard out to do the deals. With 30 years of practice behind him, Richard Wallace continued acquiring treasures on his father's death, scouring Italy for majolica and Renaissance gold, then moving most of it to London. Look for Rembrandt's portrait of his son, the Rubens landscape, the Van Dycks, and Canalettos, the French rooms, and of course the porcelain, and don't forget to say hello to Frans Hals's *Laughing Cavalier* in the Big Gallery. *Hertford House, Manchester Sq., tel. 0171/935–0687. Admission free. Open Mon.–Sat. 10–5, Sun. 2–5; closed Good Friday, May Day, Dec. 24–26, Jan. 1.*

㉟ Take a left up Wigmore Street from Duke Street, passing **Wigmore Hall,** the freshly renovated concert hall that the piano-maker Friedrich Bechstein built in 1901 (pick up a schedule for its excellent and varied concert series). Continue all the way back to Regent Street at the point where it becomes Portland Place.

**Time Out** **The Wigmore Café** in the arts-and-crafts–style basement of the concert hall is run by the same people who brought food to St. John's Smith Square, with a similar selection of salads, hot dishes, sandwiches, and cakes, served from a counter all day, every day, until 10:30 PM (Saturday from 5:30 PM).

**Portland Place,** the elegant throughway to Regent's Park, was London's widest street in the 1780s when the brothers Robert and James Adam designed it. The first sight to greet you there, drawing the eye around the awkward corner, is the succulently curvaceous

㊱ portico and pointy Gothic spire of **All Souls Church,** one part of Nash's Regent Street scheme that remains. It is now the venue for innumerable concerts and Anglican services broadcast to the nation by the British Broadcasting Corporation. The 1931 block of **Broadcasting House** next door is home to the BBC's five radio stations. It curves too, if less beautifully, and features an Eric Gill sculpture of Shakespeare's Ariel (aerial—get it?) over the entrance, from which the playful sculptor was obliged to excise a portion of phallus lest it offend public decency—which the modified model did in any case.

㊲ The **Langham Hotel** across the street was built in 1864 to resemble a Florentine palace and duly played host to exiled royalty (Napoléon III of France, Haile Selassie of Ethiopia) and the *beau monde* of the next 85 years until falling afoul of fashion (new luxury hotels were built farther west) and then, in 1940, a German land mine. Now it has been restored and reopened by the Hilton group.

Turn right about halfway up Portland Place into New Cavendish Street, left onto Great Portland Street, proceed as far as Clipstone

㊳ Street, and look to your right. That giant glass pencil is **British Telecom Tower,** imposed on London by the Post Office in 1965 (everyone still calls it the Post Office Tower) to field satellite phone calls and beam radio and TV signals around. It has a habit of popping up on the skyline from the most surprising locations, but here it reveals its full 620 feet. A terrorist bomb went off upstairs in 1975, and the great view from the top has been off-limits ever since.

# Soho and Covent Garden

*Numbers in the margin correspond to points of interest on the Soho and Covent Garden map.*

Yet another quadrilateral—this one described by Regent Street, Coventry/Cranbourn Streets, Charing Cross Road, and the eastern half of Oxford Street—encloses Soho, the most fun part of the West End. This appellation, unlike the New York neighborhood's similar one, is not an elision of anything, but a blast from the past—derived (as far as we know) from the shouts of "So-ho!" that royal huntsmen in Whitehall Palace's parklands were once heard to cry. One of Charles II's illegitimate sons, the Duke of Monmouth, an early resident, his dubious pedigree setting the tone for the future: For many years Soho was London's strip show/peep show/clip joint/sex shop/brothel center. The mid-'80s brought legislation that granted expensive licenses to a few such establishments and closed down the rest; most prostitution had already been ousted by the 1959 Street Offences Act. Only a cosmetic smear of red-light activity remains now, plus a shop called "Condomania" and one or two purveyors of couture fetishwear for outfitting trendy club goers.

These clubs, which cluster around the Soho grid, are the diametric opposite of the St. James's gentlemen's museums—they cater to youth, change soundtrack every month, and have tyrannical fashion police at the door. Another breed of Soho club is the strictly members-only media haunts (the Groucho, the Academy, Browns, Fred's), salons for carefully segregated strata of high-income hipster. The same crowd populates the astonishing selection of restaurants, but then so does the rest of London and all its visitors— because Soho is gourmet country.

It was after the First World War, when London households relinquished their resident cooks en masse, that Soho's gastronomic reputation was established. It had been a cosmopolitan area since the first immigrant wave of French Huguenots arrived in the 1680s. More French came fleeing the revolution in the late 18th century, then the Paris Commune of 1870, followed by Germans, Russians, Poles, Greeks, and (especially) Italians and, much later, Chinese. Pedestrianized Gerrard Street, south of Shaftsbury Avenue, is the hub of London's compact **Chinatown,** which boasts restaurants, dim sum houses, Chinese supermarkets, and February New Year's celebrations, plus a brace of scarlet pagoda-style archways and a pair of phone booths with pictogram dialing instructions.

Soho, being small, is easy to explore, though it's also easy to mistake one narrow, crowded street for another, and even Londoners get lost here. We enter from the northwest corner, **Oxford Circus.** From here, head south about 200 yards down Regent Street, turn left into Great Marlborough Street, and head to the top of Carnaby Street.

The '60s synonym for swinging London, **Carnaby Street** fell into a post-party depression, re-emerging sometime in the '80s as the main drag of a public-relations invention called West Soho. Blank stares would greet anyone asking directions to such a place, but it is geographically logical, and the tangle of streets—Foubert's Place, Broadwick Street, Marshall Street—do cohere, at least, in type of merchandise (youth accessories, mostly, with a smattering of designer boutiques). Broadwick Street is also notable as the birthplace, in 1758, of the great visionary poet and painter William Blake at No. 74. At age 26 he came back for a year to sell prints next door, at No. 72 (now an ugly tower block), and then remained a Soho resident in Poland Street.

Turn right off Broadwick Street into Berwick (pronounced "Berrick") Street, famed as central London's best fruit and vegetable market. Then step through tiny Walker's Court (ignoring the notorious hookers' bulletin board); cross Brewer Street, named for two extinct 18th-century breweries; and you'll have arrived at Soho's hip hangout, Old Compton Street. From here, Wardour, Dean, Frith, and Greek streets lead north, all of them bursting with the aforementioned restaurants and clubs. Take either of the latter two to **❶ Soho Square,** laid out about 1680 and fashionable in the 18th century. Only two of the original houses still stand, plus the 19th-century central garden. It's now a place of peace and offices (Paul McCartney's music publishers, Bloomsbury Publishing).

In the other direction from Old Compton Street is a longstanding Gallic outpost, recognizable by the *tricolor* fluttering outside on **❷** Dean Street, the **French House.** This pub has been crammed with

84

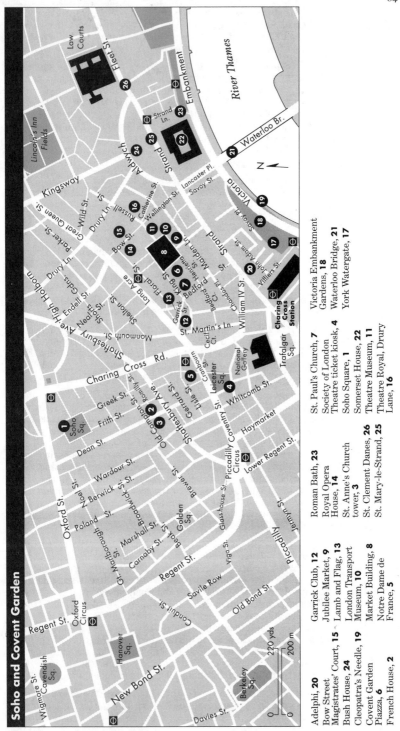

# Soho and Covent Garden

Adelphi, **20**
Bow Street
Magistrates' Court, **15**
Bush House, **24**
Cleopatra's Needle, **19**
Covent Garden
Piazza, **6**
French House, **2**

Garrick Club, **12**
Jubilee Market, **9**
Lamb and Flag, **13**
London Transport
Museum, **10**
Market Building, **8**
Notre Dame de
France, **5**

Roman Bath, **23**
Royal Opera
House, **14**
St. Anne's Church
tower, **3**
St. Clement Danes, **26**
St. Mary-le-Strand, **25**

St. Paul's Church, **7**
Society of London
Theatre ticket kiosk, **4**
Soho Square, **1**
Somerset House, **22**
Theatre Museum, **11**
Theatre Royal, Drury
Lane, **16**

Victoria Embankment
Gardens, **18**
Waterloo Bridge, **21**
York Watergate, **17**

people ever since de Gaulle's Free French Forces rendezvoused here during World War II. Nowadays the crowd isn't French—it's Soho trendies and peculiar bohemians, some heading for the trendy restaurant upstairs. No pints of beer here, but you can get a decent *vin ordinaire* or a glass of pastis beneath the signed photos of French boxers. Opposite the French House is all that remains of once-famous **St. Anne's Church,** probably the work of Wren. A German bomb in 1940 spared only the tower, and the graveyard behind it, on Wardour Street.

The street you now face is Shaftesbury Avenue, the heart of theaterland (*see* "London's Theaters" in Chapter 2, Portraits of London), and across which you'll find Chinatown.

**Time Out**   Take any excuse you can think of to visit either of Soho's wonderful rival patisseries: **Maison Bertaux** (28 Greek St.) or **Pâtisserie Valerie** (44 Old Compton St.). Both serve divine gateaux, milles-feuilles, croissants, éclairs, etc., the former in an upstairs salon, the latter in a dark room behind the cake counters.

South of Shaftesbury Avenue and Gerrard Street is **Leicester Square** (no, not "lay-sess-ter" but "lester"), of which it is no compliment to say that it is showing no sign of its great age. Looking at the neon of the major movie houses, the fast-food outlets (plus a useful Häagen-Dazs café), and the disco entrances, you'd never guess it was laid out around 1630. By the 19th century it was already bustling and disreputable, and now it's usually the only place crowded after midnight—with suburban teenagers, Belgian backpackers, and London's swelling ranks of the homeless. That said, it is not a threatening place, and the liveliness can be quite cheering. In the middle are statues of Shakespeare, Hogarth, Reynolds, and Charlie Chaplin, and underneath is an invisible new £22-million electrical substation. One landmark certainly worth visiting is the **Society of London Theatre ticket kiosk,** on the southwest corner, which sells half-price tickets for many of that evening's performances (*see* Theater in Chapter 8, The Arts and Nightlife). On the northeast corner, in Leicester Place, stands **Notre Dame de France,** with a wonderful mural by Jean Cocteau in one of its side chapels.

Charing Cross Road runs west of Leicester Square. A bibliophile's dream, it's lined with bookstores—new and second-hand, general and specialist. Although it does not qualify as a Soho street, check out little **Cecil Court,** running east off Charing Cross Road before it hits Trafalgar Square, for some of the best of the bookshops.

### Covent Garden

The best place to begin your rounds of this ever-evolving neighborhood is in its center, the former **Covent Garden Market,** now often referred to as the **Piazza** that it became in 1980. It's very close to Covent Garden tube (just stroll south down James Street). The easiest way to find the market building from Charing Cross Road is to walk down Cranbourn Street, next to Leicester Square tube, then down Long Acre, and turn right at James Street.

This has always been the sort of neighborhood alluded to as "colorful." It was originally the "convent garden" belonging to the Abbey of St. Peter at Westminster (later Westminster Abbey). The land was given to the first Earl of Bedford by the Crown after the Dissolution of the Monasteries in 1536. The Earls—later promoted to Dukes—of Bedford held on to the place right up until 1918, when the eleventh Duke managed to offload what had by then become a liability. In between, the area enclosed by Long Acre, St. Martin's Lane, Drury Lane, and assorted streets north of the Strand had gone from the height of fashion (until the nobs moved west to brand-new St. James's) to a period of arty-literary bohemia in the 18th century, followed by an era of vice and mayhem, to become the vegetable supplier of London once more when the market building went up in the 1830s, followed by the Flower Market in 1870 (Eliza Dolittle's alma mater in Shaw's *Pygmalion* and Lerner and Loewe's musical version, *My Fair Lady*).

Still, it was no Mayfair, what with 1,000-odd market porters spending their 40-shillings-a-week in the alehouses, brothels, and gambling dens that had never quite disappeared. By the time the Covent Garden Estate Company took over the running of the market from the 11th Duke, it seemed as if seediness had set in for good, and when the fruit-and-veg trade moved out to the bigger, better Nine Elms Market in Vauxhall in 1974, it left a decrepit wasteland. But this is one of London's success stories: Now the (sadly defunct) Greater London Council stepped in with a dream of a rehabilitation scheme—not unlike the one that was tried, less successfully, in the Parisian equivalent, Les Halles. By 1980, the transformation was complete. Now read on. . . .

Go all the way through the market—we'll return in a minute—exiting stage right to cross the Piazza (maybe pausing to watch the street entertainers, who have passed auditions for this coveted spot) **❼** to **St. Paul's Church.** This 1633 work of the great Inigo Jones has always been known as "the actors' church" thanks to the several theaters in its parish, and well-known actors often read the lessons at services. The matching tall, terraced houses Jones designed to form a quadrangle with the church are long since history.

With your back to St. Paul's portico (the setting for *Pygmalion*'s **❽** opening scene), you get a good view of the restored 1840 **market building** around which Covent Garden pivots. Inside, the shops are mostly higher-class clothing chains, plus a couple of cafés and some knickknack stores that are good for gifts. There's a superior crafts market on most days, too. If you turn right, you'll reach the indoor **❾** **Jubilee Market,** with stalls selling clothing, army surplus gear, more crafts, and more knickknacks. At yet another market off to the left (on the way back to the tube), the leather goods, antiques, and secondhand clothing stalls are a little more exciting. (It was undergoing expansion at press time.) In the summer it may seem that everyone you see around the Piazza (and the crowds are legion) is a fellow tourist, but there is still plenty of office life in the area, and Londoners continue to flock here.

Two entertaining museums stand at the southeastern corner of the square. First, in the old Flower Market, is the recently utterly reju- **❿** venated **London Transport Museum,** which tells the story of mass transportation in the capital. It is particularly child-friendly, with lots of touch-screen interactive stuff, live actors in costume (including a Victorian horse dung collector), old rolling-stock, period smells and sounds, and best of all, a tube driving simulator. There's also a café, and a shop selling the wonderful old London Transport posters, plus mugs, socks, bow ties, and so on, printed with that elegant London tube map, designed by Harry Beck in 1933 and still in use today. *Piazza, tel. 0171/379–6344. Admission: £3.95 adults, £2.50 children 5–16 and senior citizens, children under 5 free. Open daily 10–6; closed Dec. 24–26.*

⓫ Next door is the **Theatre Museum,** which aims to re-create the excitement of theater itself. There are usually programs in progress allowing children to get in a mess with make-up or have a giant dressing-up session. Permanent exhibits attempt a history of the English stage from the 16th century to Mick Jagger's jumpsuit, with tens of thousands of theater playbills, and sections on such topics as Hamlet-through-the-ages and pantomime—the peculiar British theatrical tradition whereby men dress as ugly women (as distinct from RuPaul), and girls wear tights and play princes. There's a little theater in the bowels of the museum and a ticket desk for "real" theaters around town, plus a café and a good bookstore. *7 Russell St., tel. 0171/836–7891. Admission: £3 adults, £1.50 children 5–14 and senior citizens. Open Tues.–Sun. 11–7; closed Good Friday, Dec. 24–26, Jan. 1.*

**Time Out**    There are so many places clamoring to feed you around Covent Garden that you could faint with hunger trying to make a decision. Both of the above museums have acceptable cafés for a snack, but for one of London's best burgers (and this is a difficult commodity to locate), try **Maxwell's** on James Street. Don't miss the mural downstairs featuring personages of our time (Mother Teresa, Jagger, the queen, Martin Luther King . . . ) drinking lurid cocktails. (*See* Covent Garden in Chapter 6, Dining).

The best way to explore the little streets around the Piazza is to follow your nose, but here are a few suggested directions to point it in, with landmarks.

You could start off, wearing your shopping hat, on **Neal Street,** which begins north of Long Acre catercorner to the tube station, and is closed to traffic halfway down. In Neal Street you can buy everything you never knew you needed—apricot tea, sitars, vintage flying jackets, silk kimonos, Alvar Aalto vases, halogen desk lamps, shoes with heel lower than toe, collapsible top hats, and so on. To the left off Neal Street, on Earlham Street, is Thomas Neal's—a new, upmarket, designerish clothing and housewares mall, which, despite trying hard, is ever underpopulated. It's named after the founder (in 1693) of the star-shaped cobbled junction of tiny streets just past there, called **Seven Dials**—a surprisingly residential enclave, with lots going on behind the tenement-style warehouse facades. Turning left into the next street off Neal Street, Shorts Gardens, you come to Neal's Yard (note the comical, water-operated wooden clock), originally just a whole-foods wholesaler, now an entire holistic village with therapy rooms, organic bakery and dairy, a great vegetarian café, and a medical herbalist's shop reminiscent of a medieval apothecary.

From Seven Dials, veer 45 degrees south into Mercer Street, turning right on Long Acre, then left into Garrick Street. Here stands a
⓬ stray from clubland (the gents version), the **Garrick Club.** Named for the 18th-century actor and theater manager David Garrick, it is, because of its literary-theatrical bent, more louche than its St. James's brothers, and famous actors, from Sir Laurence Olivier down, have always been proud to join—along with Dickens, Thack-
⓭ eray, and Trollope, in their time. Find the **Lamb and Flag** down teeny Rose Street to the left. Dickens drank in this pub, better known in its 17th-century youth as the Bucket of Blood owing to the bare-knuckle boxing matches upstairs. (You'll find that many London pubs claim Dickens as an habitué, and it's unclear whether they lie or the author was the city's premier sot.)

From Rose Street, turn right into Floral Street, another shopping spot, especially good for menswear and for the Sanctuary, a women-only day spa, with parrots, palms, and pool. At the other end you'll **⑭** emerge onto Bow Street, right next to the **Royal Opera House.** In fact, for the entire length of the block between James and Bow streets you've been walking past the theater's 1982 extension, which added much-needed rehearsal and dressing-room space to the building designed in 1858 by E. M. Barry, son of Sir Charles, the House of Commons architect. This one is the third theater on the site. The first opened in 1732 and burned down in 1808; the second opened a year later under the aegis of one John Anderson, only to succumb to fire in 1856. Anderson, who had lost two theaters already, had an appalling record when it came to keeping the limelights apart from the curtains.

Despite government subsidies, tickets for the Royal Opera are pricey, though the expense is unlikely to lead to riots as it did in 1763, 1792, and for *61 days* of protest in the Old Price Riots of 1809, when the cost of rebuilding inflated the cost of seats. (The public won.) Many British and world premiers have been staged here (including the world's first public piano recital in 1767), and the Royal Opera attracts all the glittering divas on the international circuit. Nowadays you can see some of them for free, when selected summer performances are relayed live to a giant screen in the Piazza.

**⑮** Opposite the Royal Opera's Bow Street facade is the **Bow Street Magistrates' Court,** from which the prototype of the modern police force once operated. Known as the Bow Street Runners (because they chased thieves on foot), they were the brainchild of the second Bow Street magistrate—none other than Henry Fielding, the author of *Tom Jones* and *Joseph Andrews*. The late-19th-century edifice on the site went up during one of the market improvement drives. It now houses three courts, including that of the Metropolitan Chief Magistrate, who hears all extradition applications.

Continuing on, and turning left into Russell Street, you reach Drury Lane, home to London's best-known auditorium and almost its largest, **⑯** the **Theatre Royal, Drury Lane**; its entrance is on Catherine Street. Since World War II, its forte has been musicals (*Miss Saigon* is the current resident; past ones have included *The King and I*, *My Fair Lady*, *South Pacific*, *Hello Dolly*, and *A Chorus Line*)—though David Garrick, who managed it from 1747 to 1776, made its name by reviving the works of the obscure William Shakespeare. It enjoys all the romantic accessories of a London theater—a history of fires (it burned down three times, once in a Wren-built incarnation), riots (in 1737, when a posse of footmen demanded free admission), attempted regicides (George II in 1716 and his grandson George III in 1800), and even sightings of a phantom (in the Circle, matinees).

## The Strand and Embankment

South of Covent Garden, the ¾-mile-long traffic-clogged **Strand** is one of London's oldest streets. It was already lined with mansions seven centuries ago, when it was a mere Thames-side bridle path. In 1706 Thomas Twining, the tea tycoon, moved his shop into No. 216 (it's still there); it was closely followed by a slew of coffee houses, frequented by Boswell and Johnson, that persisted for most of that century. Remember Judy Garland doing Burlington Bertie in Chaplin drag, walking down the Strand with gloves in hand, in *A Star Is Born*? William Hargreaves's song was a popular number in the Strand music halls that put the street on the map afresh in the early

1900s. Now its presence on maps is about all that the characterless Strand has to recommend it, beyond one or two high spots that we'll return to after strolling by the river.

Starting at Charing Cross Station at the southern end of the Strand, take Villiers Street down to the Thames. On Watergate Walk at the western end of Victoria Embankment stands the **York Watergate.** This was once the grand river entrance to York House, the Duke of Buckingham's mansion, built in 1625 and about the oldest building extant around here; it marks the place where the river used to flow before the road was built. A riverside road had seemed a good plan ever since Wren had come up with the idea after the Great Fire of 1666, but nobody got around to it until Sir Joseph Bazalgette set to work on the **Victoria Embankment** two centuries later. Bazalgette, incidentally, is better known for providing London with the sewer system still largely in use; he can be admired in effigy on the bronze bust right there by Hungerford Bridge.

Between the York Watergate and the Strand section of the embankment is the triangular-handkerchief **Victoria Embankment Gardens,** where office sandwich-eaters and people who call it home coexist at lunchtime. If you walk through to the river you come upon London's *very oldest thing*, predating its arbitrary namesake, and London itself, by centuries: **Cleopatra's Needle.** The 60-foot pink granite obelisk was erected at Heliopolis, in Lower Egypt, in about 1475 BC, then moved to Alexandria, where in 1819 Mohammed Ali, the Turkish Viceroy of Egypt, rescued it from its fallen state and presented it to the British. The British, though grateful, had not the faintest idea how to get the 186-ton gift home, so they left it there for years until an expatriate English engineer contrived an iron pontoon to float it to London via Spain. Future archaeologists will find an 1878 "time capsule" underneath, containing the morning papers, several bibles, a railway timetable, some pins, a razor, and a dozen photos of Victorian pinup girls.

Cross the gardens northwest from there toward the Strand, and you enter the **Adelphi.** This regal riverfront row was the work of all four brothers Adam (John, Robert, James, and William—hence the name, from the Greek *adelphoi*, meaning brothers), London's Scottish architects. All the late-18th-century design stars were roped in to beautify the interiors, but the grandeur gradually eroded, and today very few of the 24 houses remain; 7 Adam Street is the best.

Circumnavigate the Strand by sticking to the embankment walk and you'll soon reach **Waterloo Bridge,** where (weather permitting) you can catch some of London's most glamorous views, toward both the City and Westminster around the Thames bend. Look past the bridge and there you'll see the grand 18th-century classical river facade of **Somerset House,** which you enter from the Strand. Within lurks both horror and heaven, the former in a vast compilation of civil servants (cf. the red-tape-bestrewn Circumlocution Offices in Dickens's *Little Dorrit*), the latter the **Courtauld Institute Galleries,** which moved in 1990.

Founded in 1931 by the textile maven Samuel Courtauld, this is London's finest Impressionist and post-Impressionist collection, with bonus post-Renaissance works thrown in. Botticelli, Breughel, Tiepolo, and Rubens are represented, but the younger French painters (plus Van Gogh) are the stars—here, for example, are Manet's *Bar at the Folies-Bergère* and *Déjeuner sur l'Herbe* (a companion to the bigger version at the Musée d'Orsay in Paris). *The Strand, tel. 0171/873–2526. Admission: £3 adults, £1.50 children, students, and senior citizens. Open Mon.–Sat. 10–6, Sun. 2–6; closed public holidays.*

Slinking north up narrow Strand Lane between Somerset House and **King's College** (a branch of London University), you'll come upon **㉓** a curious little redbrick plunge-pool known as the **Roman Bath.** It's probably about a thousand years younger than Roman, but nobody is quite sure. To see it, you have to peer in the window at No. 5. Dickens may inadvertently have named it, in *David Copperfield*, though nobody seems quite sure of that, either.

Now you're back on the Strand, with the main entrance of Somerset House at your back, looking at the **Aldwych,** a great big croissant of a potential traffic accident, with a central island on which stand three hulking monoliths: India House, Melbourne House, and the hand- **㉔** some 1935 neo-classical **Bush House,** headquarters of the BBC World Service. Bush House shows its best face to Kingsway, to the north, with a pair of massive columns, and statues celebrating "friendship between English-speaking peoples" erected decades before the Thatcher-Reagan "special relationship."

Dwarfed by Bush House but prettier by far, and stranded (oops) in the traffic on islands in the Strand to the west, are two churches. **㉕** The 1717 **St. Mary-le-Strand,** James Gibbs's (of St.-Martin-in-the-Fields fame) first public building, was inspired by the Baroque churches of Rome that had impressed Gibbs during his studies **㉖** there. Wren's **St. Clement Danes** (with a tower appended by Gibbs) is dedicated to the Royal Air Force. Its 10 bells peal the tune of the nursery rhyme "Oranges and lemons,/Say the bells of St. Clements . . ." even though the bells in the rhyme belong to St. Clements, Eastcheap. Inside is a book listing 1,900 American airmen who were killed during World War II.

# Bloomsbury and Legal London

*Numbers in the margin correspond to points of interest on the Bloomsbury and Legal London map.*

To the north and northeast of the area we just investigated lie these two loosely delineated neighborhoods. The first is best known for its famous flowering of literary-arty bohemia during this century's first three decades, the Bloomsbury Group, and for the British Museum and the University of London, which dominate it now. The second sounds as exciting as, say, a center for accountancy or dentists, but don't be put off—it's more interesting than you might suppose.

### Bloomsbury

Let's get the Bloomsbury Group out of the way, since you can't visit them, and nothing exists to mark their territory beyond a sprinkling of Blue Plaques. (London has about 400 of these government-sponsored tablets commemorating persons who enhanced "human welfare or happiness" and have been dead for at least 20 years.) There's also a plaque in Bloomsbury Square, saying nothing about this elite clique of writers and artists except that they lived around here.

The chief Bloomsburies were Virginia Woolf, T. S. Eliot, E. M. Forster, Vanessa and Clive Bell, Duncan Grant, Dora Carrington, Roger Fry, John Maynard Keynes, and Lytton Strachey, with satellites including Rupert Brooke and Christopher Isherwood. They agreed with G. E. Moore's philosophical notion that "the pleasures of human intercourse and the enjoyment of beautiful objects . . . form the rational ultimate end of social progress." True to their beliefs, when they weren't producing beautiful objects the friends enjoyed much human intercourse, as has been exhaustively documented, not least in Virginia's own diaries. All you need do to find out more about them is read the Review supplements of the Sunday broadsheets, which are forever running Bloomsbury exposés as if they were fresh gossip.

**Bloomsbury Square** was laid out in 1660 and is therefore the earliest of the Bloomsbury squares, although none of the original houses remain; what is most remarkable about it now is that you can always find a parking spot in the huge underground garage underneath. You'll find it by exiting the tube at Tottenham Court Road—a straight, very ugly street where London buys its electrical appliances, hi-fi equipment, and computer accessories—and taking Great Russell Street east. You may never reach the square, however, because you will have had to resist entering the **British Museum.**

Allow plenty of time here. There are 2½ miles of floor space inside, split into nearly 100 galleries of astonishing artifacts and treasures bought and donated, but mostly "discovered" and looted, from everywhere in the world, some as old as humankind itself. It started in 1753, when Sir Hans Sloane, physician to Queen Anne and George II, bequeathed his personal collection of curiosities and antiquities to the nation, and then quickly grew thanks to enthusiastic kleptomaniacs after the Napoleonic Wars—most notoriously the seventh Earl of Elgin, who lifted marbles from the Parthenon and Erechtheum while on a Greek vacation between 1801 and 1804. Although Lord Elgin did a great thing in saving the marbles for posterity, their continuing presence in the British Museum is a source of embarrassment to many British subjects, who believe the Greeks should now have their "Elgin Marbles" back, as, indeed, do the Greeks.

The enormous building, with its Classical Greek–style facade featuring figures representing the Progress of Civilisation, was finished in 1847, the work of Sir Robert Smirke. Ascending the steps (dodging the eaters of ice cream), you go straight into the main entrance hall, where you can pick up a floor plan. Wherever you go there are marvels, but certain objects and collections are more important, rarer, older, or downright unique, and since you may wish to include these in your wanderings, here follows a highly edited résumé (in order of encounter) of the BM's greatest hits:

Close to the entrance hall, in the south end of Room 25, is the **Rosetta Stone,** found in 1799, and carved in 196 BC with a decree of Ptolemy V in Egyptian hieroglyphics, demotic, and Greek. It was this multilingual inscription that provided the French Egyptologist Jean-François Champollion with the key to deciphering hieroglyphics.

Maybe the **Elgin Marbles** oughtn't to be here, but since they are—and they are, after all, among the most graceful and heartbreakingly beautiful sculptures on earth—you can find them in Room 8, west of the entrance. The best part is what remains of the Parthenon frieze that girdled the interior of Athena's temple on the Acropolis, carved around 440 BC. (The handless, footless Dionysus who used to recline along the east pediment is especially well-known.) While you're in the west wing, you can see one of the Seven Wonders of the Ancient World—in fragment form, unfortunately—in Room 12: the

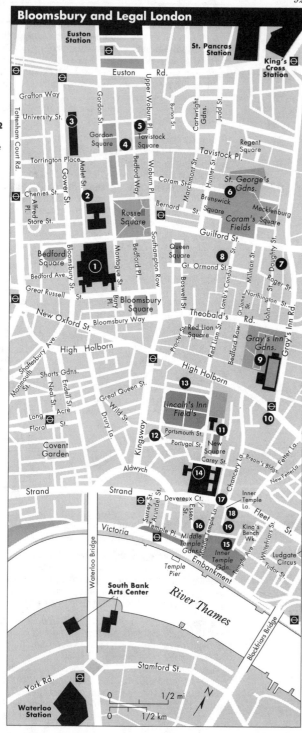

British Museum, **1**
Dickens House Museum, **7**
Gray's Inn, **9**
Hospital for Sick Children, **8**
Inner Temple, **15**
Jewish Museum, **5**
Lincoln's Inn, **11**
Middle Temple, **16**
Old Curiosity Shop, **12**
Percival David Foundation of Chinese Art, **4**
Prince Henry's Room, **18**
Royal Courts of Justice, **14**
Sir John Soane's Museum, **13**
Staple Inn, **10**
Temple Bar Memorial, **17**
Temple Church, **19**
Thomas Coram Foundation, **6**
University College, **3**
University of London, **2**

**Mausoleum of Halicarnassus.** This 4th-century tomb of Mausolus, king of Caria, was the original "mausoleum."

Also close to the entrance, but east, in Rooms 30 and 31 in the part of the British Library (*see below*) open to the public, are two of the four existing copies of that prototype census and manual of early British law, King John's 1215 charter, the **Magna Carta**, as well as the spectacularly illuminated 7th-century **Lindisfarne Gospels**, the work of a monk called Eadfrith. Also on display are handwritten manuscripts by, among others, Jane Austen, William Wordsworth, and John Lennon.

Upstairs are some of the most perennially popular galleries, especially beloved by children: Rooms 60 and 61, where the **Egyptian Mummies** live. You'll find here the preserved corpses not only of humans but also of a menagerie of animal companions discovered alongside them.

Proceeding clockwise, you'll come to Room 40, above the main entrance, where the **Mildenhall Treasure** glitters. This haul of 4th-century Roman silver tableware was found beneath the sod of a Suffolk field in 1942. Next door, in Room 41, is the equally splendid **Sutton Hoo Treasure,** which was buried at sea with (they think) Redwald, King of the Angles, in the 7th century, excavated from a Suffolk field in 1938–39, and includes swords and helmets, bowls and buckles, all encrusted with jewels.

In Room 37 lies Pete Marsh, so named by the archaeologists who unearthed the **Lindow Man** from a Cheshire peat marsh. He was ritually slain, probably as a human sacrifice, in the 1st century, and lay perfectly pickled in his bog until 1984.

Since 1759, the **British Library** has also been on this site, but in an imminent revolution in the world of English letters, the whole thing is to be decanted into its new home in St. Pancras after years of delay. The year 1991 was the intended moving date for the almost literally countless (somewhere around 18 million, actually) volumes, but the building wasn't finished, and the funding ran out, and there were problems with the new stacks, and, well, the operation will probably not have started by the time you read this. The British Library is entitled to a free copy of every single book, periodical, newspaper, and map published in the United Kingdom—a gift of George II, along with his Royal Library—which translates into two new miles of shelf space per year. Needless to say, room at the old library ran out long ago, and most of its books are not housed here. A Reader's Ticket for access to the library and entrance to the much-loved circular, copper-domed **Reading Room** is available only by written application, with proof of the serious intent of your research required. *Great Russell St., tel. 0171/636–1555 or 0171/580–1788 (recorded information). Admission free. 1½-hour guided tours, £6 per person; twice a day in winter, four times daily in summer. Phone for times. Open Mon.–Sat. 10–5, Sun. 2:30–6; closed Good Friday, May Day, Dec. 23–26, Jan. 1.*

---

**Time Out** The museum's self-service restaurant and café gets very crowded but serves a reasonable selection of not overly mass-produced meals beneath a plaster cast of a part of the Parthenon frieze that Lord Elgin didn't remove. *Open Mon.–Sat. noon–4:15, Sun. 2:45–5:15. Coffee shop open Mon.–Sat. 10–3.*

---

## Around the University of London

Leaving the Museum via the back exit leads you to Montague Place, which you should cross to Malet Street, straight ahead, to reach the ❷ **University of London.** This relatively youthful institution grew out of the need for a nondenominational center for higher education (Oxford and Cambridge both demanded religious conformity to the Church of England); it was founded by Dissenters in 1826, with its first examinations held 12 years later. Jews and Roman Catholics were not the only people admitted for the first time to an English university—women were, too, though they had to wait 50 years (until 1878) to sit for a degree. The building you see here dates only from 1911. Previously this branch of academe had borrowed Somerset House (where the Courtauld Collection is now), Burlington House (now the Royal Academy), then Burlington House's extension (now the Museum of Mankind).

On the left after you pass the university buildings is the back of the **Royal Academy of Dramatic Art,** or RADA (its entrance is on Gower Street), where at least half of the most stellar British thespians got ❸ their training. **University College** follows at the top of Malet Place—a satisfyingly classical edifice by the architect of the National Gallery, William Wilkins, with its main entrance also on Gower Street. Within its portals is the **Slade School of Fine Art,** which did for many of Britain's artists what RADA did for its actors. There is a fine collection of sculpture by one of the alumni, John Flaxman, on view inside. You can also see more Egyptology, if you didn't get enough at the BM, in the **Petrie Museum** (accessed from Malet Place), which contains one of London's weirder treasures: the clothed skeleton of one of the university's founders, Jeremy Bentham, who bequeathed himself to the college.

Circumventing the university and heading south down Gordon Street you reach **Gordon Square,** which Virginia Woolf, the Bells, John Maynard Keynes (all, severally, at No. 46), and Lytton Strachey (at No. 51) called home for a while. Here also is another of the ❹ university's collections, the **Percival David Foundation of Chinese Art,** dominated by ceramics, from the Sung to Qing dynasties—10th to 19th century, in other words. *Percival David Foundation of Chinese Art, 53 Gordon Sq., tel. 0171/387–3909. Admission free. Open weekdays 10:30–5 (sometimes closed 1–2 for lunch); closed weekends and bank holidays.*

The next square to the east, Tavistock Square, also housed Bloomsburies (Virginia and Leonard Woolf again, in No. 52), and ❺ now houses the single-room **Jewish Museum** in Adolph Tuck Hall, by the Court of the Chief Rabbi. Although it tells a potted history of the Jews in London from Norman times, the bulk of the exhibits date from the end of the 17th century (when Cromwell repealed the laws against Jewish settlement) and later. *Woburn House, Tavistock Sq., tel. 0171/388–4525. Admission: £1 adults, 50p students, children free. Open Nov.–Mar., Tues.–Thurs. 10–4, Fri. 10–12:45; Apr.–Oct., Tues.–Fri. 10–4, Sun. 10–12:45; closed national and Jewish holidays.*

Continuing south down busy Woburn Place, bypass Russell Square, Bloomsbury's biggest, on the right, and veer left down Guilford ❻ Street to reach the **Thomas Coram Foundation** in the 7-acre **Coram's Fields.** Captain Thomas Coram devoted half his life to setting up the sanctuary and hospital for London's street orphans he named the Foundling Hospital; it moved to Hertfordshire in 1926. He was a remarkable man, a master mariner and shipbuilder, who having played a major role in the colonization of Massachusetts returned to London in 1732 to sights he could not endure—abandoned babies and children "left to die on dung hills." Petitioning the lunching ladies of his day, and their lords, he raised the necessaries to set up what became the most celebrated Good Cause around, thanks partly to the sparkling benefactors he attracted. Handel gave an organ to the chapel, which he played himself in fundraising performances of his *Messiah*, and the chapel in turn became *the* place to be seen worshiping on a Sunday. Coram's great friend William Hogarth was one of several famous hospital governors, and his portrait of the founder hangs alongside other works of art (including paintings by Reynolds and Gainsborough) and mementos in the museum that now stands on the site of the hospital. *40 Brunswick Sq., tel. 0171/278–2424. Admission: £1 adults, 50p children and senior citizens. Open weekdays 10–4 unless being used for meetings or functions (check in advance); closed national holidays.*

Charles Dickens was often among the chapel congregation, since he lived a couple of blocks away, at 42 Doughty Street (turn left south of the Fields on Guilford Place, then right), which is now the **Dickens House Museum.** Blue Plaques bearing his name would litter the city if every place Dickens lived had survived, but Doughty Street is the only one still standing, and would have had a real claim to his fame in any case, since he wrote *Oliver Twist* and *Nicholas Nickleby* and finished *Pickwick Papers* here between 1837 and 1839. The house looks exactly as it would have in Dickens's day, complete with first editions, letters, and desk, plus a treat for Lionel Bart fans—his score of *Oliver!*. *48 Doughty St., tel. 0171/405–2127. Admission: £3 adults, £2 senior citizens and students, £1 children under 15. Open Mon.–Sat. 10–5; closed national holidays, Dec. 24–Jan. 1.*

Two streets west, parallel to Doughty Street, is pretty **Lamb's Conduit Street** (whose pretty pub, the Lamb, Dickens inevitably frequented); off it runs Great Ormond Street, where you will find another savior of children, the **Hospital for Sick Children.** Like Coram a century before, Dr. Charles West, its founder, was horrified at the inadequate provision made in London for the welfare of children; some 21,000 were dying every year. In 1929, Peter Pan gave the hospital a new lease of life—or rather his creator, Sir James Barrie, did, by donating the royalties from the play until 50 years after his death. (A special Act of Parliament enabled the gift to continue to this day.) Latterly, the hospital—like many in London—has been in financial difficulties again, but a new generation of benefactors has saved the day for now, and Princess Di came out of her self-imposed purdah early in 1994 to open a long-awaited new wing.

## Legal London—The Inns of Court

At the bottom of Lamb's Conduit Street you reach Theobald's Road, where you enter the time-warp territory of interlocking alleys, gardens and cobbled courts, town houses and halls, where London's legal profession grew up. The Great Fire of 1666 razed most of the city but spared the buildings you are about to explore, and the whole neighborhood oozes history. What is best about the area is that it lacks the commercial veneer of other historic sites, mostly because it is still very much the center of London's legal profession. Barristers, berobed and bewigged, may add an anachronistic frisson to your sightseeing, but they're only on their way to work.

They are headed for one of the four "Inns of Court": **Gray's Inn, Lincoln's Inn, Middle Temple,** and **Inner Temple.** Those arcane names are simply explained. The inns were just that: lodging houses for the lawyers who, back in the 14th century, clustered together here so everyone knew where to find them, and presently took over the running of the inns themselves. The temples were built on land owned by the Knights Templar, a chivalric order founded during the First Crusade in the 11th century; their 12th-century Temple Church still stands here. Few barristers (British for trial lawyers) still live in the inns, but nearly all keep chambers (British for barristers' offices) here, and all are still obliged to eat a requisite number of meals in the hall of "their" inn during training—no dinner, no career. They take exams, too.

**❾** The first inn you reach is the least architecturally interesting and the one most damaged by German bombs in the '40s, but **Gray's Inn** still has its romantic associations. In 1594, Shakespeare's *Comedy of Errors* was performed for the first time in its hall—which was lovingly restored after the World War II bombing and boasts a fine Elizabethan screen of carved oak. You must make advance arrangements to view Gray's Inn's hall, but you can stroll around the secluded and spacious gardens, first planted by Francis Bacon in 1606. *Holborn, tel. 0171/405–8164. Visits only by advance written application to the librarian. Chapel open weekdays 10–4; closed national holidays.*

You emerge from Gray's Inn onto **High Holburn** ("Hoe-bun"), heavy with traffic, since it (with the Strand) is the main route from the City to the West End and Westminster. Once it *was* the west end, or at least one of London's main shopping drags, and **Hatton Garden,** running north from Holburn Circus and still the center of London's diamond and jewelry trade, is a reminder of that. Another ghost of
**❿** former trading is **Staple Inn**—not an inn of court, but the former wool staple, where wool was weighed and traded and its merchants were lodged. It is central London's oldest surviving Elizabethan half-timbered building, and thanks to extensive restoration, with its overhanging upper stories, oriel windows, and black gables striping the white walls, looks the same as it must have in 1586 when it was brand-new.

Keep walking west, turning left down tiny Great Turnstile Row to reach one of the oldest, best preserved, and most comely of the inns,
**⓫** **Lincoln's Inn.** There's plenty to see—from the Chancery Lane Tudor brick gatehouse to the wide-open, tree-lined, atmospheric **Lincoln's Inn Fields** and the 15th-century **Chapel** remodeled by Inigo Jones in 1620. The wisteria-clad **New Square,** London's only complete 17th-century square, is not the newest part of the complex; the oldest-looking buildings are—the 1845 **Hall** and **Library,** which you must obtain the porter's permission to enter. Pass the Hall and continue around the west side of New Square, and you'll see an archway leading to **Carey Street.** You have just headed "straight for Queer Street." Since the bankruptcy courts used to stand here, you can divine what the old expression means. *Chancery La., tel. 0171/ 405–1393. Gardens and chapel open weekdays 12:30–2:30 (the public may also attend Sun. service at 11:30 in the chapel during legal terms); closed national holidays. Guided tours available.*

"Queer Street" leads you round into Portugal Street, where, at No. 13–14, stands a place of overwhelming cuteness, which a sign an-
**⓬** nounces is **The Old Curiosity Shop.** The teeny, red-roofed 16th-century "shop" (which at press time was about to become a shop once more, having been closed for a year) is probably one of the rare places in London Dickens did *not* frequent, but it sure looks like his

old curiosity shop, despite the orange-brick office block that dwarfs it.

Recross to the north side of Lincoln's Inn Fields to find a museum
⑬ that nobody who visits it ever forgets. **Sir John Soane's Museum,**
guaranteed to raise a smile from the most blasé and footsore tourist,
hardly deserves the burden of its dry name. Sir John, architect of
the Bank of England, bequeathed his house to the nation on condition that nothing be changed. We owe him our thanks, since he obviously had enormous fun with his home, having had the means to
finance great experiments in perspective and scale and to fill the
space with some wonderful pieces. In the Picture Room, for instance, two of Hogarth's *Rake's Progress* series are among the
paintings on panels that swing away to reveal secret gallery pockets
with more paintings. Everywhere mirrors and colors play tricks
with light and space, and split-level floors worthy of a fairground fun
house disorient you. In a basement chamber sits the vast 1300 BC
Sarcophagus of Seti I, lit by a domed skylight two stories up. When
Sir John acquired this priceless object for £2,000, he celebrated with
a three-day party. *13 Lincoln's Inn Fields, tel. 0171/405–2107. Admission free. Open Tues.–Sat. 10–5; closed national holidays.*

Walking the other way on Carey Street brings you to the vast Victorian Gothic pile containing the nation's principal Law Courts, the
⑭ **Royal Courts of Justice,** whose 1,000-odd rooms run off 3½ miles of
corridor all the way through to the Strand. Here are heard the most
important civil law cases—that's everything from divorce to fraud,
with libel in between—and you can sit in the viewing gallery to
watch any trial you like, for a live version of Court TV. The more
dramatic criminal cases are heard at the Old Bailey (*see* Temple Bar
to Ludgate Hill in The City, *below*). Other sights to witness include
the 238-foot-long main hall and the compact exhibition of judges'
robes. *The Strand, tel. 0171/936–6000. Admission free. Open weekdays 9–4:30; closed Aug.–Sept., national holidays.*

Leaving the Law Courts by the main door, cross the Strand and you
will be teetering on the edge of the City, at Temple Bar, ready to
⑮ ⑯ enter **Inner Temple** and **Middle Temple,** collectively known as—you
guessed it—**Temple.** The exact point of entry into the City is marked
⑰ by a young (1880) bronze griffin, the **Temple Bar Memorial.** He is the
symbol of the City, having replaced (sadly) a Wren gateway (*see*
Temple Bar to Ludgate Hill in The City, *below*). In the buildings opposite you'll see an elaborate stone arch through which you pass into
Middle Temple Lane, past a row of 17th-century timber-frame
houses, and on into Fountain Court on the right. This lane runs all
the way to the Thames, more or less separating the two Temples,
past the sloping lawns of Middle Temple Gardens, on the east border
of which you'll find the Elizabethan **Middle Temple Hall.** If it's open,
don't miss that hammer-beam roof, which is among the finest in the
land. *Tel. 0171/353–4355. Open weekdays 10–noon and (when not in
use) 3–4.*

You'll find an alternative entrance to the lawyers' sanctum farther
east where the Strand becomes Fleet Street (which we visit on the
next tour). Your landmark is the Jacobean half-timbered house
⑱ known as **Prince Henry's Room,** built in 1610 to celebrate the investi-
ture of Henry, James I's eldest son, as Prince of Wales, and marked
with his coat of arms and a "PH" on the ceiling. You can go in to visit
the small Samuel Pepys exhibition. *17 Fleet St., tel. 0171/936–2710.
Open Mon.–Sat. 11–2. Closed public holidays.*

The gateway next door leads down Inner Temple Lane as far as
**⑲ Temple Church,** built by the Knights Templar in the 12th century
and featuring "the Round"—a rare circular nave. The Red Knights
(so called after the red crosses they wore—you can see them in effigy around the nave) held their secret initiation rites in the crypt
here. Having started poor, holy, and dedicated to the protection of
pilgrims, they grew rich from showers of kingly gifts, until in the
14th century they were accused of heresy, blasphemy, and sodomy,
thrown into the Tower, and stripped of their wealth. You might suppose the church to be thickly atmospheric, but Victorian and postwar restorers have tamed the antique mystery. Still, it's a very fine
Gothic-Romanesque church, whose 1240 chancel ("the Oblong") has
been accused of perfection. *The Temple, tel. 0171/353-8462. Open
daily 10–4; closed national holidays.*

The gorgeous gardens of the Inner and Middle Temples are irritatingly off-limits to the public, but it's possible to see these, plus other
secret sights, by investing in one of the **Wig and Pen Club's Legal
Tours.** The Club is another of those St. James's–style affairs, this
time for "men of justice, journalists, and businessmen of the City"
(plus former presidents Nixon and Reagan), which has its home in
the only Strand building to have survived the Great Fire of 1666.
The tours include meals, refreshments, honorary membership for
the day (even for women), and are guided by experts. *229 Strand,
WC2, tel. 0171/583-7255. Cost: £50 (half-day) or £88 (full day).*

# The City

*Numbers in the margin correspond to points of interest on the City
map.*

If you did the previous tour, you will already have entered the City
of London. You may have assumed you had done this when your
plane touched down at Heathrow, but note that capital letter: the
City of London is not the same as the city of London. The capital-C
City is an autonomous district, separately governed since William
the Conqueror started building the Tower of London, and despite its
compact size (you may hear it referred to as the "Square Mile,"
which is almost accurate), it remains the financial engine of Britain
and one of the world's leading centers of trade.

The City is also London's most ancient part, although there is little
remaining to remind you of that fact beyond a scattering of Roman
stones. It was Aulus Plautius, Roman ruler of Britain under Claudius, who established the Romans' first stronghold on the Thames
halfway through the first century AD. The name "Londinium,"
though, probably derives from the Celtic *Lyn-dun,* meaning "fortified town on the lake," which suggests far earlier settlement. Not
much is known about the period between AD 410, when the Roman
legions left, and the 6th century, when the Saxons arrived, but it
was really after Edward the Confessor moved his court to Westminster in 1060 that the City gathered momentum. As Westminster
took over the administrative role, the City was free to develop the
commercial heart that still beats strong.

The Romans had already found Londinium's position handy for
trade—the river being navigable yet far enough inland to allow for
its defense—but it was the establishment of crafts guilds in the Middle Ages, followed in Tudor and Stuart times by the proliferation of
great trading companies (the Honourable East India Company,
founded in 1600, was the star), that really started the cash flowing.

King John had confirmed the City's autonomy by charter in 1215, and its commerce and government fed off each other, the leaders of the former electing the leaders of the latter. This is still largely the case: The Corporation of London has control over the Square Mile and elects a Lord Mayor just as it did in the Middle Ages, when the famous folk hero Richard Whittington was four times (not thrice, as in *Dick Whittington*, the pantomime) voted in.

Three times the City has faced devastation—and that's not counting the "Black Monday" of 1992, when sterling crashed. The Great Fire of 1666 spared practically none of the labyrinthine medieval streets—a blessing in disguise, actually, since the Great Plague of the year before had wiped (or driven) out most of the population and left a terrible mess in the cramped, downright sordid houses. With the wind in the west, they said, you could smell London from Tilbury. The fire necessitated a total reconstruction, in which Sir Christopher Wren had a big hand, contributing not only his masterpiece, St. Paul's Cathedral, but 49 further parish churches (*see* "Wren and the Great Fire of London" in Chapter 2, Portraits of London).

The third wave of destruction, after the plague and the fire, was, of course, dealt by the German bombers of the Second World War, who showered the City with 57 days and nights of special attention, wreaking as much havoc as the Great Fire had managed. The ruins were rebuilt, but slowly, and with no overall plan, leaving the City a patchwork of the old and the new, the interesting and the flagrantly awful. Since a mere 8,000 or so people call it home, the financial center of Britain is deserted outside the working week, with restaurants shuttered and streets forlorn and windswept. Do this tour on a weekday—there's little to see unless you see it in action.

## Temple Bar to Ludgate Hill

Begin at the gateway to the City—and we mean that literally. Until the 18th century there were eight such gates, all but one of which survive in name only (Cripplegate, Ludgate, Bishopsgate, Moorgate, and so on). The surviving one, just to be confusing, is a gate neither in name nor in form, being called **Temple Bar**, and having evolved from the chain between wooden posts that it was in the 13th century into the bronze griffin you see today on the Strand opposite the **Royal Courts of Justice**. Panels around the base recall earlier entrances, as does the ritual still performed when the sovereign wants to enter the City: She has to ask the Lord Mayor's permission, which he grants by letting her hold his Sword of State.

Temple Bar, then, marks the western edge of the Square Mile, which does cover 677 acres (a square mile is 640), though not in a remotely straight-sided fashion. The curvy shape described by its boundaries—Smithfield in the north, Aldgate and Tower Hill in the east, and the Thames on the south—resembles nothing so much as an armadillo, with Temple Bar at snout level.

Walking, as it were, toward the tail, you will soon find yourself on **Fleet Street**, which follows the course of, and is named after, one of London's ghost rivers. The Fleet, so called by the Anglo-Saxons, spent most of its centuries above ground as an open sewer, offending local noses until banished below in 1766. It still flows underfoot, now a sanctioned section of London's sewer system. The street's sometime nickname, "Street of Shame," has nothing to do with the stench. It refers to the trade that made it famous: the press. Since the end of the 15th century, when Wynkyn de Worde set up

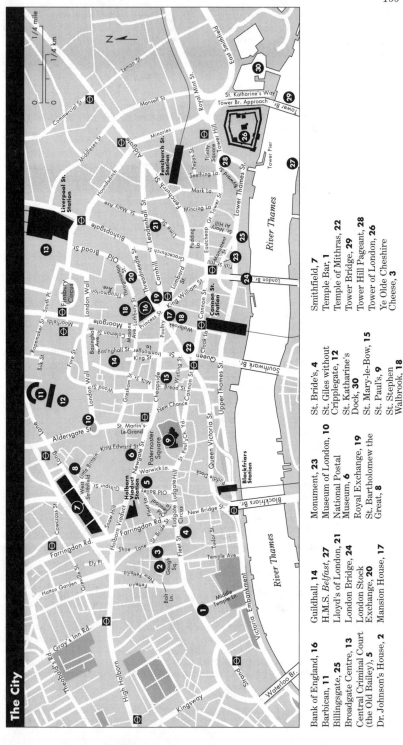

# The City

Bank of England, **16**
Barbican, **11**
Billingsgate, **25**
Broadgate Centre, **13**
Central Criminal Court
  (the Old Bailey), **5**
Dr. Johnson's House, **2**

Guildhall, **14**
H.M.S. *Belfast*, **27**
Lloyd's of London, **21**
London Bridge, **24**
London Stock
  Exchange, **20**
Mansion House, **17**

Monument, **23**
Museum of London, **10**
National Postal
  Museum, **6**
Royal Exchange, **19**
St. Bartholomew the
  Great, **8**

St. Bride's, **4**
St. Giles without
  Cripplegate, **12**
St. Katharine's
  Dock, **30**
St. Mary-le-Bow, **15**
St. Paul's, **9**
St. Stephen
  Walbrook, **18**

Smithfield, **7**
Temple Bar, **1**
Temple of Mithras, **22**
Tower Bridge, **29**
Tower Hill Pageant, **28**
Tower of London, **26**
Ye Olde Cheshire
  Cheese, **3**

England's first printing press here, and especially after 1702, when the first newspaper, the *Daily Courant*, moved in, followed by (literally) all the rest, "Fleet Street" has been synonymous with newspaper journalism. The papers themselves all moved out in the 1980s, but the British press is still collectively known as "Fleet Street." (Don't miss the black-glass-and-chrome Art Dèco *Daily Mirror* building.)

Turn left on Bolt Court to reach Gough Square, where Samuel Johnson lived between 1746 and 1759, in the worst of health, compiling his famous dictionary in the attic. Like Dickens, he lived all over town, but, like Dickens's House, **Dr. Johnson's House** is the only one of his abodes remaining today. It is a shrine to the man possibly more attached to London than anyone else, ever, and includes a first edition of his dictionary among the Johnson-and-Boswell mementos. *17 Gough Sq., tel. 0171/353-3745. Admission: £2.50 adults, £1.50 children under 16 and senior citizens. Open May–Sept., Mon.–Sat. 11–5:30; Oct.–Apr., Mon.–Sat. 11–5; closed national holidays.*

One of the places Dr. Johnson drank (like Dickens, he is claimed by many a pub) was his "local" around the corner in Wine Office Court, **Ye Olde Cheshire Cheese,** which retains a venerable open-fires-in-tiny-rooms charm when not too packed with tourists. Among 19th-century writers who followed Johnson's footsteps to the bar here were Mark Twain and, yes, Charles Dickens.

Back on Fleet Street, you come to the first of Wren's city churches—one of the bomb-damaged ones, reconsecrated only in 1960 after a 17-year restoration: **St. Bride's.** As St. Paul's, Covent Garden is the actor's church, so St. Bride's belongs to journalists, many of whom have been buried or memorialized here, as reading the wall plaques will tell you. Even before the press moved in, it was a popular place to take the final rest. By 1664 the crypts were so crowded that Samuel Pepys had to bribe the grave digger to "justle together" some bodies to make room for his deceased brother. Now the crypts house a museum of the church's rich history, and a bit of Roman sidewalk. *Fleet St., tel. 0171/353-1301. Admission free. Open Mon.–Sat. 9–5, Sun. between the services at 11 and 6:30.*

**Time Out**  **Bagel Express** (62 Fleet St.), a designer sandwich shop, is like a slice of Manhattan, complete with Korean supermarket–inspired salad bar. Try a three-cheese melt on a spinach bagel or one of the daily specials.

The end of Fleet Street is marked by the messy traffic intersection called **Ludgate Circus,** which you should cross to Ludgate Hill to reach **Old Bailey,** second on the left. At the top, on the site of the courts we are about to visit, **Newgate Prison** stood from the 12th century right until the beginning of this one. Few survived for long in the version pulled down in 1770. Those who didn't starve were hanged, or pressed to death in the Press Yard, or they succumbed to the virulent gaol (as the British sometimes spell "jail") fever—any of which must have been preferable to a life in the stinking, subterranean, lightless Stone Hold, or to suffering the robberies, beatings, and general victimization endemic in what Henry Fielding called the "prototype of hell." The next model lasted only a couple of years before being torn down by insane mobs during the anti-Catholic Gordon Riots of 1780, to be replaced by the Newgate that Dickens visited several times (in between pubs) and used in several novels— Fagin ended up in the Condemned Hold here in *Oliver Twist*, from which he would have been taken to the public scaffold which replaced the Tyburn Tree and stood outside the prison until 1868.

Instead of a hanging, the modern visitor can watch a trial by jury in the **Central Criminal Court,** better known as the Old Bailey, which replaced Newgate in 1907. The most famous, and most interesting, feature of the solid Edwardian building is the gilded statue of blind-(folded) Justice perched on top, scales in her left hand, sword in her right. Ask the doorman which current trial is likely to prove juicy, if you're that kind of ghoul—you may catch the conviction of the next Crippen or Christie (England's most notorious wife-murderers, both tried here). *Public Gallery open weekdays 10–1, 2–4; queue forms at the Newgate St. entrance. Check the day's hearings on the sign outside.*

From mass murderers to stamp collectors . . . A right turn on Newgate Street at the top of Old Bailey, then a left onto King Edward Street brings you to the **National Postal Museum.** This landmark for philatelists was founded in 1965, but the collection is as old as the postal service itself, and is one of the world's best. *King Edward Bldg., King Edward St., tel. 0171/239–5420. Admission free. Open Mon.–Thurs. 9:30–4:30, Fri. 9:30–4; closed national holidays.*

The road turns into Little Britain farther along, then emerges at **Smithfield,** London's main meat market. Nowadays the meat is dead, but up to the middle of last century, it was livestock that was sold here, by human meatheads, who liked to get blind drunk and stampede their herds around the houses—"like a bull in a china shop," which is where that phrase comes from. This "smooth field" was already a market in the 12th century, but the building you see today, modeled on the Victorian Crystal Palace, was not opened until 1868. Although threatened by various European Community directives, not to mention the disappearance of the artisan butcher, Smithfield still bustles like nowhere else, frenetic porters (actor Michael Caine's father was one) slinging sides of beef about, dripping blood down their aprons, then repairing to pubs that have special early alcohol licenses for breakfast. Visitors, although welcome, had better (a) get up very early, because the show's over by 9:30, (b) keep out of the way, or get sworn at, and (c) not be vegetarian.

**Time Out**   The **Fox and Anchor** (115 Charterhouse St.) serves beer alongside its famous Brobdingnagian mixed grills, from 6:30 AM.

Backtracking a few steps down Little Britain, you'll see on the left a perfect half-timbered gatehouse atop a 13th-century stone archway. Enter here to reach one of London's oldest churches, the Norman **St. Bartholomew the Great.** Along with its namesake on the other side of the road, St. Bartholomew's Hospital, the church was founded by Rahere, Henry I's court jester. At the Dissolution of the Monasteries, Henry VIII had most of it torn down, so that the Romanesque choir is all that survives from the 12th century. The hospital across the street is one of London's two main teaching hospitals. (The other one, Guy's, in Southwark, was being threatened with closure at press time in a long-running scandal of government mismanagement.)

### St. Paul's Cathedral

You can slip around by the back route to reach the City's star sight by recrossing Newgate Street and continuing straight through Cathedral Place, or you can go all the way around via Ludgate Hill, but

Admiral Collingwood, **21**

Admiral Earl Howe, **20**

The American Memorial Chapel, **13**

All Souls' Chapel, **1**

Bishop's Throne, **18**

Chapel of Modern Martyrs, **11**

Chapel of St. Michael and St. George , **27**

Crypt Entrance, **19**

Dean's Vestry, **16**

The Donne Effigy, **15**

Dr. Johnson by John Bacon, **8**

Duke of Wellington, **5**

General Gordon Monument, **4**

Geometric Staircase and Dean's Door, **28**

High Altar and Baldachino, **12**

J.M.W. Turner, **22**

The Lady Chapel, **14**

Lord Leighton Monument, **3**

Lord Mayor's Stall, **17**

Lord Mayor's Vestry, **6**

Minor Canons' Vestry, **9**

Nelson, **23**

St. Dunstan's Chapel, **2**

St. Paul's Watch Memorial Stone, **26**

Sanctuary Screens and Tijou Gates, **10**

Sir John Moore, **24**

Sir Joshua Reynolds by Flaxman, **7**

Staircase to Whispering Gallery, Dome, and Golden Gallery, **25**

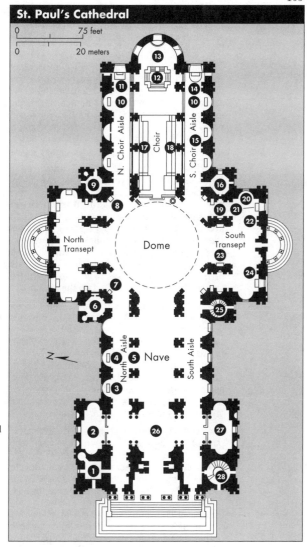

## St. Paul's Cathedral

❾ whichever way you approach **St. Paul's,** your first view of it will take your breath away. In fact, the dome—the world's third largest—will already be familiar, since you see it peeping through on the skyline from many an angle.

The cathedral is, of course, Sir Christopher Wren's masterpiece, completed in 1710 after 35 years of building and much argument with the royal commission, then, much later, miraculously (mostly) spared by the World War II bombs. Wren had originally been commissioned to restore Old St. Paul's, the Norman cathedral that had replaced, in its turn, three earlier versions, but the Great Fire left so little of it behind that a new cathedral was deemed necessary.

Wren's first plan, known as the New Model, did not make it past the drawing board, while the second, known as the Great Model, got as far as the 20-foot oak rendering you can see here today before being rejected, too, whereupon Wren is said to have burst into tears. The third, however, known as the **Warrant Design** (because it received the royal warrant), was accepted, with the fortunate coda that the architect be allowed to make changes as he saw fit. Without that, there would be no dome, since the approved design had featured a steeple. Parliament felt that building was proceeding too slowly (in fact, 35 years is lightning speed, as cathedrals go) and withheld half of Wren's pay for the last 13 years of work. He was pushing 80 when Queen Anne finally coughed up the arrears.

When you enter and see the **dome** from the inside, you may find that it seems smaller than you expected. You aren't imagining things; it *is* smaller, and 60 feet lower, than the lead-covered outer dome. Between the inner and outer domes is a brick cone, which supports the familiar 850-ton lantern, surmounted by its golden ball and cross. Nobody can resist making a beeline for the dome, so we'll start beneath it, standing dead center, on top of Wren's memorial, which his son composed and had set into the pavement, and which reads succinctly: *Lector, si monumentum requiris, circumspice*—"Reader, if you seek his monument, look around you."

Now climb the 259 spiral steps to the **Whispering Gallery.** This is the part of the cathedral with which you bribe children, who are fascinated by the acoustic phenomenon: Whisper something to the wall on one side, and a second later it transmits clearly to the other side, 107 feet away. The only problem is identifying "your" whisper from the cacophony of everyone else's, since this is a popular game. Look down onto the Nave from here, and up to the frescoes of St. Paul by Sir James Thornhill (who nearly fell off while painting them), before ascending farther to the **Stone Gallery,** which encircles the outside of the dome and affords a spectacular panorama of London. Up again (careful—you will have tackled 627 steps altogether) and you reach the **Golden Gallery,** from which you can view the lantern through a circular opening called the oculus.

Back downstairs there are the inevitable monuments and memorials to see, though fewer than one might expect, since Wren didn't want his masterpiece cluttered up. The poet John Donne, who had been Dean of St. Paul's for his final 10 years (he died in 1631), lies in the south choir aisle, his the only monument remaining from Old St. Paul's. The vivacious choir stall carvings nearby are the work of Grinling Gibbons, as is the organ, which Wren designed and Handel played. The painters Sir Joshua Reynolds and J. M. W. Turner are commemorated, as is George Washington. The American connection continues behind the high altar in the **American Memorial Chapel,** dedicated in 1958 to the 28,000 GIs stationed here who lost their lives in World War II.

A visit to the **crypt** brings you to Wren's tomb, the black marble sarcophagus containing Admiral Nelson (who was pickled in alcohol for his final voyage here from Trafalgar), and an equestrian statue of the Duke of Wellington on top of his grandiose tomb. *Tel. 0171/248–2705. Admission to cathedral, ambulatory (American Chapel), crypt, and treasury: £2.50 adults, £2 senior citizens, £1.50 children; to galleries: £2.50 adults, £2 senior citizens, £1.50 children; combined ticket: £4.50 adults, £3.50 senior citizens, £2.50 children. Cathedral open for sightseeing Mon.–Sat. 8:30–4:30 (closed occasionally for special services); ambulatory, crypt, and galleries open Mon.–Sat. 9:30–4:15.*

Surrounding St. Paul's is . . . nothing. Various plans to redevelop the area, which was flattened by bombing and obviously rebuilt in a hurry, have been dogged by bickering and delay for decades. The conflicting designs of Paternoster Square, to the west, are the paradigm: one moment modernist and exciting, the next pseudo-Italianate and safe. No progress will have been made by the time you read this.

## The Museum of London and the Barbican

Find Little Britain yet again, taking its right fork to cross Aldersgate Street to **London Wall,** named for the Roman rampart that stood along it. It's a dismal street, now dominated by post-modern architect Terry Farrell's late-'80s follies, but about halfway along you can see a section of 2nd-to-4th-century wall at St. Alphege Garden. There's another bit in an appropriate spot back at the start of London Wall, outside the **Museum of London,** which you can view better from a window inside the museum itself, near the Roman monumental arch the museum's archaeologists reconstructed a mere two decades ago. Anyone with the least interest in how this city evolved will adore the museum, especially said reconstructions and the dioramas—like one of the Great Fire (flickering flames! sound effects!), a 1940s air-raid shelter, a Georgian prison cell, and a Victorian street complete with fully stocked shops. There are plenty of treasures (the Cheapside Hoard of Jacobean jewelry shouldn't be missed), costumes, furniture, and domestic paraphernalia to flesh it all out, and galleries proceed chronologically for easy comprehension. *London Wall, tel. 0171/600–3699. Admission: £3 adults, £1.50 children under 18 and senior citizens, £7.50 family ticket (up to 2 adults and 3 children); admission free 4:30–6. All tickets allow unlimited return visits for three months. Open Tues.–Sat. 10–6, Sun. noon–6; closed Good Friday, Dec. 24–25.*

North of the Museum is the enormous concrete maze Londoners love to hate—the **Barbican,** home of the Royal Shakespeare Company and its two theaters, the London Symphony Orchestra and its auditorium, the Guildhall School of Music and Drama, a major gallery for touring exhibitions, two cinemas, a convention center, and apartments for a hapless two-thirds of the City's residents (most part-time). The name comes from a defensive fortification of the City, and defensive is what Barbican apologists (including architects Chamberlain, Powell, and Bon) became when the complex was finally revealed in 1982, after 20 years as a building site. There ensued an epidemic of jokes about getting lost forever in the Barbican bowels. A hasty rethink of the contradictory signposts and nonsensical "levels" was performed, and navigatory yellow lines materialized, Oz-like, on the floors, but it didn't help much—the Barbican remains difficult to navigate. Time has mellowed the elephant-gray concrete into a darker blotchy brownish-gray, and Londoners have come to accept the place, if not exactly love it, because of its contents. Actors rate the theater acoustics especially high, and the steep bank of the seating makes for a good stage view. The visiting exhibitions are often worth a trek, as are the free ones in the foyer.

Negotiating the windy walkways of the deserted residential section, then descending in elusive elevators to the lower depths of the Centre (where the studio auditorium, the aptly-named Pit, lives), spotting stray sculptures and water gardens, receiving electric shocks from the brass rails—all this has its perverse charm, but there is one unadulterated success in the Barbican, though unfortunately it's not often open to the public. Secreted on an upper floor is an enormous, lush conservatory in a towering glass palace, big enough for full-grown trees to flourish. *Silk St., tel. 0171/638–4141. Admission free. Open Mon.–Sat. 9 AM–11 PM, Sun. noon–11 PM. Gallery: admission £3.50 adults, £1 children and senior citizens; open Mon.–Sat. 10–7:30, Sun. and national holidays noon–7:30. Conservatory: admission 80p adults, 60p children and senior citizens; open Sat.–Sun. noon–5:30 when not in use for private function (always call first). Tours (minimum 10 people; book in advance), tel. 0171/628–0183; cost: £3.50 adults, £2.50 children and senior citizens. RSC backstage tours, tel. 0171/628–3351.*

**Time Out** The Barbican Centre's **Waterside Café** has salads, sandwiches, and pastries; they're unremarkable but are served in a tranquil enclosed concrete (naturally) waterside terrace. Sometimes customers are serenaded by practice sessions of the Guildhall School of Music and Drama's orchestra next door.

South of the Barbican complex stands one of the only City churches to have withstood the Great Fire, only to succumb to the Blitz bombs three centuries later, **St. Giles without Cripplegate.** The tower and a few walls survived; the rest was rebuilt to the 16th-century plan in the 1950s, and now the little church struggles hopelessly for attention amongst the Barbican towers, whose parishioners it tends. Past parishioners include Oliver Cromwell, married here in 1620, and John Milton, buried here in 1674.

Before heading south to the City's financial heart, detour east to see one of the more successful recent development schemes, the **Broadgate Centre,** at the north end of Old Broad Street, hanging on the tails of the redeveloped **Liverpool Street Station.** In contrast to the Barbican, this collection of offices, shops, and restaurants got good notices as soon as it opened in 1987, especially for its circular courtyard surrounded by hanging gardens. The courtyard is iced over in winter to become London's only outdoor skating rink; it hosts bands and performers in summer.

### The Guildhall and the Financial Center

Back on London Wall, turn south into Coleman Street, then right onto Masons Avenue to reach Basinghall Street and the **Guildhall,** symbolic nerve center of the City. The Corporation of London ceremonially elects and installs its Lord Mayor here as it has done for 800 years. The Guildhall was built in 1411, and though it failed to avoid either the 1666 or 1940 flames, its core survived, with a new roof sensitively appended in the 1950s and further cosmetic embellishments added in the '70s.

The fabulous hall is a psychedelic patchwork of coats of arms and banners of the City Livery Companies, which inherited the mantle of the medieval trade guilds, which invented the City in the first place. Actually, this honor really belongs to two giants, Gog and Magog, the pair of mythical beings who founded ancient Albion, and who glower upon the prime minister's annual November banquet from their west gallery grandstand in 9-foot painted limewood form.

The 94 modern Livery Companies are more than symbolic banner-bearers, since they fund education and research in the trades they represent, and many offer apprenticeships. Most are modern and useful, like the Vintners', Plaisterers', Grocers', and Insurers' Companies. Other, older ones have had to move with the times and diversify—the Tallow Chandlers' Company has gone into the oil trade, and the Paviors' Company, no longer required to dispose of scavenging pigs, now concentrates on street construction. *Gresham St., tel. 0171/606–3030. Admission free. Open Mon.–Sat. 10–5; closed national holidays.*

The 1970s west wing houses the **Guildhall Library**—mainly City-related books and documents, plus a collection belonging to one of the Livery Companies, **the Worshipful Company of Clockmakers,** with over 600 timepieces on show, including a skull-faced watch that belonged to Mary, Queen of Scots. *Tel. 0171/606–3030. Admission free. Open weekdays 10–5; closed national holidays.*

As you might guess, many streets around here were named for their own medieval craft guild, including the dairymen's lane, Milk Street, which you now follow south to **Cheapside.** Chepe being Old English for "market," you might also divine that this street was where the bakers of Bread Street, the cobblers of Cordwainers Street, the goldsmiths of Goldsmith Street, and all their brothers gathered to sell their wares.

**⑮** You come now to another symbolic center of London, **St. Mary-le-Bow,** Wren's 1673 church (and the spire survives intact). The bells are the symbolic part, since a Londoner must be born within the sound of them to qualify as a true cockney. The origin of that idea was probably the curfew rung on the Bow Bells during the 14th century, even though "cockney" only came to mean Londoner three centuries later, and then it was an insult.

**Time Out** **The Place Below** is literally below the church, in St. Mary-le-Bow's crypt, and gets packed with City workers weekday lunchtimes, since the self-service soup and quiche are particularly good. It's also open for breakfast, and Thursday and Friday evenings feature a posh and sophisticated vegetarian set dinner.

Walk to the east end of Cheapside. Here seven roads meet and financial institutions converge in a tornado of fiscal activity that is bereft of life on weekends. Turn to your left, and you will be facing the cita-
**⑯** del-like **Bank of England,** known familiarly for the past couple of centuries as "The Old Lady of Threadneedle Street," after someone's parliamentary quip. The bank, which has been central to the British economy since 1694, manages the national debt and the foreign exchange reserves, issues banknotes, sets interest rates, looks after England's gold, and regulates its banking system. Sir John Soane (*see* Legal London—The Inns of Court, *above*) designed the neo-classical hulk in 1788, wrapping it in windowless walls (which are all that survives of his building) to suggest a stability that the ailing economy of the post-Thatcher years tends to belie. The larger history of this economy, and the role that the Bank of En-

gland played in it, is traced in the **Bank of England Museum.** *Bartholomew La., tel. 0171/601–5545. Admission free. Open Easter–Sept., Mon.–Fri. 10–5, Sun. and public holidays 11–5; Oct.–Easter, Mon.–Fri. 10–6; closed public holidays Oct.–Easter.*

**⑰** With your back to the bank you will see the mid-18th-century Palladian facade of the Lord Mayor's abode, **Mansion House.** What you won't see is the colonnaded Egyptian Hall, or the cell where the suffragette Emmeline Pankhurst was held early in this century, or any of the state rooms where the mayor entertains his fellow dignitaries, since the building is closed to public scrutiny.

**⑱** At the mayor's back door stands the parish church many think is Wren's best, **St. Stephen Walbrook,** on the street of the same name. Possibly you are beginning to think that *every* Wren church shares that distinction, but this one really does shine, by virtue of its practice dome, which predates the Big One at St. Paul's by some 30 years. Two inside sights warrant investigation: Henry Moore's 1987 central stone altar, which sits beneath the dome ("like a lump of Camembert," say critics), and, well, a telephone—an eloquent tribute to that genuine savior of souls, Rector Chad Varah, who founded the Samaritans, givers of phone help to the suicidal, here in 1953.

**⑲** The third **Royal Exchange** to inhabit the isosceles triangle between Threadneedle Street and Cornhill was blessed by Queen Victoria at its 1844 opening. Sir William Tite designed the massive temple-like building, its pediment featuring 17 limestone figures (Commerce, plus merchants) supported by eight sizable Corinthian columns, to house the then thriving futures market. This has now moved on (*see below*), leaving the Royal Exchange, which you may no longer enter, as a monument to money.

**⑳** In back of the Bank of England at the start of Old Broad Street is yet another venerable trading institution that has completely changed, the **London Stock Exchange.** A mere 14 years after this building opened (again, the third on its site), it was rendered practically useless, when the "Big Bang," the stock market crash of late 1986, put a stop to trading in equities on the floor. The London Traded Options Market persisted in one corner, which visitors could spy on from the Viewing Gallery, until security-consciousness following an IRA bomb in July 1990 closed *that* down. It was due to close anyway, because in February 1992 that last bastion of the jobbers and brokers of the stock exchange floor merged with the London International Financial Futures Exchange (LIFFE, pronounced "life"), everyone packed their phones, and they all decamped to deal at **Cannon Bridge Station** in nearby Cousin's Lane (tel. 0171/623–0444; tours available by arrangement), leaving the dealing floor at the Stock Exchange echoing with red-suspendered, stripe-shirted '80s phantoms. All you can visit there now is the reception desk, where a long-suffering security guard says you can't go in and somewhat tetchily hands over an information booklet.

**㉑** Continue along Cornhill to Leadenhall Street. The final tale of fiscal fortunes on this route is contained in what most agree is the most exciting recent structure London can boast, the **Lloyd's of London** tower, Richard Rogers's (of Paris Pompidou Centre fame) 1986 masterpiece. The building is a fantastical steel-and-glass medium-rise of six towers around a vast atrium, with Rogers's trademark inside-out ventilation shafts, stairwells, gantries, and so on partying all over the facades. It is definitely best seen at night, when cobalt and lime spotlights make it leap out of the deeply boring gray skyline like Carmen Miranda at a funeral.

The institution that commissioned this fabulous £163-million fun house has been trading in insurance for two centuries and is famous the world over for several reasons: (1) having started in a coffee house; (2) insuring Marilyn Monroe's legs; (3) accepting no corporate responsibility for losses, which are carried by its investors; (4) having its "Names"—the rich people who underwrite Lloyd's losses; (5) seeming unassailable for a very long time . . . (6) until recently—losses in 1990 were £2.9 billion, (7) which caused the financial ruination of many Names, and worse: According to reports (possibly hyperbolic), more than 30 of the unfortunates were so devastated by the loss of an apparently safe investment that they committed suicide.

Lloyd's has been allowed to continue trading, however, and claims that good times are coming "in the not too distant future." Meanwhile, the viewing galleries over the trading floor and the museum of Lloyd's history, containing the Lutine Bell, which heralds important announcements (one ring for bad news), have all been closed to the public—not on account of recent misfortunes, but as insurance against future ones, in the form of bombs. *1 Lime St., tel. 0171/623-7100.*

---

**Time Out**  **Lloyd's Coffee House,** despite its name and its position at the foot of the Lloyd's tower, has nothing to do with the 17th-century coffee house where the institution was born but serves British "caff" food all day long nevertheless.

---

### Mithras, the Monument, and London Bridge

Now we leave the money markets and return briefly to Roman London, which you may have learned more about in the Museum of London. The museum funds an archaeological department, which has been patiently piecing together a picture of the 2nd-to-4th-century City for the past few decades, with one recent and exciting find currently in the process of assimilation: the remains of an amphitheater, discovered a decade ago on a building site by the Guildhall. It must have been one of Londinium's major attractions.

Another, minor place of pilgrimage in the Roman City was unearthed on another building site in 1954 and taken, at first, for an early Christian church. In fact, worshipers at the **Temple of Mithras** were not at all keen on Christ; they favored his chief rival during the 3rd and 4th centuries, Mithras, the Persian god of light. Mithraists aimed for all the big virtues, but still were not appreciated by early Christians, from whom their sculptures and treasures had to be concealed. These devotional objects are now on display back at the Museum of London, while here, on Queen Victoria Street, not far from the Bank of England, you can see the foundations of the temple itself.

Moving along a few centuries, the next shrine you pass, after a sharp left turn into Cannon Street, commemorates the "dreadful visitation" of the Great Fire of 1666. Known simply as **Monument,** this is the world's tallest isolated stone column—the work of Wren, who was asked to erect it "On or as neere unto the place where the said Fire soe unhappily began as conveniently may be." And so here it is—at 202 feet, exactly as tall as the distance it stands from Farriner's baking house in Pudding Lane, where the fire started. Above the viewing gallery (311 steps up—better than any StairMaster) is a flaming bronze urn, and around it a cage for the prevention of suicide, which was a trend for a while in the 19th century. *Monument St., tel. 0171/626–2717. Admission: £1 adults, 25p children. Open Apr.–Sept., weekdays 9–5:30, weekends 2–5:30; Oct.–Mar., Mon.–Sat. 9–3:30.*

**24** Just south of Monument is the latest **London Bridge.** This one dates from only 1972; it replaced the 1831 Sir John Rennie number that now graces Lake Havasu City, Arizona, the impulse purchase of someone at the McCulloch Oil Corporation, who (rumor has it) was under the impression that he'd bought the far more picturesque Tower Bridge. The version before that one, the first in stone and the most renowned of all, stood for 600 years after it was built in 1176, the focus of many a gathering thanks to the shops and houses crammed along its length, not to mention the boiled and tar-dipped heads of traitors that decorated its gatehouse after they were removed at the Tower of London. Before *that* the Saxons had put up a wooden bridge; it collapsed in 1014, which was probably the origin of "London bridge is falling down." Nobody is sure of the exact location of the very earliest London Bridge—the Roman version around which focus London grew—but it was certainly very close to the 100-foot-wide, three-span, pre-stressed concrete cantilever one that you see today.

**25** Turn left onto Lower Thames Street and you'll come to **Billingsgate,** London's principal fish market for 900 years—until 1982, when the fish moved to the Isle of Dogs farther east and the developers moved in here, leaving a sanitized, if pretty, shell, which at press time had yet to find a tenant. Next door is the Custom House, built early in the last century.

## The Tower of London

You'll have spotted the most famous of the City's sights already, as
**26** it's an easy five-minute walk from the Custom House: the **Tower of London.** The Tower, as it's generally known, has top billing on every tourist itinerary for good reason. Nowhere else does London's history come to life so vividly as in this mini-city of melodramatic towers stuffed to bursting with heraldry and treasure, the intimate details of lords and dukes and princes and sovereigns etched in the walls (literally in some places, as you'll see), and quite a few pints of royal blue blood spilled on the stones. Be warned that visitor traffic at the sight of sights is copious, meaning not only lines for the best bits, but a certain dilution of atmosphere, which can be disappointing if you've been fantasizing scenes from *Elizabeth and Essex.* At least you need no longer spend all day in line for the prize exhibit, the Crown Jewels, since they have been transplanted to a new home where moving walkways hasten progress at the busiest times.

The reason the Tower holds the royal gems is that it is still one of the royal palaces, although no monarch since Henry VIII has called it home. It has also housed the Royal Mint, the Public Records, the Royal Menagerie, and the Royal Observatory, although its most renowned and titillating function has been, of course, as a jail and place of torture and execution.

A person was mighty privileged to be beheaded in the peace and seclusion of **Tower Green** instead of before the mob at Tower Hill. In fact, only seven people were ever important enough—among them Anne Boleyn and Catherine Howard, wives two and five of Henry VIII's six; Elizabeth I's friend Robert Devereux, Earl of Essex; and the nine-days queen, Lady Jane Grey, aged 17. Tower Green's other function was as a corpse dumping ground when the chapel just got

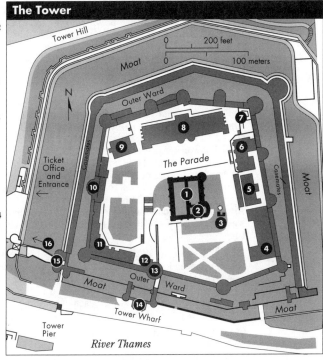

too full. You can see the executioner's block, with its charming forehead-sized dent, and his axe—along with the equally famous rack, where victims were stretched, and the more obscure scavenger's daughter, which pressed a body halfway to hell, plus assorted thumbscrews, iron maidens, etc.—in the **Martin Tower,** which stands in the northeast corner.

Before we go any farther, you should know about the excellent free and fact-packed tours that depart every half hour or so from the Middle Tower. They are conducted by the 42 Yeoman Warders, better known as "Beefeaters"—ex-servicemen dressed in resplendent navy-and-red (scarlet-and-gold on special occasions) Tudor outfits, who have been guarding the Tower since Henry VII appointed them in 1485. One of them, the Yeoman Ravenmaster, is responsible for making life comfortable for the eight ravens who live in the Tower—an important duty, since if they were to desert the Tower (goes the legend), the kingdom would fall.

In prime position stands the oldest part of the Tower and the most conspicuous of its buildings, the **White Tower.** This central keep was begun in 1078 by William the Conqueror; by the time it was completed, in 1097, it was the tallest building in London, underlining the might of those victorious Normans. Henry III (1207–1272) had it whitewashed, which is where the name comes from, then used it to house his menagerie, including the polar bear the King of Norway had given him.

The spiral staircase—winding clockwise to help the right-handed swordsman defend it—is the only way up, and here you'll find the **Royal Armouries,** Britain's national museum of arms and armor, with about 40,000 pieces on display. One of the Tower's original functions was as arsenal, supplying armor and weapons to the kings and their armies. Henry VIII started the collection in earnest, founding a workshop at Greenwich as a kind of bespoke tailor of armor to the gentry, but the public didn't get to see it until the second half of the 17th century, during Charles II's reign—which makes the Tower Armouries Britain's oldest public museum.

Here you can see weapons and armor from Britain and the Continent, dating from Saxon and Viking times right up to our own. Among the highlights are four of those armors Henry VIII commissioned to fit his ever-increasing bulk, plus one for his horse. The medieval war horse was nothing without his *shaffron*, or head protector, and here you'll find a 500-year-old example, one of the oldest pieces of horse armor in the world. Don't miss the tiny armors on the third floor—one belonging to Henry's son (who survived in it to become Edward VI), and another only just over 3 feet tall. In the **New Armouries,** added in the 17th century, are examples of almost every weapon made for the British soldier from the 17th to the 19th century.

Most of the interior of the White Tower has been much altered over the centuries, but the **Chapel of St. John,** downstairs from the armouries, is unadulterated 11th-century Norman—very rare, very simple, and very beautiful. Underneath it is "Little Ease," the cell where Guy Fawkes (*see* The Houses of Parliament in Westminster and Royal London, *above*) was held, chained to a ring in the floor.

The other fortifications and buildings surrounding the White Tower date from the 11th to the 19th century. Starting from the main entrance, you can't miss the **moat.** Until the Duke of Wellington had it drained in 1843, this was a stinking, stagnant mush, obstinately resisting all attempts to flush it with water from the Thames. Now there's a little raven graveyard in the grassed-over channel, with touching memorials to some of the old birds (who are not known for their kind natures, by the way, and you risk a savage pecking if you try to befriend them).

Across the moat, the **Middle Tower** and the **Byward Tower** form the principal landward entrance, with **Traitors' Gate** a little farther on to the right. This London equivalent of Venice's Bridge of Sighs was where the boats delivered prisoners to their cells, and so it was where those condemned to death got their last look at the outside world. During the period when the Thames was London's chief thoroughfare, this was the main entrance to the Tower.

Immediately opposite Traitors' Gate is the former Garden Tower, better known since about 1570 as the **Bloody Tower.** Its name comes from one of the most famous unsolved murders in history, the saga of the "little princes in the Tower." In 1483 the boy king, Edward V, and his brother Richard were left here by their uncle, Richard of Gloucester, after the death of their father, Edward I. They were never seen again, Gloucester was crowned Richard III, and in 1674 two little skeletons were found under the stairs to St. John's Chapel. The obvious conclusions have always been drawn—and were, in fact, even before the skeletons were discovered.

Another famous inmate was Sir Walter Raleigh, who was kept here from 1603 to 1616. It wasn't such an ordeal, as you'll see when you visit his spacious rooms, where he kept two servants, had his wife and two sons live with him (the younger boy was christened in the Tower chapel), and amused himself by writing his *History of the*

*World.* Unfortunately, he was less lucky on his second visit in 1618, which terminated in his execution at Whitehall.

Next to the Bloody Tower is the circular **Wakefield Tower,** which dates from the 13th century and once contained the king's private apartments. It was the scene of another royal murder in 1471, when Henry VI was killed mid-prayer. Henry founded Eton College and King's College, Cambridge, and they haven't forgotten: Every May 21, envoys from both institutions mark the anniversary of his murder by laying white lilies on the site.

The shiniest, the most expensive, and absolutely the most famous exhibits here are, of course, the **Crown Jewels,** now housed in the **Duke of Wellington's Barracks.** In their new setting you get so close that you could lick the gems (if it weren't for the wafers of bullet-proof glass), and they are enhanced by new laser lighting, which almost hurts the eyes with sparkle. Before you meet them in person, you are given a high-definition-film preview along with a few scenes from Elizabeth's 1953 coronation.

It's a commonplace to call these baubles (or, as the Queen Mother puts it, "Granny's chips") priceless, but it's impossible not to drop your jaw at the notion of their worth. They were, in fact, lifted once—by Colonel Thomas Blood, in 1671—though only as far as a nearby wharf. The colonel was given a royal pension instead of a beating, fueling speculation that Charles II, short of ready cash as usual, had his hand in the escapade somewhere. These days security is as fiendish as you'd expect, since the jewels—even though they would be literally impossible for thieves to sell—are *so* priceless that they're not insured.

A brief résumé of the top jewels: Finest of all is the **Royal Sceptre,** containing the earth's largest cut diamond, the 530-carat Star of Africa. This is also known as Cullinan I, having been cut from the South African Cullinan, which weighed 20 ounces when dug up from a De Beers mine at the beginning of the century. Another chip off the block, Cullinan II, lives on the **Imperial Crown of State** that Prince Charles is due to wear at his coronation—the same one that Elizabeth II wore in her coronation procession; it had been made for Victoria's in 1838. Aside from its 2,800 diamonds, it features the Black Prince's ruby, which Henry V was supposed to have worn at Agincourt, and is actually an imposter—it's no ruby, it's a semiprecious spinel. The other most famous gem is the Koh-i-noor, or "Mountain of Light" which adorns the **Queen Mother's crown.** When Victoria was presented with this gift horse in 1850, she looked it in the mouth, found it lacking in glitteriness, and had it chopped down to almost half its weight.

The little chapel of **St. Peter ad Vincula** can be visited only as part of a Yeoman Warder tour. The third church on the site, it conceals the remains of some 2,000 people executed at the Tower, Anne Boleyn and Catherine Howard among them. Being traitors, they were not so much buried as dumped under the flagstones, but the genteel Victorians had the courtesy to rebury their bones during renovations.

One of the more evocative towers is **Beauchamp Tower,** built west of Tower Green by Edward I (1272–1307). It was soon designated as a jail for the higher class of miscreant, including Lady Jane Grey, who is thought to have added her Latin graffiti to the many inscriptions carved by prisoners that you can see here.

Just south of the Beauchamp Tower is an L-shaped row of half-timbered Tudor houses, with the **Queen's House** at the center. Built for the governor of the Tower in 1530, this place saw the interrogation or incarceration of several of the more celebrated prisoners, including Anne Boleyn and the Gunpowder Plot conspirators. The Queen's House also played host to the Tower's last-ever prisoner, Rudolph Hess, the Nazi who parachuted into London in 1941 to seek asylum.

Don't forget to stroll along the battlements before you leave; from them, you get a wonderful overview of the whole Tower of London. *H. M. Tower of London, tel. 0171/709–0765. Admission: £6.70 adults, £5.10 senior citizens, £4.40 children under 15, £19 family (2 adults, 3 children, or 1 adult, 4 children). Small additional admission charge to the Fusiliers Museum. Open Mar.–Oct., Mon.–Sat. 9:30–6:30, Sun. 2–6; Nov.–Feb., Mon.–Sat. 9:30–5; closed Good Friday, Dec. 24–26, Jan. 1. For tickets to Ceremony of the Keys (the locking of the main gates, nightly at 10), write well in advance to The Resident Governor and Keeper of the Jewel House, Queen's House, H. M. Tower of London, EC3. Give your name, the dates you wish to attend (including alternate dates), and number of people (up to 7), and enclose a self-addressed stamped envelope. Yeoman Warder guides leave daily from Middle Tower, subject to weather and availability, at no charge (but a tip is always appreciated), about every 30 min until 3:30 in summer, 2:30 in winter.*

From the riverside, walk to the front of the Tower: There is a good
**27** view across the river to **H.M.S.** *Belfast* and the new building developments along the south bank of the Thames (*see* Butler's Wharf to Old St. Thomas's in The South Bank, *below*).

To the west of the Tower is London's first "dark-ride" museum, the
**28** **Tower Hill Pageant,** where automated cars take you past mock-ups of scenes from most periods of London's past, complete with "people," sound effects, and even smells. There's also an archaeological museum with finds from the Thames, set up by the Museum of London. *Tower Hill Terrace, tel. 0171/709–0081. Admission: £4.95 adults, £2.95 children under 16 and senior citizens. Open Apr.–Oct., daily 9:30–5:30; Nov.–Mar., daily 9:30–4:30; closed Dec. 25.*

## Tower Bridge and St. Katharine's Dock

The eastern edge of the City is rich indeed in symbols of London, as you will gather when staggering out from the Tower only to be con-
**29** fronted with the aptly named **Tower Bridge.** Despite its venerable, nay medieval, appearance, Tower Bridge is a Victorian youngster that celebrated its centenary in June 1994. Constructed of steel, then clothed in Portland stone, it was deliberately styled in the Gothic persuasion to complement the Tower next door, and is famous for its enormous bascules—the "arms," which open to allow large ships through. Nowadays this rarely happens, but when river traffic was dense, the bascules were raised about five times a day.

The bridge's 100th-birthday gift was a new exhibition, which is one of London's most imaginative and fun. You are conducted in the company of "Harry Stoner," an animatronic bridge construction worker worthy of Disneyland, back in time to witness the birth of the Thames's last downstream bridge. History and engineering lessons are painlessly absorbed as you meet the ghost of the bridge's architect, Sir Horace Jones, see the bascules work, and wander the walkways with their grand upstream–downstream views annotated by interactive video displays. Be sure to hang on to your ticket and follow the signs to the Engine Rooms for part two, where the original steam-driven hydraulic engines gleam, and a cute rococo theater is the setting for an Edwardian music-hall production of the bridge's story. *Tel. 0171/403–3761. Admission: £5 adults, £3.50 children under 15 and senior citizens. Open Apr.–Oct., daily 10–6:30; Nov.– Mar., daily 10–5:15 (last entry 1¼ hours before closing); closed Good Friday, Dec. 24–25, Jan. 1.*

**③⓪** You've left the City now, but still worth a look is **St. Katharine's Dock,** which you reach from the wharf underneath Tower Bridge. Finished in 1828, St. Katharine's thrived until container ships and their cargoes grew too big for the little river docks to handle, and it was shut down in 1968. Developers moved in and created this enclave of shops and luxury apartments, whose inhabitants moor their luxury yachts in the marina alongside a few old Thames sailing barges (which you can charter) and the converted-warehouse Dickens Inn, with its waterside terrace. (Dickens did not drink here.)

# The East End

*Numbers in the margin correspond to points of interest on the East End map.*

Whitechapel and Spitalfields, Shoreditch, Mile End, and Bethnal Green began as separate villages, melding together during the population boom of the 19th century—a boom that was shaped by French Huguenot and Jewish refugees, by poverty, and, in the past several decades, by a growing Bengali community. If you visit on a Sunday morning, the East End has a festive air: About half the neighborhood sprouts hundreds of market stalls (especially in and around Middlesex Street, Brick Lane, and Columbia Road). After shopping, you could go on to take brunch among cows and sheep on a farm, then play at being Georgians in a restored, candlelit 18th-century town house. You would miss out on a few weekday-only sights, but—as a Victorian peep-show barker might say—you pays yer money and you takes yer choice. Our tour begins in Whitechapel, enters Spitalfields, heads north to Bethnal Green, then south through Mile End back to Whitechapel.

## Whitechapel

The easiest way to reach Whitechapel High Street is via the District Line to Aldgate East tube (one stop past Tower Hill, where the previous tour ended). Whitechapel is where the Salvation Army was founded and the original Liberty Bell was forged, but what everyone remembers about it is that its Victorian slum streets were stalked by **Jack the Ripper.** Accordingly, we begin at the site of **George Yard Buildings,** where the notorious slasher's first victim, Martha Turner, was discovered in August 1888, punctured 29 times by his knife. Turning left out of the tube station, you come immediately to the place behind which George Yard Buildings used to stand:

**❶ Bloom's,** the United Kingdom's most famous kosher restaurant, run by the same family for over 70 years. You can clog your arteries here with *heimische* latkes, gefilte fish, and Bloom's famous salt beef, all at bargain rates (90 Whitechapel High St., tel. 0171/247–6001; meals served Sun.–Thurs. 11–9:30, Fri. 11–2). Sephardic Jews settled around here in the late 17th century, but the biggest wave of Jewish refugees were those fleeing the pogroms of Eastern Europe between the 1880s and the outbreak of World War I. Though most of London's Jews have now moved out of the East End, they have a sort of potted history written into the walls around here, as you will see.

# The East End

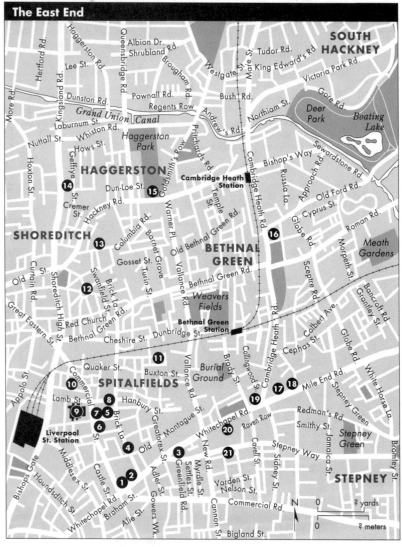

Practically next door is the striking 1901 Art Nouveau arched doorway of the **Whitechapel Gallery.** The gallery has an international
reputation for its shows, often on the cutting edge of contemporary
art. The American "action painter" Jackson Pollock showed here in
the '50s, the pop artist Robert Rauschenberg in the '60s, and David
Hockney had his first solo show here in the '70s. More recently the
Tate Gallery visited the Whitechapel and bought the American Bill
Viola's powerful video installation, the *Nantes Triptych,* which
shows Viola submerged underwater, his wife giving birth on one
side, his mother dying in a hospital on the other. Other exhibitions
highlight the local community and culture, and there are programs
of lectures, too. *Whitechapel High St., tel. 0171/377–0107. Admission free (fee for some exhibitions). Open Tues.–Sun. 11–5, Wed.
11–8. Closed Dec. 25–26, Jan. 1, and for exhibition installation.*

**Time Out**   The **Whitechapel Café** in the gallery serves remarkably inexpensive
home-cooked whole-food hot meals, soups, and cakes.

Continue east until you reach Fieldgate Street on the right, where
you'll find the **Whitechapel Bell Foundry,** responsible for some of the
world's better-known chimes. Before moving to this site in 1738, the
foundry cast Westminster Abbey's bells (in the 1580s), but its biggest work, in every sense, was the 13-ton Big Ben, cast in 1858 by
George Mears, and requiring 16 horses to transport from here to
Westminster. Its other important work was casting the original Liberty Bell (now in Philadelphia) in 1752, and both it and Big Ben can
be seen in pictures, along with exhibits about bell making, in a little
museum in the shop. You can even buy a small table bell (for about
£36) if they have them in stock, though the actual foundry is off-limits. *34 Whitechapel Rd., tel. 0171/247–2599. Admission free. Open
Mon.–Fri. 8:30–5:30; closed public holidays.*

Retracing your steps, turn right from Whitechapel Road into
Osborn Street, which soon becomes **Brick Lane.** In its time, this
long, narrow street has seen the manufacture of bricks (in the 16th
century, when it was named), beer, and bagels, but nowadays it is
the center of the East End's Bengali community. (You can still get
the bagels, though, at No. 159, the 24-hour **Beigel Bake.**) All along
here you'll see shops selling psychedelic saris and stacks of sticky
Indian sweets, video stores renting Indian movies, and Bengali,
Bangladeshi, and Pakistani restaurants, well known among Londoners for the most authentic and least expensive curries in town.
On Sunday morning the entire street is packed with stalls in a market parallel to the more famous **Petticoat Lane** (*see* Street Markets
in Chapter 4, Shopping), three blocks to the west on Middlesex
Street—it was renamed by the prudish Victorians circa 1830.

Brick Lane itself and the narrow streets running off it offer a paradigm of the East End's development. Its population has always been
in flux, with some moving in to find refuge here as others were escaping its poverty. Just before the start of Brick Lane you can take a
short detour (turn left, then right) to see the birthplace of one who
did just that. **Flower and Dean Street,** past the ugly 1970s housing
project on Thrawl Street and once the most disreputable street in
London, was where Abe Sapperstein, founder of the *Harlem Globe-
trotters,* was born in 1908.

### Spitalfields

**Fournier Street,** two blocks into Brick Lane, displays over two centuries' worth of such changes. The French Huguenots fled to

Spitalfields after the Edict of Nantes (which had allowed them religious freedom in Catholic France) was revoked in 1685. The neighborhood gave them not only religious sanctuary but also work in the nascent silk industry, and those who became master weavers grew rich. Most of the early 18th-century Huguenot silk weavers' houses along the north side of Fournier Street have now been restored by conservationists. Others still contain textile sweatshops—only now **❺** the workers are Bengali. On the Brick Lane corner is the **Jamme Masjid,** where local Muslims worship. *Umbra summus* ("We are shadows"), announces the inscription above the entrance, an apt epitaph for the successive communities who have had temporary claim on the building. Built in 1742 as a Huguenot chapel, it converted to Methodism in 1809, only to become the Spitalfields Great Synagogue when the Orthodox Machzikei Hadath sect bought it in 1897.

**❻** At the other (west) end of Fournier Street, on the left, towers **Christ Church, Spitalfields,** Wren's associate Nicholas Hawksmoor's 1729 masterpiece. Hawksmoor built only six London churches; this one was commissioned as part of Parliament's 1711 "Fifty New Churches Act." The idea was to score points for the Church of England against such Nonconformists as the Protestant Huguenots. (It must have worked; in the churchyard, you can still see some of their gravestones, with epitaphs in French.) The silk industry declined as 19th-century machinery made hand weaving redundant, and the church fell into disrepair, its gardens acquiring a reputation as a tramps' ground (and the sobriquet "Itchy Park"). By 1958 the structure was crumbling to bits and had to be closed. It was saved from demolition—but only just—and reopened in 1987, though restoration work won't be complete until 1998 or so. Until then, opening hours are restricted, but there are occasional evening concerts (and a music festival in June), and always a fine view of the colonnaded portico and tall spire from Brushfield Street to the west. *Commercial Street, tel. 0171/377–0287. Admission free (charge for concerts). Open Mon.–Fri. noon–2:30; Sun. services.*

Follow Wilkes Street north of the church, where you'll find more 1720s Huguenot houses, and turn immediately right into **Princelet Street,** once important to the Jewish settlers. No. 19 is now the **❼** **Spitalfields Heritage Centre,** dedicated to research into local immigrant communities and the preservation of the neighborhood's historic buildings. Huguenots rented the 1720 house—it still has their silk weaving attic—but in 1870 the little **United Friends Synagogue** was grafted onto the back. You can still see its wooden ark, pulpit, seats, and boards listing benefactors, complete with Hebrew errors. London's third-oldest (purpose-built) synagogue sometimes houses exhibitions and presents videos about the Jewish East End; otherwise, the Heritage Centre remains rather erratic as a museum, since it is in the process of (underfunded) restoration. *19 Princelet St., tel. 0171/377–6901. Admission free. Normally open weekdays 10–5, but phone first.*

Farther along Princelet Street, where No. 6 stands now, the first of several thriving **Yiddish Theaters** opened in 1886, playing to packed houses until the following year, when disaster struck. A false fire alarm during a January performance ended with 17 people being crushed to death, and so demoralized the theater's actor-founder, Jacob Adler, that two months later he moved his troupe to New York, where he played a major role in founding that city's great Yiddish theater tradition—which, in turn, had a significant effect on Hollywood.

Now you reach Brick Lane again. Turn left; at Hanbury Street is the ❽ **Black Eagle Brewery,** the only one of the several East End breweries still standing. And a very handsome example of Georgian and 19th-century industrial architecture it is, too, along with its mirrored 1977 extension. It belonged to Truman, Hanbury, Buxton & Co., which in 1873 was the largest brewery in the world (the English always did like their bitter). The building now houses the East End Tourism Trust offices and the modern Truman brewery's administration. You can't go in except to look at the old stables and vat house on the east side. Opposite, however, the old brewery canteen has been turned into the little **Brick Lane Music Hall,** a cute and shabby theater serving up an *echt* East End dinner (latkes feature on most menus) and an old-fashioned laugh-a-minute cabaret show. *Brewery: 91 Brick La. Music Hall: 152 Brick La., tel. 0171/377–8787; dinner and show £15–£20, Wed.–Sat. 7:30 PM.*

As you stroll safely west down Hanbury Street, reflect that it was here, in 1888, behind a seedy lodging house at No. 29, that **Jack the Ripper** left his third mutilated murderee, "Dark" Annie Chapman. A double murder followed, and then, after a month's lull, came the death on this street of Marie Kelly, the Ripper's last victim and his most revolting murder of all. He had been able to work indoors this time, and Kelly, a young widow, was found strewn all over the room, charred remains of her clothing in the fire grate. Of course, Jack the Ripper's identity never has been discovered, although to this day theories are still bandied about.

Hanbury Street becomes Lamb Street, where you'll find the two ❾ northern entrances to **Spitalfields Market.** Fruit-and-veg were sold here from the mid-17th century until 1991, but it has now been transmogrified into something far more exciting. Until the 3-acre glass-roofed market buildings are redeveloped in 1999, they have been leased to the folks who invented Camden Lock (*see* Shopping Districts and Street Markets in Chapter 4, Shopping), and the whole place now overflows with crafts and design shops and stalls, a sports hall, restaurants and bars, and different markets every day of the week. The nearer the weekend, the busier it all gets, culminating in the Sunday arts-and-crafts and greenmarket. The latest additions are an opera house and a swimming pool, and events are staged all the time, including the sculptor Andrew Logan's annual Alternative Miss World extravaganza, where drag queens replace beauty queens, in May, and the hip fetish and clubwear Alternative Fashion Show in March. *65 Brushfield St., tel. 0171/247–6590. Admission free. Open daily 10–7; market stalls Mon.–Fri. 11–2, weekends 9–4.*

**Time Out** There's a round-the-world smorgasbord of food stalls and cafés in **Spitalfields Market,** serving Indian and African curries, Thai noodles, German sausages, Mexican fajitas, French pastries . . .

Retracing your steps east on Lamb Street and then turning left on Commercial Street will bring you to Folgate Street, where in a restored early 18th-century terrace one of London's most extraordi-❿ nary experiences awaits you at **Dennis Sever's House.** Sever, a performer/designer/scholar from Escondido, California, has dedicated his life not only to the restoration of his Georgian house but also to raising the ghosts of a fictitious Jervis family who might have inhabited it over two centuries. Sever himself lives a replica of Georgian life, without electricity but with a butler in full 18th-century livery to light the candles and lay the fires—for the Jervises. Three evenings a week he stages a performance, or a "time travel experience," of philosophical bent, trailing the Jervises through 10 rooms and five generations (from 1724 to 1919, to be precise), always missing them by moments. Sever's stunning house, sans Jervises, is also open one Sunday afternoon a month. *18 Folgate St., tel. 0171/247– 4013. Admission: £5 Sun., £30 evenings. Reservations essential. No children. Open first Sun. of the month 2–5; 3 performances per week (days vary) 7:30–10:20 PM.*

Head back to Brick Lane, turn left, make the third right into Pedley Street, and you won't believe your ears. The source of the moos, ⓫ bleats, and quacks is **Spitalfields City Farm,** which is just what it sounds like—a sliver of rural England squashed between housing projects. It's one of about a dozen such places in London, which exist to educate city kids in country matters. Available are pony rides, local history tours by horse and cart, a Sunday brunch, summer barbecues, and an altogether surreal experience. *Pedley St., tel. 0171/ 247–8762. Admission free. Open Tues.–Sun. 9:30–5:30. Sun. brunch 11–3; barbecue June–Sept. (approx.), Wed. 7 PM (call to confirm). Horse and cart tours, Sun. 11 and 2:30 (weather permitting), start at £3 adults, £1.50 children.*

## Bethnal Green

It's about a half-mile's walk to the next few sights. If you go back west through Folgate Street, you reach Shoreditch High Street, where you can catch Bus 22a, 22b, or 149 north to Kingsland Road. If you walk—an especially good plan on Sunday—cross Bethnal Green Road at the north end of Brick Lane, turn left, then right onto Club Row (which was one enormous pet market until it was closed down in ⓬ the 1980s by animal-rights campaigners), which leads to **Arnold Circus.** Suddenly you're standing in a perfect circle of arts-and-crafts– style houses around a raised bandstand in the middle. This is the center of the Boundary Estate—"model" housing built by Victorian philanthropists and do-gooders for the slum-dwelling locals, and completed as the century began.

⓭ Two streets north (running west to east) is **Columbia Road,** which is the reason you should consider skipping the bus ride Sunday. Once a week this street gets buried under forests of potted palms, azaleas, ivy, ficuses, and freesias, tiger lilies, carnations, roses, and hosts of daffodils in London's main plant and flower market. Prices are ultra-low, and lots of the Victorian shop windows around the stalls are filled with wares—terra-cotta pots, vases, gardening tools, hats, and antiques. *Open Sun. 7 AM–2 PM.*

Cross Hackney Road and slip up Waterson Street to wide, busy Kingsland Road, where soon, on the right, you'll come to a row of ⓮ early 18th-century almshouses: the **Geffrye Museum.** This small, perfectly formed museum re-creates domestic English interiors of every period from Elizabethan through postwar '50s utility, all in sequence, so that you walk through time. The best thing about the Geffrye (named after the 17th-century Lord Mayor of London whose land this was) is that its rooms are not the grand parlors of the gentry one normally sees in historic houses but copies of real family homes, as if talented movie set designers had been let loose instead of academic museum curators. There's also a walled, scented herb garden and a full program of accessible lectures, including regular "bring a room to life" talks, and a new set of 20th-century rooms is in the offing. *Kingsland Rd., tel. 0171/739–9893. Admission free. Open Tues.–Sat. 10–5, Sun. and bank holiday Mon. 2–5. Period*

*Room Talks: Sat. 2 and 3:30. Closed Good Friday, Dec. 24–26, Jan. 1.*

**⑮** Head east about 500 yards on Hackney Road (Cremer Street, south of the museum, gets you there) and you come to the **Hackney City Farm.** This one is smaller than Spitalfields' (*see above*), and so are its animals. Bees and butterflies are the stars here, along with the kinds of wildflowers they like, as well as an ecologically sound pond. If you're walking this route, drop in and buy a pot of London honey. *1A Goldsmiths Row, tel. 0171/729–6381. Admission free. Open Tues.–Sun. 10–4:30.*

Going south down Warner Place (across Hackney Road opposite the farm entrance) takes you to Old Bethnal Green Road, at the end of which a right turn brings you to a primary-colored sign announcing **⑯** the **Bethnal Green Museum of Childhood.** The East End outpost of the Victoria and Albert museum, this entire iron, glass, and brown-brick building was transported here from South Kensington in 1875; since then, believe it or not, its contents have grown into the biggest toy collection *in the world.* The central hall is a bit like the Geffrye Museum zapped into miniature, since here are doll's houses of every period, including royal ones. Each genre of plaything has its own enclosure, so if teddy bears are your weakness, you need waste no time with the train sets. Soon—when the upstairs social-history-of-childhood galleries are completed—the museum's title will be justified. Until then, if you have a special interest in such things, you may arrange to view them by calling in advance. *Cambridge Heath Rd., tel. 0181/980–4315. Admission free. Open Mon.–Thurs. and Sat. 10–5:50, Sun. 2:30–5:50. Free art workshops for children over 3: Sat. 11 and 2. Closed May Day holiday, Dec. 24–26, Jan. 1.*

### Mile End

Now you can either catch Bus 106 or 253 or walk south about half a mile down Cambridge Heath Road as far as the Mile End Road. Turning left, you'll find four historical landmarks, which provide, let's be honest, more food for thought than thrills for the senses. On the north side of the street, a redbrick student hostel cunningly con-**⑰** ceals its interesting origin as the **Trinity Almshouses,** built (possibly with Wren's help) in 1695 for "28 decayed Masters and Commanders of Ships or ye widows of such," bombed during World War II, and restored thus by London County Council. Behind, even better concealed, is the oldest Jewish cemetery in Britain, founded by the Sephardic community in 1657 after Cromwell allowed them back into the country. (If you would like to view the cemetery, call the United Synagogues Cemetery Maintainance Department, tel. 0171/790–1445.)

On the south side of the street stands the third visually uninteresting landmark—a stone inscribed "Here William Booth commenced the work of the Salvation Army, July 1865." It marks the position of the first Sally Army platform, while back on the north side a few **⑱** steps past the almshouses, a **statue of William Booth** stands on the very spot where the first meetings were held.

Turn around now, and on the northwest corner of Cambridge Heath Road you'll see a Victorian pub with the completely un-p.c. name of **⑲** **The Blind Beggar.** You've just beheld the sites of the first Sally Army platform and the first Sally Army meetings; this den of iniquity was where William Booth preached his first sermon. Booth didn't supply the pub's main claim to fame, though. The Blind Beggar's real notoriety dates only from March 1966, when Ronnie Kray—one of the Kray twins, the former gangster kings of London's East End underworld—shot dead rival "godfather" George Cornell in the saloon bar.

**Time Out** | In addition to sermons and murders, **The Blind Beggar** serves bar snacks and hot meals at lunchtime, best consumed in its conservatory or garden, and washed down with real ales from the bar.

**㉕** The hulk of a building opposite Whitechapel tube, a few yards west of the pub, is the **Royal London Hospital.** The hospital was founded in 1740, and its early days were as nasty as its then-neighborhood near the Tower of London. Waste was carried out in buckets and dumped in the street; bedbugs and alcoholic nurses were problems, but according to hospital records, nobody died—they were "relieved." Anyone who lived but refused to give thanks to both the hospital committee and God went on a blacklist, banned from further treatment. In 1759, the hospital moved to a new building, the core of the one you see today. By then it had become the best hospital in London, and it was enhanced further by the addition of a small medical school in 1785, and then, 70 years later, an entire state-of-the-art medical college. Thomas John Barnado, who went on to found the famous Dr. Barnado's Homes for orphans, came to train here in 1866. Ten years later, with the opening of a new wing, the hospital became the largest in the United Kingdom, and now, though mostly rebuilt since World War II, it remains one of London's most capacious.

**㉑** Behind the buildings, the **Royal London Hospital Archives** have displays of medical paraphernalia, objects, and documentation to illustrate the 250-year history of this East London institution. *Crypt of St. Augustine with St. Philip's Church, Newark St., tel. 0171/377–7000, ext. 3364. Admission free. Open Mon.–Fri. 10–4:30; closed Dec. 24–26, Jan. 1.*

# The South Bank

*Numbers in the margin correspond to points of interest on the South Bank map.*

If you head back to Tower Bridge, cross it, and follow the river upstream, you soon enter London's oldest "suburb," **Southwark.** Just across the river from London Bridge yet conveniently outside the City walls and laws, it was the ideal location for the taverns and cock-fighting arenas that served as after-hours entertainment in the Middle Ages. By Shakespeare's time it had become a veritable den of iniquity, famous above all for the "Southwark stews," or brothels, and for being very rough. The Globe Theatre, in which Shakespeare acted and held shares, was one of several established here after theaters were banished from the City in 1574 for encouraging truancy in young apprentices and being generally rowdy and insalubrious. The Globe was as likely to stage a few bouts of bear-baiting as the latest Shakespeare.

Southwark was heavily bombed during World War II, then neglected for a few decades while more central parts of London were repaired. The active ports had moved downstream by then anyway, so Southwark's 19th-century warehouses and winding alleys had little to recommend them to developers. This circumstance began to change when theater returned to the Bankside environs (Bankside being the street along the South Bank from Southwark to Blackfriars Bridges) in the form of the national arts complex that opened downstream in 1976, but it took another decade or so for developers and local authorities to catch on to the potential farther east. Now the pockets of the new and the renovated—Gabriel's Wharf, London Bridge City, Hay's Galleria, Butler's Wharf—have practically connected to form a South Bank that even Londoners, who have an attitude problem about crossing the river, have been known to admire and even frequent.

## Butler's Wharf to Old St. Thomas's

**①** Start your walk scenically at the end of **Tower Bridge** opposite the one where our City tour finished, finding the steps on the east (left) side, which descend to the start of a pedestrians-only street, Shad Thames. Now turn your back on the bridge and follow this quaint path between cliffs of good-as-new warehouses. These were once the seedy, dingy, dangerous shadowlands where Dickens killed off evil
**②** Bill Sikes in *Oliver Twist* but are now part of **Butler's Wharf,** an '80s development that is maturing gracefully. Many apartments in its deluxe loft-style warehouse conversions and swanky new blocks still lack inhabitants, but there *is* life here, thanks partly to London's saint of the stomach, Sir Terence Conran (also responsible for Bibendum and Quaglino's—*see* St. James's in Chapter 6, Dining). He gave it his "Gastrodrome" of three restaurants, a vintner's, a deli, a bakery, and who knows what else by now. You'll find it to your left.

Conran was also responsible for the other success on this riverside
**③** site, the **Design Museum,** which you come to next. Opened in 1989, it's the first museum in the world to elevate the everyday design we take for granted to the status of exhibit, slotting it into its social and cultural context. On the top floor, the **Collection** traces the evolution of mass-produced goods, with cases full of telephones and washing machines, plates and hi-fi equipment, computers and Coke bottles, and plenty of back-up material from ads to films. Alongside the Collection, the regularly revamped **Review** looks deeply into a particular aspect of the consumer durable. Special exhibitions are held downstairs on the first floor, and there's also a program of lectures and events, as well as the very good **Blueprint Café** with its own river terrace. *Butler's Wharf, tel. 0171/403-6933. Admission: £3.50 adults, £2.50 children and senior citizens. Open daily 10:30–5:30; closed Dec. 24–26, Jan. 1.*

Turn around and veer away from the river, just before you get back to Tower Bridge, along Horsleydown Lane, then follow Tooley Street. Take the right turn at Morgan Lane and you'll be hit by the
**④** unlikely spectacle of a vast gray battleship—**H.M.S.** *Belfast,* at 656 feet one of the largest and most powerful cruisers the Royal Navy ever had. It played a role in the D-day landings off Normandy, left for the Far East after the war, and has been becalmed here since 1971. On board there's an outpost of the Imperial War Museum, which tells the Royal Navy's story from 1914 to the present and shows you what life on board a World War II battleship was like, from mess decks and bakery, punishment cells, and operations room to engine room and armaments. *Morgan's La., Tooley St., tel. 0171/ 407-6434. Admission: £4 adults, £3 senior citizens, £2 children under 16. Open mid-Mar.–Oct., daily 10–5:30; Nov.–mid-Mar., daily 10–4; closed Dec. 24–26, Jan. 1.*

**⑤** From the *Belfast,* take a short riverside stroll to reach **Hay's Galleria.** Hay's Wharf was built by Thomas Cubitt in 1857 on the spot where the port of London's oldest wharf had stood since 1651. It

# The South Bank

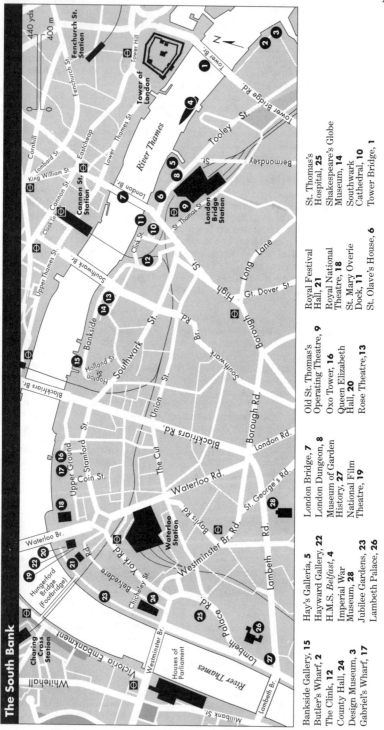

440 yds
400 m

N

Fenchurch St. Station

Fenchurch St.

Tower Hill

Tower of London

Tower Br.

Tower Bridge Rd.

River Thames

Cornhill

Lombard St.

King William St.

Cannon St.

Eastcheap

Lower Thames St.

Clock La.

Upper Thames St.

Cannon St. Station

London Br.

Bermondsey

Tooley St.

St. Thomas St.

London Bridge Station

Long Lane

Gt. Dover St.

Borough High St.

Southwark Br.

Southwark St.

Clink St.

Bankside

Holland St.

Hopton St.

Blackfriars Br.

Union St.

The Cut

Stamford St.

Coin St.

Upper Ground

Borough Rd.

London Rd.

St. George's Rd.

Waterloo Rd.

Waterloo Station

Boyle's Rd.

Westminster Br. Rd.

Lambeth Rd.

Hungerford Bridge (Footbridge)

Waterloo Br.

York Rd.

Belvedere Rd.

Chicheley St.

Lambeth Palace Rd.

Lambeth Br.

Charing Cross Station

Whitehall

Victoria Embankment

Houses of Parliament

River Thames

Millbank St.

Bankside Gallery, **15**
Butler's Wharf, **2**
The Clink, **12**
County Hall, **24**
Design Museum, **3**
Gabriel's Wharf, **17**

Hay's Galleria, **5**
Hayward Gallery, **22**
H.M.S. *Belfast*, **4**
Imperial War
Museum, **28**
Jubilee Gardens, **23**
Lambeth Palace, **26**

London Bridge, **7**
London Dungeon, **8**
Museum of Garden
History, **27**
National Film
Theatre, **19**

Old St. Thomas's
Operating Theatre, **9**
Oxo Tower, **16**
Queen Elizabeth
Hall, **20**
Rose Theatre, **13**

Royal Festival
Hall, **21**
Royal National
Theatre, **18**
St. Mary Overie
Dock, **11**
St. Olave's House, **6**

St. Thomas's
Hospital, **25**
Shakespeare's Globe
Museum, **14**
Southwark
Cathedral, **10**
Tower Bridge, **1**

was known as "London's larder" on account of the edibles landed here until it wound down gradually, then closed in 1970. In 1987 it was reborn as this Covent Gardenesque parade of bars and restaurants, offices, and shops, all weatherproofed by an arched glass atrium roof supported by tall iron columns. The centerpiece is a fanciful kinetic sculpture by David Kemp, *The Navigators*, which looks like the skeleton of a pirate schooner crossed with a dragon and spouts water from various orifices. Inevitably, jugglers, string quartets, and crafts stalls abound. This courtyard hub of the developing **London Bridge City** needed all the help it could get in its early days, but it has settled in nicely now with its captive crowd of office workers from the adjacent new developments.

**Time Out** For lunch in the galleria, drop by **Café Rouge,** one of a growing chain of reasonably priced faux-Parisian bistros. Alternatively, buy something to take out and eat it on a bench overlooking the river, enjoying the view across to the Custom House.

Step out onto Tooley Street again and you come upon the former Hay's Wharf offices, an exciting black-and-white-and-gold-striped Art Deco block built in 1931 by H. S. Goodhart-Rendel and called **St. Olave's House** after the church it replaced. The shiny square edifice has far more style than the newer buildings around it, and quite puts them to shame. At the end of Tooley Street (difficult to see how, but the name is a corruption of St. Olave's) stands the 1972 version of **London Bridge.**

Coming up to the left on the same street is the gory, grisly, gruesome **London Dungeon.** Here realistic waxwork people are subjected in graphic detail to all the historical horrors the Tower of London merely suggests. Tableaux depict famous bloody moments—like Anne Boleyn's decapitation, or the martyrdom of St. George—alongside the torture, murder, and ritual slaughter of more anonymous victims, all to a soundtrack of screaming, wailing, and agonized moaning. London's times of deepest terror—the Great Fire and the Great Plague—are brought to life, too, and so are its public hangings. And did you ever wonder what a disembowelment actually looks like? See it here. Children absolutely adore this place, which is among London's top tourist attractions and usually features long lines. *28–34 Tooley St., tel. 0171/403–0606. Admission: £6 adults, £5 students, £4 children under 14 and senior citizens. Open Apr.–Sept. daily 10–5:30, Oct.–Mar. daily 10–4:30; closed Dec. 24–26.*

To continue the theme of pain and blood after the dungeons, turn left into Joiner Street underneath the arches of London's first (1836) railway, then right onto St. Thomas Street, where you'll find the **Old St. Thomas's Operating Theatre.** This is all that remains of one of England's oldest hospitals, which stood here from the 12th century until the railway forced it to move in 1862, and was where women went under the knife. The theater was bricked up and forgotten for a century but has now been restored into an exhibition of early 19th-century medical practices: the operating table onto which the gagged and blindfolded patients were roped, the box of sawdust underneath for catching their blood, the knives, pliers, and handsaws the surgeons wielded, and—this was a theater in the round—the spectators' seats. Next door is a sweeter show: the **Herb Garret,** with displays of medicinal herbs used in the same period. *9A St. Thomas St., tel. 0171/955–4791. Admission: £2 adults, £1.50 senior citizens, £1 children. Open Tues.–Sun. 10–4.; closed Dec. 15–Jan. 5.*

## Southwark Cathedral to Coin Street

🔟 Just across Borough High Street you reach **Southwark Cathedral** (pronounced suth-uck). Despite having still-standing 12th-century parts (which make it the second-oldest Gothic church in London, next to Westminster Abbey) and housing some remarkable memorials, not to mention a program of lunchtime concerts, it is little visited. It was promoted to cathedral status only in 1905, before that having been the priory church of St. Mary Overie (as in "over the water"—on the South Bank). Look for the gaudily renovated 1408 tomb of the poet John Gower, friend of Chaucer, and for the Harvard Chapel, named after John Harvard, founder of the college, who was baptized here in 1608. Another notable buried here is Edmund Shakespeare, brother of William.

Walk down Cathedral Street to the water and you'll be in another of the South Bank's recent office developments, **St. Mary Overie Dock.** The three-masted topsail schooner *Kathleen & May,* kept in an enclosed dock, maintains the maritime theme. Early this century hundreds like it hauled cargoes of coal, cement, timber, and even gunpowder around the British coast, but now the *Kathleen & May* is the only one left. You can board it to view an exhibition about this brand of seafaring life, plus a rare film of the ship itself under sail. *St. Mary Overie Dock, tel. 0171/403–3965. Admission: £1 adults, 50p children under 16 and senior citizens. Open daily 10–5; closed Dec. 25, Jan. 1.*

Incorporated in the St. Mary Overie development is the west wall, with rose window outline, of Winchester House, palace of the Bishops of Winchester until 1626. Attached to this palace was a prison whose name still serves as a general term for jail: **the Clink.** One of five Southwark prisons, it was the first to detain women, most of whom were "Winchester Geese"—another euphemism the bishops donated to the language, meaning prostitutes. The oldest profession was endemic in Southwark, especially around the bishops' area of jurisdiction, which was known as "The Liberty of the Clink." Their graces' sensible solution was to license prostitution rather than ban it, but a Winchester goose who flouted the rules ended up, of course, in the Clink. Now there is a museum tracing the history of prostitution in "the Liberty" and showing what the Clink was like in its 16th-century prime. *1 Clink St., tel. 0171/403–6515. Admission: £2 adults, £1 children and senior citizens. Open daily 10–6. Closed Dec. 25–26.*

Shakespeare's Globe Theatre was also "within the Liberty," and if you continue to the end of Clink Street onto Bankside, the paved riverside walk, and under Southwark Bridge, you will come to a reconstruction of it. First, though, turn left up Rose Alley, where in 1989 the remains of another famous Jacobean theater, the **Rose Theatre,** were unearthed. Depending, however, on what stage (no pun intended) the office development that will surround the preserved foundations has reached, there may not be much to see.

The next little alley is Bear Gardens, and it is here that you'll find **Shakespeare's Globe Museum.** For more than two decades, until he died in 1993, the American actor and film director Sam Wanamaker worked ceaselessly to raise funds for this ambitious project. In addition to a replica of Shakespeare's open-roofed 1599 Globe Playhouse now being constructed with authentic Elizabethan materials and craft techniques, he planned a second, indoor theater, which is to be built to a design of the 17th-century architect Inigo Jones. Inside you'll find a thriving museum, which outlines the project (it continues despite the loss of its champion), paints the history of Jacobean theater, and hosts many a lecture, performance, reading, and even masked ball. It stands on appropriate turf: In the 17th century this was Davies Amphitheatre, admittedly more a bull-baiting, prize-fighting sort of venue than a temple to the legitimate stage, but at least Samuel Pepys immortalized it in his diaries. (You can join the Friends of Shakespeare's Globe and help raise the couple of million the project still needs by sending £10 to Box 70, London SE1 0SU.) *Bear Gdns., tel. 0171/928–6342. Admission: £3 adults, £2 children under 18 and senior citizens. Open Mon.–Sat. 10–5, Sun. 2–5:30.*

About 100 yards farther along Bankside you reach the reconstruction of the Globe Playhouse itself, followed by the 17th-century **Cardinal's Wharf,** where, as a plaque explains, Wren lived while St. Paul's Cathedral was being built. Next you pass by the disused **⑮** Bankside Power Station and arrive at **Bankside Gallery,** a modern building in which two artistic societies—the Royal Society of Painter-Printmakers and the Royal Watercolour Society—have their headquarters. Together they mount exhibitions of current members' work, which is usually for sale, alongside artists' materials and books. *48 Hopton St., tel. 0171/928–7521. Admission: £2 adults, £1 children and senior citizens. Open Tues.–Sat. 10–5, Sun. 1–5; closed Dec. 24–Jan. 2, Easter.*

You have now reached your fourth bridge on this tour, **Blackfriars Bridge,** which you pass beneath to join the street called Upper **⑯** Ground. You may notice the **Oxo Tower** to your left, with what looks like a giants' game of tic-tac-toe written in windows on its summit. In fact, it's a 1928 billboard-advertising-regulations avoidance ploy: "Oxo" was—and is—a brand of beef bouillon (and now it also has a free ad in Fodor's). Just before it, by the bridge, is a modern pub remarkable only for its name, **Doggett's Coat and Badge.** Each July the boat race of the same name, founded by an actor named Thomas Doggett in 1716, still runs from Cadogan Pier in Chelsea to London Bridge, making it the oldest annual event in British sport.

In between pub and tower you pass yet another (fairly) new development, but one of an entirely different character from the foregoing business behemoths. **Coin Street Community Builders,** as their name suggests, is a nonprofit action group formed by local residents in the mid-'70s to create family housing and public spaces out of land that would otherwise have gone to commercial developers. You can see the human-scale homes and gardens they've already built since 1984, and adjacent Stamford Wharf, which they plan to make into a haven of housing, performance spaces, crafts workshops, and res-**⑰** taurants. In the meantime they've set up **Gabriel's Wharf,** a dinky marketplace of shops and cafés, where about 15 designers sell jewelry, ceramics, toys, etc., and music is staged in summer.

**Time Out** In Gabriel's Wharf, a goat's cheese and sun-dried tomato pizza from **The Gourmet Pizza Company** or a burger and cocktail from **Studio Six** (both open daily) may hit the spot after so many bridges have been crossed.

## The South Bank Arts Complex

The next section involves a single bridge, but several hours. At least, for anyone with any feeling for any of the arts it does, since the concrete congregation on either side of Waterloo Bridge is London's chief arts center. Continue along Upper Ground to reach the first of

**⑱** its buildings, the **Royal National Theatre,** a low-slung, multi-layered block the color of heavy storm clouds. You may be forgiven for believing you made a mistake and wandered back to the Barbican—and, indeed, Londoners generally felt the same way about Sir Denys Lasdun's brutalist function-dictates-form building when it opened in 1976, as they would a decade later about the far nastier Barbican. But whatever its merits or demerits as a landscape feature (and architects have given it an overall thumbs up), the Royal National Theatre—which is still abbreviated colloquially to the pre-royal warrant "NT"—has wonderful insides.

There are three auditoriums in the complex. The biggest one, the **Olivier,** is named after Sir Laurence, chairman of the first building commission and first artistic director of the National Theatre Company, formed in 1962. (In between the first proposal of a national theater for Britain and the 1949 formation of that building commission, an entire century passed.) The **Lyttleton** theater, unlike the Olivier, has a traditional proscenium arch, while the little **Cottesloe** mounts studio productions and new work in the round. Interspersed with the theaters are various levels of foyer, where exhibitions are mounted, bars and restaurants are frequented, and free entertainment is provided, and the whole place is lively six days a week. The Royal National Theatre Company does not rest on its laurels. It attracts many of the nation's top actors (Anthony Hopkins, for one, does time here) in addition to launching future stars. Since it's a repertory company, you'll have several plays to choose from even if your London sojourn is short, but, tickets or not, have a wander round, and catch the buzz. *South Bank, tel. 0171/928–2252 (box office). Hour-long tours of the theater backstage (tel. 0171/633–0880) Mon.– Sat. at 10:15, 12:30, and 5:30; £3.50 adults, £2.50 children and senior citizens. Foyers open Mon.–Sat. 10 AM–11 PM; closed Dec. 24–25.*

Keep walking along the wide path now. You'll find distractions all over here, especially in summer—secondhand bookstalls, entertainers, arrogant pigeons, and a series of plaques annotating the build-
**⑲** ings opposite. Underneath Waterloo Bridge is the **National Film Theatre** (or NFT). Its two movie theaters boast easily the best repertory programming in London, favoring rare, obscure, foreign, silent, forgotten, classic, noir, or short films over blockbusters. Technically it's a film club, but you can easily join for the modest fee of 40p. There's a third cinema inside MOMI, or the **Museum of the Moving Image,** but if you reckon you'll just have a quick look around before you catch a movie here, think again. MOMI may be the most fun of all London's museums, and you will get stuck for a couple of hours minimum. The main feature is a history of cinema from 4,000-year-old Javanese shadow puppets to Spielbergian special effects, and very good the displays are, too, but the supporting program is even better, and it stars *you*. Actors dressed as John Wayne or Mae West, or usherettes, or chorus girls pluck you out of obscurity to read the TV news or audition for the chorus line or fly like Superman over the Thames. They also perform, mime, improvise, and generally bring celluloid to life, while all around, various screens show clips from epoch-making giants like Hitchcock and Eisenstein, plus newsreels and ads. Techies can learn focus-pulling and satellite beaming; artists can try animation; eggheads can explore ethical issues like censorship and documentary objectivity. Needless to say, this is always a big hit with kids. *South Bank Centre, tel. 0171/401–2636. Admission: £5.50 adults, £4 children and senior citizens, £4.70 students, £16 family (2 adults, 4 children). Open daily 10–6, last admission 5 PM; closed Dec. 24–26.*

**Time Out** The NFT restaurant and cafeteria—especially the big wooden tables outside—are popular for lunch or supper. You don't have to buy a membership.

⑳ The next building you come to contains one medium and one small concert hall, the **Queen Elizabeth Hall** and the **Purcell Room,** respectively. Both offer predominantly classical recitals of international caliber, with due respect paid to 20th-century composers and the more established jazz and vocal artists. Following on, riverside,

㉑ is the largest auditorium, the **Royal Festival Hall,** with superb acoustics and a 3,000-plus capacity. It is the oldest of the blocks, raised as the centerpiece of the 1951 Festival of Britain, a postwar morale-boosting exercise. The London Philharmonic resides here, symphony orchestras from the world over like to visit, and choral works, ballet, serious jazz and pop, and even film with live accompaniment are also staged. As at the NT, there is a multiplicity of foyers, with free rotating exhibitions, several eating stations, and a very good bookstore.

㉒ Finally, tucked behind the concert halls, is the **Hayward Gallery,** one of the city's major art-exhibition spaces, its bias fixed firmly in this century. This stained and windowless bunker has come in for the most flak of all the buildings, enduring constant threats to flatten it and start again, but it's still here, topped by its multicolored neon tube sculpture, which is the most familiar feature on the South Bank skyline. *South Bank Complex, tel. 0171/928–3144. Admission varies according to exhibition. Open daily 10–6, Tues. and Wed. until 8; closed Good Friday, May Day, Dec. 25–26, Jan. 1.*

**Time Out** Very handy for post-theater meals, **The Archduke** (153 Concert Hall Approach, tel. 0171/928–9370) is a bright converted warehouse under Hungerford Bridge, next to the Festival Hall, featuring live jazz, quiche, salads, pâtés, and sausages, and a wide selection of wines by the glass.

### Westminster Bridge to the Imperial War Museum

Now make your way to the final two bridges on this tour, eyes glued to the opposite bank for the quintessential postcard vista of the Houses of Parliament, best in the late afternoon when the last westerly rays silhouette the towers and catch on the waves of the Thames—if it's not raining.

㉓ This view is good from **Jubilee Gardens,** the rectangle of grass planted in 1977 to mark the queen's 50th year on the throne; it is the site of arts festivals and often, during summer, a visiting circus. It

㉔ gets better as you pass **County Hall,** a curved, colonnaded neo-classical hulk, which took 46 years (1912–1958; two world wars interfered) to build and was home to London's local government, the Greater London Council (or GLC, which mutated out of the London County Council in 1965) until it disbanded in 1986. Since then the question of whether a new citywide governing body would enhance London has been a contentious issue. (It's politicians who wrangle; most Londoners would like to have one.) Whatever happens, any son-of-GLC would have to find a new home, since County Hall is being transformed into a gigantic hotel.

㉕ Past Westminster Bridge the river is fronted by **St. Thomas's Hospital,** which few bother to look at since you are now finally at the spot precisely opposite Westminster Hall. You may remember the remains of Old St. Thomas's from the Southwark leg of this tour; here is where the hospital reopened, in 1868, to the specifications of the founder of the first school of nursing, "The Lady with the Lamp," Florence Nightingale. Most of it was bombed to death in the Blitz, then rebuilt to become one of London's teaching hospitals. Since 1989 it has also housed the **Florence Nightingale Museum,** where you can learn all about the most famous of nursing reformers. Here is a reconstruction of the barracks ward at Scutari (Turkey), where she tended soldiers during the Crimean War (1854–56) and earned her nickname; here is a Victorian East End slum cottage showing what she did to improve living conditions among the poor; and here is The Lamp. *2 Lambeth Palace Rd., tel. 0171/620–0374. Admission: £2.50 adults, £1.50 children and senior citizens. Open Tues.–Sun. and public holidays 10–4; closed Good Friday., Easter, Dec. 25–26, Jan. 1.*

**26** Having seen the remains of the palace of the Bishops of Winchester at St. Mary Overie Dock, you now arrive at **Lambeth Palace,** a bishop's palace that is still standing, complete with (occasionally) resident *arch*bishop. For 800 years this has been the London base of the Archbishop of Canterbury, top man in the Church of England. Much of the palace is hidden behind great walls, and even the Tudor gatehouse, which is visible from the street, is closed to the public, but you can stand here and absorb the historical vibrations echoing from such momentous events as the 1381 storming of the palace during the Peasants' Revolt against the poll tax (a modern version of which Thatcher recently reinstated, whereupon modern riots ensued, and the tax was sheepishly repealed), and the 1534 clash of wills when Thomas More refused to sign the Oath of Supremacy claiming Henry VIII (and not the pope) as leader of the English Church, was sent to the Tower, and executed for treason the following year.

**27** Adjacent to the palace is **St. Mary's,** which you certainly can visit. It belongs to the Tradescant Trust, which is named after John Tradescant (c. 1575–1638), botanist extraordinaire, who brought to these shores the lilac, larch, jasmine, and spiderwort (named Tradescantia in his honor), and which founded the **Museum of Garden History** here when the old church was deconsecrated in 1977. In the nave are changing horticulturally themed exhibitions, supplemented by a reconstructed—or regrown—17th-century knot garden. Tradescant's tomb in the graveyard is carved with scenes from his worldwide plant-discovery tours and surrounded with the plants he discovered. Near it, William Bligh, captain of the *Bounty*, is buried, which suits the theme—the *Bounty* was on a breadfruit-gathering mission in 1787 when the crew mutinied. *Lambeth Palace Rd., tel. 0171/261–1891. Admission free; donations welcome. Open weekdays 11–3, Sun. 10:30–5; closed mid–Dec.–early Mar.*

En route to the next museum, if you take a detour to the right off Lambeth Road, you could be "doing the Lambeth Walk" down the street of the same name. A cockney tradition ever since the 17th century, when there was a spa here, the Sunday stroll was immortalized in a song from the 1937 musical *Me and My Gal*, which recently proved a hit all over again in the West End and on Broadway. A little farther east along Lambeth Road you reach an elegant domed and colonnaded building erected in the early 19th century to house the Bethlehem Hospital for the Insane, better known as the infamous Bedlam. In fact, though, by 1816, when the patients were moved to this location, they were no longer kept in cages to be taunted by tourists (see the final scene of Hogarth's *Rake's Progress* at Sir John Soane's Museum for an idea of how horrific it was), since reformers—and George III's madness—had effected more humane confinement.

The pair of giant guns outside have nothing to do with restraint of patients, however, since Bedlam moved to Surrey in 1930. The building now houses the **Imperial War Museum.** Pacifists, don't stop reading. Despite its title, this museum of 20th-century warfare does not glorify bloodshed but attempts to evoke what it was like to live through the two world wars. Of course, there is hardware for martial boys—a Battle of Britain Spitfire, a German V2 rocket, tanks, guns, submarines—but there is an equal amount of war art (David Bomberg, Henry Moore, John Singer Sargent, Graham Sutherland, to name a few), poetry, photography, and documentary film footage. One very affecting exhibit is *The Blitz Experience*, which is what it sounds like—a 10-minute taste of an air raid in a street of acrid smoke with sirens blaring and searchlights glaring. More recent wars attended by British forces are thoughtfully commemorated, too, right up to the Gulf War of 1991. *Lambeth Rd., tel. 0171/416–5000. Admission: £3.70 adults, £2.65 senior citizens, £1.85 children under 16. Open daily 10–6; closed Dec. 24–26, Jan. 1.*

# Chelsea and Belgravia

*Numbers in the margin correspond to points of interest on the Chelsea and Belgravia map.*

It would be unfair to London to pretend there's nothing of interest south of the river between Lambeth and Battersea, but space forbids its exploration here, so we gloss over such sights as Kennington's cricket valhalla, **the Oval,** and the new fruit-and-veg wholesale market at **Nine Elms,** Vauxhall, into which Covent Garden was decanted, and the no-longer-used four-chimney landmark **Battersea Power Station,** beloved by Londoners out of all proportion to its usefulness (which is negligible—nobody will buy it), and big, beautiful **Battersea Park,** and aim directly for the third bridge upstream from Lambeth Bridge to return to the north bank.

## Chelsea

**Albert Bridge,** a hybrid cantilever-suspension model, went up in 1873 and is probably London's favorite (except to those trapped on it daily by rush-hour traffic) on account of its prettiness, especially when fairy-lit by night. On its north side is Chelsea, a neighborhood as handsome as its real estate is costly. Strolling its streets you will often notice gigantic windows adorning otherwise ordinary houses. They are now mostly used to hike property values a few notches higher, but these remnants of Chelsea's 19th-century bohemian days once lit artists' studios; many famous artists and writers have lived here. Latterly Chelsea—especially the King's Road—gave birth to Swinging '60s London, then to '70s punk youth culture. The '90s version is not really the center of anything, but it's hard not to like walking it.

Stretching in both directions from Albert Bridge is very expensive **Cheyne Walk** (it rhymes with "rainy"), featuring some beautiful Queen Anne houses (particularly Norman Shaw's ornamental 1876 Cheyne House, to the right) and a storm of Blue Plaques marking famous ex-residents' abodes. George Eliot died at No. 4 in 1880; Dante Gabriel Rossetti annoyed the neighbors of No. 16 with his peacock collection (there's still a clause in the lease banning the birds); at Carlyle Mansions (after the King's Head and Eight Bells

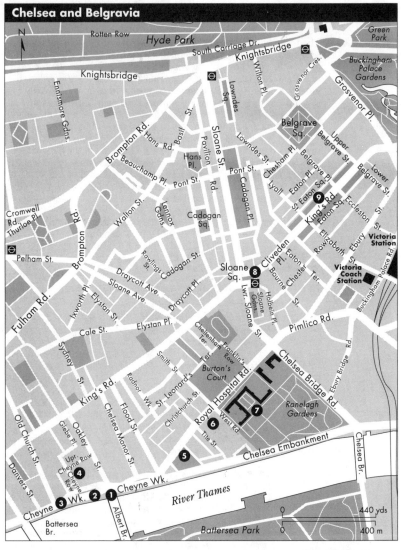

## Chelsea and Belgravia

*132*

Albert Bridge, **1**

Carlyle's House, **4**

Chelsea Physic Garden, **5**

Cheyne Walk, **2**

Eaton Square, **9**

National Army Museum, **6**

Royal Court Theatre, **8**

Royal Hospital, **7**

Thomas More statue, **3**

pub), Henry James died, and T. S. Eliot and Ian Fleming lived. The western reaches was painters' territory, most notabl·· James McNeill Whistler, who lived at No. 96 and then No. 101, and J. M. W. Turner, who used No. 119 as a retreat, shielding his identity behind the name Admiral "Puggy" Booth.

Also toward the western end, outside the church of All Saints, is a ❸ golden-faced **Thomas More** (who wouldn't sign the Oath of Supremacy at Lambeth Palace in 1534 and was executed as a traitor; *see* Westminster Bridge to the Imperial War Museum in The South Bank, *above*), looking pensive and beatific on a throne facing the river, in a 1969 addition to the Walk. Double back and turn left into Cheyne ❹ Row to reach one literary residence you can visit. **Carlyle's House** was a thriving salon of 19th-century authors attracted by the fame of Thomas Carlyle (who wrote a then-blockbuster, since all-but-forgotten history of the French Revolution, and founded the London Library), and by the wit of his wife, the poet Jane Carlyle. Dickens, Thackeray, Tennyson, and Browning were regular visitors, and you can see the second-floor drawing room where they met just as they saw it, complete with leather armchair, decoupage screen, fireplace, and oil lamps, all in ruddy Victorian hues. *24 Cheyne Row, tel. 0171/352-7087. Admission: £2.80 adults, £1.40 children under 17. Open Apr.-Oct., Wed.-Sun. and public holidays 11-5 (last admission 4:30); closed Good Friday, Dec. 24-26, Jan. 1.*

At the point where the east end of Cheyne Walk runs into Royal Hospital Road, gardeners and herbalists should make a beeline for the ❺ **Chelsea Physic Garden,** first planted by the Society of Apothecaries in 1673 for the study of medicinal plants and still in use for the same purpose today. These herbs and shrubs and flowers, planted to a strict plan but tumbling rurally over the paths nevertheless, are interspersed with woodland areas, England's first rock garden, and ancient trees, some of which were tragically uprooted in a 1987 hurricane. In the middle stands a statue of Sir Hans Sloane, Queen Anne and George II's physician, whose collection formed the basis of the British Museum, and who saved the garden from closure in 1722, making sure nobody would ever be allowed to build over it. *Swan Walk, 66 Royal Hospital Rd., tel. 0171/352-5646. Admission: £2.50 adults, £1.30 children under 16 and students. Open Apr.-Oct., Sun. and Wed. 2-5; daily noon-5 during the Chelsea Flower Show in the 3rd week of May.*

Turn right after the garden on Royal Hospital Road. The Imperial War Museum (*see* Westminster Bridge to the Imperial War Museum in The South Bank, *above*) tells of British warfare during this centu-❻ ry; the **National Army Museum** covers the history of British land forces from the Yeoman of the Guard (the first professional army, founded 1485 and ancestors of the Tower's beefeaters) to the present. Again, a great deal of effort is made to convey the experience of those who lived through the wars, and a visit should enhance anyone's grasp of London's history and its personages. *Royal Hospital Rd., tel. 0171/730-0717. Admission free. Open Mon.-Sat. 10-5:30, Sun. 2-5:30; closed Good Friday, May Day, Dec. 24-26, Jan. 1.*

Royal Hospital Road takes its name from the institution next door to ❼ the museum, the magnificent **Royal Hospital.** Charles II founded this hospice for elderly and infirm soldiers in 1682—some say after a badgering from his soft-hearted, high-profile mistress, Nell Gwynn, but more probably as an act of expedience, since his troops had hitherto enjoyed not so much as a meager pension and were growing restive after the civil wars of 1642–46 and 1648. Charles wisely appointed the great architect of burned-out City churches, Sir Christopher Wren, to design this small village of red brick and Portland stone, set in manicured gardens (which you can visit) surrounding the "Figure Court"—named after the 1692 bronze figure of Charles II dressed up as a Roman soldier—and the Great Hall (dining room) and chapel. The latter is enhanced by the choir stalls of Grinling Gibbons (who did the bronze of Charles, too), the former by a vast oil of Charles on horseback by Antonio Verrio, and both are open to inspection.

No doubt you will run into some of the 400-odd residents. Despite their advancing years, these "Chelsea Pensioners" are no shrinking violets. In summer and for special occasions they wear dandy scarlet frock coats with gold buttons and breastfuls of medals, and natty tricorne hats, and, being of proven good character (a condition of entry, along with old age and loyal service), might offer to show you around—in which case you may wish to supplement their daily beer and tobacco allowance with a tip.

May is the big month at the Royal Hospital. The 29th is **Oak Apple Day,** when the pensioners celebrate Charles II's birthday by draping oak leaves on his statue and parading around it in memory of a hollow oak tree that expedited the king's miraculous escape from the 1651 Battle of Worcester. In the same month the **Chelsea Flower Show,** the year's highlight for thousands of garden-obsessed Brits, is also held here (*see* Festivals and Seasonal Events in Chapter 1, Essential Information). *Royal Hospital Rd., tel. 0171/730–0161. Admission free. Open Mon.–Sat. 10–noon and 2–4, Sun. 2–4; closed national holidays and Sun. Oct.–Mar.*

A left turn up Franklin's Row and Cheltenham Terrace brings you to famous **King's Road,** where the miniskirt was born in the '60s and Vivienne Westwood and Malcolm McLaren clothed the Sex Pistols in bondage trousers from their shop, Sex, in 1975, thus spawning punk rock. Westwood, Britain's most innovative fashion star, still has her shop at No. 430, where the road kinks. Both boutique and neighborhood are called **World's End,** possibly because Chelsea-ites believe that's what it does here—the less-fancy Fulham begins around this stretch. The other end of King's Road, leading into Sloane Square, has various fashion stores (no longer style-setters, on the whole) and some rather good antiques shops and markets along the way; check out **Antiquarius** at No. 135–141.

The **Pheasantry** at No. 152 is recognizable by some over-the-top Grecian statuary in a fancy portico. Named in its mid-19th-century pheasant-breeding days, it had a phase from 1916 to 1934 as a ballet school where Margot Fonteyn and Alicia Markova learned the first position. Now it's a club-restaurant haunted by the braying breed of Chelsea yuppie, dubbed "Sloane Rangers" by '80s style-watchers. **Peter Jones** department store marks the exit from the north of Chelsea and the beginning of Belgravia: Sloane Square.

---

**Time Out**  **Oriel,** near the tube station on Sloane Square's east side, has a restaurant on the right, a bar and brasserie on the left, and a cappuccino bar in the middle, so weary shoppers can choose between a full French meal, coffee and pastries, or a gin and tonic.

---

You may remember Sir Hans Sloane from the Chelsea Physic Garden, which he saved for posterity, and the British Museum, which his collection started. This is his territory, since he bought the manor of Chelsea in 1712, and Sloane Square, laid out late that century, ❽ is named in his honor. Of chief interest here now is the **Royal Court**

**Theatre,** which is dedicated to new work and has seen many a first night of future star playwrights. It was here that John Osborne's *Look Back in Anger* premiered in 1956. Fifty years earlier, many of George Bernard Shaw's plays had their first public airings here, too.

## Belgravia

The neighborhood between Sloane Square and Hyde Park Corner is aristocratic **Belgravia,** with King's Road and Knightsbridge its southern and northern borders, Sloane Street and Grosvenor Place its western and eastern ones, and vast Belgrave Square, home to many embassies, in the middle. Belgravia is relatively young: It was built between the 1820s and the 1850s by the builder-developer-entrepreneur Thomas Cubitt (who had as great an influence on the look of London in his day as Wren and Nash had in theirs), under the patronage of Lord Grosvenor, and was intended to rival Mayfair for spacious snob value and expense.

Well, it did, and it does. The grand, white-stucco houses have
**9** changed not at all since the mid-19th century, and **Eaton Square** remains such a desirable address that the rare event of one of its houses coming on the market makes all the property pages. Its most famous residents were fictional: The enduringly popular period soap, *Upstairs Downstairs*, was set here.

# Knightsbridge, Kensington, and Holland Park

*Numbers in the margin correspond to points of interest on the Knightsbridge, Kensington, and Holland Park map.*

East of Belgravia and north of Chelsea lies salubrious Knightsbridge, with approximately equal doses of elite residential streets and ultra-shopping opportunities. To *its* east is one of the highest concentrations of important artifacts anywhere, the "museum mile" of South Kensington, with the rest of Kensington offering peaceful strolls, a noisy main street, and another palace. The Holland Park neighborhood is worth visiting for its big, fancy, tree-shaded houses and its exquisite and surprising park. This is an all-weather tour—museums and shops for rainy days, grass and strolls for sunshine.

## Knightsbridge

When you surface from the Knightsbridge tube station—one of London's deepest—you are immediately engulfed among the angry drivers, professional shoppers, and ladies-who-lunch who comprise the local population. If you're in a shopping mood, **Harvey Nichols**—right at the tube—has six floors of total fashion, and **Sloane Street,** leading south, is strung with the boutiques of big French and English designers. (*See* Chapter 4, Shopping.)

**1** There's no point pretending you don't want to see **Harrods,** so we'll head there next, going west down Brompton Road and soon colliding with the store's domed terra-cotta Edwardian bulk, which is outlined in thousands of white lights by night. The 15-acre Egyptian-owned store's sales weeks are world-class, and the store is as frenetic as a stock market floor, since its motto, *Omnia, omnibus, ubique* ("everything, for everyone, everywhere") is not too far from the

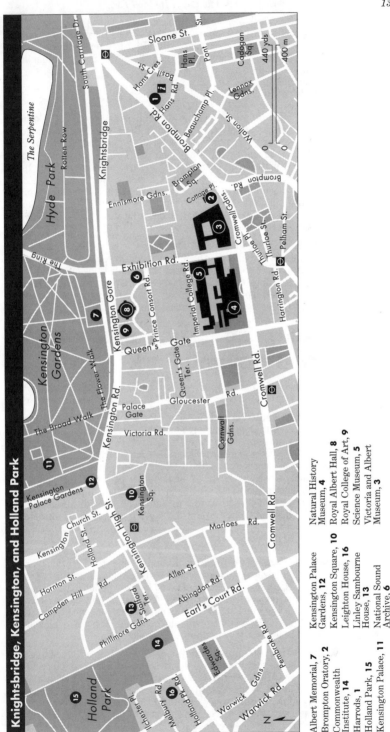

# Knightsbridge, Kensington, and Holland Park

The Serpentine

Hyde Park

Rotten Row

South Carriage Dr.

Sloane St.

Hans Cres.

Basil St.

Hans Pl.

Pont

Cadogan Sq.

Lennox Gdns.

Brompton Rd.

Beauchamp Pl.

Walton St.

Knightsbridge

Ennismore Gdns.

Brompton Sq.

Cottage Pl.

Brompton Rd.

Cromwell Gdns.

Thurloe Pl.

Thurloe St.

Pelham St.

Exhibition Rd.

Cromwell Pl.

Harrington Rd.

Kensington Gore

Prince Consort Rd.

Imperial College Rd.

Queen's Gate

The Ring

Kensington Gardens

The Flower Walk

The Broad Walk

Kensington Rd.

Queen's Gate Ter.

Gloucester Rd.

Cromwell Rd.

Palace Gate

Victoria Rd.

Cornwall Gdns.

Kensington Palace Gardens

Kensington Church St.

Kensington High St.

Kensington Sq.

Marloes Rd.

Cromwell Rd.

Holland Park Gardens

Holland Park

Hornton St.

Campden Hill Rd.

Holland St.

Stafford Ter.

Phillimore Gdns.

Allen St.

Abingdon Rd.

Earl's Court Rd.

Ilchester Pl.

Melbury Rd.

Holland Rd.

Holland Pl.

Edwardes Sq.

Warwick Gdns.

Pembroke Rd.

Warwick Rd.

N

0      440 yds

0      400 m

Albert Memorial, **7**
Brompton Oratory, **2**
Commonwealth Institute, **14**
Harrods, **1**
Holland Park, **15**
Kensington Palace, **11**

Kensington Palace Gardens, **12**
Kensington Square, **10**
Leighton House, **16**
Linley Sambourne House, **13**
National Sound Archive, **6**

Natural History Museum, **4**
Royal Albert Hall, **8**
Royal College of Art, **9**
Science Museum, **5**
Victoria and Albert Museum, **3**

truth. Visit the pet department, a highlight for children, and don't miss the extravagant **Food Hall,** with its stunning Art Nouveau tiling in the neighborhood of meat and poultry, which continues in the fishmonger's territory, where its glory is rivaled by displays of the sea produce itself. This is the place to acquire your green-and-gold souvenir Harrods bag, since food prices are surprisingly competitive. Go as early as you can to avoid the worst of the crowds. From Harrods, continue west down the Brompton Road, pausing at Beauchamp ("Bee-chum") Place and Walton Street if shopping is your intention.

**Time Out**   **Patisserie Valerie** (215 Brompton Rd., tel. 0171/832–9971; open daily), just down the road from Harrods, offers light meals and a gorgeous array of pastries. It's perfect for breakfast, lunch, or tea.

Presently, at the junction of Brompton and Cromwell roads, you ❷ come to the pale, Italianate **Brompton Oratory,** a product of the English Roman Catholic revival of the late 19th century led by John Henry Cardinal Newman (1801–1890), who established this oratory in 1884 and whose statue you see outside. A then-unknown 29-year-old architect, Herbert Gribble, won the competition to design the place, an honor that you may assume went to his head when you see the vast, incredibly ornate interior. It is punctuated by treasures far older than the church itself, like the giant Twelve Apostles in the nave, carved from Carrara marble by Giuseppe Mazzuoli in the 1680s and brought here from Siena's cathedral. New and dastardly treasure was also found here, in the side altar, when the second pillar to the left of the pietà was unmasked as a "dead letter box"—a hot line from secret agent to KGB.

### South Kensington

You are now in museum territory. (The neighborhood's three large museums, incidentally, can be reached via a long underground passage from the South Kensington tube.) Since 1994, museum visiting has put less strain on the pocket with the launch of the **White Card**—a group ticket to the three South Kensington museums and 10 further ones. (*See* Highlights '95, before the introduction to this book, and the italicized service information, *below,* for more details.)

The next building along, at the start of Cromwell Road, is the first of ❸ the colossal museums of South Kensington, the **Victoria and Albert,** recognizable by the copy of Victoria's Imperial Crown it wears on the lantern above the central cupola, and always referred to as the V&A. It showcases the applied arts of all disciplines, all periods, all nationalities, and all tastes, and is a wonderful, generous place to get lost in, full of innovation and completely devoid of pretension. The collections are *so* catholic that confusion is a hazard—one minute you're gazing on the Jacobean oak 12-foot-square four-poster **Great Bed of Ware** (one of the V&A's most prized possessions, given that Shakespeare immortalized it in *Twelfth Night*); the next, you're in the 20th-century end of the equally celebrated **Dress Collection,** coveting a Jean Muir frock you could actually buy at Harrods.

Prince Albert, Victoria's adored consort, was responsible for the genesis of this permanent version of the 1851 Great Exhibition, and his queen laid its foundation stone in her final public London appearance in 1899. From the start, the V&A had an important role as a research institution, and that role continues today, with many resources available to scholars, designers, artists, and conservators. Two of the latest are the **Textiles and Dress 20th Century Reference Centre,** with ingenious space-saving storage systems for thousands of bolts of cloth, and the **Textile Study Galleries,** which perform the same function for 2,000 years' worth of the past.

Follow your own whims around the 7 miles of gallery space, but try to reach the latest addition, the spectacular **Glass Gallery,** where a collection spanning four millennia is reflected between room-size mirrors, under young designer Danny Lane's breathtaking glass balustrade. *Cromwell Rd., tel. 0171/938–8500. Suggested contribution: £3.50 adults, £1 children and senior citizens. Open Mon. noon–5:50, Tues.–Sun. 10–5:50; closed Good Friday, May Day, Dec. 24–26, Jan. 1.*

*Prices for the 1995 **White Card,** available here (see Highlights '95 for other locations), had not been set at press time. 1994 cost: 3-day card £10, 7-day card £20; 3-day family card (2 adults, 2 children) £25, 7-day family card £50.*

**Time Out** Rest your overstimulated eyes in the brick-walled V&A café, where full meals and small snacks are available, and the Sunday Jazz Brunch (11–5), accompanied by live music and Sunday papers, is fast becoming a London institution.

The museum that follows provides clues to its contents in relief panels scattered across its outrageously ornate French Romanesque-style terra-cotta facade. Alfred Waterhouse, the architect of the **❹ Natural History Museum,** carved living creatures to the left of the entrance, extinct ones to the right, a categorization that is sort of continued in reverse inside, with **Dinosaurs** on the left and the **Ecology Gallery** on the right. Both these newly renovated exhibits (the former with life-size *moving* dinosaurs, the latter complete with moonlit "rainforest") make essential viewing in a museum that realized it was getting crusty and has consequently invested millions overhauling itself in recent years.

The **Creepy Crawlies Gallery** features a nightmarish superenlarged scorpion, yet ends up making tarantulas cute (eight out of 10 animal species, one learns here, are arthropods). Other wonderful bits include the **Human Biology Hall,** which you arrive in through a birth-simulation chamber; the full-size blue whale; and in the east wing, which was once the separate Geological Museum, an earthquake machine (not for L.A. residents) in the **Earth Galleries.** Understandably, this place usually resembles grade-school recess. *Cromwell Rd., tel. 0171/938–9123. Admission: £4.50 adults, £2.20 children under 17 and senior citizens, £12 family (2 adults, 4 children). Admission free weekdays 4:30–5:50, weekends 5–5:50. White Card available (see above). Open Mon.–Sat. 10–5:50., Sun. 11–5:50; closed Dec. 24–26, Jan. 1.*

**❺** The last of the three big museums, the **Science Museum,** stands behind the Natural History Museum in a far plainer building. This one features even more hands-on exhibits, with entire schools of children apparently decanted inside to play with them; but it is, after all, painlessly educational. Highlights include the **Launch Pad** gallery, which demonstrates basic scientific principles (try the beautiful plasma ball, where your hands attract "lightning"—if you can get them on it); the **Computing Then and Now** show, which gets the most crowded of all; *Puffing Billy,* the oldest train in the world; and the actual **Apollo 10** capsule, which took U.S. astronauts around the moon in 1969 and now sits beside a mock-up moon-base in the space exploration segment. Food technology, medical history, flight, navigation, transport, meteorology—all these topics are explored, and the entire height of the museum is used for a **Foucault's Pendulum** that has been there, in perpetual motion thanks to the movement of the earth, from the start. *Exhibition Rd., tel. 0171/938–8000. Admission: £4 adults, £2.10 children under 15 and senior citizens. White Card available (see above). Open Mon.–Sat. 10–6, Sun. 11–6; closed Dec. 24–26, Jan. 1.*

**Time Out**   **Daquise** (20 Thurloe St., tel. 0171/589–6117), at the southern tip of Exhibition Road (near South Kensington tube station), is a cozy Polish restaurant that is as happy to dispense coffee and pastries as it is to serve up its large portions of inexpensive, somewhat stodgy East European home cooking (*see* South Kensington in Chapter 6, Dining).

Turn left to continue north up Exhibition Road, a kind of unfinished cultural main drag that was Prince Albert's conception, toward the road after which British moviemakers named their fake blood, Kensington Gore. Near the end on the left is the aural outpost of the ⑥ British Library, the **National Sound Archive,** in which you may listen to the queen who made this entire tour possible: The million recordings held here include one of Victoria speaking sometime in the 1880s, but you have to book in advance to hear her or anyone else. There's a small exhibit of early recording equipment and ephemera, too. *29 Exhibition Rd., tel. 0171/589–6603. Admission free. Open weekdays 10–5 (Thurs. 10–9); closed public holidays, Dec. 24–26, Jan. 1.*

Having heard Victoria, you can now see Albert, across Kensington Gore in the grandiose temple that his grieving widow had erected on the spot where his Great Exhibition had stood a mere decade before his early death from typhoid in 1861. To tell the truth, all you can ⑦ actually see of the **Albert Memorial** is the world's tallest free-standing piece of scaffolding, since the intricate structure housing the 14-foot bronze statue of Albert is crumbling so assiduously that conservationists have sentenced it to be shielded indefinitely from the elements.

Just opposite, on the south side of the street, stands a companion— ⑧ and, this time, shriekingly visible—memorial, the **Royal Albert Hall.** The Victorian public donated funds to build this domed, circular 8,000-seat auditorium (as well as the Albert Memorial), but more money was raised by selling 1,300 future seats at £100 apiece—not for the first night, but for every night for 999 years. (Some descendants of purchasers still use the seats.) The Albert Hall is best-known and best-loved for its annual July–September Henry Wood Promenade Concerts (the "Proms"), with bargain standing (or promenading, or sitting-on-the-floor) tickets sold on the night of the world-class classical concerts. London also enjoys the "Erics," when the rock guitarist Eric Clapton services adoring fans for 10 days there every February. *Kensington Gore, tel. 0171/589–3203. Admission varies according to event.*

The building adjacent to the Albert Hall could hardly contrast more sharply with all this sentimental Victoriana: the glass-dominated ⑨ **Royal College of Art,** designed by Sir Hugh Casson in 1973. Famous in the '50s and '60s for processing David Hockney, Peter Blake, and Eduardo Paolozzi, the RCA is still one of the country's foremost art schools, and there's usually an exhibition, lecture, or event here open to the public. *Kensington Gore, tel. 0171/584–5020. Admission free. Open weekdays 10–6; phone first to check exhibition details.*

**Kensington**

You've already entered Kensington, but now you're drawing closer
to the heart of it. It first became the *Royal* Borough of Kensington
(& Chelsea) by virtue of a king's asthma. William III, who suffered
terribly from the Thames mists over Whitehall, decided in 1689 to
buy Nottingham House in the rural village of Kensington so that he
could breathe more easily; besides, his wife and co-monarch, Mary
II, felt confined by water and wall at Whitehall. Courtiers and func-
tionaries and society folk soon followed where the crowns led, and by
the time Queen Anne was on the throne (1702–14), Kensington was
overflowing. In a way, it still is, since most of its grand houses, and
the later, Victorian ones of Holland Park, have been divided into
apartments, or else are serving as foreign embassies.

**⑩** Begin with a stroll around the covetable houses of **Kensington
Square,** laid out around the time William moved to the palace up the
road, and therefore one of London's oldest squares. A few early
18th-century houses remain, with Nos. 11 and 12 the oldest. Return
to Kensington High Street up Derry Street, with the offices of
London's local paper, the *Evening Standard*, on the right, and what
was once Derry and Tom's department store—it closed down in the
'70s—on the left. The best feature of the store was its magical roof
garden, complete with palm trees, ponds, and flamingos; it's still
there, now part of a nightclub owned by Richard Branson, the high-
profile London figure who also owns Virgin Atlantic Airways.

---

**Time Out**  The next left turn from Derry Street is Wright's Lane, where you'll
find **The Muffin Man,** a cozy anachronism of a tea shop. Here floral-
aproned waitresses serve toasted sandwiches, cream teas, and, yes,
English muffins.

---

Follow the road east until you reach Kensington Gardens, where
**⑪** **Kensington Palace** stands close to the western edge. It did not enjoy
a smooth passage as royal residence. Twelve years of renovation
were needed before William and Mary could move in; it continued to
undergo all manner of refurbishment during the next three monarchs' times. By coincidence, these monarchs happened to suffer
rather ignominious deaths. First, William III fell off his horse when
it stumbled on a molehill, and succumbed to pleurisy in 1702. Then,
in 1714, Queen Anne (who, you may recall, was fond of brandy) suffered an apoplectic fit brought on by over-eating. Next, George I,
the first of the Hanoverian Georges, had a stroke as a result of "a
surfeit of melons"—admittedly not at Kensington, but in a coach to
Hanover, in 1727. Worst of all, in 1760, poor George II burst a blood
vessel while on the toilet (the official line was, presumably, that he
was on the throne).

The best-known royal Kensington story, though, concerns the 18-
year-old Princess Victoria of Kent, who was called from her bed in
June 1837, by the Archbishop of Canterbury and the Lord Chamberlain. Her uncle, William IV, was dead, they told her, and she was to
be queen. The **state rooms** where Victoria had her ultrastrict up-
bringing are arranged in early 19th-century style. On the first floor,
you can also see the **Court Dress Collection,** which conveys a great
deal about royal protocol alongside the ladies' and gentlemen's outfits dating from 1750 to Princess Diana's 1981 wedding dress. The
other half of the palace is off-limits, since Princess Margaret lives
here when in London. *Kensington Gdns., tel. 0171/937–9561. Admission: £3.90 adults, £2.95 senior citizens, £2.60 children under*

16. *Open Mon.–Sat. 9–5, Sun. 11–5 (last admission 4:15); closed Good Friday, Dec. 24–26, Jan. 1.*

Behind the palace runs one of London's rare private roads, guarded and gated both here and at the Notting Hill Gate end, **Kensington Palace Gardens.** If you walk it, you will see why it earned the nickname "Millionaires' Row"—it is lined with palatial white-stucco houses designed by a selection of the best architects of the mid-19th century. The novelist Thackeray, author of *Vanity Fair*, died in 1863 at No. 2—a building that now houses an embassy (Israeli), as do most of the others. **Kensington Church Street** also leads up to Notting Hill Gate, with the little 1870 St. Mary Abbots Church on its southwest corner and a cornucopia of expensive antiques in its shops all along the way.

Rather than walk the traffic-laden Kensington High Street, take the longer, scenic route, first turning left off Kensington Church Street into Holland Street and admiring the sweet 18th-century houses (Nos. 10, 12–13, and 18–26 remain). As you cross Hornton Street you'll see to your left an orange-brick 1970s building, the Kensington Civic Centre (donor of parking permits, home of the local council), and Holland Street becomes the leafy Duchess of Bedford's Walk, with **Queen Elizabeth College,** part of London University, on the right.

Turn left before Holland Park into Phillimore Gardens (perhaps detouring east into Phillimore Place to see No. 44, where Kenneth Grahame, author of *The Wind in the Willows,* lived from 1901 to 1908), then left again into Stafford Terrace to reach **Linley Sambourne House.** The Victorian Society has perfectly preserved this 1870s home of the political cartoonist Edward Linley Sambourne, complete with William Morris wallpapers and illustrations from the (recently deceased) satirical magazine *Punch,* including many of Sambourne's own, adorning the walls. *18 Stafford Terr., tel. 0181/994–1019. Admission: £3 adults, £1.50 children under 16. Open Mar.–Oct., Wed. 10–4, Sun. 2–5.*

Step back to High Street, turn right, pass the gates of Holland Park (we'll enter them soon), and you'll see one of London's more eccentric structures—the swimming-pool-blue walls and asymmetric copper tent roof of the **Commonwealth Institute.** A wander round the open-plan walkways of this lovable museum is like a trip around the world, or at least around the 50 Commonwealth nations, with lifestyles and histories of other continents captured in dioramas and displays that are more like art than education. Education is an important part of the work done at this vibrant institute (it hosts a lot of music, art, and film events, too)—which makes it all the sadder that, at press time, it was in trouble. Funding may be withdrawn in early 1996, so if you like it, sign its petition. *230 Kensington High St., tel. 0171/603–4535. Admission: £1 adults, 50p children. Open Mon.–Sat. 10–5, Sun. 2–5; closed Good Friday, Dec. 24–26, Jan. 1.*

## Holland Park

Stepping through the gates you just passed, you find yourself in a haven of wildlife, flora, and even culture, **Holland Park.** These former grounds of the Jacobean **Holland House** opened to the public only in 1952; since then, many treats have been laid on within its 22 hectares. Holland House itself was nearly flattened by World War II bombs, but the east wing remains, now incorporated into a youth hostel and providing a fantastical stage for the April–September **Open Air Theatre** (box office, tel. 0171/602–7856). The glass-walled

**Orangery** also survived to host art exhibitions and wedding receptions, while next door, the Garden Ballroom has become the **Belvedere** restaurant (*see* Kensington and Notting Hill Gate in Chapter 6, Dining).

From the Belvedere's terrace you see the formal **Dutch Garden,** planted by Lady Holland in the 1790s with the first English dahlias. North of that are woodland walks, lawns populated by peacocks and guinea fowl and the odd emu, a fragrant rose garden, great banks of rhododendrons and azaleas (which bloom profusely in May), a well-supervised children's **Adventure Playground,** and even a **Japanese water garden,** legacy of the 1991 London Festival of Japan. If that's not enough, you can watch cricket on the **Cricket Lawn** on the south side, or tennis on the several courts.

**Time Out** Since the **Holland Park Café** is run by an Italian family, it serves a homemade risotto or pasta, and good cappuccino, alongside the sandwiches, cakes, and tea you'd expect. There are lots of bucolically tree-shaded outside tables.

Exit the park at the gate by the tennis courts (near the Orangery) onto Ilchester Place, follow Melbury Road a few yards, and turn ⑯ right onto Holland Park Road to reach **Leighton House.** The main reason to tour the home of Frederic Leighton—painter, sculptor, president of the Royal Academy, endowed with a peerage by Victoria (unfortunately, he died a month later)—is the incredible **Arab Hall.** George Aitchison designed this Moorish fantasy in 1879 to show off Leighton's valuable 13th- to 17th-century Islamic tile collection, and, adorned with marble columns, dome, and fountain, it is exotic beyond belief. The rest of the rooms are more conventionally, stuffily Victorian, but they do feature many paintings by Leighton, plus Edward Burne-Jones, John Millais, and other leading Pre-Raphaelites. *12 Holland Park Rd., tel. 0171/602–3316. Admission free. Open Mon.–Sat. 11–5; closed national holidays.*

Late last century, **Melbury Road** was a veritable colony of artists, though the Victorian muse they followed failed to appeal to later sensibilities, and they're now an obscure bunch—excepting Dickens's illustrator, Marcus Stone, who had No. 8 built in 1876. From here you could turn right onto Addison Road (just off our map) to see the Technicolor tiles rioting over Sir Ernest Debenham's "Peacock House" at No. 8 (he founded the eponymous Oxford Street department store). If you continue north, you reach the Parisian boulevardesque, plane tree–lined Holland Park Avenue, main thoroughfare of an expensive residential neighborhood, which is most pleasant to stroll.

# Hyde Park, Kensington Gardens, and Notting Hill

*Numbers in the margin correspond to points of interest on the Hyde Park, Kensington Gardens, and Notting Hill map.*

Many Londoners, not to mention visitors, love the city above all for its huge chunks of green, which cut right through the middle of town. The two we visit here together form by far the biggest of central London's royal parks (Richmond Park, in the far west, is larger; *see* Richmond in The Thames Upstream, *below*). It's probably been centuries since any major royal had a casual stroll here, but the parks remain the property of the Crown, and it was the Crown that saved them from being devoured by the city's late-18th-century growth spurt.

Hyde Park, along with the smaller St. James's and Green Parks to the east, started as Henry VIII's hunting grounds. He had no altruistic intent but—you could say—stole the land for his pleasure, from the monks at Westminster at the 1536 Dissolution of the Monasteries. James I was more generous and allowed the public in at the beginning of the 17th century, as long as they were "respectably dressed." Nowadays, as summer visitors can see, you may wear whatever you like—a bathing suit will do.

North of the parks—which are separate, although the boundary is virtually invisible—lie Bayswater, Queensway, and Notting Hill, the last of these a multicultural neighborhood that has really come into its own in the past few years.

## Hyde Park

Where else would you enter Hyde Park but at Hyde Park Corner? The most impressive of the many entrances is here, beside Apsley House (*see* Piccadilly in St. James's and Mayfair, *above*). Officially **❶** it's the Hyde Park Screen, but it's usually called **Decimus Burton's Gateway** because it was he who designed this triple-arched monument in 1828. The next gate along to the north was a 90th-birthday gift to Queen Elizabeth the Queen Mother (who is as old as the century), and we don't know what she thought of it. Public reception of **❷** the gaudy unicorns-and-lions-rampant **Queen Mother's Gate,** wrought in scarlet-, cobalt-, white-, and gold-painted metal, was derisive, but see what you think.

Your first landmark in all the greenery is a sand track that runs **❸** along the south perimeter, called **Rotten Row.** It was Henry VIII's royal path to the hunt—hence the name, a corruption of *route du roi*. Contemporary horses still use it, ridden by the rich who own them, the fairly well-heeled who hire them (*See* Participant Sports and Fitness in Chapter 5, Sports), or the Household Cavalry who **❹** ride for the queen. You can see the latter's **Knightsbridge Barracks**—a high rise and a long, low, ugly red block—to the left. This is the brigade that mounts the guard at the palace, and you can see them leave to perform this duty, in full regalia, plumed helmet and all, at around 10:30, or await the return of the exhausted ex-guard about noon.

You can follow either Rotten Row or Serpentine Road west, or you can stray over the grass, but the next landmark to find is the long, **❺** narrow, man-made (in 1730) lake, the **Serpentine.** It is a loved place, much frequented in summer, when the south shore **Lido** resembles a beach and the water is dotted with hired rowboats. If you rise very early, you might catch the Serpentine Swimming Club—a band of eccentrics guaranteed to appear on TV at the first hard frost each winter, since they dive in here at 6 AM every single day of the year, breaking the ice first if necessary. Walk the bank and you will soon **❻** reach the picturesque stone **Serpentine Bridge,** built in 1826 by George Rennie.

**Time Out**  The restaurant at the eastern end of the Serpentine seems to change hands every few months, but it still offers sandwiches, hot dishes, tea, coffee, and snacks in an eye-achingly green setting.

# Hyde Park, Kensington Gardens, and Notting Hill

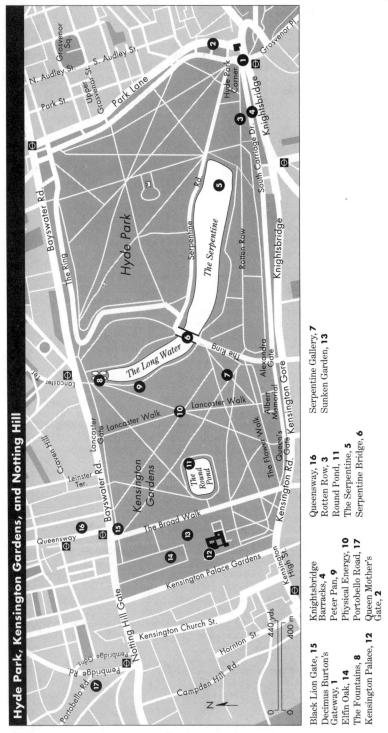

**Kensington Gardens**

In passing the bridge, you leave Hyde Park and enter **Kensington Gardens.** On the south side of the bridge is the **Serpentine Gallery,** which hangs several exhibitions of modern work a year, often very avant-garde indeed, and always worth a look. *Kensington Gardens, tel. 0171/402–6075. Admission free. Open daily 10–6; closed Christmas week.*

Kensington Gardens is more formal than its neighbor, since it was first laid out as palace grounds. Continue along the south bank of the lake, which is called the Long Water on this side of the bridge, to the top, to reach the formal, paved Italian garden called, for obvious reasons, **The Fountains.**

On your way, you will have passed a statue that children have loved since George Frampton cast it in 1912—a bronze of the boy who lived on an island in the Serpentine and never grew up, **Peter Pan.** His creator, J. M. Barrie, lived at 100 Bayswater Road, not 500 yards from here. There's another statue worth seeking southwest of Peter at the intersection of several paths: George Frederick Watts's 1904 bronze of a muscle-bound horse and rider, entitled **Physical Energy.**

Next on your westward stroll comes another water feature, the **Round Pond,** a magnet for model-boat enthusiasts and duck feeders. You may happen onto an exciting remote-controlled shipwreck, or ice thick enough for skating, which is allowed here. Next you reach **Kensington Palace** (*see* Kensington, *above*), with an early 19th-century **Sunken Garden** north of it, complete with a living tunnel of lime trees and golden laburnam. **The Broad Walk** between the pond and the palace runs south-to-north, from the bottom to the top of the park. Following it all the way north to the Bayswater Road, you'll see, on the left, a **playground** full of the kind of children who have nannies and whose nannies take them to the remains of a tree carved with scores of tiny woodland creatures, Ivor Innes's **Elfin Oak.**

Leaving the park by **Black Lion Gate,** you are almost opposite Bayswater's main drag, **Queensway,** a rather peculiar, cosmopolitan street of ethnic confusion, late-night cafés and restaurants, a skating rink, and the Whiteleys shopping-and-movie mall. The road expresses Bayswater's nature quite aptly: This is a neighborhood that looks fancy, with its grand white-stucco terraced houses and leafy squares, but is somewhat disreputable, as demonstrated by the 1963 Profumo sex scandal—involving a government minister, a teenage showgirl, and a Soviet naval attaché—which unfurled behind closed Bayswater doors and toppled a government (see the movie *Scandal* for the whole story). You'll notice dozens of identical medium-priced hotels along the streets east of Queensway, but probably won't notice the prostitution, of which there's a certain amount still going on around here, too.

**Time Out**　About halfway down Queensway (No. 127), **Maison Pechon** is a patisserie, but one which serves full English breakfasts, omelets, jacket potatoes, and salads alongside its French tarts, brioches, cream cakes, and cookies.

**Notting Hill**

As you walk west, the Bayswater Road turns into **Notting Hill Gate,** a wide, windy crossroads of functional shops. Turn right at Pembridge Road, however, and you've reached the start of a happening neighborhood, a trendsetting square mile of multi-ethnicity, music, and markets, with lots of see-and-be-seen-in restaurants and the younger, more egalitarian and adventurous versions of the Cork Street commercial modern-art galleries. The style-watching media dub the musician/novelist/filmbiz/drug-dealer/fashion-victim local residents and hangers-out Notting Hillbillies.

🄪 The famous **Portobello Road** starts soon on the left and runs about a mile north. What it's famous for is its Saturday antiques market, which begins around Chepstow Villas and continues for about three blocks before giving way to fruit and veg stalls. Lining the sloping street are also dozens of antiques shops and indoor markets, open most days (*see* Chapter 4, Shopping). Where the road levels off, youth culture kicks in and continues to the **Westway** overpass ("flyover" in British), where London's best flea market (high-class, vintage, antique, and second-hand clothing and jewelry) happens Friday and Saturday, then on up to Goldbourne Road. There's a strong West Indian flavor to Notting Hill, with a Trinidad-style **Carnival** centered along Portobello Road on the August bank-holiday weekend.

# Regent's Park and Hampstead

*Numbers in the margin correspond to points of interest on the Regent's Park and Hampstead map.*

This walk is a long one. We start at the Georgian houses superimposed on medieval Maryburne, where London's most overpopulated tourist attraction now lies, and continue around John Nash's Regency facades, and his park, home now to everything from elephants to softball. Next, we visit North London's canalside youth center, then climb up to the city's prettiest, most expensive "village," which wraps around its most bucolic park, before finishing, fittingly, at its most famous cemetery. You may well want to divide this tour into segments, using the notoriously inefficient Northern Line of the tube to jump between neighborhoods.

Begin at the tube station whose name will thrill the Sherlock Holmes fan: **Baker Street.** It sits on **Marylebone Road** (pronounced "Marra-le-bun"), remarkable for its permanent traffic jam. The aforementioned Conan Doyle reader may wish to pay homage to the fictional detective, who lived at 221B Baker Street. Walking past the Abbey National Building Society's head office at Abbey House, 215–229 Baker Street (sparing a thought for the poor mail-room attendant who still wades through letters asking Holmes and Watson for
❶ help), you reach No. 237–9, the **Sherlock Holmes Museum,** distinguishable by the actor dressed as a Victorian policeman outside, and by the sign that claims this as 221B, though we know it's lying. Inside, "Holmes's housekeeper" conducts you into a series of Victorian rooms, full of Sherlockabilia. *"221B" Baker St., tel. 0171/ 935–8866. Admission: £5 adults, £3 children under 16 and senior citizens. Open daily 10–6; closed Dec. 25, Jan. 1.*

❷ Around the corner again on Marylebone Road, follow the line of tour buses to one of London's busiest sights, **Madame Tussaud's.** It is nothing more, nothing less, than the world's premier exhibition of lifelike waxwork models of celebrities. Madame T. learned her craft while making death masks of French Revolutionary victims and in 1835 set up her first show of the famous ones near this spot. Nowa-

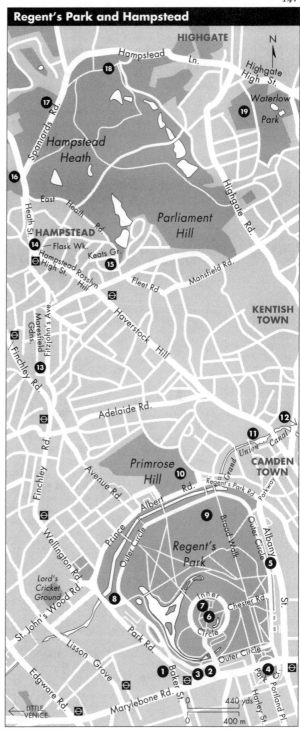

## Regent's Park and Hampstead

days, "Super Stars" of entertainment, in their own hall of the same name, outrank any aristo in popularity, along with the newest segment, "The Spirit of London," a "time taxi ride" that visits every notable Londoner from Shakespeare to Benny Hill. But top billing still goes to the murderers in the Chamber of Horrors, who stare glassy-eyed at you—this one from the electric chair, that one next to the tin bath where he dissolved several wives in quicklime. What, aside from ghoulish prurience, makes people stand in line to invest in London's most expensive museum ticket? It must be the thrill of rubbing shoulders with Shakespeare, Martin Luther King, the queen, and the Beatles—most of them dressed in their own clothes—in a single day. *Marylebone Rd., tel. 0171/935-6861. Admission: £7.40 adults, $5.50 senior citizens, £4.75 children under 15; or joint ticket with planetarium (see below). Open Sept.–June, Mon.–Fri. 10–5:30, Sat.–Sun. 9:30–5:30; July–Aug., daily 9:30–5:30; closed Dec. 25.*

❸ Next door is the green dome of the **London Planetarium,** which could hardly provide greater contrast with the waxworks (though you can save a bit of cash by combining them in a single visit). The stars here, of course, are the ones in the sky, simulations of which are projected on the dome's insides by the Zeuss projector and accompanied by gosh-wow-fancy-that narration. The shows, which change daily, are good enough to leave children addicted to astronomy. The "Space Trail" of interactive planet and spacecraft models is also worth seeing, and there are occasional laser shows and rock music extravaganzas. *Marylebone Rd., tel. 0171/486–1121. Admission: £4 adults, £3.10 senior citizens, £2.50 children under 15. Joint ticket with Madame Tussaud's: £9.40 adults, £7.95 senior citizens, £5.65 children. Shows every 40 min., weekdays 12:40–4:40, weekends 10:40–5:20; extra shows during school vacations.*

Now, hope for good weather, because the next leg of the tour keeps you outdoors. Continuing east up Marylebone Road, you pass by **Harley Street**—an English synonym for private (as opposed to state-funded) medicine, since it's lined with the consulting rooms of the country's top specialist doctors. Next you reach the first part of John Nash's impressive Regent's Park scheme, the elegantly curva-
❹ ceous **Park Crescent.** Nash planned it as a full circus at the northern end of his ceremonial route from St. James's, but only this southern semicircle was built (1812–1818). It was later wrecked during World War II, reconstructed, and rebuilt behind the repaired facade in the 1960s—as, indeed, were all the Nash houses you will see around the park. Crossing the street, you enter **Regent's Park** at the Outer Circle.

## Regent's Park and the Zoo

This, the youngest of London's great parks, was laid out in 1812 by John Nash, working, as ever, for his patron, the Prince Regent (hence the name), who was crowned George IV in 1820. The idea was to re-create the feel of a grand country residence close to the center of town, with all those magnificent white-stucco terraces facing in on the park. As you walk the Outer Circle, you'll see how successfully Nash's plans were carried out, although the center of it all, a palace for the prince, was never built—George was too busy fiddling with the one he already had, Buckingham Palace.

The most famous and impressive of Nash's terraces, appearing soon on your right, was extra ornamental, since it would have been in the
❺ prince's line of vision from the planned palace. **Cumberland Terrace**

has a central block of Ionic columns surmounted by a triangular Wedgwood-blue pediment that is like a giant cameo. Snow-white statuary personifying Britannia and her empire (the work of the on-site architect, James Thomson) further single it out from the pack.

Turn left into the park from this road. As in all London parks, planting is planned with the aim of having something in bloom in all seasons, but if you hit the park in May, June, or July, head first to the

**❻ Inner Circle.** Your nostrils should lead you to **Queen Mary's Gardens,** a fragrant 17-acre circle that riots with roses in summer, and heathers, azaleas, and evergreens in other seasons. Close by is the

**❼ Open-Air Theatre,** which has been mounting mostly Shakespeare productions since 1932. *A Midsummer Night's Dream* is the one to catch—never is that enchanted Greek wood more lifelike than it is here, augmented by genuine bird squawks. The park can get chilly, so bring a blanket—and rain stops the play only when heavy, so an umbrella may be wise, too. *Open Air-Theatre, Regent's Park, tel. 0171/486-2431. Open June–Aug.*

Rejoin the **Broad Walk** from Chester Road, look west past the mock-Tudor prefab tearoom, and before you stretches what is practically London's only uninterrupted open vista. From here you can watch a Technicolor sunset over the minaret and glittery gilt dome of the

**❽ London Central Mosque** on the far west side of the park, or—if it's a summer evening or a Sunday afternoon—witness a remarkable recent phenomenon. Wherever you look, the sport being enthusiastically played (subject to the ritual annual banning by the park authorities) is not cricket but softball, now Britain's fastest-growing participant sport (bring your mitt). Actually, you're likely to see cricket, too.

Continue along the Broad Walk and you will reach an institution that opened in 1828, peaked in the 1950s (when more than 3 million visitors passed through its turnstiles every year), but recently faced the

**❾** prospect of closing its gates forever: the **London Zoo.** The problems started when animal-crazy Brits, apparently anxious about the morality of caging wild beasts, simply stopped visiting. But the zoo fought back, pulling heartstrings with a *Save Our Zoo* campaign and tragic predictions of mass euthanasia for homeless polar bears, and, at the 11th hour, found commercial sponsorship that was generous enough not only to keep the wolves from the door (or the wolves indoors) but also to fund a great big modernization program.

Zoo highlights that will remain include the Brutalist **Elephant and Rhino Pavilion,** which closely resembles the South Bank Arts Complex; the graceful **Snowdon Aviary,** spacious enough to allow its tenants free flight; and the 1936 **Penguin Pool,** where feeding time sends small children into raptures. Plans include the construction of a desert swarming with locusts; a rainforest alive with butterflies, bats, and hummingbirds; and a cave lit by fireflies. This being the headquarters of the Zoological Society of London, much work is done here in wildlife conservation, education, and the breeding of endangered species, and the new funding will enable even more emphasis to be placed on these spheres, and more displays to help explain them to visitors. *Regent's Park, tel. 0171/722-3333. Admission: £6.50 adults, £5 senior citizens, £4 children under 14, under 4 free. Penguin feed, 2:30; aquarium feed, 2:30; reptile feed, 2:30 Fri. only; elephant bath, 3:45. Open summer, daily 9–6; winter, daily 10–4; closed Dec. 25.*

From here, you can take the water bus and spy on the back gardens along the **Grand Union Canal** (which everyone calls the Regent's Canal) to Little Venice. Don't get *too* excited—the canal you're on (constructed 1812–1820) is the only one there is, but this peaceful little bit of London does have an atmosphere unique to it, with enormous white wedding-cake houses set back from the banks, and it's a good strolling location. (For more on canal trips, *see* Guided Tours in Chapter 1, Essential Information.)

**❿** North of the zoo, cross Prince Albert Road to **Primrose Hill,** a high point (literally, at 206 feet), and the best place to be on the night of November 5, when London's biggest bonfire burns a Guy Fawkes effigy (*see* The Houses of Parliament in Westminster and Royal London, *above*), and there's a spectacular fireworks display. Heading east from here (Regent's Park Road, then left down Parkway is the easiest route) brings you to the center of Camden Town, the neighborhood that, according to recent censuses, houses London's highest concentration of single people in their twenties.

This demographic will quickly become obvious as you flail in seas of creative haircuts and store after store of identical T-shirts, clompy boots, vintage frocks, and cheap leathers. Camden definitely has its charms, though. Gentrification has been layered over a once overwhelmingly Irish neighborhood, vestiges of which coexist with the youth culture: Inverness Street fruit-and-veg market alongside the Arlington House homeless shelter, architects' offices, and antiques stores. Dominating everything are the markets that brought in the crowds. Turning left at the foot of Parkway, and battling north along Camden High Street (actually, the crowds are unbearably dense only on the weekend), you reach **Camden Lock,** which is indeed a pair of locks on the Grand Union Canal, now developed into a vast market that sells just about everything, but mostly crafts, clothing (vintage, ethnic, and young designer), and antiques.

**⓫**

**Time Out** You will not go hungry in Camden Town. Among the countless cafés, bars, pubs, and restaurants, the following stand out for good value and good food: **Marine Ices** (8 Haverstock Hill, past the lock) has a window dispensing ice cream to strollers, or pasta, pizza, and sundaes inside. **Bar Gansa** (2 Inverness St., near the tube) offers Spanish tapas—small dishes for sharing. **Cottons Rhum Shop, Bar and Restaurant** (55 Chalk Farm Rd., past the lock) is a Caribbean island in miniature, with great rum cocktails and jerk chicken.

Escaping the mayhem is easy if you take the canal towpath in either direction. Going west—a green and pleasant stroll in summer—you reach Regent's Park in no time, with some fancy houses to admire along the way. The easterly walk is less scenic by far, but interesting: You pass by housing projects and light-industrial buildings on the way to **King's Cross,** site of one of London's main train stations, of the new British Library building, of vast acres belonging to British Rail (where a massive redevelopment scheme has currently stalled), and of the city's highest concentration of streetwalkers.

About a mile along the towpath, in a former ice storage house, is the **⓬** quirky little **London Canal Museum.** Here you can learn about the rise and fall of London's once extensive canal network: the trade, the vessels, and the way of life. Outside, on the Battlebridge Basin, float the gaily painted narrow boats of modern canal dwellers—a few steps and a world away from what remains one of London's least salubrious neighborhoods, despite recent police action to clean up street activities like drug dealing and prostitution. *12–13 New Wharf Rd., N1, tel. 0171/713–0836. Admission: £2.50 adults, £1.25*

*children and senior citizens. Open Apr.–Sept., Tues.–Sun. 10–4;
call for winter hours; closed national holidays.*

## Hampstead

You can walk about a mile up Haverstock Hill, then Rosslyn Hill (the same street) to reach Hampstead, in which case you get to stop off at ⑬ the **Freud Museum.** The father of psychoanalysis lived here for only a few months, between his escape from Nazi persecution in his native Vienna in 1938 and his death in 1939. Many of his possessions emigrated with him and were set up by his daughter, Anna (herself a pioneer of child psychoanalysis), as a shrine to her father's life and work. Four years after Anna's death in 1982, the house was opened as a museum. It replicates the atmosphere of Freud's famous consulting rooms, particularly through the presence of The Couch. You'll find Freud-related books, lectures, and study groups here, too. *20 Maresfield Gdns., tel. 0171/435–2002. Admission: £2.50 adults, £1.50 children under 12 and senior citizens. Open Wed.–Sun. noon–5; closed Easter, Dec. 24–26, Jan. 1.*

If you skip Freud's house, three stops on the Northern Line from Camden Town tube (make sure you take the Edgware branch) will plant you squarely 181 feet below central Hampstead, in London's deepest tube station. The cliché about **Hampstead** is that it is just like a pretty little village—albeit one with designer shops, expensive French delicatessens, restaurants, cafés, cinemas, and so on. In fact, like so many London neighborhoods, Hampstead did start as a separate village, when plague-bedeviled medieval Londoners fled the city to this clean hilltop 4 miles away. By the 18th century its reputation for cleanliness had spread so far that its water was being bottled and sold to the hoi polloi down the hill as the Perrier of its day. That was the beginning of Hampstead's heyday as an artistic and literary retreat attracting many famous writers, painters, and musicians to its leafy lanes—as it still does today. Just strolling around here is rewarding: Not only are the streets incredibly picturesque, they also harbor some of London's best Georgian buildings.

The very best, and most concentrated, collection is strung along ⑭ **Church Row,** said to be London's most complete Georgian street. At the west end is the 1745 "village" church of **St. John's,** where the painter John Constable is buried. **Flask Walk** is another pretty street, narrow and shop-lined at the High Street end, then widening after you pass The Flask—the pub it is named for, which in turn is named for the flasks that contained that therapeutically clean Hampstead spa water. The pub has a pretty courtyard, by the way. Nearby **Well Walk** was where the spring surfaced, its place now marked by a dried-up fountain. John Constable lived here, as well as John Keats and, later, D. H. Lawrence.

⑮ Keats moved on in 1818, though, to what is now known as **Keats House** in, well, Keats Grove. Here you can see the plum tree under which the young Romantic poet composed the *Ode to a Nightingale,* many of his original manuscripts, his library, and other possessions he managed to acquire in his short life. He died in Rome of consumption, aged 25, two years after moving in here. *Keats House, Wentworth Pl., Keats Grove, tel. 0171/435–2062. Admission free. Open Apr.–Oct., weekdays 10–6, Sat. 10–5, Sun. and national holidays 2–5; Nov.–Mar., weekdays 1–5, Sat. 10–5, Sun. 2–5; closed 1 hour at lunch and Easter, May Day, Dec. 24–26, Jan. 1.*

**Time Out** Hampstead is another neighborhood full of eating places, including a few that have been here forever. Try **The Coffee Cup** (74 Hampstead High St.), serving all-day English breakfasts, pastries, and things-on-toast; or the **Hampstead Tea Rooms** (9 South End Rd.) for its sandwiches, pies, and its great windowful of pastries and cream cakes.

However pretty the houses may be, quite the nicest thing about Hampstead is **Hampstead Heath,** which spreads for miles to the north, and is utterly wild in parts. On the southwest corner stands ⑯ the rebuilt version of a famous inn, **Jack Straw's Castle.** It is named after the Peasant Revolt leader who hid out and was captured here in 1381 after destroying Sir Robert Hales's residence and Priory, the Prior of St. John. Hales was hated for enforcing the poll tax, which led to the uprising—and which, when reintroduced in 1990, proved as unpopular the second time around.

Another historic pub stands off the northwest edge of the Heath, on ⑰ Hampstead Lane. The **Spaniards Inn** is, in contrast to the above, little changed since the early 18th century, when (they say) the notorious highwayman Dick Turpin hung out here. Keats also drank here, as did Shelley and Byron—but not Dickens. When his eternal pub crawl brought him up to Hampstead, he preferred Jack Straw's Castle.

The main sight on the Heath, aside from the woods, ponds, and overall rural bliss, is **Kenwood House.** This magnificent mansion was ⑱ first built in 1616 and remodeled by Robert Adam in 1764. Adam refaced most of the exterior and added the glorious library, which, with its curved, painted ceiling and gilded detailing, is the highlight of the house. The other unmissable part is the **Iveagh Bequest**—a collection of paintings the Earl of Iveagh gave the nation in 1927, starring a Rembrandt self-portrait and works by Reynolds, Van Dyck, Hals, Gainsborough, Vermeer, and Turner. In front of the house, a graceful lawn slopes down to a little lake crossed by a dinky bridge—all in perfect 18th-century upper-class taste. Nowadays the lake is dominated by its **concert bowl,** which stages a popular summer series of orchestral concerts, including at least one performance of Handel's *Music for the Royal Fireworks*, complete with fireworks. *Hampstead La., tel. 0181/348–1286. Admission free. Open Easter–Sept., 10–6, Oct.–Easter, 10–4; closed Christmas.*

**Time Out** The café in the former stables at Kenwood serves sandwiches, salads, light lunches, and pastries, and has many outside tables in its sheltered courtyard.

To the east of Hampstead, and also topping a hill, is the former village of **Highgate,** which has some fine houses, especially along its Georgian High Street, and retains a peaceful period atmosphere. ⑲ What it is most famous for is **Highgate Cemetery,** a sprawling early Victorian graveyard featuring many an overwrought stone memorial, especially on its older, west side—which can be visited only by a tour given by the Friends of Highgate Cemetery, a group of volunteers who virtually saved the place from ruin. The shady streets of the dead, Egyptian Avenue and the Circle of Lebanon on the west side, are particularly Poe-like, but the famous graves are mostly on the newer, less atmospheric east side, which is still in use and may be wandered freely. Karl Marx's enormous black bust is probably the most visited place, but George Eliot is also buried here. This is not London's oldest cemetery—that distinction belongs to Kensal Green, with its spine-chilling catacombs and Gothic mausolea (*see*

Off the Beaten Track, *below*). *Swains La., Highgate, tel. 0181/340–1834. Admission: east side, £1; west side tour, £2. East side open Apr.–Oct., daily 10–4:45; Oct.–Mar., daily 10–3:45. West side tours: Apr.–Oct., weekdays 2 and 4 PM, weekends periodically 11–4; Nov.–Mar., weekdays noon, 2, and 3; weekends periodically 11–3. Closed Dec. 25 and for funerals.*

**Time Out** **Lauderdale House** in nearby Waterlow Park was built in the 16th century by a master of the Royal Mint and is now a community and arts center, with a great café serving homemade hot meals as well as snacks.

# Greenwich

*Numbers in the margin correspond to points of interest on the Greenwich map.*

About 8 miles downstream—which means seaward, to the east—from central London lies a neighborhood you'd think had been designed to provide the perfect day out. **Greenwich** is another of London's self-contained "villages," only one with unique and splendid sights surrounding the residential portion. Sir Christopher Wren's Royal Naval College and Inigo Jones's Queen's House reach architectural heights; the Old Royal Observatory measures time for our entire planet; and the Greenwich Meridian divides the world in two—you can stand astride it with one foot in either hemisphere. The National Maritime Museum and the proud clipper ship *Cutty Sark* are thrilling to seafaring types, and landlubbers can stroll the green acres of parkland that surround the buildings, the quaint 19th-century houses, and the weekend crafts and antiques markets.

The journey to Greenwich is fun in itself, especially if you approach by river, arriving to the best possible vista of the Royal Naval College, with the Queen's House behind. On the way, the boat glides past famous sights on the London skyline (there's a guaranteed spine chill on passing the Tower) and ever-changing docklands, and there's always a cockney navigator enhancing the views with wiseguy commentary. The trip takes about an hour from Westminster Pier (next to Big Ben), 25 minutes from the Tower of London. (*See* Guided Tours in Chapter 1, Essential Information.)

The least interesting, but fastest, route to Greenwich is on the Network SouthEast train from Charing Cross, which takes about 10 minutes. This is London's oldest railway line, but you can also take the newest: the Docklands Light Railway (DLR). This high-speed elevated track, which opened in 1987, connects with the tube network at Bank; alternatively, you can pick it up at Tower Gateway, a two-minute walk from the Tower Hill tube stop. The DLR brings you to Island Gardens, exactly opposite the Royal Naval College, with the finest possible view, of course. You can't miss the squat little circular brick building with its glass-domed roof. This is also the entrance to the Greenwich Foot Tunnel, where an ancient elevator takes you down to a walkway under the Thames that brings you up very close to the *Cutty Sark*.

Since the pleasure boats also land hereabouts, we'll start at this romantic tea clipper, which happens to provide a great way into the Greenwich riches. The ***Cutty Sark*** was built in 1869, one of fleets and fleets of similar wooden tall-masted clippers, which during the 19th century plied the seven seas trading in exotic commodities—tea, in this case. The *Cutty Sark*, the last to survive, was also the

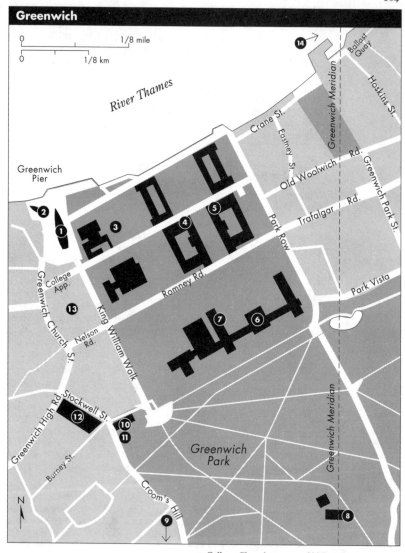

# Greenwich

fastest, sailing the China–London route in 1871 in only 107 days. Now the photogenic vessel lies in dry dock, a museum of one kind of seafaring life—and not a comfortable kind for the 28-strong crew, as you'll see. The collection of figureheads is amusing, too. *King William Walk, tel. 0181/858–3445. Admission: £3.25 adults, £2.25 children under 16 and senior citizens. Open Apr.–Sept., Mon.–Sat. 10–6, Sun. and public holidays noon–6; Oct.–Mar., Mon.–Sat. 10–5, Sun. and public holidays noon–5. Last admission 30 min. before closing. Closed Dec. 24–26.*

**②** While you're there, don't miss the adjacent dry-docked **Gipsy Moth IV,** the boat in which Sir Francis Chichester achieved the first single-handed circumnavigation of the globe in 1966. Inside you'll see the tiny space the sailor endured for 226 days, and the ingenious way everything he needed was installed. The queen knighted him on board here, using the same sword with which the previous Elizabeth had knighted that other seagoing Francis, Sir Francis Drake, three centuries before. *King William Walk, tel. 0181/858–3445. Admission: 50p adults, 30p children and senior citizens. Open Apr.–Oct., Mon.–Sat. 10–6, Sun. noon–6; closed Nov.–Mar.*

Now that you have some salt in your veins, you can begin penetrating to the heart of Greenwich. By continuing along King William **③** Walk, you come to the wrought-iron gates of the **Royal Naval College,** which Wren began in 1694 as a home, or hospital (cf. the Royal Hospital in Chelsea), for ancient mariners, but which became this school for young ones in 1873. You'll notice how the blocks part to reveal the Queen's House across the central lawns. Wren, with the help of his assistant, Hawksmoor, was at pains to preserve the river vista from the house, and there are few more majestic views in London than the awe-inspiring symmetry he achieved. Behind the col- **④** lege are two buildings you can visit. The **Painted Hall,** the college's dining hall, derives its name from the baroque murals of William and Mary (reigned 1609–1782) and assorted allegorical figures, the whole supported by *trompe l'oeil* pillars that Sir James Thornhill (who decorated the inside of St. Paul's dome, too) painted between **⑤** 1707 and 1717. In the opposite block stands the **College Chapel,** which was rebuilt after a fire in 1779 and is altogether lighter, in a more restrained, neo-Grecian style. At Christmas 1805, Admiral Nelson's body was brought from the battle of Trafalgar to lie in state here. *Royal Naval College, King William Walk, tel. 0181/858–2154. Admission free. Open daily except Thurs. 2:30–4:45.*

From the south end of the Naval College, you approach the building **⑥** that Wren's majestic quadrangles frame, the **Queen's House.** The queen whom Inigo Jones began designing it for in 1616 was James I's Anne of Denmark, but she died three years later, and it was Charles I's French wife, Henrietta Maria, who inherited the building when it was completed in 1635. It is no less than Britain's first classical building—the first, that is, to use the lessons of Italian Renaissance architecture—and is therefore of enormous importance in the history of English architecture. Inside, the Tulip Stair, named for the fleur-de-lys–style pattern on the balustrade, is especially fine, spiraling up, without a central support, to the Great Hall. The Great Hall itself is a perfect cube, exactly 40 feet in all three directions, and decorated with paintings of the Muses, the Virtues, and the Liberal Arts. *Admission: £3.50 adults, £2.50 children; see below for joint admission prices. Open as below.*

The Queen's House forms part of Greenwich's star attraction, the **⑦** **National Maritime Museum,** which you come to now. The place contains everything to do with the British at sea, in the form of paintings, models, maps, globes, sextants, uniforms (including the one Nelson died in at Trafalgar, complete with bloodstained bullet hole), and—best of all—actual boats, including a collection of ornate, gilded royal barges. *Romney Rd., tel. 0181/858–4422. Joint admission with Royal Observatory (*see below*): £3.75 adults, £2.75 children 7–16 and senior citizens. Day passport ticket (includes entrance to Queen's House, Old Royal Observatory, and Cutty Sark, and free repeat visits for 12 months): £7.45 adults, £5.45 children and senior citizens; family ticket (2 adults, 5 children) £14.50. Open Mon.–Sat. 10–6, Sun. noon–6; closed Good Friday, May Day, Dec. 24–27, Jan. 1.*

**Time Out** The **Dolphin Coffee Shop** on the museum grounds is a good place to recuperate after the rigors of the museum; non-museum visitors are also welcome.

❽ Now head up the hill in Greenwich Park overlooking the Naval College and Maritime Museum to the **Old Royal Observatory,** founded in 1675 by Charles II. That same year, Wren built it for John Flamsteed, the first Astronomer Royal, but the red ball you see on its roof has been there only since 1833. It drops every day at 1 PM, and you can set your watch by it, as the sailors on the Thames always have. In fact, nearly everyone sets their watch by it, since this "Greenwich Timeball," along with the Gate Clock inside the observatory, are the most visible manifestations of Greenwich Mean Time, since 1884 the ultimate standard for time around the world. Also here is the **Prime Meridian,** a brass line laid on the cobblestones at zero degrees longitude, one side being the eastern, one the western hemisphere. In 1948, the Old Royal Observatory lost its official status: London's glow had grown too intense, and the astronomers moved to Sussex, while the Astronomer Royal decamped to Cambridge. They left various telescopes, chronometers, and clocks for you to view in their absence. *Greenwich Park, tel. 0181/858–4422. Joint admission with National Maritime Museum (*see above*). Opening hours as for National Maritime Museum.*

**Greenwich Park** itself is one of London's oldest royal parks. It had been in existence for well over 200 years before Charles II commissioned the French landscape artist Le Nôtre (who was responsible for Versailles and for St. James's Park) to redesign it in what was, in the 1660s, the latest French fashion. The Flower Garden on the southeast side and the deer enclosure nearby are particularly pleasant. Look also for **Queen Elizabeth's Oak** on the east side, around which Henry VIII and his second queen, Anne Boleyn, Elizabeth I's mother, are said to have danced.

❾ Just outside the park boundaries, on the southwest side, stands the **Ranger's House,** a handsome early 18th-century mansion, which was the Greenwich Park Ranger's official residence during the 19th century, and now houses collections of Jacobean portraits and early musical instruments. Concerts are regularly given here. *Chesterfield Walk, Blackheath, tel. 0181/853–0035. Admission free. Open daily Apr.–Sept. 10–6, Oct.–Mar. 10–4 except for 1 hour at lunch; closed Good Friday, Dec. 24–26, Jan. 1.*

Walking back through the park toward the river, you'll enter the pretty streets of Greenwich Village to the west. There are plenty of bookstores and antiques shops for browsing, and, at the foot of ❿ Crooms Hill, the modern **Greenwich Theatre.** Officially a West End theater, despite its location, it mounts well-regarded, often star-spangled productions. *Tel. 0181/858–7755.*

**Time Out**   The **Theatre Restaurant** serves good food and even has a salad bar. You can eat here at lunchtime, or before or after a show.

Immediately opposite the theater, in two newly restored houses dating from the 1820s, is the highly unusual **Fan Museum.** The 2,000 fans here, which date from the 17th century onward, comprise the world's only such collection, and the history and purpose of these often exquisitely crafted objects are explained satisfyingly. It was the personal vision—and fan collection—of Helene Alexander that brought it into being in 1991, and the workshop and conservation and study center that she has also set up ensure that this anachronistic art has a future. *10–12 Croom's Hill, tel. 0181/858–7879. Admission: £2.50 adults, £1.50 children under 15 and senior citizens. Open Tues.–Sat. 11–4:30, Sun. noon–4:30; closed Dec. 24–26, Jan. 1.*

If you're visiting on a weekend, there are two excellent markets. The **Greenwich Antique Market** (open 8–4), on Burney Street near the museum and theater, has a lot of bric-a-brac and books, too, and is well-known among the cognoscenti as a good source for vintage clothes. The Victorian **Covered Crafts Market** (open 9–5) you'll find by the *Cutty Sark*, on College Approach. As you'd expect, this one features crafts, but there are more of the sort of ceramics, jewelry, knitwear, and leather goods that you might actually want to own than is common in such places, and you get to buy them off the people who made them.

A few miles farther downstream—another 25-minute boat ride away (though you can also get here by Network SouthEast trains from Greenwich or Charing Cross to Charlton)—is the amazing **Thames Barrier,** a mammoth piece of civil engineering that will come in handy if the water table ever again rises as high as it did in 1928 and 1953 and London is threatened with another flood. This curiously haunting ¼-mile-long barrier, with its ten upstanding steel gates, contains enough concrete to build 10 miles of six-lane freeway, and looks like a cross between the Sydney Opera House and a line of submerged alien beings. You can't visit the control room, but there's an exhibition, with videos explaining why it's necessary and how it works, and you can walk along the riverbank close to it, though the best view is from out on the river. Also here is **Hallett's Panorama,** an incongruous re-creation, with oils and sculpture, of the city of Bath. *Unity Way, off Woolwich Rd., tel. 0181/854–1373. Admission (including Hallett's Panorama): £2.25 adults, £1.40 children and senior citizens. Open weekdays 10:30–5, weekends 10:30–5:30; closed Dec. 25–26, Jan. 1.*

# The Thames Upstream

The Thames is Britain's longest river. It winds its way through the Cotswolds, beyond the "dreaming spires" of Oxford and past majestic Windsor Castle—far more the lazy, leafy country river than the dark gray urban waterway you see in London. Once you leave the city center, going west, or upstream, you reach a series of former villages—Chiswick, Kew, Richmond, Putney—that, apart from the roar of aircraft coming in to land at Heathrow a few miles farther west, still retain a peaceful, almost rural atmosphere, especially in places where parkland rolls down to the riverbank. In fact, it was really only at the beginning of this century that these villages expanded into London proper. The royal palaces and grand houses that dot the area were built not as town houses but as country residences with easy access to London by river.

Each of the places we list here could easily absorb a whole day of your time (Hampton Court is especially huge), and it might be wise to resist attempting to see everything. Access is fairly easy: The District Line of the Underground runs out to Kew and Richmond, as does Network SouthEast from Waterloo, which also serves Twickenham and Hampton Court. Chiswick House can be reached by tube to Turnham Green, then the E3 bus; or by tube to Hammersmith and Bus 290.

Of course, the best, if slowest, way to go is by river. Boats depart Westminster Pier (just by Big Ben) for Kew (1½ hours), Richmond (2–3 hours), and Hampton Court (4 hours) several times a day in summer, less frequently from October through March. As you can tell from those sailing times, the boat trip is worth taking only if you make it an integral part of your day out, and even then, be aware that it can get very breezy on the water and that the scenery going upstream is by no means constantly fascinating. *Westminster Pier, tel. 0171/930–4097.*

## Chiswick and Kew

**Chiswick** is the nearest of these Thames-side destinations to London, with Kew just a mile or so beyond it. Much of Chiswick today is a nondescript suburb developed at the beginning of this century. But, incongruously stranded among the terraced houses, a number of fine 18th-century houses and a charming little village survive. The peacock of the flock is **Chiswick House,** built circa 1725 by the Earl of Burlington as a country residence in which to entertain friends, and as a kind of temple to the arts. It is the very model of a Palladian villa, inspired by the Villa Capra near Vicenza in northeastern Italy. The house fans out from a central octagonal room in perfect symmetry, guarded by statues of Burlington's heroes, Palladio himself and his disciple Inigo Jones. Burlington's friends—Pope, Swift, Gay, and Handel among them—were well qualified to adorn a temple to the arts.

This is the Lord Burlington of Burlington House, Piccadilly, home of the Royal Academy and, of course, Burlington Arcade. It goes without saying that he was a great connoisseur, and an important patron, of the arts, but he was also an accomplished architect in his own right, fascinated—obsessed even—by the architecture and art of the Italian Renaissance and ancient Rome, with which he'd fallen in love during his Italian grand tour (every well-bred boy's rite of passage). Along with William Kent (1685–1748), who designed the interiors and the rambling gardens here, Burlington did an awful lot to disseminate the Palladian ideals around Britain: Chiswick House sparked enormous interest, and you'll see these forms reflected in hundreds of subsequent English stately homes both small and large. *Burlington La., tel. 0181/995–0508. Admission: £2.20 adults, £1.60 senior citizens, £1.10 children under 16. Open Apr.–Sept., daily 10–6; Oct.–Mar., daily 10–4; closed 1 hour at lunch and Dec. 25–26, Jan. 1.*

Close to Chiswick House, but unprotected from the six-lane Great West Road, which remains a main route to the West Country, is **Hogarth's House,** where the painter lived from 1749 until his death in 1764. Although the poor house is besieged by the surrounding traffic, it contains a little museum consisting mostly of the amusingly moralistic engravings for which Hogarth is best known, including the most famous one of all, *The Rake's Progress* series of 1735. *Hogarth La., tel. 0181/994–6757. Admission free. Open Apr.–Sept.,*

*Mon.–Sat. 11–6, Sun. 2–6; Oct.–Mar., Mon.–Sat. 11–4, Sun. 2–4; closed Good Friday, first 3 weeks of Sept., last 3 weeks of Dec., Jan. 1.*

**Church Street** (reached by an underpass) is the nearest thing to a sleepy country village street in all of London, despite its proximity to the Great West Road. Follow it down to the Thames and turn left at its foot to reach the sturdy 18th-century riverfront houses of **Chiswick Mall.** The half-mile walk along here takes you far away from London and into a world of elegance and calm.

**Time Out** You will pass several riverside pubs as you head along this stretch of the Thames toward Hammermith Bridge. The **Dove** is the prettiest, if the most crowded, with its terrace hanging over the water, though the food is better at the **Blue Anchor,** which you reach first.

There's a similarly peaceful walk to be had about a mile to the west, along the 18th-century river frontage of **Strand-on-the-Green,** whose houses look over the narrow towpath to the river, their tidy brick facades covered with wisteria and roses in summer. Strand-on-the-Green ends at Kew Bridge, opposite which is **Kew Green,** where local teams play cricket on summer Sundays. All around it are fine 18th-century houses, and, in the center, a church in which the painters Gainsborough and John Zoffany (1733–1810) are buried.

The village atmosphere of Kew is still distinct, making this one of the most desirable areas of outer London. What makes Kew famous, though, are the Royal Botanic Gardens, known simply as **Kew Gardens:** a spectacular 300 acres of public gardens, containing more than 60,000 species of plants. In addition, this is the country's leading botanical institute, with strong royal associations. Until 1840, when Kew Gardens was handed over to the nation, it had been the grounds of two royal residences: the White House (formerly Kew House), and Richmond Lodge, or the Dutch House. George II and Queen Caroline lived at Richmond Lodge in the 1720s, while their eldest son, Frederick, Prince of Wales, and his wife, Princess Augusta, came to the White House during the 1730s.

The royal wives were keen gardeners. Queen Caroline got to work on her grounds, while next door Frederick's pleasure garden was developed as a botanic garden by his widow after his death. She introduced all kinds of "exotics," foreign plants brought back to England by botanists. Caroline was aided by a skilled head gardener and by the architect Sir William Chambers, who built a series of temples and follies, of which the crazy 10-story **Pagoda** (1762), visible for miles around, is the star turn. The celebrated botanist Sir Joseph Banks (1743–1820) then took charge of Kew, which developed rapidly in both its roles—as a beautiful landscaped garden, and as a center of study and research.

In 1802, George III, who had been brought up largely at Kew, united the two estates, knocking down the White House, which he intended to rebuild on a more lavish scale, and living in the Dutch House meanwhile. But George was, famously, losing his reason, and the new palace never got built. The Dutch House became known as **Kew Palace** and remains to this day quietly domestic. The little formal gardens to its rear were redeveloped in 1969 as a 17th-century garden. These, too, are a pleasure to see, with their trim hedges, statuary, and carefully laid-out plants and flowers. *Tel. 0181/940–3321. Admission: £1.20 adults, 90p senior citizens, 80p children under 16. Open Apr.–Sept., daily 11–5:30.*

It is not the palace that makes anyone remember a visit to Kew, though, but the two great 19th-century greenhouses filled with tropical plants, many of which have been there as long as their housing. Both the **Palm House** and the **Temperate House** were designed by Sir Decimus Burton, the first opening in 1848, the second in 1899 (though it had been begun 40 years earlier). The older Palm House, with its ornate cast-iron supports and curvaceous glass walls, is generally more celebrated than the later building, although on its completion the latter was the biggest greenhouse in the world and today contains the biggest greenhouse plant in the world, a Chilean wine palm rooted in 1846. You can climb the spiral staircase almost to the roof and look down on this and the dense tropical profusion from the walkway.

The **Princess of Wales Conservatory,** the latest and the largest plant house at Kew, was opened in 1987 by Princess Diana. Under its bold glass roofs, designed to maximize energy conservation, there are no less than 10 climatic zones, their temperatures all precisely controlled by computer. Within a few minutes you can move from the humid pool-and-swamp habitats, where the Amazon water lily flourishes, to the cloud-forest zone, which reproduces the conditions on the upper reaches of tropical mountains, through to the savanna of eastern Africa.

The **Centre for Economic Botany** is housed in the newly constructed Joseph Banks Building, the majority of which is devoted to Kew's research collection on economic botany and to its library. But the public can enjoy exhibitions here on the theme of plants in everyday life. *Admission free. Open Mon.–Sat. 9:10–4:30, Sun. 9:30–5:30.*

The plant houses make Kew worth visiting even in the depths of winter, but in spring and summer the gardens come into their own. In late spring, the woodland nature reserve of **Queen Charlotte's Cottage Gardens** is carpeted in bluebells; a little later, the **Rhododendron Dell** and the **Azalea Garden** become swathed in brilliant color. High summer features glorious displays of roses and water lilies, while fall is the time to see the heather garden, near the pagoda. Whatever time of year you visit, something is in bloom, and your journey is never wasted. *Royal Botanic Gardens, tel. 0181/940–1171. Admission: £3.50 adults, £1.80 senior citizens and students, £1.30 children under 16. Gardens open at 9:30 daily, glasshouses at 10; closing time varies according to sunset, usually 4 PM in winter, later in summer.*

**Time Out**    **Maids of Honour** (288 Kew Rd.), the most traditional of Olde Worlde English tearooms, is named for the famous tarts invented here and still baked by hand on the premises. It's only open for tea (Tues.–Sat. 2:45–5:30).

## Osterley Park

You reach **Osterley Park** by getting off the Piccadilly Line five stops before Heathrow Airport, then making a 15-minute walk from the station. A unique hybrid of Tudor and 18th-century architecture, Osterley was built in the 1560s, then tinkered with extensively by Robert Adam two centuries later. The result is a Tudor brick mansion with a pepper-pot tower at each corner and a sweeping central staircase leading to an incongruous Doric-columned doorway with a carved pediment. The inside is maximum Adam, down to much of the furniture. The architect himself described it as being all "delicacy, gaiety, grace, and beauty," with "fanciful figures and winding foliage." Sir Horace Walpole, on the other hand, found much of it "too theatric"—an attribute rather in its favor if you don't have to live in it but are just visiting. The outrageously elaborate neo-Gothic blue, green, and gold ceiling (with matching frilly window blinds and handloomed carpet) in the Drawing Room, and the all-over fresco work of the Etruscan Room ("like Wedgwood's vase," said Walpole) are nothing if not arresting. When it all gets to be too much, you can retire to the gardens, designed by William Chambers (who was responsible for much of Kew Gardens, too), with an Adam greenhouse. *Isleworth, tel. 0181/560–3918. Admission: £3.50 adults, £1.75 children under 16. Open Apr.–Oct., Wed.–Sat. 1–5, Sun. 11–5; closed Nov.–Mar.*

## Richmond

Named after the palace Henry VII built here in 1500, **Richmond** is still a welcoming and extremely pretty riverside "village" with many handsome (and mountainously expensive) houses, many antiques shops, a Victorian theater, and, best of all, the biggest of London's royal parks, **Richmond Park.** Charles I enclosed this one in 1637, as with practically all the parks, for hunting purposes. Unlike the others, however, Richmond Park still has wild red and fallow deer roaming its 2,470 acres of grassland and heath, among the oldest oaks you're likely to see—vestiges of the medieval forests that once encroached on London from all sides. **White Lodge,** inside the park, was built for George II in 1729. Edward VIII was born here; now it houses the Royal Ballet School. You can walk from the park past the fine 18th-century houses in and around **Richmond Hill** to the river, admiring first the view from the top. At the Thames, you may notice Quinlan Terry's recent **Richmond Riverside** development, which met with the approval of England's architectural advisor, Prince Charles, for its classical facades, and was vilified by many others for playing it safe.

**Time Out** **The Cricketers** on Richmond Green serves a good pub lunch. The modern, partially glass-roofed **Caffé Mamma,** on Hill Street, serves inexpensive Italian food. **Beeton's,** on Hill Rise, offers a good, traditional English breakfast, lunch, and afternoon tea, as well as proper dinners.

## Ham House and Marble Hill House

To the west of Richmond Park, overlooking the Thames and nearly opposite the oddly named Eel Pie Island, stands **Ham House.** The house was built in 1610 by Sir Thomas Vavasour, knight marshal to James I, then refurbished later the same century by the Duke and Duchess of Lauderdale, who, although not particularly nice (a contemporary called the duchess "the coldest friend and the most violent enemy that ever was known"), managed to produce one of the finest houses in Britain at the time. Now that £2 million has been sunk into restoring Ham House—a project overseen by the National Trust, and still in progress—its splendor can be appreciated afresh. The formerly empty library has been filled with 17th- and 18th-century volumes; the original decorations in the Great Hall, Round Gallery, and Great Staircase have been replicated; and all the furniture and fittings, on permanent loan from the V&A, have been cleaned and restored. The 17th-century gardens, too, merit a visit in their own right. You can reach Ham from Richmond on Bus 65 or 371, or by one of Greater London's most pleasant rural walks, along the eastern riverbank south from Richmond Bridge for half an hour or so. *Ham St., Richmond, tel. 0181/940–1950. Admission: £4 adults, £2 children under 16 and senior citizens; admission to gardens free. Open Mar.–Oct., Sat.–Wed. 1–5; Nov.–Dec., weekends 1–5. Closed Jan.–Feb.*

On the northern bank of the Thames, almost opposite Ham House, stands another mansion, this one a near-perfect example of a Palladian villa. **Marble Hill House** was built in the 1720s by George II for his mistress, the "exceedingly respectable and respected" Henrietta Howard. Later the house was occupied by Mrs. Fitzherbert, who was secretly married to the Prince Regent (later George IV) in 1785. Marble Hill House was restored in 1901 and opened to the public two years later, looking very much like it did in Georgian times. A ferry service operates during the summer from Ham House across the river; access by foot is via a half-hour walk south along the west bank from Richmond Bridge. *Richmond Rd., Twickenham, tel. 0181/892–5115. Admission free. Open Easter–Sept., daily 10–6; Oct.–Easter, daily 10–4; closed Dec. 24–25, Jan. 1.*

## Hampton Court Palace

Some 20 miles from central London, on a loop of the Thames upstream from Richmond, lies **Hampton Court,** one of London's oldest royal palaces, more like a small town in size, and requiring a day of your time to do it justice. The magnificent Tudor brick house was begun in 1514 by Cardinal Wolsey, the ambitious and worldly lord chancellor (roughly, prime minister) of England and archbishop of York. He wanted it to be the absolute best palace in the land, and in this he succeeded so effectively that Henry VIII grew deeply envious, whereupon Wolsey felt obliged to give Hampton Court to the king. Henry moved in in 1525, adding a great hall and chapel, and proceeded to live much of his rumbustious life here. James I made further improvements at the beginning of the 17th century, but by the end of the century the palace was getting rather run-down. Plans were drawn up by the joint monarchs William III and Mary II to demolish the building and replace it with a still larger and more splendid structure in conscious emulation of the great palace of Versailles outside of Paris. However, the royal purse wouldn't stretch quite that far. It was decided to keep the original buildings but add a new complex adjoining them at the rear, for which Wren was commissioned, and his graceful South Wing is one of the highlights of the whole palace. (A serious fire badly damaged some of Wren's chambers in 1986, but they were restored and opened again in 1992, with some of the Tudor features he had covered up uncovered again.) William and, especially, Mary loved Hampton Court and left their mark on the place—see their fine collections of Delftware and other porcelain.

The site beside the slow-moving Thames is perfect. The palace itself, steeped in history, hung with priceless paintings, full of echoing cobbled courtyards and cavernous Tudor kitchens, complete with deer pies and cooking pots—not to mention the ghost of Catherine Howard, who is still abroad, screaming her innocence (of adultery) to an unheeding Henry VIII—is set in a fantastic array of ornamental gardens, lakes, and ponds. Among the horticultural highlights are an Elizabethan Knot Garden, Henry VIII's Pond Garden, the enormous conical yews around the Fountain Garden, and the Great Vine near the Banqueting House, planted in 1768 and still

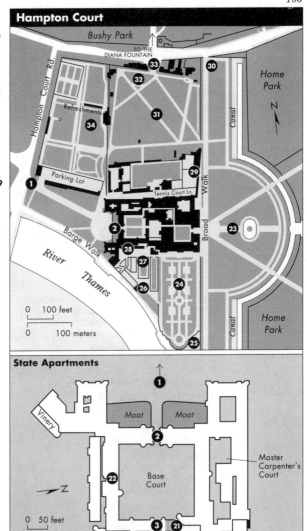

**Hampton Court**

Bushy Park

TO THE DIANA FOUNTAIN

Home Park

Hampton Court Rd.

Refreshments

Parking Lot

Tennis Court Ln.

Barge Walk

River Thames

Broad Walk

Canal

Home Park

N

0   100 feet

0   100 meters

**State Apartments**

Vinery

Moat   Moat

Base Court

Master Carpenter's Court

N

0   50 feet

0   20 meters

Colonnade

Wren's

Clock Court

Round Kitchen Court

Fountain Court

Chapel Court

producing Black Hamburg grapes, which you can buy in season. Best of all is the celebrated maze, which you enter to the north of the palace. It was planted in 1714 and is truly fiendish.

Royalty ceased living here with George III; poor George preferred the seclusion of Kew, where he was finally confined in his madness. The private apartments that range down one side of the palace are now occupied by pensioners of the Crown. Known as "grace and favor" apartments, they are among the most covetably positioned homes in the country, with a surfeit of peace and history on their doorsteps. *East Molesey, tel. 0181/977–8441. Admission: apartments and maze £6.50 adults, £4.90 senior citizens, £4.30 children under 16; maze only £1.50 adults and senior citizens, £1 children; grounds free. State apartments open Apr.–Oct., Tues.–Sun. 9:30–6, Mon. 10:15–6; Nov.–Mar., Tues.–Sun. 9:30–4:30, Mon. 10:15–4:30; grounds open daily 8–dusk. Closed Good Friday, Dec. 24–25, Jan. 1.*

# Sightseeing Checklists

## Historic Buildings and Sites

**Buckingham Palace.** *See* Westminster and Royal London.
**Clarence House.** *See* St. James's and Mayfair.
**Downing Street.** *See* Westminster and Royal London.
**Lambeth Palace.** *See* The South Bank.
**Lancaster House.** *See* St. James's and Mayfair.
**Mansion House.** *See* The City.
**Marlborough House.** *See* St. James's and Mayfair.
**Palace of Westminster.** *See* Westminster and Royal London.
**St. James's Palace.** *See* St. James's and Mayfair.
**Somerset House.** *See* Soho and Covent Garden.

## Museums and Galleries

**Bank of England Museum.** *See* The City.
**Bankside Gallery.** *See* The South Bank.
**Banqueting House.** *See* Westminster and Royal London.
**Barbican Gallery.** *See* The City.
**Battle of Britain Museum.** *See* **Royal Air Force Museum.**
**Bethnal Green Museum of Childhood.** *See* The East End.
**H.M.S.** *Belfast.* *See* The South Bank.
**British Museum.** *See* Bloomsbury and Legal London.
**Cabinet War Rooms.** *See* Westminster and Royal London.
**Canal Museum.** *See* Regents Park and Hampstead.
**Carlyle's House.** *See* Chelsea and Belgravia.
**Centre for Economic Botany.** *See* The Thames Upstream.
**Chelsea Royal Hospital.** *See* **Royal Hospital and Museum.**
**Chiswick House.** *See* The Thames Upstream.
**Clink Prison.** *See* The South Bank.
**Clock Museum.** *See* The City.
**Commonwealth Institute.** *See* Knightsbridge, Kensington, and Holland Park.
**Court Dress Collection.** *See* **Kensington Palace.**
**Courtauld Institute Art Galleries.** See Soho and Covent Garden.
**Crown Jewels.** *See* **Tower of London.**
*Cutty Sark.* *See* Greenwich.
**Design Museum.** *See* The South Bank.
**Dickens House.** *See* Bloomsbury and Legal London.

**Dulwich Picture Gallery.** *See* Off the Beaten Track.
**Fan Museum.** *See* Greenwich.
**Faraday's Laboratory and Museum.** *See* St. James's and Mayfair.
**Florence Nightingale Museum.** *See* The South Bank.
**Foundling Hospital Art Treasures.** *See* Bloomsbury and Legal London.
**Freud Museum.** *See* Regent's Park and Hampstead.
**Geffrye Museum of Furniture and Decorative Arts.** *See* The East End.
*Gipsy Moth IV*. *See* Greenwich.
**Guards Museum.** See Westminster and Royal London.
**Guildhall.** *See* The City.
**Ham House.** *See* The Thames Upstream.
**Hampton Court Palace.** *See* The Thames Upstream.
**Hayward Gallery.** *See* The South Bank.
**Heinz Gallery.** The gallery of the Royal Institute of British Architects, with a changing program of exhibitions. *21 Portman Sq., tel. 0171/580–5533. Admission free. Open weekdays (during exhibitions) 11–5, Sat. 10–1; closed national holidays and Aug.*
**Hogarth's House.** *See* The Thames Upstream.
**Horniman Museum and Library.** *See* What to See and Do with Children.
**Imperial War Museum.** *See* The South Bank.
**Institute of Contemporary Arts.** *See* Westminster and Royal London.
**Iveagh Bequest.** *See* Regent's Park and Hampstead.
**The Jewish Museum.** *See* Bloomsbury and Legal London.
**Dr. Johnson's House.** *See* The City.
*Kathleen & May*. *See* The South Bank.
**Keats House.** *See* Regent's Park and Hampstead.
**Kensington Palace and Court Dress Collection.** *See* Knightsbridge, Kensington, and Holland Park.
**Kenwood House.** *See* **Iveagh Bequest.**
**Kew Palace.** *See* The Thames Upstream.
**Leighton House Museum and Art Gallery.** *See* Knightsbridge, Kensington, and Holland Park.
**Linley Sambourne House.** *See* Knightsbridge, Kensington, and Holland Park.
**London Toy and Model Museum.** *See* What to See and Do with Children.
**London Transport Museum.** *See* Soho and Covent Garden.
**Marble Hill House.** *See* The Thames Upstream.
**The Monument.** *See* The City.
**Museum of Garden History.** *See* The South Bank.
**Museum of London.** *See* The City.
**Museum of the Moving Image.** *See* The South Bank.
**National Army Museum.** *See* Chelsea and Belgravia.
**National Gallery.** *See* Westminster and Royal London.
**National Maritime Museum.** *See* Greenwich.
**National Portrait Gallery.** *See* Soho and Covent Garden.
**National Postal Museum.** *See* The City.
**Natural History Museum.** *See* Knightsbridge, Kensington, and Holland Park.
**North Woolwich Old Station Museum.** *See* Off the Beaten Track.
**Old Royal Observatory.** *See* Greenwich.
**Old St. Thomas's Hospital Operating Theatre Museum.** *See* The South Bank.
**Osterley Park House.** *See* The Thames Upstream.
**Percival David Foundation of Chinese Art.** *See* Bloomsbury and Legal London.
**Pollock's Toy Museum.** An 18th-century house containing a treasure

trove of dolls, dolls' houses, toy theaters, teddy bears, and folk toys. *1 Scala St., tel. 0171/636–3452. Admission: £2 adults, 75p children. Open Mon.–Sat. 10–5. Check for national holiday opening.*

**Prince Henry's Room.** *See* Bloomsbury and Legal London.

**Public Records Office Museum.** Exhibitions of historic documents, including a copy of the Magna Carta. *Chancery La., tel. 0171/876– 3444. Admission free. Open weekdays 9:30–4:45; closed national holidays, first half of Oct.*

**Queen's Gallery.** *See* Westminster and Royal London.

**Queen's Tower.** *See* Knightsbridge, Kensington, and Holland Park.

**Ranger's House.** *See* Greenwich.

**Royal Academy of Arts.** *See* St. James's and Mayfair.

**Royal Air Force Museum.** *See* Off the Beaten Track.

**Royal Hospital and Museum.** *See* Chelsea and Belgravia.

**Royal London Hospital Archives.** *See* The East End.

**Royal Mews.** *See* Westminster and Royal London.

**Royal Naval College.** *See* Greenwich.

**St. Bride's Crypt Museum.** *See* Bloomsbury and Legal London.

**Science Museum.** *See* Knightsbridge, Kensington, and Holland Park.

**Serpentine Gallery.** *See* Hyde Park, Kensington Gardens, and Notting Hill.

**Shakespeare's Globe Museum.** *See* The South Bank.

**Sir John Soane's Museum.** *See* Bloomsbury and Legal London.

**Tate Gallery.** *See* Westminster and Royal London.

**Theatre Museum.** *See* Soho and Covent Garden.

**Tower Bridge.** *See* The City.

**Tower Hill Pageant.** *See* The City.

**Tower of London.** *See* The City.

**Victoria and Albert Museum.** *See* Knightsbridge, Kensington, and Holland Park.

**Wallace Collection.** *See* St. James's and Mayfair.

**Wellington Museum.** *See* St. James's and Mayfair.

**Westminster Abbey Undercroft, Pyx Chamber, and Treasury.** *See* Westminster and Royal London.

**Whitechapel Gallery.** *See* The East End.

**William Morris Gallery.** An 18th-century house in northeast London where the artistic polymath William Morris (craftsman, painter, and writer) lived for eight years, containing many examples of his work and that of his fellows in the Arts and Crafts Movement. *Water House, Lloyd Park, Forest Rd., tel. 0181/527–3782. Open Tues.– Sat. 10–1 and 2–5, first Sun. each month 10–12 and 2–5; closed national holidays.*

**Wimbledon Lawn Tennis Museum.** Displays on the history and development of the game in a building immediately behind the celebrated Centre Court. *Church Rd., tel. 0181/946–6131. Admission: £2 adults, £1 children under 16 and senior citizens. Open Tues.–Sat. 11–5, Sun. 2–5; closed national holidays, Dec. 24–Jan. 2 and during the 2-week Championship each June.*

## Parks and Gardens

The majority of London's large open spaces are the **Royal Parks,** now administered by a government department but formerly all owned by the royal family and used for hunting and other relaxations. Those in central London are:

**Green Park.** *See* St. James's and Mayfair.

**Hyde Park.** *See* Hyde Park, Kensington Gardens, and Notting Hill.

**Kensington Gardens.** *See* Hyde Park, Kensington Gardens, and Notting Hill.
**Primrose Hill.** *See* Regent's Park and Hampstead.
**Regent's Park.** *See* Regent's Park and Hampstead.
**St. James's Park.** *See* Westminster and Royal London.

The Royal Parks in outer London are:

**Bushey Park,** near Hampton Court
**Hampton Court Park.** *See* The Thames Upstream.
**Richmond Park.** *See* The Thames Upstream.
*All the above parks are open daily from dawn to dusk.*

Also well worth exploring is **Hampstead Heath** on the range of hills overlooking central London to the north (*see* Regent's Park and Hampstead).

Two specialist gardens regularly open to the public are:

**Chelsea Physic Garden.** *See* Chelsea and Belgravia.
**Royal Botanic Gardens.** *See* The Thames Upstream.

## Churches

The following is no more than a small selection of London's many interesting historic churches. Note that since most small churches are staffed entirely by voluntary helpers, opening times may vary. Visitors are always welcome to attend Sunday services; remember that, in the City especially, weekday services are frequently held as well. Admission to churches is nearly always free, but donations are always welcome; churches receive no government assistance toward the cost of building maintenance.

**All Saints, Margaret Street.** An outstanding example of ornate mid-19th century Gothic Revival style. *Margaret St., tel. 0171/ 636–1788. Open daily 7–7; closed after morning service national holidays.*
**All Souls, Langham Place.** *See* St. James's and Mayfair.
**Brompton Oratory.** *See* Knightsbridge, Kensington, and Holland Park.
**Chapel Royal, St. James's Palace.** *See* St. James's and Mayfair.
**Ely Chapel.** *See* St. Etheldreda.
**Grosvenor Chapel.** *See* St. James's and Mayfair.
**Guards Chapel.** *See* Westminster and Royal London.
**Queen's Chapel.** *See* St. James's and Mayfair.
**St. Bartholomew the Great.** *See* The City.
**St. Bride.** *See* The City.
**St. Clement Danes.** *See* Soho and Covent Garden.
**St. Etheldreda** (Ely Chapel). A 13th-century chapel restored to Roman Catholicism in the 19th century and renovated in the 1930s. The oldest Roman Catholic place of worship in London. *Ely Pl., tel. 0171/405–1061. Open daily 7–7.*
**St. George, Hanover Square.** *See* St. James's and Mayfair.
**St. James's, Piccadilly.** *See* St. James's and Mayfair.
**St. Margaret's Westminster.** *See* Westminster and Royal London.
**St. Martin-in-the-Fields.** *See* Westminster and Royal London.
**St. Mary-le-Bow.** *See* The City.
**St. Mary-le-Strand.** *See* Soho and Covent Garden.
**St. Mary Woolnoth.** Damaged in the Great Fire, this church was repaired by Wren but rebuilt by Hawksmoor in the 1720s in the English Baroque style. *Lombard St., tel. 0171/626–9701. Open weekdays 8–5; closed national holidays.*
**St. Paul's Cathedral.** *See* The City.

**St. Stephen Walbrook.** *See* The City.
**Savoy Chapel.** An early 16th-century chapel rebuilt in the mid-19th century. Since the 18th century it has been a chapel of the British monarch, and it's also the chapel of the Royal Victorian Order. *Savoy Hill, The Strand. Open Tues.–Sat. 11:30–3:30, Sun. services 11:15. Closed Aug.–Sept.*
**Southwark Cathedral.** *See* The South Bank.
**Temple Church.** *See* Bloomsbury and Legal London.
**Westminster Abbey.** *See* Westminster and Royal London.
**Westminster Cathedral.** *See* Westminster and Royal London.

### Other Places of Interest

**Barbican Arts Centre.** *See* The City.
**Brass-Rubbing Centre.** *See* Westminster and Royal London.
**Chessington World of Adventures.** *See* What to See and Do with Children.
**Guinness World of Records.** *See* Soho and Covent Garden.
**Highgate Cemetery.** *See* Regent's Park and Hampstead.
**Lloyd's of London.** *See* The City.
**London Brass-Rubbing Centre.** *See* Westminster and Royal London.
**London Dungeon.** *See* The South Bank.
**London Planetarium.** *See* Regent's Park and Hampstead.
**London Stock Exchange.** *See* The City.
**London Zoo.** *See* Regent's Park and Hampstead.
**Madame Tussaud's.** *See* Regent's Park and Hampstead.
**Thames Barrier Visitor Centre.** *See* Off the Beaten Track.
**Wembley Stadium.** *See* Off the Beaten Track.

# What to See and Do with Children

On London's traditional sightseeing circuit, make for the **Royal Mews** (*see* Westminster and Royal London), where some of the queen's horses can be seen up close, the **Changing of the Guard,** with its colorful pomp and circumstance (*see* Westminster and Royal London), the **Whispering Gallery** in **St. Paul's Cathedral** (*see* The City), where it is fun to try the echo, and the gruesome instruments of torture on show in the **Martin Tower** in the **Tower of London** (*see* The City). Climb the 311 steps to the top of the **Monument** (*see* The City), or see the interactive video-annotated views from the walkways of **Tower Bridge** (*see* The City). At **Hampton Court** see who can find their way out of the maze first.

**Kidsline** is a computerized information service with details on current events that might interest children. Call 0171/222–8000 during office hours for information.

Museums of specific interest to children include the **London Transport Museum** in Covent Garden (*see* Soho and Covent Garden); the **Science Museum,** where there are lots of opportunities for hands-on discovery; the **London Toy and Model Museum** in Paddington, with its many model trains; the **Bethnal Green Museum of Childhood** in east London (*see* The East End), which has traditional toys, dolls, dolls' houses, and puppets; and the **Horniman Museum,** an educational museum set in 16 acres of gardens in south London with well-displayed ethnographic and natural history collections, a Music Gallery, and a colony of honey bees visibly at work in their glass-fronted hive. Many other museums—e.g., the Natural History Museum, the

Museum of London, and the National Gallery—provide children's quizzes and vacation activities.

**London Toy & Model Museum,** *21–23 Craven Hill, tel. 0171/262–9450. Admission: £3.50 adults, £2.50 senior citizens, £2 children under 15. Open Tues.–Sat. 10–5:30, Sun. 11–5:30; closed all Mons. except national holidays, Good Friday, Dec. 24–25, Jan. 1.*

**Horniman Museum,** *100 London Rd., Forest Hill, tel. 0181/699–1872/2339. Admission free. Open Mon.–Sat. 10:30–6, Sun.2–6.*

Other attractions of interest include **Guinness World of Records,** in the Trocadero Centre at Piccadilly Circus (*see* Soho and Covent Garden), the **London Dungeon,** in Tooley Street (*see* The South Bank)—though the latter isn't suitable for young children or for sensitive children of any age—and the **London Zoo** in Regent's Park (*see* Regent's Park and Hampstead).

Older children might appreciate the Madame Tussaud's offshoot, **Rock Circus,** where replicas of everyone from Elvis to Madonna go through their paces amid the odd laser and a *loud* soundtrack. At the other extreme of automated entertainment, the **Cabaret Mechanical Theatre** is a charming small exhibition of hand-built wood and metal sculptures large and small, which move when buttons are pressed or handles cranked. Some are very funny and more suitable for adults.

A novel idea might be to try brass rubbing, at the **Brass-Rubbing Centre** in Westminster Abbey or at the **London Brass-Rubbing Centre** at St. Martin-in-the-Fields Church in Trafalgar Square (*see* Westminster and Royal London).

There are two sophisticated theme parks on the very edge of the built-up area of the capital city: **Chessington World of Adventures,** to the south, where there is also a zoo, and **ThorpePark,** toward the west.

**Cabaret Mechanical Theatre,** *33–34 The Market, Covent Garden Piazza, tel. 0171/379–7961. Admission: £1.75 adults, £1 children and senior citizens. Open Tues.–Sun. 10–6:30, Mon. noon–6:30.*

**Chessington World of Adventures,** *Leatherhead Rd., Chessington, Surrey, tel. 013727/27227. Admission: £13 adults, £10.75 children, £5.75 senior citizens. Open daily 10–5. Oct.–Mar. the zoo alone is open.*

**Rock Circus,** *London Pavilion, Piccadilly Circus, tel. 0171/734–8025. Admission: £6.50 adults, £4.50 children, $5.50 senior citizens. Open Sun., Mon., Wed., Thurs. 11–9, Tues. noon–9, Fri. and Sat. 11–10; closed Dec. 25.*

**Thorpe Park,** *Staines Rd., Chertsey, Surrey, tel. 01932/562633. Admission: £9.95 adults, £8.95 children under 14, £7 senior citizens. Open daily Apr.–Oct. 10–6.*

**Chiselhurst Caves,** on the southeastern edge of the city, are the remains of old chalk mines said to date from Roman times; the tours take place by lamplight. *Old Hill, Chiselhurst, tel. 0181/467–3264. Admission: £2.50 adults, £1.20 children under 16. Open Easter–Sept., daily 11–5; Oct.–Easter, weekends 11–4:30. Long tours Sun. at 2:30. Cost of tours: £4 adults, £2 children.*

**Hampstead Heath** (*see* Regent's Park and Hampstead) is a superb place for a walk. Join the kite-flyers on Parliament Hill Fields on the southern slopes of the heath throughout the year, and if there's snow get your hands on a toboggan—this is one of London's best tobogganing spots.

Another fun outdoor activity is boating on the **Serpentine,** the lake in **Hyde Park** (*see* Hyde Park, Kensington Gardens, and Notting Hill).

Places where children might actually enjoy shopping are **Covent Garden** and **Hamley's,** the huge toy shop in Regent's Street. At Christmas, a visit to Father Christmas at **Selfridges,** on Oxford Street, is generally reckoned to be the best in London; be prepared for lengthy crowds in December—those in the know come in November.

# Off the Beaten Track

**Regent's Canal** From **Camden Lock,** follow the tow path of the **Regent's Canal** (*see* Regent's Park and Hampstead) east for a fascinating view of London and Londoners at home. The canal runs past the elegant houses of Islington and then through increasingly less prosperous areas, eventually reaching the Thames at Limehouse. There's a great deal of interest for the curious observer—private homes and semisecret back gardens running down to the water, wide views south to the tower blocks of the City, and old industrial areas. The canal runs alongside Victoria Park in Hackney, one of the capital's first public parks. Follow it the other way and you're led the back way around the perimeter of Regent's Park and on through Paddington (part posh villas, part housing projects) to Little Venice, literally one of London's more hidden backwaters. Refresh yourself at the picturesque Bridge House pub (Delamere Terr.). There are numerous exits from the canal towpath to the surrounding streets.

**Docklands** London's most rapidly changing neighborhood has emerged from what only a decade ago was an even less frequented area—partly low-cost residential, partly working docks, partly wasteland. Now it houses national newspaper offices, a brand new riverside business community containing Britain's tallest building, sports facilities, and even a farm. Its boundaries are roughly defined by **Tower Bridge** and the **Design Museum** to the west (*see* Butler's Wharf to Old St. Thomas's in The South Bank, *above*), and **London City Airport** and the **Royal Docks** to the east, though the area inside a loop of the Thames called the **Isle of Dogs** is of most interest. Take the high-tech **Docklands Light Railway** (DLR) to Crossharbour (change at Bank) and pick up a free map at the **London Docklands Visitors Centre,** where an exhibition, information desk, and film introduce the area. *3 Limeharbour, Isle of Dogs, E14, tel. 0171/512–1111. Open weekdays 9–6, weekends and holidays 10–4:30. Bus tours of the area depart Tues. at 2, Thurs. at 10:30, Sun. at 11:30.*

Off season, the upbeat tone is belied by the absence of crowds, and indeed, Docklands is by no means an unmitigated success story. More than 16,000 new homes have been constructed, but many remain unsold; and much of the 28 million square feet of commercial and industrial development lies empty. **Canary Wharf,** with its 50-story **Tower** (1 Canada Sq.) by the architect of New York City's World Trade Center, Cesar Pelli, is the most notorious development project Britain has seen in years. Olympia & York, the Canadian developers, went bust; bomb scares closed the observation deck; the arts funding ran out; shops stayed unlet; jokes were made. But here are waterfront promenades and pubs, a new London piazza called **Cabot Square,** a large concert hall, and a (rather unexciting) shopping mall. *Canary Wharf Visitor Center, Cabot Pl. E, E14, tel. 0171/418–2000.*

# American Express offers Travelers Cheques built for two.

Cheques *for Two*<sup>SM</sup> from American Express are the Travelers Cheques that allow either of you to use them because both of you have signed them. And only one of you needs to be present to purchase them.

Cheques *for Two* are accepted anywhere regular American Express Travelers Cheques are, which is just about everywhere. So stop by your bank, AAA* or any American Express Travel Service Office and ask for Cheques *for Two*.

A different approach is to get off the DLR at **Island Gardens** for a spectacular view across the river to the Naval College of Greenwich—which you can walk to via the **Greenwich Foot Tunnel** under the Thames. There's a small information center next to the DLR station (open weekdays 10–4:30). Or on a summer's evening, you can bring a picnic to the Isle of Dogs and watch the cricket in **Millwall Park** across Manchester Road. North of the park, **Mudchute Farm** is a real working farm, complete with animals and a riding school. *E. Ferry Rd., tel. 0171/515–5901. Admission free. DLR: Mudchute.*

**Dulwich**   **Dulwich Village** in southeast London has handsome 18th-century houses strung out along its main street. Most of the land around here belongs to the Dulwich College Estate—founded in the early 17th century by the actor Edward Alleyn—which keeps strict control of modern development. The village is a pleasant place to wander on a sunny summer day. **Dulwich Park** is a well-kept municipal park with a particularly fine display of rhododendrons in late May. Opposite the park gates is the **Dulwich Picture Gallery,** a lovely small gallery with works by Rembrandt, Van Dyck, Rubens, Poussin, and Gainsborough, among others; the gallery was designed by Sir John Soane (*see* Bloomsbury and Legal London). To get to Dulwich take the Network South East surface train from Victoria to West Dulwich or from London Bridge to North Dulwich. *College Rd., tel. 0181/693–5254. Admission: £2 adults, children under 16 free, £1 senior citizens. Open Tues.–Fri. 10–1, 2–5, Sat. 11–5, Sun. 2–5; closed national holidays.*

If you have enough energy left after exploring Dulwich and the Picture Gallery, walk through the park and then south for about half a mile to another delightful small museum, the **Horniman Museum** (*see* What to See and Do with Children, *above*).

**The Royal Air**   **The Royal Air Force Museum** in north London is a must for flying and
**Force Museum**   military enthusiasts. The story of the R.A.F. is told in great detail, and there are uniforms, guns, and radar equipment on display, as well as detailed sections on World War I and World War II exploits, including the work of the Bomber Command. The **Battle of Britain Museum** in the same complex (no extra charge) explains how the R.A.F. fought off the German Luftwaffe in 1940. The nearest tube stop is Colindale, a 15-minute walk from the museum. *Grahame Park Way, Hendon, tel. 0181/205–2266. Admission: £4.90 adults, £2.45 children under16 and senior citizens. Open daily 10–6; closed Dec. 25–26, Jan. 1.*

**North**   After visiting the Thames Barrier (*see* Greenwich), make your way
**Woolwich Old**   east into Woolwich, take the open-deck car ferry across the river,
**Station**   and visit the **North Woolwich Old Station Museum.**This has displays
**Museum**   on the history of railways in east London, as well as locomotives, rolling stock, and a reconstructed 1910 booking office. Return to central London by overground train from North Woolwich. *Pier Rd., N. Woolwich, tel. 0171/474–7244. Admission free. Open Mon.– Sat. 10–5, Sun. and national holidays 2–5; telephone to check Christmas and Easter week opening times.*

**Kensal Green**   Heralding itself as "London's first Necropolis," this west London
**Cemetery**   cemetery was established in 1832 and beats the more famous Highgate for atmosphere, if only because it's less populated with live people. Within its 77 acres are more freestanding mausolea than in any other cemetery in Britain, some of them almost the size of small churches, and most of them constructed while their future occupants were still alive. Those who balked at burial but couldn't afford a mausoleum of their own could opt for a position in the

catacombs, and these, with their stacks of moldering caskets, are a definite highlight for seekers of the macabre, though they can only be seen as part of a tour. In the cemetery you will find the final resting places of the novelists Trollope, Thackeray, and Wilkie Collins; of the great engineer Isambard Kingdom Brunel (1806–1859); and of Decimus Burton, Victorian architect of the Athenaeum Club, the Wellington Arch, the Kew Gardens greenhouses, and many other bits of London you'll have just seen. To get here, take the Bakerloo line tube to Kensal Green, then Bus 18, which stops outside the gates. *Harrow Rd. W10, tel. 0181/969–0152. Suggested donation: £2. Open Mon.–Sat. 9–5:30, Sun. 10–5:30 (times may vary Nov.–Feb., so call first). 2-hr guided tours (including catacombs) Mar.–Oct., weekends 2:30; Oct.–Feb., Sun. 2. Catacomb tours first Sun. of the month; phone for times.*

# 4 Shopping

## Shopping Districts

**Camden Town**  Crafts and vintage clothing markets and shops cluster in and around picturesque but over-renovated canalside buildings in this frenetic mecca for Generation X. Things are quieter midweek. It's a good place for boots and T-shirts, cheap leather jackets, and recycled trendywear.

**Chelsea**  Chelsea centers on the King's Road, which is no longer synonymous with ultra-fashion but still harbors some designer boutiques, plus antiques and home furnishings emporia.

**Covent Garden**  A something-for-everyone neighborhood. The restored 19th-century market building features mainly high-class clothing chain stores, plus crafts and design shops, with stalls selling vintage, army-surplus, and ethnic clothing around it. Neal Street and the surrounding alleys offer amazing gifts of every type—bikes, kites, tea, herbs, beads, hats . . . you name it. Floral Street and Long Acre have designer and chain-store fashion in equal measure. Good for people-watching, too.

**Hampstead**  For picturesque peace and quiet with your shopping, stroll around here midweek. Upscale clothing stores and representatives of the better chains share the half-dozen streets with cozy boutique-size shops for the home and stomach.

**Kensington**  Kensington Church Street features expensive antiques, plus a little fashion. The main drag, Kensington High Street, is a smaller, less crowded, and classier version of Oxford Street, with some good-quality mid-price clothing shops and larger stores at the eastern end.

**Knightsbridge**  Harrods dominates Brompton Road, but there's plenty more, especially for the well-heeled and fashion-conscious. Harvey Nichols is the top clothes stop, with many expensive designers' *boites* along Sloane Street. Walton Street and narrow Beauchamp (pronounced "beecham") Place offer more of the same, plus home furnishings and knickknacks, and Brompton Cross, at the start of Fulham Road, is the most design-conscious corner of London, with the Conran Shop and Joseph leading the field.

**Mayfair**  Here is Bond Street, Old and New, with desirable dress designers, jewelers, plus fine art (old and new) on Old Bond Street and Cork Street. South Molton Street has high-priced high-style fashion—especially at Browns—and the tailors of Savile Row are of worldwide repute.

**Oxford Street**  Crowded Oxford Street is past its prime and lined with tawdry discount shops. There are some good stores, however—particularly Selfridges, John Lewis, and Marks and Spencer—and interesting boutiques secreted in little St. Christopher's Place and Gees Court.

**Piccadilly**  Though the actual number of shops is small for a street of its length (Green Park takes up a lot of space), Piccadilly manages to fit in several quintessentially British emporia. Fortnum and Mason is its star, and the arcades are an elegant experience even for shopphobics.

**Regent Street**  At right angles to Oxford Street, this wider, curvier version has another couple of department stores, including what is possibly London's most pleasant, Liberty's. Hamley's is the capital's toy center; other shops tend to be either somewhat dull, or airline offices. "West Soho," around Carnaby Street, stocks designer youth paraphernalia and 57 varieties of T-shirt.

**St. James's** Where the English gentleman shops. Here are hats, handmade shirts and shoes, silver shaving kits and hip flasks, as well as the Prince of Wales's aftershave supplier and possibly the world's best cheese shop. Nothing is cheap, in any sense.

## Specialty Stores

**Antiques** Investment pieces or lovable junk, London has lots. Try markets first—even for pedigree silver, the dealers at these places often have the best wares and the knowledge to match. Camden Passage, Portobello Road, and Bermondsey (*see* Street Markets, *below*) are the best, and the former two are surrounded by shops open outside market hours. Kensington Church Street is *the* antiques shopping street, with prices and quality both high. Out of the hundreds of stores, we list five to whet your appetite.

**Antiquarius** (131–141 King's Rd., SW3), at the Sloane Square end of the King's Road, is an indoor antiques market with more than 200 stalls offering a wide variety of collectibles, including things that won't bust your baggage allowance: Art Deco brooches, meerschaum pipes, silver salt cellars . . . (*See* map B.)

Movie art directors do research at the **Gallery of Antique Costume and Textiles** (2 Church St., NW8) to get the period just right, because everything here, from bedspreads to bloomers, was stitched before 1930—except for the wonderful range of copycat brocade vests. It lies off our maps, but is easily found three blocks north of the Edgware Road tube.

**Gray's Antique Market** (58 Davies St., W1) and **Gray's Mews** (1–7 Davies Mews, W1) around the corner are conveniently central. Both collect dealers specializing in everything from Sheffield plate to Chippendale furniture. Bargains are not impossible, and proper pedigrees are guaranteed.(*See* map A.)

Just one of the many specialist stores around here, **Hope and Glory** (131a Kensington Church St., W8) has commemorative china and glass from 1887 to the present, with many affordable lesser pieces. (*See* map B.)

**Books** Charing Cross Road is London's booksville, with a couple of dozen stores there or thereabout. The many antiquarian booksellers tend to look daunting (deceptively, as Helen Hanff found by correspondence with No. 84), but there are many new bookshops, too. Especially large, though it has to be the most chaotic and confusing shop in London, with a staff that doesn't know anything, is **Foyle** (No. 119). **Waterstone** (No. 121–125) is part of an admirable, and expanding, chain with long hours and a program of author readings and signings. **Hatchards** (187–188 Piccadilly, WC2) and **Dillons** (82 Gower St., WC1) both have not only a huge stock, but also a well-informed staff to help you choose. (*See* map A.)

**Books for Cooks** (4 Blenheim Cres., W11) and its near neighbor, **The Travel Bookshop** (No. 13), are exactly what they say, and worth the trip for enthusiasts. Travel books and maps are the specialty of **Stanford** (12 Long Acre, WC2); art books of **Zwemmer** (24 Litchfield St., WC2) just off Charing Cross Rd.; and sci-fi, fantasy, horror, and comic books of **Forbidden Planet** (71 New Oxford St., WC1). (*See* map A.)

Back on the Charing Cross Road, **Silver Moon** at No. 64 is an accessible and friendly women's bookshop. Just off the south end, in **Cecil Court**—a pedestrians-only lane where every shop is a specialty

# Shopping A (Mayfair, Soho, and Covent Garden)

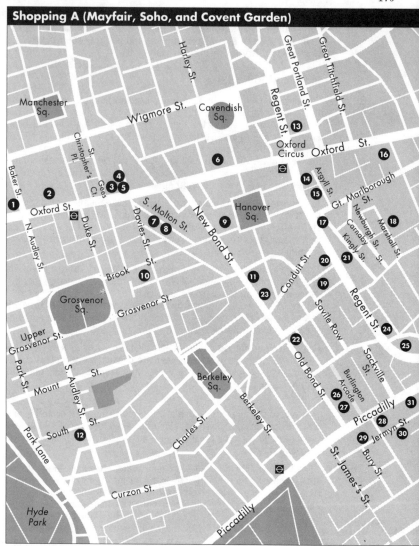

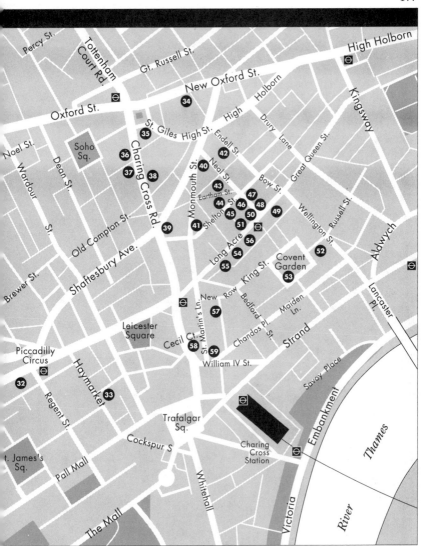

Mulberry, **3**
Naturally British, **57**
Neal Street East, **50**
Nicole Fahri, **4**
Outlaws Club, **42**
Paddy Campbell, **5**
Paul Smith, **56**
Penhaligon's, **52**

Pleasures of Times
Past, **58**
Ray Man, **41**
Rebecca, **48**
Sam Walker, **43**
Selfridges, **2**
Silver Moon, **38**
Simpson, **32**
Sportspages, **35**

Stanford, **55**
Tea House, **46**
Thomas Goode, **12**
Tom Gilbey, **19**
Turnbull & Asser, **30**
Warehouse, **14**
Waterstone, **36**
Whistles, **53**
Zwemmer, **39**

178

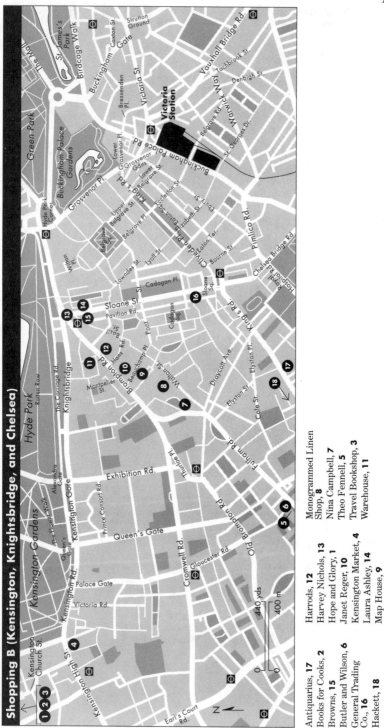

# Shopping B (Kensington, Knightsbridge, and Chelsea)

Antiquarius, **17**
Books for Cooks, **2**
Browns, **15**
Butler and Wilson, **6**
General Trading
Co., **16**
Hackett, **18**

Harrods, **12**
Harvey Nichols, **13**
Hope and Glory, **1**
Janet Reger, **10**
Kensington Market, **4**
Laura Ashley, **14**
Map House, **9**

Monogrammed Linen
Shop, **8**
Nina Campbell, **7**
Theo Fennell, **5**
Travel Bookshop, **3**
Warehouse, **11**

bookstore—**Bell, Book and Radmell** (No. 4) has quality antiquarian volumes and modern first editions; **Marchpane** (No. 16) stocks covetable rare and antique illustrated children's books; **Dance Books** (No. 9) has—yes—dance books; and **Pleasures of Times Past** (No. 11) indulges the collective nostalgia for Victoriana. At the north end, **Sportspages** (Caxton Walk) is London's only sports bookshop—it's so comprehensive there's even a good baseball section. (*See* map A.)

**China and Glass**  English Wedgwood and Minton china are as collectible as they ever were, and most large department stores carry a selection, alongside lesser varieties with smaller price tags. Regent Street has several off-price purveyors, and, if you're in search of a bargain, Harrods's sale can't be beat—but sharpen your elbows first. For a selection of the best formal china and leaded crystal, **Thomas Goode** (19 S. Audley St., W1) is the one-stop shop. (*See* map A.)

**Clothing**  London is one of the world's four fashion capitals (along with Paris, Milan, and New York), and every designer you've ever heard of is sold here somewhere. As well as the top names, though, London retains a reputation for quirky street style, and many an exciting young designer has cut his or her teeth selling early collections at a London street market. Don't just go by the label, and you could be the first to wear clothes by a future star. Traditional British men's outfitters are also rather well-known. From the Savile Row suit, handmade shirt, and custom shoes to the Harris-tweeds-and-Oxford-brogues English country look that Ralph Lauren purloined, England's indigenous garments make for real investment dressing.

*General*  **Aquascutum** (100 Regent St., W1) is known for its classic raincoats, but also stocks the garments to wear underneath, for both men and women. Style keeps up with the times but is firmly on the safe side, making this a good bet for solvent professionals with an anti-fashion attitude. (*See* map A.)

The shopfitters at **Burberrys** (161–165 Regent St., W1, and 18–22 The Haymarket, SW1) have done their best to evoke an English Heritage ambience, with mahogany closets and stacks of neatly folded neckerchiefs alongside the trademark "Burberry Check" tartan, which adorns—in addition to those famous raincoat linings—scarves, umbrellas, and even pots of passion-fruit curd and tins of shortbread, in the newish British provisions line. (*See* map A.)

**Herbert Johnson** (30 New Bond St., W1) is one of a handful of gentleman's hatters who still know how to construct deerstalkers, bowlers, flat caps, and panamas—all the classic headgear, and Ascot hats for women, too. (*See* map A.)

**Kensington Market** (49–53 Kensington High St., W8) is the diametric opposite of sober British stiff-upper-lip anti-fashion.For more than two decades it has been a principal purveyor of the constantly changing, frivolous, hip London street style. Hundreds of stalls—some shop-size, others tiny—are crammed into this building, where you can get lost for hours trying to find the good bits. (*See* map B.)

**Lord's** (66–70 Burlington Arcade, W1) softly irresistible supply of cashmere for men and women—plus shirts, ties, and scarves in abundance—provides a very good reason for visiting the seductive Burlington Arcade. Their paisley-patterned bathrobes would have made Noël Coward's eyes gleam. (*See* map A.)

**Marks & Spencer** (458 Oxford St., W1 and 173 Oxford St., W1) is a major chain of stores that's an integral part of the British way of life—sturdy practical clothes, good materials and workmanship, and basic accessories, all at moderate, though not bargain basement, prices. "Marks and Sparks," as they are popularly known, have never been renowned for their high style, though that is changing as they continue to bring in (anonymously) big-name designers to spice up their ranges. What they *are* renowned for is underwear. All of England buys theirs here. The Marble Arch branch (458 Oxford St.) has the highest turnover of any shop in the land. (*See* map A.)

**Mulberry** (11–12 Gees Ct., W1) outdoes Ralph Lauren in packaging the English look. Covetable, top-quality leather bags, belts, and cases, wool riding jackets, coats, and sweaters, and corduroy and linen pants are the sort of things found here—at a price. (*See* map A.)

**Simpson** (203 Piccadilly, W1) is a quiet, pleasant store with a thoughtful variety of designer and leisure wear, luggage, and gifts. It is the home of the Daks' brand of classic British design. There are a barbershop, restaurant, and wine bar to add to the store's conveniences. It's just a block west of Piccadilly Circus.(*See* map A.)

*Women's Wear* **Browns** (23–27 South Molton St., W1) was the first notable store to populate the South Molton Street pedestrian mall, and seems to sprout more off shoots every time you see it. Well-established, collectible designers (Jean Muir, Donna Karan, Romeo Gigli, Jasper Conran, Jil Sander) rub shoulder pads here with younger, funkier names (Dries Van Noten, Jean Paul Gaultier, Yohji Yamamoto), and Browns also has its own label. Its July and January sales are famed. Also at 6C Sloane St., SW1. (*See* both maps.)

**Droopy & Browns** (99 St. Martin's La., WC2) features beautifully constructed, extravagantly theatrical frocks and suits, made up in raw silks and fine linens, brocades and velvets. Colors are strong, tailoring is unimpeachable, and kind salespeople don't turn up their noses at larger ladies. (*See* map A.)

**The Hat Shop** (58 Neal St., WC2) is keeping the art of millinery alive and bringing it within reach of the average pocket. The stock here ranges from classic trilbies, toppers, panamas, and matador hats to frivolous tulle-and-feather constructions, with scores of inexpensive, fun titfers in between. The shop is so tiny that only 10 people are allowed in at a time. (*See* map A.)

**Janet Reger** (2 Beauchamp Pl., SW3) pioneered the surge of luxurious lingerie that now froths out from every store. This is the one, though, to visit for the real thing. (*See* map B.)

**Jigsaw** (21 Long Acre, Covent Garden, WC2, and other branches) is popular for its separates that don't sacrifice quality to fashion, are reasonably priced, and suit women in their twenties to forties. (*See* map A.)

**Laura Ashley** (256–258 Regent St., W1; also at 183 Sloane St., SW1, and other branches) offers design from the firm founded by the late high priestess of English traditional. Country dresses, blouses, and skirts, plus wallpapers and fabrics in dateless patterns that rely heavily on flowers, fruit, leaves, or just plain stripes, have captured the nostalgic imagination of the world. (*See* both maps.)

**Nicole Farhi** (25–26 St. Christopher's Pl., W1; also at 27 Hampstead High St., NW3, and other branches), a store specially recommended for the career woman of taste, stocks a desirable range of practical clothes. Prices are on the high side, but there is some affordable wear as well, especially the sporty, casual Diversion range. Farhi offers an equally desirable men's line as well. (*See* map A.)

**Paddy Campbell** (8 Gees Ct., W1) designs elegant matching separates in natural fabrics and subtle colors. Prices are reasonable for this level of workmanship, and the staff will alter garments for a perfect fit. (*See* map A.)

**Warehouse** (19 Argyll St., W1; also at 76 Brompton Rd., SW3, as well as other locations) stocks practical, stylish, reasonably priced separates in easy fabrics and lots of fun colors. The finishing isn't so hot, but style, not substance, counts here, and the shop's youthful fans don't seem to mind. The stock changes very quickly, so it always presents a new face to the world. (*See* both maps.)

**Whistles** (The Market, Covent Garden, WC2; also at Heath St., Hampstead, and other branches) is a small chain stocking its own high-fashion, mid-price label, plus several European (mostly French) designers. Clothes are hung color-coordinated in shops like designers' ateliers. (*See* map A.)

*Men's Wear*  Most stores we list above under General Clothing stock excellent men's wear. Try Aquascutum, Burberrys, and Simpson. All the large department stores, too, carry a wide range of men's clothing, Selfridges and Harrods especially.

**Blazer** (36 and 117 Long Acre, WC2) stocks medium-priced formal wear at the first branch and a casual range at the second. Clothes tend toward the classic, but with style-conscious details and rich colors. (*See* map A.)

**Hackett** (65B New King's Rd., SW6) started as a posh thrift store, recycling cricket flannels, hunting pinks, Oxford brogues, and similar Britishwear. Now they make their own, and they have become a genuine—and very good—gentlemen's outfitters. (*See* map B.)

**Paul Smith** (41 Floral St., WC2) is your man if you don't want to look outlandish but you're bored with plain pants and sober jackets. His well-tailored suits have a subtle quirkiness, his shirts and ties a sense of humor, and his jeans and sweats a good cut. (*See* map A.)

**Sam Walker** (41 Neal St., WC2) provides a refined way to buy secondhand clothes. They specialize in men's vintage clothing at prices that *almost* reflect their near-museum quality. Much of the stock is pre–World War II, and there's also a women's version, called **Rebecca,** at No. 66. (*See* map A.)

**Tom Gilbey** (2 New Burlington Pl., W1) is a custom tailor, but the exciting part of his shop is the Waistcoat Gallery, where exquisite vests, some in silk or brocades or embroidered by hand, others marginally plainer, are essential accessories for the dandy. (*See* map A.)

**Turnbull & Asser** (71 & 72 Jermyn St., W1) is *the* custom shirtmaker. Unfortunately for those of average means, the first order must be for a minimum of six shirts, from around £100 each. But there's a range of less expensive, still exquisitely made ready-to-wear shirts, too. (*See* map A.)

*Crafts*  With the current interest in alternate ways of living, whole food eating, and preserving the environment, there has been an enormous increase in public awareness of the value of traditional crafts, and London has more than its share of stores that stock the work of traditional and innovative designer-makers.

Some of the best British potters joined to found the **Craftsmen Potters Shop** (7 Marshall St., W1) as a cooperative venture to market their wares. The result is a store that carries a wide spectrum of the potter's art, from thoroughly practical pitchers, plates, and bowls to ceramic sculptures. Prices range from the reasonable to way up. (*See* map A.)

**Craftworks** (31 Southend Rd., NW3; tube stop: Hampstead) is a haven packed with handmade table- and glassware, ceramics, candlesticks, wall hangings, and mirrors from all over the world—and also from just down the road.

At **Contemporary Applied Arts** (43 Earlham St., WC2), a mixed bag of designers and craftspeople display their wares over two floors. Anything from glassware and jewelry to furniture and lighting can be found here. (*See* map A.)

As its name suggests, **Naturally British** (13 New Row, WC2) stocks the traditional end of the crafts spectrum, with items made by woodcarvers and leather toolers and silversmiths and knitters across the British Isles. Here you can find Aran sweaters, Celtic silver, Dorset cream fudge, and Welsh woolen blankets without leaving town. (*See* map A.)

They're not indigenous, but Italian hand-marbled papers from **Nina Campbell** (9 Walton St., SW3), in the form of address books, letter racks, stationery sets, and photo albums, make gorgeous gifts and keepsakes. (*See* map B.)

**Gifts** Of course, virtually anything from any shop in this chapter has gift potential, but these selections lean toward stores with a lot of choice, both in merchandise and price. Chances are you'll be wanting the recipients of your generous bounty to know how far you traveled to procure it for them, so our suggestions tend toward identifiable Britishness. You should also investigate the possibilities in the shops attached to the major museums, most of which offer far more than racks of souvenir postcards these days. Some of the best are at the **British Museum,** the **V&A,** the **Royal Academy,** and the **London Transport Museum.**

**The Armoury of St. James's** (17 Piccadilly Arcade, SW1) offers perfect playthings for overgrown schoolkids in the form of antique and new painted lead soldiers (most wars with British involvement can be fought in miniature), plus medals, brass buttons, and military prints. (*See* map A.)

**Conran Shop** (Michelin House, 81 Fulham Rd., SW3) is the domain of Sir Terence Conran, of course, who has been informing British middle-class taste since he opened Habitat in the '60s; this is the grown-up, upmarket version. Home enhancers from furniture to stemware, both handmade and mass-produced, famous name and young designer, are displayed in a suitably gorgeous building.

**Fortnum & Mason** (181 Piccadilly, W1), the queen's grocer, is, paradoxically, the most egalitarian of gift stores, with plenty of irresistibly packaged luxury foods, stamped with the gold "by appointment" crest, for under £5. Try the teas, preserves, blocks of chocolate, tins of pâté, or a box of Duchy Originals oatcakes—like Paul Newman, the Prince of Wales has gone into the retail food business with these.

**General Trading Co.** (144 Sloane St., SW1) "does" just about every upper-class wedding gift list, from Charles and Diana's down, but caters also to slimmer pockets with its merchandise shipped from far shores (as the name suggests) but moored securely to English taste. (*See* map B.)

**Halcyon Days** (14 Brook St., W1) specializes in enamelware. It's best known for its little pillboxes: These can be selected from a range of pastoral scenes or Regency dandies or even plain colors, and personalized with initials or messages, and will add mere ounces to your luggage weight. (*See* map A.)

**Hamleys** (188–196 Regent St., W1) has six floors of toys and games for both children and adults. The huge stock ranges from traditional teddy bears to computer games and all the latest technological gimmickry. Try to avoid it at Christmas, when police have to rope off a section of Regent Street for Hamleys customers. (*See* map A.)

**Maison** (47–49 Neal St., WC2) is a cool, spacious two floors of homage to design. Among the gorgeous goods displayed like museum pieces are lots of witty ideas for presents, from the sublime (Alvar Aalto vases) to the ridiculous (chocolate sardines). (*See* map A.)

**Neal Street East** (5 Neal St., WC2) isn't big on British, no, but this importer of Oriental everything does carry stock with universal appeal. There are several floors of what you'd expect in the way of woks, chopsticks, bowls, books, kimonos, and toys, but also glorious lacquered boxes, woven baskets, amber and silver jewelry, silk flowers, Japanese kites, and loads of fun gifts for under a fiver. (*See* map A.)

**Penhaligon's** (41 Wellington St., WC2; also at 55 Burlington Arcade, W1; 69 Moorgate, EC2; and 20A Brook St., W1) was established by William Penhaligon, court barber at the end of Queen Victoria's lengthy reign. He blended perfumes and toilet waters in the back of his shop, using essential oils and natural, often exotic ingredients, and you can buy the very same formulations today, along with soaps, talcs, bath oils, and accessories, with the strong whiff of Victoriana both inside and outside the pretty bottles and boxes. (*See* map A.)

**Ray Man** (Shelton St., WC2), for "Eastern Musical Instruments," is probably the only place in Europe you can buy an erhhu, which is, of course, a two-stringed coconut fiddle. It's an amazing place, perfect for gifts for the weird. You can pick up a set of ankle bells or pan pipes for a song. (*See* map A.)

**The Tea House** (15A Neal St., WC2) purveys everything to do with the British national drink; you can dispatch your entire gift list here. Alongside every variety of tea—including strange or rare brews like orchid, banana, Japanese Rice, and Russian Caravan—are teapots in the shape of a British bobby or a London taxi, plus books, and what the shop terms "teaphernalia"—strainers, and trivets, and infusers, and other gadgets that need explaining. (*See* map A.)

**Jewelry** Jewelry—precious, semiprecious, and totally fake—can be had by just rubbing an Aladdin's lamp in London's West End. Of the department stores, Liberty and Harvey Nichols are particularly known for their fashion jewelry, but here are a few more suggestions for baubles, bangles, and beads.

**Asprey's** (165–169 New Bond St., W1) has been described as the "classiest and most luxurious shop in the world." It offers a range of exquisite jewelry and gifts, both antique and modern. If you're in the market for a six-branched Georgian candelabrum or a six-carat emerald-and-diamond brooch, you won't be disappointed. (*See* map A.)

All that glisters at **Butler and Wilson** (20 South Molton St., W1; also at 189 Fulham Rd., SW3) isn't gold. This store is designed to set off its irresistible costume jewelry to the very best advantage—against a dramatic black background. It has some of the best displays in town, and keeps very busy marketing silver, diamanté, French gilt, and pearls by the truckload. (*See* both maps.)

**Cartier** (175 New Bond St., W1) boasts an exclusivity that captures the very essence of Bond Street. It combines royal connections—Cartier's was granted its first royal warrant in 1902—with the last word in luxurious good taste. Many of the Duchess of Windsor's trinkets were wrought here. The store also sells glassware, leather goods, and stationery. (*See* map A.)

**Garrard** (112 Regent St., W1) has connections with the royal family going back to 1722 (Prince Charles bought Diana her engagement ring here), and the company is still responsible for keeping the Crown Jewels in glittering condition. But they are also family jewelers, and offer an enormous range of items in jewelry or silver, from antique to modern. (*See* map A.)

**The Outlaws Club** (49 Endell St., WC2) stocks the work of around 100 designers, with prices ranging from a few pounds up to £200. The dominant style is avant-garde, meaning that this shop has been a favorite with fashion writers for a decade. (*See* map A.)

Blue-blooded **Theo Fennell** (177 Fulham Rd., SW3) designs pieces that are instantly recognizable—exquisitely detailed miniatures, and covetable jewelry (in gold studded with precious stones) that is reminiscent of the ecclesiastical. (*See* map B.)

**Linen**     Among the traditional crafts that can still be bought in London, fine linen ranks high. Again, many of the department stores, Liberty and Harrods among them, carry a fair range of linengoods, but here are three specialty stores that you might want to try for more personal service.

**The Irish Linen Co.** (35–36 Burlington Arcade, W1) is a tiny store bursting with crisp, embroidered linen for the table, the bed, and the nose. Exquisite handkerchiefs should be within reach of everyone's pocket. (*See* map A.)

**The Linen Cupboard** (21 Great Castle St., W1) is stacked with piles of sheets and towels of all sorts and has by far the lowest-priced fine Irish linens and Egyptian cottons in town. (*See* map A.)

Try **The Monogrammed Linen Shop** (168 Walton St., SW3) for a wide range of fine Italian bed linen with matching towels, bathrobes, and nightshirts, as well as tablecloths, place mats, and napkins—all of which you can have monogrammed. Proud grandparents may want to buy a superbly embroidered christening gown here. (*See* map B.)

**Prints**     London harbors trillions of prints, and they make great gifts—for yourself, perhaps. We list two West End stores, but try also street markets, and Cecil Court (*see* Books, *above*), just north of Trafalgar Square.

**Grosvenor Prints** (28–32 Shelton St., WC2) sells antiquarian prints, but with an emphasis on views and architecture of London—and dogs! It's an eccentric collection, and the prices range widely, but the stock is so odd that you are bound to find something interesting and unusual to meet both your budget and your taste. (*See* map A.)

At **The Map House** (54 Beauchamp Pl., SW3), antique maps can run from a few pounds to several thousand, but the shop also has excellent reproductions of maps and prints, especially of botanical subjects and cityscapes. (*See* map B.)

## Department Stores

London's department stores range from Harrods—which every tourist is obliged to visit—through many serviceable middle-range stores, devoted to the middle-of-the-road tastes of the middle class, to a few cheap jack ones that sell merchandise you would find at a better rate back home. Most of the best and biggest department stores are grouped in the West End around Regent Street and Oxford Street, with two notable exceptions out in Knightsbridge.

You will recognize **Liberty** (200 Regent St., W1) by its wonderful black-and-white mock-Tudor facade, a peacock among pigeons in humdrum Regent Street. Inside, it is a labyrinthine building, full of nooks and crannies, all stuffed with goodies like a dream of an eastern bazaar. Famous principally for its fabrics, it also has an Oriental department, rich with color; men's wear that tends to the traditional; and women's wear that has lately been spiced up with extra designer ranges. It is a hard store to resist, where you may well find an original gift—especially one made from those classic Liberty prints. (*See* map A.)

A short distance from Liberty, two blocks west on Oxford Street, is **John Lewis** (278 Oxford St., W1), a store whose motto is "Never knowingly undersold," and for sensible goods at sensible prices this store is hard to beat. For the visitor to London who's handy with the needle, John Lewis has a wonderful selection of dress and furnishing fabrics. Many's the American home with John Lewis drapes. (*See* map A.)

Ten blocks west on Oxford Street—crowded blocks in the middle of the day or at sale time—lies **Selfridges** (400 Oxford St.,W1). This giant, bustling store is London's upscale version of Macy's, and was started early this century by an American. If this all-rounder has an outstanding department, it has to be its Food Hall, onto which attention has lately been lavished—or else its frenetic cosmetics department, which seems to perfume the air the whole length of Oxford Street. In recent years, Selfridges has made a specialty of high-profile popular designer fashion. Even more important for the visitor to town, there's a branch of the London Tourist Board on the premises, a theater ticket counter, and a branch of Thomas Cook, the travel agent, in the basement. (*See* map A.)

**Harrods** (87 Brompton Rd., SW1), being the only English department store classed among monuments and museums on every visitor's list, hardly needs an introduction. In fact, its Englishness is tentative these days, since it is owned by the Egyptian Al Fayed brothers—but who cares? It is swanky and plush and deep-carpeted as ever, its spectacular food halls are alone worth the trip, and it stands out from the pack for fashion these days, too. You can forgive the store its immodest motto, *Omnia, omnibus, ubique* ("everything, for everyone, everywhere"), since there are more than 230 departments, including a pet shop rumored to supply aardvarks to zebras on request, and the toy department—sorry, *kingdom*—which does the same for plush versions. During the pre-Christmas period and the sales, the entire store is a menagerie. (*See* map B.)

**Harvey Nichols** (109 Knightsbridge, SW1) is just a few blocks from Harrods, but is not competing on the same turf, since its passion is fashion, all the way. There are five floors of it, including departments for dressing homes and men, but the woman who invests in her wardrobe is the main target. Accessories are strong suits, especially jewelry, scarves, and make-up—England's first MAC counter here was 10-deep for months. (*See* map B.)

## Street Markets

London is as rich in street markets as it is in parks, and they contribute as much to the city's culture. Practically every neighborhood has its own cluster of fruit-and-veg stalls, but we list here the bigger, specialist sort of market, which provides not only (if you luck out) a bargain, but a great day out. A Sunday morning strolling the stalls of Brick Lane and breakfasting on the native bagels (smaller than New York's, but just as good), or a Saturday antiquing in the Portobello Road are Londoners' pastimes as much as they are tourist activities, and markets are a great way to see the city from the inside out.

**Bermondsey** (Tower Bridge Rd., SE1). Also known as the New Caledonian Market, this is London's best antiques market, one of the largest, and the one the dealers frequent. Thanks to their professional presence, the Fridays-only market starts at the unearthly hour of 4 AM, and it's then that the really great buys will be snapped up. You should still be able to find a bargain or two if you turn up a bit later. *To get here, take Bus 15 or 25 to Aldgate, then Bus 42 over Tower Bridge to Bermondsey Sq., or take the tube to London Bridge and walk. Open Fri. 4 AM–1.*

**Camden Lock Market** (NW1). Visit the lock on a sunny August Sunday if you want your concept of a crowd redefined. Camden is actually several markets gathered around a pair of locks in the Regent's Canal, and was once very pretty. Now that further stalls and a new *faux* warehouse have been inserted into the surrounding brick railway buildings, the haphazard charm of the place is largely lost, although the variety of merchandise is mindblowing—vintage and new clothes (design stars have been discovered here), antiques and junk, jewelry and scarves, candlesticks, ceramics, mirrors, toys . . . But underneath it's really a meat market for hip teens. The neighborhood is bursting with shops and cafés, and further markets, and is a whole lot calmer, if stall-free, midweek. *Take the tube or Bus 24 or 29 to Camden Town. Shops open Tues.–Sun. 9:30–5:30, stalls weekends 8–6.*

**Camden Passage** (Islington, N1). Despite the name, this one is not in Camden but a couple of miles away in Islington, a neighborhood first gentrified by media hippies in the '60s. Around 350 antiques dealers set up stalls here Saturday and Wednesday, with a curtailed version on Thursday, and it remains a fruitful, fair-priced, and picturesque hunting ground. *Bus 19 or 38 or a tube to the Angel will get you here. Open Wed. and Sat. 8:30–3.*

**Greenwich Antiques Market** (Greenwich High Rd., SE10). If you're planning to visit Greenwich, then combine your trip with a wander around this open-air market near St. Alfege Church. You'll find one of the best selections of secondhand and antique clothes in London—quality tweeds and overcoats can be had at amazing prices. The market for antiques is open on Saturday and Sunday only. *Take a British Rail train to New Gate Cross and then Bus 117, or a bus direct to Greenwich. Antiques, crafts, and clothes weekends 9–5; fruit and vegetables weekdays 9–5.*

**Leadenhall Market** (EC3). The draw here is not so much what you can buy—plants and food, mainly—as the building itself. It's a handsome late-Victorian structure, ornate and elaborate, with plenty of atmosphere. *Take the tube to Bank or Monument. Open weekdays 9 AM–5 PM.*

**Petticoat Lane** (Middlesex St., E1). Actually, Petticoat Lane doesn't exist, and this Sunday clothing and fashion market centers on Middlesex Street, then sprawls in several directions, including east to Brick Lane. Between them, the crammed streets turn up items of dubious parentage (CD players, bikes, car radios), alongside clothes (vintage, new, and just plain tired), jewelry, books, underwear, antiques, woodworking tools, bedlinens, jars of pickles, and outright junk in one of London's most entertaining diversions. *Liverpool St., Aldgate, or Aldgate East tubes are the closest. Open Sun. 9–2.*

**Portobello Market** (Portobello Rd., W11). London's most famous market still wins the prize for the all-round best. It sits in a most lively and multicultural part of town, the 1,500-odd antiques dealers don't rip you off, and it stretches over a mile, changing character completely as it goes. The top (Notting Hill Gate) end is antiques-land (with shops midweek); the middle is where locals buy fruit and veg, and hang out in trendy restaurants; the section under the elevated highway called the Westway boasts the best flea market in town; and then it tails off into a giant rummage sale among record stores, vintage clothing boutiques, and art galleries. *Take Bus 52 or the tube to Ladbroke Grove or Notting Hill Gate. Fruit and vegetables Mon.–Wed. and Fri. 8–5, Thurs. 8–1; antiques Fri. 8–3; both on Sat. 6–5.*

**Spitalfields** (Brushfield St., E1). Until it eventually becomes shops and offices, the developers of Camden Lock have got hold of the old 3-acre indoor fruit market near Petticoat Lane and installed food, crafts, and clothes stalls, cafés, performance and sports facilities (including an opera house and a swimming pool), and a city farm. There's a different market every day; Saturday is antiques, Sunday a green market. *Directions as for Petticoat Lane, above. Open weekdays 11–3, Sun. 9–3.*

## VAT Refunds

To the eternal fury of Britain's storekeepers, who struggle under cataracts of paperwork, Britain is afflicted with a 17½% Value Added Tax. Foreign visitors, however, need not pay VAT if they take advantage of the Personal Export Scheme. Of the various ways to get a VAT refund, the most common are **Over the Counter** and **Direct Export.** Note that though practically all larger stores operate these schemes, information about them is not always readily forthcoming, so it is important to ask. Once you have gotten on the right track, you'll find that almost all of the larger stores have export departments that will be able to give you all the help you need.

The easiest and most usual way of getting your refund is the **Over the Counter** method. There is normally a minimum of £75, below which VAT cannot be refunded. You must also be able to supply proof of your identity—your passport is best. The salesclerk will then fill out the necessary paperwork, Form 407 VAT. (Be sure to get an addressed envelope as well.) Keep the form and give it to customs when you leave the country. Lines at major airports are usually long, so leave plenty of time, and pack the goods you have purchased in your carry-on bags—you'll need to be able to produce them. The form will then be returned to the store and the refund forwarded to you, minus a small service charge, usually around $3. You can specify how you want the refund. Generally, the easiest way is to have it credited to your charge card. Alternatively, you can have it in the form of a sterling check, but your bank will charge a fee to convert it. Note also that it can take up to eight weeks to receive the refund.

The **Direct Export** method—whereby you have the store send the goods to your home—is more cumbersome. You must have the VAT Form 407 certified by customs, police, or a notary public when you get home and then send it back to the store. They, in turn, will refund your money.

If you are traveling to any other EC country from Britain, the same rules apply, except in France, where you can claim your refund as you leave the country.

However, in 1988 the **Tourist Tax-Free Shopping** service came into operation. This service, which uses special VAT refund vouchers, rather than Form 407, expedites your refund, provided that you make your purchases at a store (identified by the red, white, and blue Tax-Free for Tourists sign) offering the service. If you are going on from Britain to the Continent, you can even get cash refunds. Full details and a list of stores offering the Tax-Free service are available from the British Tourist Authority, 40 West 57th St., New York, NY 10019; and the British Travel Centre, 12 Regent St., London SW1Y 4PQ.

## Clothing Sizes

**Men**  Suit and shirt sizes in the United Kingdom and the Republic of Ireland are the same as U.S. sizes.

**Women**
*Dresses/Coats*

| U.S. | 4 | 6 | 8 | 10 | 12 | 14 | 16 |
|---|---|---|---|---|---|---|---|
| U.K./Ireland | 6 | 8 | 10 | 12 | 14 | 16 | 18 |

*Blouses/*
*Sweaters*

| U.S. | 30 | 32 | 34 | 36 | 38 | 40 | 42 |
|---|---|---|---|---|---|---|---|
| U.K./Ireland | 32 | 34 | 36 | 38 | 40 | 42 | 44 |

*Shoes*

| U.S. | 4 | 5 | 6 | 7 | 8 | 9 | 10 |
|---|---|---|---|---|---|---|---|
| U.K./Ireland | 2 | 3 | 4 | 5 | 6 | 7 | 8 |

# 5 Sports an the Outdoors

There are the Wimbledon Tennis Championships, and there's cricket, and then there's soccer, and that's about all there is for the sports fan in London, right? Wrong. London is a great city for the weekend player of almost anything, and really comes into its own in summer, when the parks sprout nets and goals and painted white lines, outdoor swimming pools open, and a season of spectator events gets underway. The listings below concentrate on facilities available to the casual visitor in a whole range of sports and on the more accessible or well-known spectator events. Bring your kit, and branch out from that hotel gym.

# Participant Sports and Fitness

If your sport is missing from those listed below, or if you need additional information, **Sportsline** (tel. 0171/222–8000, weekdays 10–6) supplies details about London's clubs, events, and facilities. It's a free service.

Aerobics You don't need to buy a membership at any of the following studios, which offer a range of classes for all levels of fitness and are open daily. The price range for an hour's worth of sweating is £3–£5.

**Drill Hall Arts Centre** (16 Chenies St., W1, tel. 0171/631–5107). Yes, you read that right, this is an arts center, which means there are acrobatics and dance classes mixed into the program. "Below the Belt" lower-body conditioning is popular, and Mondays are women-only days.

**Jubilee Hall** (30 The Piazza, Covent Garden, WC2, tel. 0171/379–0008). Many are addicted to Jamie Addicoat's "Fatbuster" classes, but there are plenty more, from bodysculpting and step to pilates and jazz dance.

**Portobello Green Fitness Centre** (3–5 Thorpe Close, W10, tel. 0181/960–2221). It's under the Westway overpass, and you'll have to battle through flea-market shoppers on weekends to reach the bargain (£3) classes.

**Seymour Leisure Centre** (Seymour Pl., W2, tel. 0171/402–5795). The best classes in the "Move It" program here—especially Julie Corsair's amazing hip-hop rave classes—fill to the brim, but the spacious studios can take the pressure. Arrive early for step; you'll need a ticket.

Bicycling London is reasonably cycle-friendly for a big city, with special lanes marked for bicycles on some major roads, but it is never safe to ride without a helmet. You can rent new mountain bikes from **Go By Cycle** (9 Templeton Pl., SW5, tel. 0171/373–3657) from £10/day or £35/week plus deposit. It's a good idea to reserve in advance.

Boxing These two spots offer training-only sessions, but if you happen to be a fighter, All Stars is one of the gyms where world champs train when they're in town.

**All Stars Gym** (576 Harrow Rd., W10, tel. 0181/960 7724). The "KO Circuit" at this friendly gym in a converted church is a two-hour intensive workout, with shadowboxing, heavy bags, pad work, skipping, weights, and a lengthy warm-up, cool-down, and stretch. It pulls in both serious fighters and dilettantes, and an average male-to-female ratio of 7 to 3. Total beginners are shown the ropes, too. *Mon.–Thurs. 7:30 PM, Sat. 10 AM.*

**Boxerobics** (Danceworks, 16 Balderton St., W1, tel. 0171/629–6183). Ex-pro fighter Paul Connolly's hour-long hybrid of a boxer's training session and an aerobics circuit includes shadowboxing, skipping, double-end bag, and speedbag, but no gloves. *Tues. 7 PM, Sat. 3:30.*

**Dance** There's a lot of dance action around, but only space to list a few of the more general studios. Check the listings in *Time Out* for specialized classes.

**Danceworks** (16 Balderton St., W1, tel. 0171/629–6183). You'll find what is probably the widest-ranging program of classes here, catering to all standards from beginner to professional. Ballet, jazz, flamenco, Egyptian, and tap are regulars, but there's more.

**Pineapple** (7 Langley St., WC2, tel. 0171/836–4004). This is where the '80s fitness boom was launched in London, though modern dance has always been its real business. Classes are highly regarded by the sort of dancers who appear a lot on MTV.

**The Place** (17 Dukes Rd., WC2, tel. 0171/388–8430). It really *is* the place for modern dance, since it houses the Contemporary Dance Trust and the London Contemporary Dance School, plus a dance theater, in addition to holding all grades of class.

**Golf** Golf is as huge in England as it is in the States, but if you want to play a round in London, you'll have to hit the outer boroughs.

**Regent's Park Golf and Tennis School** (Outer Circle, Regent's Park, NW1, tel. 0171/724–0643). You don't have to travel far to get here—it's just by the zoo—but driving ranges and putting greens are all you'll get. The instructors have a good reputation.

**Richmond Park** (Roehampton Gate, SW15, tel. 0181/876–1795). There are two well-kept but very busy 18-hole courses here. You don't have to be a member of anything, and can hire half or full sets of clubs, plus buggies and trollies.

**Trent Park Golf Club** (Bramley Rd., Southgate N14, tel. 0181/366–7432). Here you do have to pay a modest fee to join, but it's worth considering for regular visitors, since the setting of this countrified 18-hole course is beautiful, and it's easily reached on the Piccadilly line to Oakwood.

**Horseback Riding** **Rotten Row** and the surrounding network of Hyde Park sand tracks make up the only place to ride in central London—better for posing in the saddle than serious maneuvers, and no galloping allowed. Outer London offers more scope, plus lessons.

**London Equestrian Centre** (Frith Manor Farm, Lullington Garth, N12, tel. 0181/349–1345). This big, bustling north London stable caters to all stages of rider, even nervous beginners. Cross-country, dressage, jumping, and even side-saddle lessons are available, too. You must submit to a half-hour assessment first.

**Ross Nye** (8 Bathurst St., Mews, W2, tel. 0171/262–3791). The only public stable left for Hyde Park riding keeps about 16 horses, mostly on the stolid side (they call it "bomb-proof" in England). Early morning (it opens at 7) is the best time to avoid the park crowds.

**Trent Park Stables** (East Pole Farm, Bramley Rd., N14, tel. 0181/363–8630). You'll think you've left London as you hack through 300 acres of near-rural Middlesex. You can't ride alone because of insurance restrictions, but all standards are accommodated, and indoor and outdoor lessons, from beginners' to dressage and jumping, are available.

**Ice Skating** Hockey is actually becoming pretty popular, but the rinks below are for recreational fun. Skating has a slight image problem in Britain, where it's perceived as downscale. This can mean a certain amount of loutishness on the ice.

**Broadgate Arena** (3 Broadgate, EC2, tel. 0171/588–6565). It's a tiny circle, but it's outdoors—and therefore unique in London. Open from November to April, it's a fun place to skate because of the audience of City workers and the silly team games you can join. Skate hire is available.

**Queens Ice Skating Club** (Queensway, W2, tel. 0171/229–0172). A figure-skating rink with disco tendencies, this is central London's only serious ice venue, and you can take a lesson should your outside edge be rusty. You can hire skates here, too. Queensway tube is next door.

**Martial Arts** You can learn everything from *ba gua zhang* (a Chinese internal martial art) to *silat perisai diri* (Indonesian self-defense), but the places we list teach the pronounceable ones.

**Academy** (16 Hoxton Sq., N1, tel. 0171/729–5789). One of London's best martial arts centers, the Academy is close to the City in a former school building.

**Jubilee Hall** (30 The Piazza, Covent Garden, WC2, tel. 0171/379–0008). This venue offers regular tai chi, tae kwon do, and karate classes, plus wu shu (Chinese boxing).

**YWCA Central Club** (16–22 Great Russell St., WC1, tel. 0171/636–7512). The Y holds tai chi classes for beginners and advanced students, plus xing yi quan, a more combative form.

**Rock Climbing** This is not something you can do outdoors in London, but there are interior "mountains" behind doors.

**NLRC** (Cordova Rd., Bow, E3, tel. 0181/980–0289). It's a little hard to locate (it's near Mile End tube), but worth it, because here are four buildings with every possible rockface—transverse, vertical, and completely upside-down—plus abseiling in the Tower. Classes and equipment are available, as well as national champions to watch when you're exhausted.

**Sobell Sports Centre** (Hornsey Rd., N7, tel. 0171/609–2166). Islington's all-purpose, council-owned center has three walls, plus instruction and equipment.

**Running** London is just perfect for joggers. If you're after a crowd, the more popular routes include **Green Park,** which gets a stream of runners armed with maps from the Piccadilly hotels, and—to a lesser extent—adjacent **St. James's Park.** Both can get perilous with deck chairs during summer days. **Hyde Park** and **Kensington Gardens** together supply a 4-mile perimeter route, or you can do a 2½-mile run in Hyde Park alone if you start at Hyde Park Corner or Marble Arch and encircle the Serpentine. Most Park Lane hotels offer jogging maps for this, their local green space. **Regent's Park** has probably the most populated track, since it's a sporting kind of place; the Outer Circle loop measures about 2½ miles.

Away from the center, there are longer, scenic runs over more varied terrain at **Hampstead Heath,** connecting with **Kenwood** and **Parliament Hill,** London's highest point, where you'll get a fabulous panoramic sweep over the entire city. **Richmond Park** is the biggest green space of all, but don't run into the deer during rutting season (Oct.–Nov.). Back in town, there's a rather traffic-heavy 1½-mile riverside run along **Victoria Embankment** from Westminster Bridge to Embankment at Blackfriars Bridge, or a beautiful mile among the rowing clubs and ducks along the Malls—Upper, Lower, and Chiswick—from **Hammersmith Bridge.**

*Group Runs* If you don't want to run alone, call the **London Hash House Harriers** (tel. 0181/995–7879). They organize noncompetitive hour-long runs round interesting bits of town, with loops and checkpoints built in. Cost: £1.

**Softball** Control your mirth—the sport is huge here; in fact, it's the fastest-growing participatory sport in England. Pick up a game Sunday afternoon in **Regent's Park,** or on the south edge of **Hyde Park.**

**Squash** Racquetball is unknown to the English, but squash is played, though less now than during the '80s, when it boomed. Most courts belong to clubs requiring membership, but the ones we list don't.

**Ironmonger Row** (Ironmonger Row, EC1, tel. 0171/253–4011). There are 10 courts in this popular City sports center. You can't book by phone without a membership, but office hours are less busy, as are weekends.

**Portobello Green Fitness Centre** (3–5 Thorpe Close, W10, tel. 0181/960–2221). Only three courts here, but they're inexpensive.

**Sobell Sports Centre** (Hornsey Rd., N7, tel. 0171/609–2166). This is a popular place, but you can usually get court time.

**Swimming** London does not lack for public swimming pools—clean, lifeguarded, and usually open long hours.

*Indoor Pools* **Chelsea** (Chelsea Manor St., SW3, tel. 0171/352–6985). This renovated turn-of-the-century 27-by-10-yard pool is just off the King's Road, so it's busy, and packed with kids on weekends.

**Seymour Leisure Centre** (Seymour Pl., W2, tel. 0171/402–5795). There's usually a lane roped off for laps at this very central 44-by-20-yard pool, unless the aquaerobics class has taken over.

**Swiss Cottage** (Winchester Rd., NW3, tel. 0171/586–5989). A little out-of-the-way (but next to the Swiss Cottage tube), this is one of the largest (37 by 16 yards) and best for serious lap swimming. There's a shallow children's pool, too.

*Indoor/Outdoor* **Oasis** (32 Endell St., WC2, tel. 0171/831–1804). And it is just that,
*Pools* with a heated outdoor pool (open May–Sept.) right in Covent Garden, and a 30-by-10-yard one indoors. Needless to say, they both get packed in summer.

*Spa Pools* **Ironmonger Row** (Ironmonger Row, EC1, tel. 0171/253–4011). Old Street is the tube nearest to this 33-by-12-yard City pool. It's in a '30s complex that includes a Turkish bath, not quite as beautiful as Porchester's (*see below*). There are separate sessions for men and women.

**Porchester Baths** (Queensway, W2, tel. 0171/229–9950). Here there's a 33-by-11-yard pool for serious lap swimmers, plus a 1920s Turkish bath, sauna, and spa of gorgeous, slightly faded grandeur. It, too, has separate sessions for men and women.

*Beaches* **Serpentine Lido** (Hyde Park, W2, tel. 0171/262–5484). Okay, so it's a beach on a lake, but a hot day in Hyde Park is surreally reminiscent of the seaside. There are changing facilities, and the swimming section is chlorinated. Open May–Sept.

**Hampstead Ponds** (co-ed: East Heath Rd., NW3, tel. 0171/435–2366; women only: Millfield La., N6, tel. 0171/348–1033). These Elysian little lakes are surrounded by grassy lounging areas. The women's one is particularly secluded—and crowded in summer, though it's open all year. The "Mixed Pond" is open May through September. Both have murky-looking, but clean, fresh water.

**Tennis** Poor England never wins its own Grand Slam tournament. Some blame that circumstance on its being a nation of mere park players, which, for the visitor, has obvious benefits.

**Holland Park** (Kensington High St., W8, tel. 0171/602–2226). This is the best, most central, and prettiest place to play, with six hard courts available April through September.

**Islington Tennis Centre** (Market Rd., N7, tel. 0171/700–1370). It's about the only place where you don't need membership to play indoors (year-round), though you need it to reserve by phone. There are four outdoor courts, too, and coaching is available. Caledonian Road tube is nearby.

**Paddington Sports Club** (Castelain Rd., W9, tel. 0171/286–4515). A surprisingly large and busy green space provides a set of eight hard courts where you compete for attention with track runners and soccer, cricket, and softball players.

**Weight Training** If your hotel lacks a gym, these are central and sell either daily or monthly temporary membership.

**Albany Fitness Centre** (St. Bede's Church, Albany St., NW1, tel. 0171/383–7131). This is a deconsecrated church (buy a "work off thy last supper" T-shirt), which means tons of space. There's Keiser equipment, free weights, cardio machines, and aerobics/sculpting classes. The cost is £15/day, with lower weekly rates negotiable. The tube is Great Portland Street.

**Central YMCA** (112 Great Russell St., WC1, tel. 0171/637–8131). As you'd expect from the Y, this place boasts every facility and sport, including a great 25-meter pool and a very well-equipped gym. Weekly membership costs £32.50.

**Jubilee Hall** (30 The Piazza, Covent Garden, WC2, tel. 0171/379–0008). The day rate is £5, monthly £40 (£55 including classes) at this very crowded but very happening and super-well-equipped central gym.

**The Peak** (Hyatt Carlton Tower Hotel, 2 Cadogan Pl., SW1, tel. 0171/235–1234). This hotel club is expensive (£20/day or £200/month) but has top equipment, great ninth-floor views over Knightsbridge, and a sauna—with TV—in the full beauty spa.

**Seymour Leisure Centre** (Seymour Pl., W2, tel. 0171/402–5795). A fee of £4.50 buys you entrance to the gym plus a cardio center that overlooks a hall full of soccer, b-ball, or badminton players.

**Yoga** This discipline is becoming very popular in London, as it is in the United States.

**The Life Centre** (15 Edge St., W8, tel. 0171/221–4602). London's newest, and without a doubt best, yoga school specializes in the dynamic, energetic Vinyasa technique imported from Germany by chief instructor Godfrey Devereux. Beautiful premises enhance the experience.

# Spectator Sports

**Boating**  One of London's most beloved sporting events (since 1845) is also the easiest to see, and it's free. The only problem with the late-March **Oxford and Cambridge Boat Race** is securing a position among the crowds who line the Putney-to-Mortlake route (mostly at pubs along the Hammersmith Lower and Upper Malls, or on Putney Bridge). The Saturday start time varies from year to year according to the tides. The **Head of the River Race** is the professional version, only this time up to 420 crews of eight row the university course in the other direction. It usually happens the Saturday before the university race, or sometimes later the same day.

**Cricket**  **Lord's** (St. John's Wood, NW8, tel. 0171/289–1611) has been hallowed turf for worshipers of England's summer game since 1811. The World Series of cricket, the Tests, are played here, but tickets are hard to procure. One-day internationals, though, can usually be seen by queuing up on the day, and top-class county matches are similarly accessible—whether the rules are is quite another matter.

**The Oval** (Kennington Oval, SE11, tel. 0171/582–6660) is a far easier place to witness the *thwack* of leather on willow. At London's second-string ground, you can see the home teams, Middlesex and Surrey, play county games of very high standard.

**Equestrian Events**  It's one of those clichés based in truth that, from the queen down, the English are in love with the horse, as proved by the United Kingdom's Olympic medals. If you require further proof, attend one of these:

*Parades*  You can see all the city's working horses at the Easter Monday **London Harness Horse Parade** (Inner Circle, Regent's Pk., NW1; 9:30 AM–1 PM). The show competitions have categories like "Heavy Horse" and "Single Horsed Commercial Van." Something similar happens to recreational animals at the **London Riding Horse Parade,** on the first Sunday in August in (where else?) Rotten Row.

*Racing*  The main events of "the Season," which is as much social as sporting, occur just outside the city. Her actual Majesty attends **Royal Ascot** (Grand Stand, Ascot, Berkshire, tel. 01344/22211) in mid-June, driving from Windsor in an open carriage, and processing before the plebs daily at 2. **Derby Day** (The Grandstand, Epsom Downs, Surrey, tel. 01372/726311), on the first Wednesday in June, is the other big one. One of the world's greatest races for three-year-olds, it kicks off at 3:45.

*Show Jumping*  The **Horse of the Year Show** (Wembley Arena, tel. 0181/900–1234) in late October is the top international competition, with lots of fun events alongside the serious. Best of all are the Pony Club Games, where child riders perform virtual gymnastics on horseback.

**Football**  You'll have to call this "American Football" while in London, or everyone will think you're talking about soccer. Amazingly enough, London has a team in the World Football League, and the team is about the best of a mediocre bunch. See the **London Monarchs** at Wembley Stadium (Wembley, Middlesex, tel. 0181/900–1234) during March and April. Also at Wembley is the August **NFL Bowl,** when two American teams come to play. London likes the Raiders.

**Rugby**  This is not a million miles from gridiron, but players are unpadded. It raises the British (and especially Welsh) blood pressure like no other sport, with the 15-a-side amateur game, Rugby Union, or rugger, thrilling purists far more than the pro 13-a-side Rugby League.

The **Rugby League Final** is played at Wembley Stadium (Wembley, Middlesex, tel. 0181/900–1234) on the last Saturday in April, while the Rugby Union **Pilkington Cup** is fought a week later at the Twickenham Rugby Football Ground (Whitton Rd., Twickenham, Middlesex, tel. 0181/892–8161). Tickets for both are more precious than gold. But you can see international matches at Twickenham during the September-to-April season or catch the home games of the London teams, the **Saracens** (Dale Green Rd., N14, tel. 0181/449–3770) and **Rosslyn Park** (Priory La., Upper Richmond Rd., SW15, tel. 0181/876–1879).

**Running**  Starting at 9 AM on the third Sunday in April, some 25,000 runners in the huge **London Marathon** race from Blackheath or Greenwich to Westminster Bridge or the Mall. Entry forms for the following year are available starting in May (tel. 01891/234234).

**Soccer**  To refer to the national winter sport as "soccer" is to blaspheme. It is Football, and the British season culminates in the televised Wembley Stadium **FA Cup Final,** for which tickets are about as easy to get as they are for the Superbowl. International matches at Wembley during the August-to-May season are easier to attend (tel. 0181/900–1234).

For a real taste of this British obsession, though, nothing beats a match at the home ground of one of the three London clubs competing in the Premier League. More than likely you won't see a hint of the infamous hooliganism but will be quite carried away by the electric atmosphere only a vast football crowd can generate. **Tottenham Hotspur,** or "Spurs" (White Hart La., 748 High Rd., N17, tel. 0181/808–3030), and **Arsenal** (Avenell Rd., Highbury, N5, tel. 0171/359–0131) have north Londoners' loyalties about equally divided, while **Chelsea** (Stamford Bridge, Fulham Rd., SW6, tel. 0171/385–5545) is adored by the slightly more genteel west London fan.

**Tennis**  **The Wimbledon Lawn Tennis Championships**—famous among fans for the green, green grass of Centre Court, for strawberries and cream, and for rain, which always falls, despite the last-week-of-June/first-week-of-July high-summer timing—comprise, of course, one of the top three Grand Slam events of the tennis year. Whether you can get tickets is literally down to the luck of the draw, since there's a ballot system for advance purchase. To apply, send a self-addressed, stampled envelope between October and December to All England Lawn Tennis & Croquet Club, Box 98, Church Rd., Wimbledon SW19 5AE (tel. 0181/946–2244), then fill in the application form, then hope.

But there are other ways to see the tennis. A block of Centre Court tickets is kept back to sell each day, but fanatics queue all night for these, especially in the second week. Each afternoon, though, tickets collected from departed spectators are resold (profits go to charity). These can provide grandstand seats (with plenty to see—play continues till dusk), since those who care so little about tennis are often on expensive business freebies or company season tickets. You can also buy entry to the grounds to roam matches on the outer courts, where even the top-seeded players compete early in the fortnight. For up-to-date information, the London Tourist Board operates a **Wimbledon Information Line** from the beginning of June (tel. 01839/123417; cost: 48p/min., 36p cheap rate).

# 6 Dining

During the past, oh, five years, London has undergone an incredible transformation. The city is now—and longtime absentees must suspend disbelief here—among the top places in the world for dining out. It has long been possible to get a good meal in London, especially by spending big bucks or going ethnic, but it's more than that. A new generation of chefs has emerged, weaned in restaurants and familiar with the cuisines of six continents. They watch each other's work and cross-pollinate. Collectively they've precipitated a fresh style of cooking, which you could call "London," though most have dubbed it "Modern British." Everyone's got an opinion on it, since newspapers now devote pages to food columns and restaurant reviews, which everyone reads. Everyone dines out. England has become a nation of foodies.

Even before the current healthy restaurant scene crystallized, successive waves of immigrants had done their best to help the city out. There are a handful still extant of the venerable French and Italian places that were once the last word in fancy; and there are still the thousands of (mostly northern) Indian restaurants that have long ensured that Londoners see a good tandoori as their birthright. Chinese—Cantonese, mostly—places in London's tiny Chinatown have been around a long time, too, as have Greek tavernas; Thai restaurants are the latest to proliferate. Malaysian, Spanish, a hint of Japanese (with more on the way?), Russian, and Korean places have also been opening. After all this, traditional British food, lately revived from its deathbed, appears as one more exotic cuisine in the pantheon.

These listings comprise a taste of London's variety. Largely absent are those aforementioned Indian restaurants, not because they're no good, but because they're nearly all good, and inexpensive, too. Try your local one, or go to Brick Lane in the East End (the **Clifton** is recommended); take a Brit along to do the ordering.

As for cost, the democratization of restaurants means lighter checks than during the '80s, with many experiments in fixed-price menus, but still London is not an inexpensive city. Damage-control methods include making lunch your main meal—the very top places often have bargain lunch menus, halving the price of evening à la carte—and ordering a second appetizer instead of an entrée, to which few places should object. Seek out fixed-price menus, and watch for hidden extras on the check: "cover," bread and vegetables charged separately, and service.

Most restaurants exclude service charges from the menu (which the law obliges them to display outside), then add 10%–15% to the check or else stamp SERVICE NOT INCLUDED along the bottom, in which case you should add the 10%–15% yourself. Don't pay twice for service—unscrupulous restaurateurs may add service, then leave the total in the credit card slip blank, hoping for more.

One final caveat: beware of Sunday. Many restaurants are closed on this day, especially in the evening; likewise public holidays. Over the Christmas period, London shuts down completely—only hotels will be prepared to feed you. When in doubt, call ahead. It's as well to book a table anyway. After all, everyone eats out nowadays.

Highly recommended restaurants are indicated by a star ★.

| Category | Cost* |
|----------|-------|
| $$$$ | over £40 |
| $$$ | £25–£40 |
| $$ | £15–£25 |
| $ | under £15 |

*per person for a three-course meal, excluding drinks, service, and VAT*

## Mayfair

**$$$$**
**French**
**Four Seasons.** This, one of Great Britain's great hotel dining rooms, came to fame under the aegis of Bruno Loubet, who, at press time, was seeking premises for a second place of his own, cooking at his wonderful Bistrot Bruno (*see* Soho, *below*) meanwhile. Young star Jean-Christophe Novelli now holds the reins in this opulent salon (the kind where sniffy waiters flourish silver domes), and early reports have been universal raves. His style is not unrelated to Loubet's *cuisine de terroir*; his *assiette des saveurs*, for instance, consists of pig's trotter and tail, calf's liver and kidneys, and oxtail. The expensive ingredients of haute cuisine are also present and correct, however, and his skill with game has been noted. Here also, there's a "bargain" £25 set lunch. *Four Seasons Hotel, Hamilton Place, Park La., W1, tel. 0171/499–0888. Reservations required at least 2 days in advance. Jacket and tie required. AE, DC, MC, V.*

★ **Le Gavroche.** Albert Roux has handed the toque to his son, Michel, who has yet to regain the third Michelin star that was dropped in '93. But many still consider this London's finest restaurant. The excellent service and the discreetly sumptuous decor complement the positively Lucullan *haute cuisine*—seafood velouté with champagne, lobster roasted with cepes and rosemary. The basement dining room is comfortable and serious, hung with oil paintings, its darkness intensified by racing-green walls. Yet again, the set lunch is relatively affordable at £40 (for canapés and three courses, plus mineral water, a half-bottle of wine, coffee, and petit fours, service *compris*). In fact, it's the only way to eat here if you don't have a generous expense account at your disposal—as most patrons do. *43 Upper Brook St., W1, tel. 0171/408–0881. Reservations advised at least 1 week in advance. Jacket and tie required. AE, DC, MC, V. Closed weekends, 10 days at Christmas, national holidays.*

**Nico at Ninety.** Those with refined palates and very deep pockets would be well advised not to miss Nico Ladenis's exquisite cuisine, served in this suitably hushed and plush Louis XV dining room next to the Grosvenor House Hotel. Autodidact Nico is one of the world's great chefs, and he's famous for knowing it. The menu is in French and untranslated; vegetarians and children are not welcome. There is no salt on the table—ask for some at your peril. It's all more affordable in daylight, proffering a £25 set menu at lunchtime in place of à la carte. *90 Park La., W1, tel. 0171/409–1290. Reservations required. Jacket and tie required. AE, DC, MC, V. Closed weekends, public holidays, 3 weeks in Aug.*

**French/**
**Traditional**
**English**
★
**The Connaught.** This charming and very grand mahogany-paneled, velvet-upholstered, and crystal-chandeliered dining room belongs to the absolutely exclusive eponymous hotel (*see* Chapter 7, Lodging). Waiters wear tails, tables must be booked far in advance, and prices are fearsome; but the restaurant remains London's most respected traditional dining room, with famed French chef

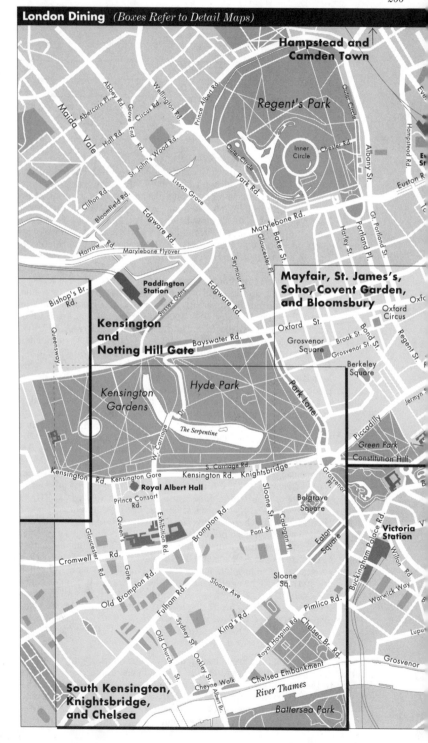

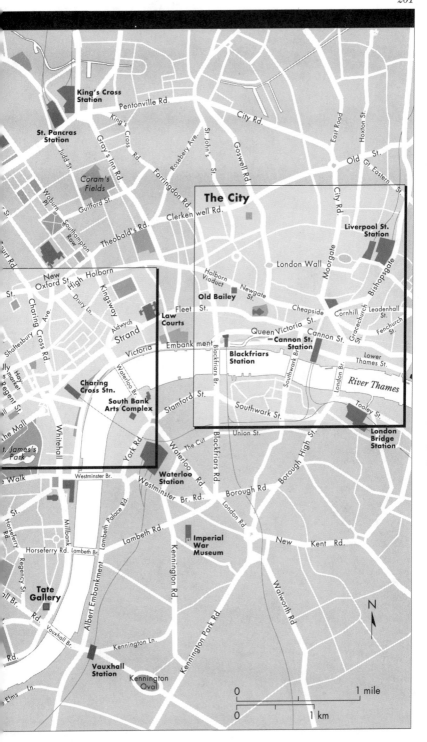

King's Cross Station

St. Pancras Station

Pentonville Rd.

City Rd.

East Road

Hoxton St.

King's Cross Rd.

Gray's Inn Rd.

St. John's St.

Goswell Rd.

Old Gt. Eastern St.

Judd St.

Woburn Pl.

Coram's Fields

Guilford St.

City Rd.

Southampton Row

Theobald's Rd.

Clerkenwell Rd.

**The City**

London Wall

Moorgate

**Liverpool St. Station**

Bishopsgate

New Oxford St.

High Holborn

Kingsway

Drury Ln.

Charing Cross Rd.

Shaftesbury Ave.

Aldwych

Strand

Holborn Viaduct

**Old Bailey**

Newgate St.

Cheapside

Cornhill

Leadenhall St.

Gracechurch St.

Fenchurch St.

Fleet St.

**Law Courts**

Queen Victoria St.

Cannon St.

**Cannon St. Station**

Victoria

Embankment

Blackfriars Br.

**Blackfriars Station**

Southwark Br.

London Br.

Lower Thames St.

*River Thames*

**Charing Cross Stn.**

Waterloo Br.

**South Bank Arts Complex**

Stamford St.

Southwark St.

Tooley St.

**London Bridge Station**

Whitehall

York Rd.

The Cut

Blackfriars Rd.

Union St.

Borough High St.

St. James's Park

the Mall

he Walk

Westminster Br.

**Waterloo Station**

Westminster Br. Rd.

Borough Rd.

London Rd.

New Kent Rd.

Lambeth Palace Rd.

Lambeth Br.

Lambeth Rd.

Kennington Rd.

**Imperial War Museum**

Walworth Rd.

Horseferry Rd.

Millbank

Horseferry Rd.

Regency St.

**Tate Gallery**

Albert Embankment

Kennington Ln.

Kennington Park Rd.

Vauxhall Br.

**Vauxhall Station**

Kennington Oval

Elms Ln.

N

0      1 mile

0      1 km

# Dining in Mayfair, St. James's, Soho, Covent Garden, and Bloomsbury

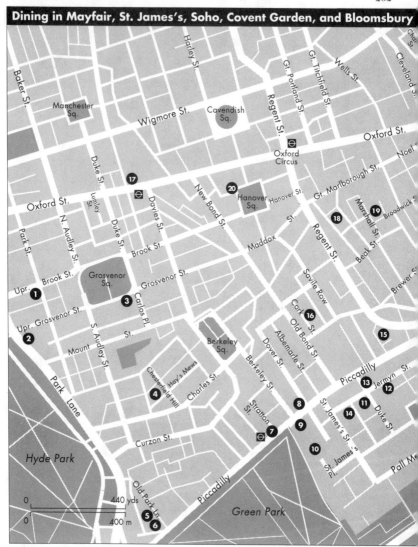

Alastair Little, **30**
Bahn Thai, **28**
Bertorelli's, **41**
Bistrot Bruno, **29**
Café Fish, **36**
Café Flo, **48**
Café Pacifico, **40**
Café Piazza, **43**
Chez Gerard, **21**

Chicago Pizza Pie
Factory, **20**
Connaught, **3**
Crank's, **19**
Criterion, **35**
Deal's West, **18**
dell'Ugo, **31**
Down Mexico Way, **15**
Fatboy's Diner, **46**

Food for Thought, **39**
Fountain, **13**
Four Seasons, **5**
Fung Shing, **34**
The Greenhouse, **4**
Green's, **11**
Hard Rock Café, **6**
Ivy, **38**
Joe Allen's, **50**
Langan's Brasserie, **7**

Le Caprice, **10**
Le Gavroche, **1**
L' Escargot, **27**
Mandeer, **23**
Maxwell's, **42**
Mulligans, **16**
Museum Street Café, **25**
New World, **32**
Nico at Ninety, **2**

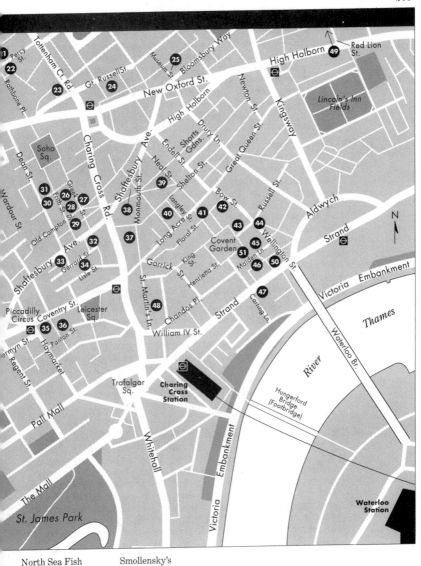

Map labels:
1, 22, Percy St., Tottenham Ct. Rd., Rathbone Pl., 23, Gt. Russell St., Museum St., 25, Bloomsbury Way, New Oxford St., High Holborn, 24, High Holborn, 49, Red Lion St., Newton St., Kingsway, Lincoln's Inn Fields, Dean St., Soho Sq., Shorts Gdns., Drury Ln., Great Queen St., Aldwych, Wardour St., 31, 30, 26, 27, 28, 29, Great Fifth St., Old Compton St., Charing Cross Rd., Shaftesbury Ave., Monmouth St., Neal St., Endell St., Shelton St., 39, 38, 40, 41, 42, Langley St., Long Acre St., Bow St., Russell St., Strand, N, Shaftesbury Ave., 32, 33, 34, Gerrard St., Lisle St., 37, Floral St., King St., Garrick St., Henrietta St., Covent Garden, 43, 44, 45, 51, 46, 50, Wellington St., Maiden Ln., Piccadilly Circus, Coventry St., Leicester Sq., 35, 36, Panton St., St. Martin's Ln., 48, Chandos Pl., Strand, Carting Ln., 47, Jermyn St., Haymarket, Regent St., Pall Mall, William IV St., Trafalgar Sq., Charing Cross Station, Hungerford Bridge (Footbridge), Victoria Embankment, Thames, River, Waterloo Br., The Mall, St. James Park, Whitehall, Embankment, Victoria, Waterloo Station

North Sea Fish
Restaurant, **49**
Now & Zen, **37**
Orso, **44**
Porter's, **51**
Quaglino's, **14**
Ritz, **9**
Rules, **45**
Savoy Grill, **47**

Smollensky's
Balloon, **8**
Soho Soho, **26**
Tai Wing Wa, **33**
Wagamama, **24**
White Tower, **22**
Wilton's, **12**
Zoe, **17**

Michel Bourdin still in charge of the kitchens after many years. This is the place for game—venison, guineafowl, pigeon (not local birds . . . )—presented with traditional trimmings or perhaps with some confection of wild mushrooms. "Luncheon dishes" change according to the day of the week (if this is Friday, it must be oxtail) and are not as exorbitant as they seem at first, since the price includes a starter and dessert. The Connaught is by no means a fashionable place, but it is never out of fashion. *Carlos Pl., W1, tel. 0171/499–7070. Reservations advised at least 1 week in advance. Jacket and tie required. MC. Closed weekends and national holidays.*

**$$$**
**British**
**The Greenhouse.** Tucked away behind the Mayfair mansions in a cute, cobbled mews is this elegant salon for people who like their food big and strong. You sit among extravagant topiary and men in ties to partake of Gary Rhodes's much-praised British food. Alone, he handles the P.R. for faggots (a type of meatball, once reviled) and braised oxtails; but he invents new things, too, like smoked eel risotto, and he is the master of the stew—venison and bacon in red wine, perhaps. This is the place for stodgy, sticky English desserts like bread-and-butter pudding and steamed syrup sponge. (At press time, Mr. Rhodes was threatening to open a place of his own, and may have deserted the Greenhouse by now.) *27A Hay's Mews, W1, tel. 0171/499–3331. Reservations required. Dress: smart. AE, DC, MC, V. Closed Sat. lunch, Sun. dinner, Christmas.*

**French/**
**Traditional**
**English**
**Langan's Brasserie.** Langan's is partly owned by Michael Caine, and although the infamous *bon vivant* and insult artist Peter Langan is no longer with us, it is still a place that makes it into the occasional gossip column. You'll find here contemporary art on the walls, a hundred or so dishes on the menu (including the famous spinach soufflé with anchovy sauce—not served in the quieter upstairs room), and frank, efficient waiters who'll tell you which daily specials are best. *Stratton St., W1, tel. 0171/491–8822. Reservations required. Dress: casual but neat. AE, DC, MC, V. Closed Sat. lunch, Sun., Christmas, national holidays.*

**Irish**
**Mulligans.** You'd think there'd be more Emerald Isle cooking in London, but it is a very rare commodity, especially done this well. Mulligans is straight out of Dublin, down to the draught Guinness and copies of *The Irish Times* in the upstairs bar. Traditional dishes like steak, Guinness and oyster pie, and Irish stew avoid heaviness while retaining flavor, and homey accompaniments like colcannon (buttery mashed potatoes with cabbage) make you feel pampered and pleased, as do the big puddings and friendly service. *13–14 Cork St., W1, tel. 0171/409–1370. Reservations advised. Dress: smart casual. AE, MC, V. Closed Sat. lunch, Sun. dinner, Dec. 25–26, Jan. 1.*

**$$**
**American**
**Smollensky's Balloon.** This American-style bar restaurant is useful for those with children in tow, especially on weekends, when the young are fed burgers, fish sticks, and "Kids' Koktails," and taken off your hands by sundry clowns and magicians. The grown-ups' menu is absolutely committed to red meat, with several cuts of steak the specialty, all served with fries and a choice of sauces. There are also a handful of weekly specials, a single vegetarian pick, and a salmon steak, though you should not travel far for these. *1 Dover St., W1, tel. 0171/491–1199. Reservations advised Fri.–Sun. Dress: casual. AE, DC, MC, V. Closed Dec. 24–26, Jan. 1.*

**Mediterranean**
**Zoe.** Handy for West End shopping, this two-level place serves two-level food—proper dinners downstairs in a sunlit basement of jazzy colors; and posh cocktails, coffee, and sandwiches ("hot spicy pork

with prunes and crispy bacon" is typical) upstairs. It's another Antony Worrall Thompson place (*see* Bistrot 190 in South Kensington, *below*) and so features the trademark heartiness. The schizophrenic restaurant menu is half smart "City" dishes (corn crab cakes, poached eggs, hollandaise, and wilted greens), half huge "Country" ensembles (poached ham, parsley sauce, pease pudding, and hot potato salad), most offered in two sizes, rendering decisions impossible. *St. Christopher's Pl., W1, tel. 0171/224–1122. Reservations advised. Dress: casual. AE, DC, MC, V. Closed Sat. lunch, Sun. (bar open 7 days), Christmas.*

**$**
**American**

**The Chicago Pizza Pie Factory.** The first of expat American Bob Payton's "My Kinda Town" legion of inexpensive, Chicago-style places, this one serves enormous deep-dish pies with the usual toppings, in a wood-floored basement, loud with the sounds of WJMK, the Windy City's oldies station. The restrooms are labeled "Elton John" and "Olivia Newton John."*17 Hanover Sq., W1, tel. 0171/629–2669. Reservations advised for lunch. Dress: casual. AE, MC, V. Closed Dec. 25–26.*

**The Hard Rock Café.** People (especially tourists) stand in line for hours to get into this huge, split-level room with ceiling fans, pool lamps, long tables, and ear-splitting rock music. Favorites include BLT sandwiches, ice-cream sodas, calorific desserts, and, of course, hamburgers and steaks. *150 Old Park La., W1, tel. 0171/629–0382. No reservations. Dress: casual. V. Closed Dec. 24–26.*

**Mexican**

**Down Mexico Way.** Many of London's proliferating Mexican joints serve horrid food, but this one's good. The fine lumpy guacamole is fresh, not factory-packed, and amongst the usual tortillas and burritos are a few adventurous numbers like fish in almond-chili sauce, with sides of cheese and jalapeño muffins or spiced spinach. Look for the beautiful Spanish ceramic tiles and avoid evenings if you want a quiet night out—the place is often taken over by party animals. *25 Swallow St., W1, tel. 0171/437–9895. Reservations advised. Dress: casual. AE, MC, V. Closed Dec. 25–26.*

**Modern British**
**★**

**Criterion.** This palatial neo-Byzantine mirrored marble hall, which first opened in 1874, is now back on the map. When the huge blue-lit glass clock says 2:30, it's teatime (£7.50); otherwise you can choose from a commendably unpretentious "nouveau Brit" menu of appetizers like grilled squid on spinach with lemon vinaigrette, or penne and mussels in a fennel cream, then cod and crab cakes, or grilled tuna with mushroom chutney. More London restaurants should copy the Criterion's generous attitude toward set-priced dining: About half the dishes on the main menu are offered at £10 for two courses, any time (desserts like sticky toffee pudding or lemon tart are an extra £4.50 or so). Cooking and service, though not smooth as mayonnaise, are certainly more assured than one has a right to expect at the price, and this is a pretty setting to while away a wet Sunday over the noon-to-5:30 brunch. Altogether a welcome oasis in the Piccadilly desert. *Piccadilly Circus, W1, tel. 0171/925–0909. Reservations advised. Dress: casual. AE, DC, MC, V. Closed Christmas.*

## St. James's

**$$$$**
**French/**
**Traditional**
**English**

**The Ritz.** The British cuisine here hasn't always lived up to its setting, but since this Louis XVI marble, gilt, and trompe l'oeil treasure, with its view over Green Park, is known as London's most magnificent dining room, that's not such a crime. The latest chef, David Nicholls, retains the French accent and ingredients as rich as the decor (foie gras terrine with fig preserves; lobster thermidor), but he also offers British specialties—Irish stew, braised oxtail, steak and kidney pie, and a daily roast—which are the most enticing part of the menu. A three-course prix fixe lunch at £26 and a four-course dinner at £39.50 make the check more bearable, but the wine list is pricey. *Piccadilly,W1, tel. 0171/493–8181. Reservations required. Jacket and tie required. AE, DC, MC, V.*

*Traditional English*  **Green's Restaurant and Oyster Bar.** The oyster side of things and the comfy-wood-paneled-restaurant angle are in equal balance at this reliable purveyor of the British dining experience, complete with the whiff of public (meaning private and exclusive) school, and coteries of lunching ladies. Oysters, of course, are served in season (which is whenever there's an "R" in the month), alongside smoked fish, lobster cocktail, grilled sole, fish cakes, and so on, but there are comforting English unfishy dishes, like shepherd's pie, too, and—the proper ending to a nanny-sanctioned meal—warm and fattening "nursery puddings," like steamed sponge with custard, and treacle tart. *36 Duke St., St. James's, SW1, tel. 0171/930–4566. Reservations required. Jacket and tie required. AE, DC, MC, V. Closed Sun. dinner, national holidays.*

**Wilton's.** The search for the British Establishment stops here, among Edwardian booths full of politicians in a restaurant that traces its pedigree back to 1742 and offers a taste of the adjacent gentlemen's clubs—for which you pay through the nose. Fish is the mainstay of a plainspeaking menu, from which grilled Dover sole is probably ordered most often, with sherry trifle for afters, and an old-fashioned savory like angels on horseback (crisp bacon wrapped around oysters) with the port. Service is buttoned to the neck; one feels one ought to ask permission to use the bathroom here. *55 Jermyn St., SW1, tel. 0171/629–9955. Reservations advised 2 days in advance. Jacket and tie required. AE, DC, MC, V. Closed Sat. lunch, Sun., last week in July and first 2 weeks in Aug., 10 days at Christmas.*

*$$$ Modern British*  **Le Caprice.** It's just behind the Ritz, and its interior, designed by Eva Jiricna, is filled with equally sophisticated diners tucking into an eclectic selection of dishes from all over Europe—pastas and risottos, peasanty rabbit with polenta, Catalan fish stew, English sausage and mash, dietetic salads or tomato-basil galette for the model types who don't eat. For those who do, desserts are good, as is the wine list, but the main reason to book at Le Caprice is for the best people-watching in town. (Also try sister restaurant, the Ivy; *see* Covent Garden, *below*.) *Arlington House, Arlington St., SW1, tel. 0171/629–2239. Reservations required. Dress: casual but neat. AE, DC, MC, V. Closed Sat. lunch.*

**Quaglino's.** Sir Terence Conran—of Bibendum, Conran Shop, Cantina del Ponte, and Pont de la Tour fame (*see below*)—lavished £2.5 million doing up this famous pre–World War II haunt of the rich, bored, and well-connected. Now in its third year, "Quags" is *the* out-of-towners' post-theater or celebration destination, while Londoners like its late hours. The gigantic sunken restaurant boasts a glamorous staircase, "Crustacea Altar," small dance floor, and large bar. The food is fashionably pan-European, with plenty of small fowl (duck magret with olives and noodles), game (rabbit with prosciutto and herbs), and seafood (crab with mirin and soy, roast crayfish, plateaux de fruits de mer, etc., etc.). Desserts come from somewhere between the Paris bistro and the English nursery (raspberry sablé, parkin pudding with butterscotch sauce), and wine from the Old World and the New, some bottles at modest prices. *16*

*Bury St., SW1, tel. 0171/930–6767. Reservations required. Dress: smart casual. AE, DC, MC, V. Closed Christmas.*

**$$** **Café Fish.** Just to the east of St James's proper, this cheerful, bus-
*French* tling restaurant has an encyclopedic selection of fish (shark and tur-
bot join the trout, halibut, salmon, and monkfish, some of which is
brought daily from Normandy), arranged on the menu according to
cooking method: chargrilled, steamed, *meunière*; smoked fish pâté
is brought with the bread to help you choose. Downstairs there's an
informal wine bar with a smaller selection of dishes. *39 Panton St.,
SW1, tel. 0171/930–3999. Reservations advised. Dress: casual. AE,
DC, MC, V. Closed Sat. lunch, Sun., Dec. 25–26, Jan. 1.*

**$** **The Fountain.** At the back of Fortnum and Mason's is this old-fash-
*Traditional* ioned restaurant, frumpy and popular as a boarding school matron,
*English* serving delicious light meals, toasted snacks, sandwiches, and ice-
★ cream sodas. During the day, go for the Welsh rarebit or cold game
pie; in the evening, a no-frills fillet steak is a typical option. Just the
place for afternoon tea and ice-cream sundaes after the Royal Acad-
emy or Bond Street shopping, or for pre-theater meals. *181 Picca-
dilly, W1, tel. 0171/734–4938. Reservations accepted for dinner
only. Dress: casual. AE, DC, MC, V. Closed Sun., national holi-
days.*

## Soho

**$$$** **Alastair Little.** Little is one of London's most original chefs, drawing
*Modern British* inspiration from practically everywhere—Thailand, Japan, Scandi-
★ navia, France—and bringing it off brilliantly.His restaurant is
starkly modern, so all attention focuses on the menu, which changes
not once but twice daily in order to take advantage of the best ingredients. There will certainly be fish, but other than that it's hard to
predict. Anyone truly interested in food will not be disappointed. *49
Frith St., W1, tel. 0171/734–5183. Reservations advised. Dress: casual. No credit cards. Closed weekends, national holidays, 2 weeks
at Christmas, 3 weeks in Aug.*

**$$** **L'Escargot.** This ever-popular media haunt serves Anglo-French
*Anglo-French* food in its ground floor brasserie and its more formal upstairs res-
taurant. A comprehensive, reasonably priced wine list sets off a ro-
bust ragout of spiced lamb or a simple, fresh poached or grilled fish.
This place is reliable and relaxed. *48 Greek St., W1, tel. 0171/437–
2679. Reservations advised upstairs, not taken downstairs. Dress:
casual but neat. AE, DC, MC, V. Closed Sun., public holidays.*

*Chinese* **Fung Shing.** This comfortable, cool green restaurant is a cut above
★ the Lisle/Wardour Street crowd in both service and ambience, as
well as in food. The usual Chinatown options are supplemented by
some exciting dishes. Salt-baked chicken, served on or off the bone
with an accompanying bowl of intense broth, is essential, and the ad-
venturous might try intestines—deep-fried cigarette-shaped mor-
sels, which are far more delicious than you'd think. *15 Lisle St.,
WC2, tel. 0171/437–1539. Reservations suggested. Dress: casual.
AE, DC, MC, V. Closed Dec. 25.*

*French* **Bistrot Bruno.** Bruno is Bruno Loubet, who earned three Michelin
★ stars at the Four Seasons (he has since left to find a home of his own),
and may be the most dedicated and original chef in London. Here he
does everything but cook, but the menu is unmistakably his work,
dotted with bits of animals you wouldn't want in your freezer, which
in his hands become balanced, beautiful *cuisine du terroir* dishes.
His fromage de tête, or brawn (a pâté from the Lorraine made from

pig's head in aspic), or tripes niçoise (cow's stomach, frankly) may not sound appetizing, but on the plate, they are irresistible. Cowards can order scallops on puff pastry or an amazing shallot tarte tatin, or duck leg confit with crushed potato and cepe sauce, then an iced meringue and cherry slice. Coffee arrives with mini-sorbets encased in chocolate. *63 Frith St., W1, tel. 0171/734–4545. Reservations required. Dress: smart casual. MC, V. Closed Sat. lunch, Sun., Christmas.*

**Soho Soho.** The ground floor is a lively café bar with a (no booking) rotisserie, while upstairs is a more formal and expensive restaurant. Inspiration comes from Provence, both in the olive-oiled cooking style and the decor, with its murals, primary colors, and pale ocher terra-cotta floor tiles. The rotisserie serves omelets, salads, charcuterie, and cheeses, plus a handful of bistro dishes like Toulouse sausages with fries; herbed, grilled poussin; and tarte tatin. Or you can stay in the café-bar and have just a kir or a beer. *11–13 Frith St., W1, tel. 0171/494–3491. Reservations advised upstairs. Dress: casual. AE, DC, MC, V. Closed Sun., Sat. lunch upstairs, Dec. 25–26, Jan. 1.*

*Mediterranean* **dell'Ugo.** A three-floor Mediterranean café-restaurant from the stable of Antony Worrall Thompson (*see* Bistrot 190 in South Kensington, *below*). You can choose light fare—bruschetta loaded with marinated vegetables, mozzarella, Parmesan etc., Tuscan soups, and country bread—or feast on wintry, warming one-pot ensembles and large platefuls of sunny dishes like spicy sausages and white bean casserole with onion confit. The place gets overrun with hormone-swapping youth some weekends, but trendiness, on the whole, doesn't mar pleasure. *56 Frith St., W1, tel. 0171/734–8300. Reservations required for restaurant, not taken for café. Dress: casual. AE, MC, V. Closed Sun., Christmas.*

*Thai* **Bahn Thai.** Many people find this the best of London's many Thai restaurants (you can see at least four others from the door), better still now that its ancient, gloomy decor has been excised, leaving a brasserie on the first floor for casual eating. Upstairs, an immensely long menu features little chili symbols for the nervous of palate, plus easy options like chargrilled poussin marinated in honey and spices with a plum dipping sauce. Other Thai dishes are well explained. *21A Frith St., W1, tel. 0171/437–8504. Reservations advised for dinner. Dress: casual. AE, MC, V. Closed Dec. 25–26.*

*Thai/American* **Deal's West.** Viscount Linley and his two partners have hit on a winning formula here (and in the two other Deal's, at Chelsea Harbour and Hammersmith): an unlikely sounding merger between America and Thailand. Off Carnaby Street in a relaxed, barn-like diner with exposed brick walls, wooden floors and beams, loudish music accompanies ribs, salads, and burgers—as well as Thai curries. Cocktails, extended hours, and live jazz on weekends make this popular with a young, after-work crowd. *14–16 Fouberts Pl., W1, tel. 0171/287–1050. Reservations advised for dinner. Dress: casual. AE, DC, MC, V. Closed Sun. dinner, public holidays.*

**$** **New World.** A cavernous dim sum palace—probably the best-known *Chinese* one in London's small Chinatown—serving from trollies between 11 and 6 daily. Demanding gourmets might not enjoy. *1 Gerrard Pl., W1, tel. 0171/734–0677. Reservations not necessary (700 seats). Dress: casual. AE, DC, MC, V. Closed Christmas.*

**Tai Wing Wa.** This relative newcomer does good dim sum for beginners—there's a menu in English, and the waiters are friendly. *7–9 Newport Pl., tel. 0171/287–2702. Reservations advised. Dress: casual. AE, DC, MC, V. Closed Sat., Christmas.*

**Vegetarian** **Crank's.** This is a popular vegetarian chain (there are other branches at Covent Garden, Great Newport Street, Adelaide Street, Tottenham Street, and Barrett Street), bought out by the management in 1992, and now serving more up-to-date meatless meals than the '60s menu that made their name. They remain always crowded and, irritatingly, insist on closing at 8. *8 Marshall St., W1, tel. 0171/437–9431. Dress: casual. AE, DC, MC, V. Closed Sun., national holidays.*

## Covent Garden

**$$$$** **Savoy Grill.** The grill continues in the first rank of power dining loca-
**French/** tions. Politicians, newspaper barons, and tycoons like the comfort-
**Traditional** ing food and impeccably discreet and attentive service in the low-
**English** key, yew-paneled salon. On the menu, an omelet Arnold Bennett (with cheese and smoked fish) is perennial, as is beef Wellington on Tuesday and roast Norfolk duck on Friday. Playgoers can split their theater menu, eating part of their meal before the show, the rest after. *Strand, WC2, tel. 0171/836–4343. Reservations essential for lunch, and for Thurs.–Sat. dinner. Jacket and tie required. AE, DC, MC, V. Closed Sat. lunch, Sun.*

**$$$** **Now & Zen.** This spectacular restaurant, with its audacious shop-
**Chinese** window front, glass pavement, and glass waterfall connecting the three floors, would be worth patronizing for the visuals alone; lucki-ly the food measures up, since this is one of the Zen chain, which practices the creed of freshness, regional dishes, minimal sodium, and no MSG. Menu notes without capital letters encourage balanced ordering—a fried dish to accompany a steamed one; sushi, perhaps, from the short Japanese menu first, or coriander (cilantro) and cut-tlefish (squid) cakes. Waitering here is an art form. Tiny, perfectly formed, immaculately black-clad people wrap crispy Szechuan duck pancakes with one hand behind their back. Downstairs in the Lower Deck, you can pay a set price and order all night from a list of 50 small dishes, like Thai chicken with port wine or coriander prawn croquettes. *4A Upper St. Martin's La., WC2, tel. 0171/497–0376. Reservations advised. Dress: smart casual. AE, DC, MC, V. Closed Dec. 25–26, Jan. 1.*

**International** **The Ivy.** This seems to be everybody's favorite restaurant—every-
★ body who works in the media or the arts, that is. In a Deco dining room with blinding white tablecloths, and Hodgkins and Paolozzis on the walls, the celebrated and the wannabes eat Caesar salad, roast grouse, shrimp gumbo, braised oxtail, and rice pudding with Armagnac prunes or sticky toffee pudding. *1 West St., WC2, tel. 0171/836–4751. Reservations advised. Dress: casual but neat. AE, DC, MC, V. Closed Christmas.*

**Italian** **Orso.** The Italian brother of Joe Allen's (*see below*)—a basement
★ restaurant with the same snappy staff and a glitzy clientele of showbiz types and hacks. The Tuscan-style menu changes every day, but always includes excellent pizza and pasta dishes, plus en-trées based perhaps on grilled rabbit or roast sea bass and first courses of roquette (arugula) with shaved Parmesan or deep-fried zucchini flowers stuffed with ricotta. Food here is never boring, much like the place itself. *27 Wellington St., WC2, tel. 0171/240–5269. Reservations required. Dress: casual but neat. No credit cards. Closed Dec. 25–26.*

**Traditional** **Rules.** A London institution—an Edwardian restaurant that was a
**English** great favorite of Lily Langtry's, among others. After decades the restaurant remains interesting for its splendid period atmosphere,

but annoying for its slow service. For a main dish, try the seasonal entrées on the list of daily specials, which will, in season, include game from Rules's own Scottish estate (venison is disconcertingly called "deer"). It is more than a little touristy, but that's because it's so quaint. *35 Maiden La., WC2, tel. 0171/836–5314. Reservations advised at least 1 day in advance. Dress: casual but neat. AE, DC, MC, V. Closed Christmas.*

**$$**
*British* **Porters.** Good British food (really), an Olde Worlde public house interior, a nob owner (the Earl of Bradford), and a reasonable check, with vegetables and service included—no wonder Americans invariably like this place. Pies star on the menu—lamb-and-apricot or chicken-and-chili alongside the traditional fish or steak-and-kidney—with steamed sponges and custard for afters. The budget alternative to Rules. *17 Henrietta St., WC2, tel. 0171/836–6466. Reservations required for weekend dinner. Dress: casual. AE, MC, V. Closed Christmas.*

*American* **Joe Allen's.** Long hours (thespians flock after the curtain falls in
★ theaterland), a welcoming, if loud, brick-walled interior mean New York Joe's London branch is still swinging after nearly two decades. The fun, California-inflected menu helps: Roast, stuffed poblano chili, or black bean soup are typical starters; entrées might feature barbecue ribs with black-eyed peas and London's only available corn muffins, or roast monkfish with sun-dried-tomato salsa. There are the perennial egg dishes and huge salads, too, and Yankee desserts like grilled banana bread with ice cream and hot caramel sauce. It can get chaotic, with long waits for the cute waiters, but at least there'll be famous faces to ogle in the meantime. *13 Exeter St., WC2, tel. 0171/836–0651. Reservations required. Dress: casual. No credit cards. Closed Easter, Dec. 25–26.*

*Italian* **Bertorelli's.** Right across from the stage door of the Royal Opera
★ House, Bertorelli's is quietly chic, the food better than ever now that Maddalena Bonnino (formerly of 192) is in charge. Poached cotechino sausage with lentils; monkfish ragout with fennel, tomato and olives; and garganelli with French beans, cob nuts, and Parmesan are typical dishes. Downstairs is a very relaxed inexpensive wine bar serving a simpler menu of pizza, pasta, salads, and a few big dishes and daily specials. *44A Floral St., WC2, tel. 0171/836–3969. Reservations required for restaurant; advised downstairs for dinner. Dress: smart casual. AE, DC, MC, V. Closed Christmas.*

**$**
*American* **Fatboy's Diner.** One for the kids, this is a 1941 chrome trailer transplanted from the banks of the Susquehanna in Pennsylvania and now secreted, unexpectedly, in a backstreet, complete with Astroturf "garden." A '50s jukebox accompanies the dogs, burgers, and fries. *21 Maiden La., WC2, tel. 0171/240–1902. No reservations. Dress: casual. No credit cards. Closed Christmas.*
**Maxwell's.** London's first-ever burger joint, 21 in '93, cloned itself and then grew up. Here's the result, a happy place under the Opera House serving the kind of food you're homesick for: quesadillas and nachos, Buffalo chicken wings, barbecue ribs, Cajun chicken, chef's salad, a real NYC Reuben, and a burger to die for. *8–9 James St., WC2, tel. 0171/836–0303. Reservations advised weekends. Dress: casual. AE, DC, V. Closed Christmas.*

*French* **Café Flo.** This useful brasserie serves the bargain "Idée Flo"—soup or salad, *steak-frites* or *poisson-frites*, and coffee—a wide range of French café food, breakfast, wines, *tartes*, espresso, fresh orange juice, simple set-price weekend menus . . . everything for the Francophile on a budget. There are branches in Hampstead, Islington,

Fulham, and Kensington. *51 St. Martin's La., WC2, tel. 0171/836–8289. Reservations advised. Dress: casual. MC, V. Closed Dec. 25, Jan. 1.*

*Italian* **Café Piazza.** It doesn't look like much with its standard-issue bent-
★ wood chairs and undressed tables, but this usefully central brasserie enjoys the services of a young Florentine chef far, far better than the low prices suggest. Weekly specials (osso bucco, a smoked cheese and leek risotto, *linguine alla bottarga*—with mullet roe) augment a menu of Italian greatest hits (minestrone, seafood salad, wood-oven pizzas), plus surprises (ricotta and spinach ravioli with walnut sauce, entrecote marinated in juniper and bay), cooked with great flair. *16–17 Russell St., WC2, tel. 0171/379–7543. Reservations advised evenings. Dress: casual. AE, MC, V.*

*Mexican* **Café Pacifico.** Reasonably priced Chicano and straight Mexican food is served in this young, lively converted warehouse. The bar boasts a full range of tequilas (including frozen margaritas). If you go on a Sunday night, live music accompanies your *ceviche* (spiced fish marinated in lime juice) or *fajitas* (marinated beef/chicken with onions, peppers, tortillas, cheese, and guacamole). *5 Langley St., WC2, tel. 0171/379–7728. Reservations not accepted for dinner. Dress: casual. MC, V. Dinner only. Closed national holidays, Jan. 1.*

*Vegetarian* **Food for Thought.** This simple basement restaurant (no liquor li-
★ cense) seats only 50 and is extremely popular, so you'll almost always find a line of people down the stairs. The menu—stir-fries, casseroles, salads, and desserts—changes every day, and each dish is freshly made; there's no microwave. *31 Neal St., WC2, tel. 0171/836–0239. No reservations. Dress: casual. No credit cards. Closed after 8 PM, 2 weeks at Christmas, national holidays.*

## Bloomsbury

$$$ **The White Tower.** Barely changed in six decades, the White Tower is
*Greek* quite different from the average London Greek, its three Georgian stories lined with antique pistols and prints (and a portrait of that most famous Hellenist, Lord Byron), and its verbose menu listing many unusual dishes, like the cracked wheat, fruit, and nut-stuffed duck you must order in advance, or the chicken Paxinou, served with fried banana and aubergine (eggplant). The *taramasalata*—cod's roe dip, which all too often resembles Pepto-Bismol—is the best in town, was the first in town, and is always ordered by the many establishment types who love this place. *1 Percy St., W1, tel. 0171/636–8141. Reservations required. Jacket and tie required. AE, DC, MC, V. Closed weekends, national holidays, 3 weeks in Aug., 1 week at Christmas.*

$$ **Chez Gerard.** One of a chain of three steak-frites restaurants, this
*French* one has updated itself of late, widening the choice on the utterly Gallic menu to include more for non–red meat eaters—brioche filled with wild mushrooms and artichoke hearts, for instance, plus fish dishes and something for vegetarians, like stuffed roast onion. Steak, served with shoestring fries and béarnaise sauce, remains the reason to visit, though. *8 Charlotte St., W1, tel. 0171/636–4975. Reservations advised. Dress: casual. AE, DC, MC, V. Closed Christmas.*

*Modern British* **The Museum Street Café.** This tiny restaurant near the British Museum serves a limited selection of impeccably fresh dishes, intelligently and plainly cooked by the two young owners. The evening menu might feature grilled, maize-fed chicken with pesto, followed with a rich chocolate cake; at lunchtime you might choose a sandwich of Stilton on walnut bread and a big bowl of soup. Bring your own wine (check first—they were applying for a liquor license at press time), and don't smoke. *47 Museum St., WC1, tel. 0171/405–3211. Reservations required for dinner. Dress: casual. No credit cards. Closed weekends, public holidays.*

**$**
*Indian*
**Mandeer.** Buried in a basement, with tiled floors, brick walls, and temple lamps, the Mandeer is useful for being central (off Tottenham Court Road, where there's nothing much else), and extremely cheap at lunchtime, when you help yourself to the vegetarian buffet. *21 Hanway Pl., W1, tel. 0171/580–3470. No reservations at lunch. Dress: casual. AE, DC, MC, V. Closed Sun., national holidays, 2 weeks over New Year.*

*Japanese*
★
**Wagamama.** London's gone wild for Japanese noodles in this big basement. It's high-tech (your order is taken on a hand-held computer) and high-volume—there are always crowds, with which you share wooden refectory tables, so the noise level is inevitably high. You can choose ramen in or out of soup, topped with sliced meats or tempura; or "raw energy" dishes—rice, curries, tofu, and so on. *4 Streatham St., WC1, tel. 0171/323–9223. No reservations. Dress: casual. No credit cards. Closed Christmas.*

*Seafood*
★
**The North Sea Fish Restaurant.** This is the place for the British national dish of fish-and-chips—battered and deep-fried whitefish with thick fries shaken with salt and vinegar. It's a bit tricky to find—three blocks south of St. Pancras station, down Judd Street. Only freshly caught fish is served, and you can order it grilled—though that would defeat the object. You can take out or eat in. *7–8 Leigh St., WC1, tel. 0171/387–5892. Reservations advised. Dress: casual. AE, DC, MC, V. Closed Sun., national holidays, Christmas.*

## South Kensington

**$$$$**
*French*
★
**Bibendum.** Bibendum is in the reconditioned Michelin House, with its Art Deco decorations and brilliant stained glass, Conran Shop (*see* Chapter 4), and Oyster Bar. For some years now it has been home to Simon Hopkinson's enormous talent. He is famous for preparing simple dishes perfectly. Thus you can order herrings with sour cream, a risotto, or leeks vinaigrette followed by steak au poivre or the perfect boeuf bourgignon, or you might try brains or tripe as they ought to be cooked. The £25 set-price menu at lunchtime is money well spent. *Michelin House, 81 Fulham Rd., SW3, tel. 0171/581–5817. Reservations required. Dress: casual. MC, V. Closed Sun.*

**$$**
*French*
★
**Lou Pescadou.** This place is like a little *tranche* of the South of France, with the sea-themed decor and emphatically French staff. The menu changes often and is based on fish—don't miss the *soupe de poisson* with croutons and *rouille* (rose-colored, garlicky mayonnaise) if it's on—but there are other dishes, too, from steak-frites to, perhaps, delicate braised *cervelles*—brains. *241 Old Brompton Rd., SW5, tel. 0171/370–1057. No reservations. Dress: casual. AE, DC, MC, V. Closed Aug., Christmas.*

*Mediterranean*
**Bistrot 190.** Chef-restaurateur and popular guy Antony Worrall Thompson dominates this town's medium-priced eating scene with his happy, hearty food from Southern Europe (liver and wild mushroom terrine; chargrilled squid with red and green salsa; lemon tart) in raucous hardwood-floor-and-art settings. This place, which

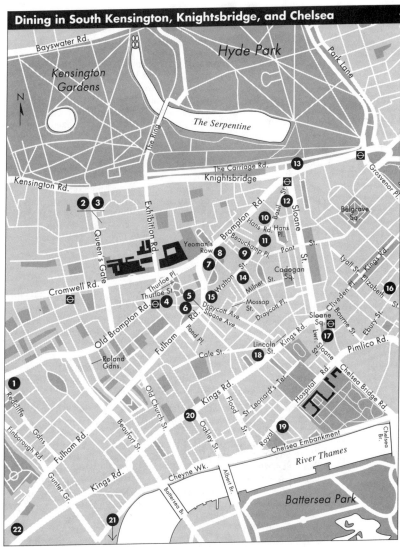

# Dining in South Kensington, Knightsbridge, and Chelsea

Bibendum, **5**
Bistrot 190, **2**
The Canteen, **21**
Capital, **10**
Caravela, **9**
Chelsea Kitchen, **18**
Chutney Mary, **22**
Daquise, **4**
Downstairs at 190, **3**
Gavvers, **17**

Henry J. Bean's, **20**
Joe's Café, **15**
La Tante Claire, **19**
Lou Pescadou, **1**
Luba's Bistro, **8**
Marco Pierre White:
The Restaurant, **13**
Mijanou, **16**
PJ's Bar and Grill, **7**
St. Quentin, **7**

San Lorenzo, **11**
Stockpot, **12**
Waltons, **14**

was his first, is handy to museum or Albert Hall excursions. *190 Queen's Gate, SW7, tel. 0171/581–5666. No reservations. Dress: smart casual. AE, DC, MC, V. Closed Sat. lunch, Sun., Dec. 25–26, Jan. 1.*

**Downstairs at 190.** This is another Worrall Thompson creation— this time a good-value fish restaurant (*see* Bistrot 190, *above*). You can choose "Snacking Food," or appetizers, like grilled mussels and clams with garlic crumbs or smoked haddock and salmon carpaccio with anchovy ice cream, or go for lobster ravioli or a cassoulet of fishes, then attempt whisky fudge cake with caramelized oranges. *190 Queen's Gate, SW7, tel. 0171/581–5666. Reservations advised. Dress: casual. AE, DC, MC, V. Closed Sun., Christmas.*

$ **Daquise.** This venerable and well-loved Polish café by the tube sta-
*Polish* tion is incongruous in this neighborhood, since it's neither style-con-
scious nor expensive. Fill your stomach without emptying your pocketbook (or, it must be said, overstimulating your taste buds) on *bigos* (sauerkraut with garlic sausage and mushrooms), stuffed cabbage and cucumber salad, or just coffee and cakes. *20 Thurloe St., SW7, tel. 0171/589–6117. Reservations advised weekend dinner. Dress: casual. No credit cards. Closed Christmas.*

---

## Knightsbridge

$$$$ **The Capital.** This elegant, clublike dining room has chandeliers and
*French* trompe l'oeil floral urns, a grown-up atmosphere, and formal ser-
★ vice. Chef Philip Britten keeps his star bright with perhaps a subtle baked mousse of haddock and ginger, an emincé of chicken with olives, or pot-roasted pigeon with armagnac, then a perfect caramel soufflé with butterscotch sauce. Set-price menus both at lunch (£21.50 and £25) and in the evening (£25) make it somewhat more affordable. *22–24 Basil St., SW3, tel. 0171/589–5171. Reservations required. Jacket and tie required. AE, DC, MC, V.*

*Modern British* **Marco Pierre White: The Restaurant.** One fears one ought to have read the book and seen the movie before patronizing The Restaurant. Actually, if one is from London, one has. Bad boy Marco enjoys Jagger-like fame from his TV appearances, from his book *White Heat*, and from gossip column reports of his complicated love life and random eruptions of fury. He should stick to his pans, say superchef critics, meaning it literally in some cases. But, hype aside, Marco is a great chef and now gets to show off in his most serious setting yet, all valuable oils, starched napery, and batteries of flatware. If you invest in an evening here, know that he will despise you for ordering his *assiette des chocolats*, which he considers low-class. *Hyde Park Hotel, Knightsbridge, SW3, tel. 0171/259–5380. Reservations required. Jacket and tie required. AE, DC, MC, V.*

*Traditional* **Waltons.** Popular with Americans, this formal, sumptuous res-
*English* taurant has strong color schemes, acres of rich fabrics, and flowers. The cuisine is as rich as the surroundings and, though billed as British, is not so easy to categorize—try the ravioli stuffed with lobster or the steamed red mullet on a fondue of tomatoes and fresh basil. *121 Walton St., SW3, tel. 0171/584–0204. Reservations advised. Jacket and tie required. AE, DC, MC, V. Closed Christmas, Dec. 25–26, Jan. 1, and Easter.*

$$$ **San Lorenzo.** This well-established, well-heeled trattoria, with
*Italian* quiet green decor, is nothing special foodwise, but it's just the ticket if you're keen to spot celebrities or royalty, gaze into the world of ladies-who-lunch—or if you are yourself a lady-who-lunches. The usual upscale Italian dishes are here, but they nod to fashion—try

wood pigeon with polenta, or any of the veal dishes. *22 Beauchamp Pl., SW3, tel. 0171/584–1074. Reservations advised. Dress: casual stylish. AE, DC, MC, V. Closed Sun. and national holidays.*

**$$**
*French*

**St. Quentin.** A very popular slice of Paris, frequented by French expatriates and locals alike. The cuisine is meaty, Gallic, and plain, with some more modern dishes—lime and honey marinated duck breast, for instance, or sweetbreads with a hazelnut sauce. *Tartes* for dessert come from St. Quentin's gourmet food shop, Les Specialités, as do the cheeses. It can become a lot more expensive if you dine à la carte. *243 Brompton Rd., SW3, tel. 0171/589–8005. Reservations advised. Dress: casual but neat. AE, DC, MC, V.*

*Portuguese*

**Caravela.** This narrow lower-ground-floor place is one of London's few Portuguese restaurants. You can get *Caldo verde* (cabbage soup), *bacalhau* (salt-cured cod), and other typical dishes while listening (on Friday or Saturday) to the national music, fado—desperately sad songs belted out at thrash-metal volume. *39 Beauchamp Pl., SW3, tel. 0171/581–2366. Reservations advised weekend dinner. Dress: casual. AE, DC, MC, V. Closed Sun. lunch, Christmas, Easter.*

**$**
*International*

**Stockpot.** You'll find speedy service in this large, jolly restaurant, often packed to the brim with young people and shoppers. The food is filling and wholesome: try the Lancashire hot pot, for example, and the apple crumble. *6 Basil St., SW3, tel. 0171/589–8627. Reservations accepted. Dress: casual. No credit cards. Closed Christmas, national holidays. Other branches at 40 Panton St., off Leicester Sq. (tel. 0171/839–5142); 18 Old Compton St., Soho (tel. 0171/287–1066); and 273 King's Rd., Chelsea (tel. 0171/823–3175).*

*Russian*

**Luba's Bistro.** Popular for decades: long wooden tables, plain decor, and authentic Russian cooking—chicken Kiev, beef Stroganoff, etc. Bring your own wine. *6 Yeoman's Row, SW3, tel. 0171/589–2950. Reservations required. Dress: casual. MC, V. Closed Sun., national holidays.*

## Chelsea

**$$$$**
*French*
★

**La Tante Claire.** Justly famous, but cripplingly expensive. The decor is light and sophisticated, the service impeccable, the French wine list impressive, but the food is the point. From the *carte*, you might choose hot pâté de foie gras on shredded potatoes with a sweet wine and shallot sauce, roast spiced pigeon, or Pierre Koffmann's famous signature dish of pig's feet stuffed with mousse of white meat with sweetbreads and wild mushrooms. As every gourmet expense-accounter knows, the set lunch menu (£24.50) is a genuine bargain. *68 Royal Hospital Rd., SW3, tel. 0171/352–6045. Reservations advised 3–4 weeks in advance for dinner, 2–3 days for lunch. Jacket and tie required. AE, DC, MC, V. Closed weekends, 2 weeks at Christmas, Jan. 1, 10 days at Easter, 3 weeks in Aug.–Sept.*

**$$$**
*Anglo-Indian*

**Chutney Mary.** London's first-and-only Anglo-Indian restaurant provides a fantasy version of the British Raj, all giant wicker armchairs and palms. Dishes like Masala roast lamb (practically a whole leg, marinated and spiced) and "Country Captain" (braised chicken with almonds, raisins, chilis, and spices) alternate with the more familiar North Indian dishes like roghan josh (lamb curry). The best choices are certainly the dishes re-created from the kitchens of Indian chefs cooking for English palates back in the old Raj days. For this reason,the all-you-can-eat Sunday buffet is not such a great idea, since it leaves those out. Service is deferential, and desserts, unheard of in tandoori places (kulfi excepted), are worth leavingroom for. *535 King's Rd., SW10, tel. 0171/351–3113. Reservations advised. Dress: smart. AE, DC, MC, V. Closed Dec. 25 dinner, Dec. 26.*

*French* **Gavvers.** This was the original site of Le Gavroche and is now a simpler, less expensive *petit-Gavroche* run by people trained in the Michel and Albert Roux ways. Set menus are composed entirely of their inventions, and include, at dinner, a glass of kir, three courses (with choices like a sausage of goose and foie gras, then hare in a sauce of red wine and bitter chocolate), coffee, and petits fours. Lunch is simpler (and more than £10 cheaper). *61–63 Lower Sloane St., SW1, tel. 0171/730–5983. Reservations required. Dress: casual. AE, DC, MC, V.Closed for Sat. lunch, Sun., national holidays, Dec. 24–Jan. 1.*

**Mijanou.** The haunt of politicians and Whitehall civil servants. Chef Sonia Blech claims on the menu that she "merely rearranges the natural ingredients which have always existed," but she's too modest, as the likes of her quail stuffed with wild rice and pecan nuts or lobster terrine with a mild saffron sauce will prove. Smoking is banned in the entire restaurant, which is just as well, because it's tiny. There is a small patio. *143 Ebury St., SW1, tel. 0171/730–4099. Reservations required. Jacket and tie required. AE, DC, MC. Closed weekends, national holidays, 1 week at Christmas, most of Aug.*

*Modern British* **Joe's Café.** A stylish brasserie just across the road from Bibendum, serving light, chic food to suit the designer patrons and Designer Patron—he is Joseph Etedgui, the fashion maven and inventor of '80s matte black. As dishes like lemon shrimp salad or tagliatelle Nero with squid suggest, this is not really a café at all, but a none-too-cheap restaurant. Staff can be snooty. *126 Draycott Ave., SW3, tel. 0171/225–2217. Reservations advised. Dress: casual but neat. AE, DC, MC, V. Closed Sun. evening, 1 week Christmas.*

**$$**  **PJ's Bar and Grill.** The decor here evokes the Bulldog Drummond
*American* lifestyle, with wooden floors and stained glass, a vast, slowly revolving propeller from a 1940s Curtis flying boat, and polo memorabilia. A menu of all-American staples (soft shell crab, chowder, gumbo, steaks, smoked ribs), and big salads,then lemon tart, brownies, and Häagen-Dazs should please all but vegetarians, and portions are big (especially the local bankers' favorite "Confusion Solution"—half the menu with fries). Beware the sugary fruit sauces; anyway, this place is more remarkable for ambience than for food—it's open late, it's relaxed, friendly, and efficient, and it has bartenders who can mix anything. The sister PJ's in Covent Garden (30 Wellington St., tel. 0171/240–7529) is worth remembering for its excellent weekend "Fun Club" for kids. *52 Fulham Rd., SW3, tel. 0171/581–0025. Reservations advised. Dress: smart casual. AE, DC, MC, V. Closed Dec. 25–26, Jan. 1.*

*Modern British* **The Canteen.** Of all celebrity chefs, Marco Pierre White is the column-inch king, and this is his second-string place—he's joint owner (with Michael Caine, who often eats here), does the menu, trains the chefs, and hangs out here, occasionally banning people arbitrarily, but he doesn't actually lift a pan. (That he does at the immodestly named The Restaurant. *See* Knightsbridge, *above.*) It all adds up to bargain Marco. Menus read plain, taste fantastic—winter might offer a risotto of ink or roast calamari followed by grilled guinea fowl, creamed cabbage, and pommes Anna, then the tarte tatin of pears for two, straight from The Restaurant, where dinner is closer to £80 than the £30-odd it'll set you back here. *Unit G4 Harbour Yard,*

*Chelsea Harbour, SW10, tel. 0171/351–7330. Reservations essential. Dress: smart casual. MC, V. Closed Christmas.*

**$**
**American**
**Henry J. Bean's (but his friends all call him Hank) Bar and Grill.** This popular Payton place (*see* The Chicago Pizza Pie Factory in Mayfair, *above*) is a cheap and cheerful, useful dive for any homesick American prepared to endure a menu (on napkins; you order from the bar) that calls salad "a bit on the side" or "let's go gardening." It's worth it to sit in the big, lovely patio garden. Nachos, burgers, hot dogs, fried chicken, potato skins, and mud or pecan pie complete the menu, along with a score of cocktails. Loud fun. *195–197 King's Rd., SW3, tel. 0171/352–9255. No reservations. Dress: casual. No credit cards. Closed Dec. 25–26, 31.*

**International**
**Chelsea Kitchen.** This café has been crowded since the '60s with hungry people after hot, filling, and inexpensive food. Expect nothing more fancy than pasta, omelets, salads, stews, and casseroles. The menu changes every day. *98 King's Rd., SW3, tel. 0171/589–1330. No reservations. Dress: casual. No credit cards. Closed Christmas.*

## Kensington and Notting Hill Gate

**$$$**
**French**
**Boyd's.** Boyd Gilmour was a professional percussionist who decided he'd rather rattle the pans, and so built this glass-roofed conservatory garden. It's a soothing, satisfying restaurant, the cooking unpretentious—crab ravioli with ginger and scallions; wood pigeon in a black-currant sauce; chocolate terrine—the atmosphere calmer than at near-neighbor Kensington Place (*see below*). A 100-bottle wine list includes about 10 to sample by the glass. *135 Kensington Church St., W8, tel. 0171/727–5452. Reservations advised. Jacket and tie required. AE, MC, V. Closed Sun., Mon., 1 week at Christmas, Easter.*

**Chez Moi.** Sophisticated French food is served in a warm salmon-pink dining room, which, with the tables widely spaced and the lighting low, demands romantic behavior. There are dishes the menu calls "traditional" that Chez Moi's fans have depended on for a quarter century—things like rack of lamb with garlic and mint and beef tournedos with béarnaise, which are wonderful here. There are also more novel dishes like the popular "Oursins Chez Moi"—ersatz sea urchins made of shrimp and scallop, with fried angel-hair pasta "spines." The desserts are extra-good. *1 Addison Ave., W11, tel. 0171/603–8267. Reservations required for dinner. Dress: casual. AE, DC, MC, V. Open dinner only Mon.–Sat., also Sun. lunch. Closed 2 weeks over Christmas, 2 weeks in Aug., national holidays.*

**French/**
**Californian**
**Clarke's.** There's no choice on the evening menu at Sally Clarke's award-winning restaurant; her dinners feature ultrafresh ingredients, plainly but perfectly cooked, accompanied by home-baked breads. *124 Kensington Church St., W8, tel. 0171/221–9225. Reservations required. Dress: casual but neat. MC, V. Closed weekends, public holidays, 2 weeks in Aug.*

**Modern British**
**First Floor.** A place for well-off but arty locals who know and watch each other, popular both for its inventive food and its ambience—it looks like a bombed church inhabited by distressed nobility. There might be Thai fishcakes or Tuscan lamb stew in the evening, while lunch, at about half the price, consists of lighter dishes like focaccia with grilled vegetables. *186 Portobello Rd., W11, tel. 0171/243–0072. Reservations required. Dress: casual. AE, MC, V. Closed Christmas.*

★ **Kensington Place.** A favorite among the local glitterati, always packed and noisy. A huge plate-glass window and mural are back-

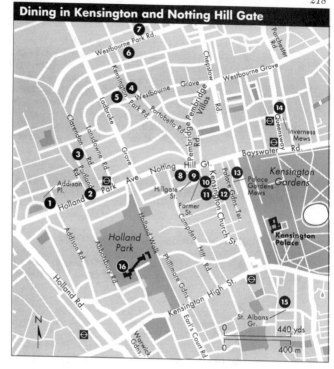

## Dining in Kensington and Notting Hill Gate

drops to fashionable food—grilled foie gras with sweet-corn pancake and baked tamarillo with vanilla ice are perennials—but it's the buzz that draws the crowds. *201 Kensington Church St., W8, tel. 0171/727–3184. Reservations advised. Dress: casual but neat. MC, V. Closed Aug. bank holiday, Christmas.*

*Traditional*
*British*

**Julie's.** This restaurant has two parts: an upstairs wine bar and a basement restaurant, both decorated with Victorian ecclesiastical furniture. The cooking is sound, old-fashioned English (salmon-and-halibut terrine, roast pheasant with chestnut stuffing and wild rowan jelly). The traditional Sunday lunches are very popular, and in summer there's a garden for outside eating. *135 Portland Rd., W11, tel. 0171/229–8331. Reservations advised for dinner and on weekends. Jacket and tie suggested. MC, V. Closed Sat. lunch, Dec. 25 and 31, Easter.*

**$$**
*French*

**L'Artiste Assoiffé.** Stanley and Sally the parrots will scold you in the bar of this eccentric Victorian house filled with antiques from Portobello Road just outside. Unadventurous French food (spinach crepes with nuts and cheese; chicken in mushroom cream sauce; chocolate mousse) is by no means expertly cooked, but the bohemian atmosphere keeps the tables full. *122 Kensington Park Rd., W11, tel. 0171/727–4714. Reservations required. Dress: casual but neat. AE, DC, MC, V. Closed Sun., national holidays.*

*French/*
*Traditional*
*English*

**Ark.** Established in the 1960s, the Ark remains popular with the locals. The atmosphere is cozy, as is the menu, made up of old-fashioned bistro-type comfort food like crab bisque and French onion soup, steak-frites and crème brûlée; smoked chicken pancakes is about as wild as it gets. The welcoming, book-lined, wood-paneled rooms, enhanced by a pretty conservatory, are filled with the hum of conversation—though, it must be said, the topic of conversation is not the food. *122 Palace Gardens Terr., W8, tel. 071/229–4024. Reservations required. Dress: casual. AE, MC, V. Closed Sun. lunch, Christmas, Easter.*

*Greek* **Kalamaras.** Here are two small, friendly, authentic Greek restaurants, one "micro" and one "mega," nearly next door to each other. The micro, which doesn't have a liquor license, is cheaper but more cramped than the mega. Menu choice here is wider than at the average Greek restaurant; try a few unusual *mezedes* (appetizers, for sharing), like artichoke hearts with broad beans and dill, or grilled mussels, then a great moussaka (a rare thing), or kavouri—baked crab. *76–78 Inverness Mews, W2, tel. 0171/727–9122. Reservations advised. Dress: casual. AE, DC, MC, V. Dinner only. Closed Sun., national holidays.*

*Mediterranean* **The Belvedere.** There can be no finer setting for a summer supper or a sunny Sunday brunch than a window table—or a balcony one if you luck out—at this stunning restaurant in the middle of Holland Park. The menu is big on shaved Parmesan, sun-dried tomatoes, and arugula, which suits the conservatory-like room, but both food and service do occasionally miss the target. Still, with a view like this, who cares about waterglasses or bland chicken? *Holland Park, off Abbotsbury Rd., W8, tel. 0171/602–1238. Reservations required weekends. Dress: smart casual. AE, DC, MC, V. Closed Sun. dinner, Christmas.*

*Modern British* **192.** Upstairs is a noisy wine bar/dining room where the local
★ trendies live, and which recently doubled in size; downstairs is a perennially popular, relaxed restaurant serving school-of-Alistair-Little (who began here) flavorsome cooking. On a menu that changes twice a day, there are always inventive salads (like romanesco, broccoli, anchovy, and gremolata), plus at least one fish (sea bass with fennel, lemon, and rosemary), and something unexpected (scallop, chickpea, chorizo, and clam casserole). Since first courses are often more exciting, many people order two of them instead of an entrée. *192 Kensington Park Rd., W11, tel. 0171/229–0482. Reservations advised. Dress: smart casual. AE, MC, V. Closed Mon., lunch, public holidays.*

*Polish* **Wódka.** This smart, modern Polish restaurant is the only one in the
★ world, as far as we know, to serve smart, modern Polish food. It is popular with elegant locals plus a sprinkling of celebs and often has the atmosphere of a dinner party. Alongside the smoked salmon, herring, caviar, and eggplant *blinis*, you might also find venison sausages or roast duck with krupnik (honey-lemon vodka). Order a carafe of the purest vodka in London (and watch the check inflate . . . ); it's encased in a block of ice and hand-flavored (with bison grass, cherries, rowanberries . . . ) by the owner, who, being an actual Polish prince, is uniquely qualified to do this. *12 St. Albans Grove, W8, tel. 0171/937–6513. Reservations required for dinner. Dress: casual but neat. AE, DC, MC, V. Closed weekend lunch, public holidays.*

$ **Tootsies.** A superior burger place, dark but cheerful, decorated with
*American* vintage advertisements and playing vintage rock. Alternatives to the burgers, which come with thick, crinkly fries, are big salads, steak, BLTs, and chili in a bottomless pan—they'll give you as much as you can take. The usual ices and pies do for dessert. There are branches in Fulham, Chiswick, and Notting Hill. *120 Holland Park*

Ave., W11, tel. 0171/229–8567. No reservations. Dress: casual. MC, V. Closed Christmas.

*Greek* **Costa's Grill.** Come for good value and such down-to-earth Greek food as grilled fish and *kleftiko* (roast lamb on the bone). The atmosphere is lively and great fun. *14 Hillgate St., W8, tel. 0171/229–3794. Reservations advised for groups of more than 4. Dress: casual. No credit cards. Closed Sun., national holidays, 3 weeks in summer.*

*Modern British* **All Saints.** One warms to the wobbly kitchen chairs and spartan plaster walls here after a bottle or two of the inexpensive house wine, and an enormous portion of home-style cooking. Serial chef changes alter the nature of the food, but not of the place, home-away-from-home for young and trendy Notting Hillbillies. Menu staples at press time included roast vegetables with aioli (garlic mayonnaise), lamb brochette with tabbouleh and hummus, and a four-inch-high creamy lemon tart. *12–14 All Saint's Rd., W11, tel. 0171/243–2808. Reservations required for dinner. Dress: casual. MC, DC, V. Closed Sun. dinner, Christmas.*

*Seafood* **Geales.** This is a cut above your typical fish-and-chips joint. The de-
★ cor is stark but the fish will have been swimming in the sea just a few hours beforehand, even the ones from the Caribbean (fried swordfish is a specialty). Geales is popular with the rich and famous, not just loyal locals. *2 Farmer St., W8, tel. 0171/727–7969. No reservations. Dress: casual. MC. Closed Sun., Mon., 2 weeks at Christmas, 3 weeks in Aug., national holidays.*

## The City

$$$ **Bubb's.** Old Bailey lawyers, stockbrokers, and diamond merchants
*French* flock here for lunch. The ambience is cozy and Gallic, the food as fresh as you'll find anywhere, and well prepared. Escargots with aioli, Barbary duck, and crème brûlée are usually available on a frequently changing menu with many daily specials. *329 Central Markets, Smithfield, EC1, tel. 0171/236–2435. Reservations required. AE, V. Jacket and tie advised. Closed dinner, weekends, national holidays, 2 weeks in Aug., 1 week at Christmas.*

★ **Le Pont de la Tour.** Sir Terence Conran's other pièce de résistance (in addition to Quaglino's and Bibendum) lies across the river, overlooking the bridge that gives it its name, and so comes into its own in summer, when the outside tables are very heaven. Inside the "Gastrodrome" (his word) there's a vintner and baker and deli, a seafood bar, a brasserie, and this '30s diner-style restaurant, smart as the captain's table. Fish and seafood (lobster salad; Baltic herrings in crème fraîche; roast halibut with aioli), meat and game (venison fillet, port and blueberry sauce; roast veal, caramelized endive) feature heavily—vegetarians are out of luck. Prune and Armagnac tart or chocolate terrine could finish a glamorous—and expensive—meal. By contrast, an impeccable salade niçoise in the brasserie is about £8. *36D Shad Thames, Butler's Wharf, SE1, tel. 0171/403–8403. Reservations required for lunch, weekend dinner. Dress: smart. MC, V. Closed Christmas.*

**Le Poulbot.** Probably the most popular set lunch in the City. It's part of the Roux brothers' empire (*see* Le Gavroche in Mayfair, *above*), and, like the other Roux restaurants, provides top-class, well-balanced food in an intimate red-plush setting. Poulbot specialties include smoked salmon flan and lamb cutlets with crème of sweet pepper, and you get three courses of them, plus an aperitif. Beware the wine list—it will double the check if you let it. *45 Cheapside, EC2, tel. 0171/236–4379. Reservations advised 2–3 days in ad-*

Bill Bentley's, **7**

Bubb's, **3**

The Eagle, **2**

Mustards Bistro à Vin, **4**

Le Pont de la Tour, **6**

Le Poulbot, **5**

Quality Chop House, **1**

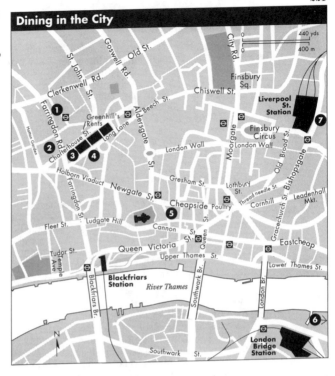

vance. *Jacket and tie required. AE, DC, MC, V. Lunch only. Closed weekends.*

**$$**
**Seafood**

**Bill Bentley's.** You can see from the bare walls and the arched ceiling that this was once a wine merchant's vaults. There are four other branches in London, all equally old-fashioned in feel, and all serving Bill Bentley's special oysters and seafood platters. *Swedeland Ct., 202 Bishopsgate, EC2, tel. 0171/283–1763. Reservations required. Jacket and tie required. MC, V. Lunch only. Closed weekends, national holidays.*

*Traditional*
*English*

**Quality Chop House.** This was converted from one of the most gorgeous "greasy spoon" caffs in town, retaining the solid Victorian fittings (including pew-like seats, which you often have to share). It is not luxurious, but the food is wonderful. It's almost a parody of caff food—bangers and mash turns out to be home-made herbed veal sausage with rich gravy, light, fluffy potato, and vegetables *à point;* egg and chips (fries) are not remotely greasy. There are also posh things like salmon fishcakes and steak, and desserts that change with the seasons. *94 Farringdon Rd., EC1, tel. 0171/837–5093. Reservations required. Dress: casual. No credit cards. Closed Sat. lunch, Sun. dinner, public holidays.*

**$**
*French*

**Mustards Bistro à Vin.** How useful this is when you're stranded in the City after dark, or need to escape the Barbican Centre caterers' clutches. Sit at the bar and order a "casse croûte" (a French grilled open sandwich), or sink into a banquette for a choucroute garnie (sauerkraut with various sausages), or the bargain (£7.95) two-course salad, steak, and fries. Many of the wines are well-priced, too. *62–63 Long La., EC1, tel. 0171/600–1111. Reservations ad-*

*vised. Dress: casual. AE, DC, MC, V. Closed weekends, Christmas, public holidays.*

Italian ★ **The Eagle.** If the name makes it sound like a pub, that's because it is a pub, albeit a superior one, with wooden floors, a few sofas, and art on the walls. It does, however, belong in the "Dining" section by virtue of the amazingly good-value nouveau Tuscan food, which you choose from the blackboard menu (or by pointing) at the bar. There are about half a dozen dishes, a pasta and/or risotto always among them. There are currently quite a few places in London charging four times the price for remarkably similar—and no better—food. *159 Farringdon Rd., EC1, tel. 0171/837–1353. No reservations. Dress: casual. No credit cards. No food served Sat., Sun. evenings.*

## Camden Town and Hampstead

$$ Anglo-French **Camden Brasserie.** The perfect neighborhood restaurant (unless you're vegetarian), this mellow, brick-walled, wood-floored haven makes its charcoal grill work hard (barbecued corn-fed chicken, salmon fillet, steak, etc., come with piles of matchstick fries) and offers a daily fish, pasta, soup, and salad, too. Convenient for market, Canal, and Zoo excursions. *216 Camden High St., NW1, tel. 0171/ 482–2114. Reservations advised weekends. Dress: casual. MC, V. Closed Christmas.*

Belgian ★ **Belgo.** To enter what must be London's least normal restaurant, you pass the wavy concrete facade and cross the spotlit "drawbridge" over the brushed-steel open kitchen. Inside, wait staff in maroon monks' habits sweep over to your refectory-like table to take your order of moules-frites (steamed mussels in various sauces with fries), waterzooi (a whitefish stew), wild boar sausages, and other authentic Belgian dishes.Try the Kriek, cherry beer brewed by Trappist monks. Improbably, it's enormous fun—and the food's great. *72 Chalk Farm Rd., tel. 0171/267–0718. Reservations required, same day only. Dress: casual. AE, MC, V. Closed Christmas.*

French **Café des Arts.** A welcome addition to the Hampstead scene, this brasserie is housed in a 17th-century cottage on the main street. Every wood-paneled wall is hung with work for sale—hence the name—and the patrons are just the sort to buy it, too. About half the beautifully presented dishes—tuna tataki (just-seared fillets) with five-spice lentils; provençale fish stew with rouille; chicken breast with lemon-herb dumplings—come in two sizes, so you can control the check. Don't miss the wicked warm chocolate soufflé. *82 Hampstead High St., NW3, tel. 0171/435–3608. Reservations advised weekends. Dress: smart casual. AE, DC, MC, V. Closed Christmas.*

Italian **San Carlo.** Lunch here on a summer Sunday, after a visit to nearby Highgate Cemetery, would make for a fine day out, since San Carlo is a sweet and pampering place, with obsequious service, lots of space, plants, and paintings, a pretty patio, an evening pianist, and a clientele of well-heeled locals. Try pappardelle with wild mushrooms from the list of classic pastas, then maybe chicken breast with a sauce of prunes, lime, and brandy. *2 Highgate High St., N6, tel. 0181/340–5823. Reservations advised. Dress: smart casual. AE, MC, V.*

**Underground Café.** Next door to the Camden Brasserie, and a close relation, this pastel-walled, terra-cotta-floored basement place serves big platefuls of irresistible Italian-esque dishes (chargrilled vegetables with polenta; roast stuffed suckling pig; seafood risotto) to loyal locals. *214 Camden High St., NW1, tel. 0171/482–0010. Reservations advised weekends. Dress: casual. MC, V. Closed Mon.–Sat. lunch, Sun. dinner, Christmas.*

**$**   **The Coffee Cup.** A Hampstead landmark for just about as long as
*English*  anyone can remember, this smoky, dingy, uncomfortable café is lovable, very cheap, and therefore always packed. You can get anything (beans, eggs, kippers, mushrooms) on toast, grills, sandwiches, cakes, fry-ups, etc.—nothing healthy or fashionable whatsoever. There are tables outside in the summer, but no liquor license. *74 Hampstead High St., NW3, tel. 0171/435–7565. No reservations. Dress: casual. No credit cards. Closed Christmas.*

*Greek*  **Lemonia.** On a very pleasant street near Regent's Park is this superior version of London Greek—large and light, friendly, and packed every evening. Besides the usual *mezedes* (appetizers), *souvlakia* (kebabs), *stifado* (beef stewed in wine), and so on, there are interesting specials: quail, perhaps, or *gemista* (stuffed vegetables). *89 Regent's Park Rd., NW1, tel. 0171/586–7454. Reservations required for dinner. Dress: casual. No credit cards. Closed Sat. lunch, Sun. dinner, Christmas.*

## Pubs

Many Londoners could no more live without their "local" than they could forego their daily dinner. The pub—or public house, to give it its full title—is ingrained in the British psyche as social center, bolthole, second home. Pub culture is still male-dominated, revolving around pints, pool, darts, and sports, but mass redecoration by the major breweries (which own most pubs) in the late '80s transformed so many ancient smoke- and spittle-stained dives into fantasy Edwardian drawing rooms that (on the whole) they feel more congenial to women than ever before. There are signs of a welcome pub-food renaissance, too, with others slowly following where the Eagle (*see* The City, *above*) led, and offering more than the antique pub fare of quiche, greasy sausages, and ploughman's lunch (bread, cheese, and pickles).

Arcane licensing laws forbid the serving of alcohol after 11 PM (10:30 on Sunday; different rules for restaurants) and have created, some argue, a nation of alcoholics, obliged to down more pints than is decent in a limited time—a circumstance you see in action at 10 minutes to 11, when the "last orders" bell signals a stampede to the bar. The list below offers a few pubs selected for central location, historical interest, a pleasant garden, music, or good food, but you might just as happily adopt your own temporary local.

**Black Friar.** A step from Blackfriars tube, this pub has an arts-and-crafts interior that is entertainingly, satirically ecclesiastical, with inlaid mother-of-pearl, wood carvings, stained glass, and marble pillars all over the place, and reliefs of monks and friars poised above finely lettered temperance tracts, regardless of which there are six beers on tap. *174 Queen Victoria St., EC4, tel. 0171/236–5650.*
**Bunch of Grapes.** A traditional (which means smoky, noisy, and antichic) pub, popular since Victoria was on the throne, in the heart of Shepherd Market, the village-within-Mayfair, and still featuring a full deck of London characters. *16 Shepherd Market, W1, tel. 0171/629–4989.*
**Crown and Goose.** The possible shape of pubs to come is exemplified by this sky-blue-walled, art-bedecked Camden Town local, where armchairs augment the tables, coffee and herb tea the beers, and great food (steak in baguette, smoked chicken salad with honey vin-

aigrette, baked and stuffed mushrooms) is served to the crowds. *100 Arlington Rd., NW1, tel. 0171/485-2342.*

**Dove Inn.** Read the list of famous ex-regulars, from Charles II and Nell Gwynn (mere rumor, but a likely one) to Ernest Hemingway, as you queue ages for a beer at this very popular, very comely 16th-century riverside pub by Hammersmith Bridge. If it's *too* full, stroll upstream to the Old Ship or the Blue Anchor. *19 Upper Mall, W6, tel. 0181/748-5405.*

**Freemason's Arms.** This place is supposed to have the largest pub garden in London, with two terraces, a summerhouse, country-style furniture, and roses everywhere. Try your hand at the 17th-century game of pell mell—a kind of croquet—or at skittles. It's a favorite Hampstead pub, and popular with local young people. *32 Downshire Hill, NW3, tel. 0171/435-2127.*

**French House.** In the pub where the French Resistance convened during World War II, Soho hipsters and eccentrics rub shoulders now. More than shoulders, actually, because this tiny, tricolore-waving, photograph-lined pub is always full to bursting. *49 Dean St., W1, tel. 0171/437-2799.*

**George Inn.** The inn sits in a courtyard where Shakespeare's plays were once performed. The present building dates from the late 17th century and is central London's last remaining galleried inn. Dickens was a regular—the inn is featured in *Little Dorrit.* Entertainments include Shakespeare performances, medieval jousts, and morris dancing. *77 Borough High St., SE1, tel. 0171/407-2056.*

**Island Queen.** Gigantic caricatures of politicians leer down at you from the ceiling in this sociable Islington (*see* Minogues, *below*) pub, which offers superior home-cooked food (better still in Mojees, the upstairs restaurant), and a fab jukebox. The playwright Joe Orton frequented; he lived—and died—next door, murdered by his lover, Ken Halliwell. *87 Noel Rd., N1, tel. 0171/226-0307.*

**Jack Straw's Castle.** Straw was one of the leaders of the Peasant's Revolt of 1381, and was hanged nearby. In Tudor times it was a favorite hangout for highwaymen, but by the 19th century it had become picturesque and respectable; artists painted charming views from it and Dickens (inevitably) stayed here. Sadly, it was blitzed during World War II, and rebuilt in the1960s. You can admire the views over Hampstead Heath and drink (weather permitting) in the large and lovely outside courtyard. *North End Way, NW3, tel. 0171/435-8885.*

**The Lamb.** Another of Dickens's locals is now a picturesque place for a summer pint, when you can drink on the patio. *94 Lamb's Conduit St., WC1, tel. 0171/405-0713.*

**Lamb and Flag.** This 17th-century pub was once known as "The Bucket of Blood," because the upstairs room was used as a ring for bare-knuckle boxing. Now, it's a trendy, friendly, and entirely bloodless pub, serving food (at lunchtime only) and real ale. It's on the edge of Covent Garden, off Garrick Street. *33 Rose St., WC2, tel. 0171/836-4108.*

**Mayflower.** An atmospheric 17th-century riverside inn, with exposed beams and a terrace, this is practically the very place from which the Pilgrims set sail for Plymouth Rock. The inn is licensed to sell American postage stamps alongside its superior pub food. *117 Rotherhithe St., SE16, tel. 0171/237-4088.*

**Minogues.** A little out of the way in Islington (but perfect for the Almeida theater or Camden Passage antiquing expeditions), this is a friendly, gentrified version of an Irish pub, with Guinness on tap, excellent live traditional folk, and equally excellent Irish food in the adjoining brasserie. *80 Liverpool Rd., N1, tel. 0171/354-4440.*

**Museum Tavern.** Across the street from the British Museum, this gloriously Victorian pub makes an ideal resting place after the rigors of the culture trail. With lots of fancy glass—etched mirrors and stained glass panels—gilded pillars, and carvings, the heavily restored hostelry once helped Karl Marx to unwind after a hard day in the Library. He could have spent his kapital on any one of six beers available on tap. *49 Great Russell St.,WC1, tel. 0171/242-8987.*

**Pheasant and Firkin.** David Bruce single-handedly revived the practice of serving beer that's been brewed on the premises (then sold the thriving business), and this is one of his jolly microbrewery/ pubs, all named the something and Firkin (a small barrel), serving beers called "dogbolter" or "rail ale," and selling T-shirts printed with *bons mots* like "I had a Pheasant time at the Firkin pub." Students like this a lot. *166 Goswell Rd., EC1, tel. 0171/235-7429.*

**Prospect of Whitby.** Named after a ship, this historic riverside tavern dates back to 1520. Once upon a time it was called "The Devil's Tavern," because of the numbers of low-life criminals—thieves and smugglers—who congregated here. It's ornamented with pewter ware and nautical memorabilia. *57 Wapping Wall, E1, tel. 0171/481-1095.*

**Sherlock Holmes.** This pub used to be known as the Northumberland Arms, and Arthur Conan Doyle popped in regularly for a pint. It figures in *The Hound of the Baskervilles*, and you can see the hound's head and plaster casts of its huge paws among other Holmes memorabilia in the bar. *10 Northumberland St., WC2, tel. 0171/930-2644.*

**Spaniards Inn.** This is another historic, oak-beamed pub on Hampstead Heath, boasting a gorgeous rose garden, scene of the tea party in Dickens's *Pickwick Papers.* Dick Turpin, the highwayman, used to frequent the inn; you can see his pistols on display. Romantic poets—Shelley, Keats, Byron—hung out here, and so, of course, did Dickens. It's extremely popular, especially on Sunday when Londoners take to the Heath in search of fresh air. *Spaniards Rd., NW3, tel. 0171/455-3276.*

**The Sun.** Near the Lamb (*see above*) by Coram's Fields, this no-frills pub prides itself on the 20 or so beers from independent breweries it keeps in peak condition. The place tends to be testosterone-heavy, since real ale connoisseurs are not, on the whole, female. *63 Lamb's Conduit St., tel. 0171/405-8278.*

**Three Greyhounds.** Usefully Soho-central, this welcoming, reconditioned mock-Tudor pub serves a great bar meal—homemade scotch eggs (hard boiled, wrapped in sausage meat, and deep fried in bread crumbs), matzo-coated southern fried chicken, sandwiches of home-cured ham or herring, oysters by the half dozen. Its other claim to fame is its youthful landlady's name—say hi to Roxy Beaujolais. *25 Greek St., W1, tel. 0171/734-8799.*

**Windsor Castle.** One to rest at on a Kensington jaunt, and sample the traditional sort of pub food (steak and kidney pudding is good here), which you order from a Cruikshank-illustrated menu, in keeping with the general Dickensian ambience. In winter there are blazing fires; in summer, an exquisite walled patio garden. *114 Campden Hill Rd., W8, tel. 0171/727-8491.*

**Ye Olde Cheshire Cheese.** Yes, it is a tourist trap, but this most historic of all London pubs (it dates from 1667) deserves a visit anyway, for its sawdust-covered floors, low wood-beamed ceilings, the 14th-century crypt of Whitefriars' monastery under the cellar bar, and the set of 17th-century pornographic tiles upstairs. This was the most regular of Dr. Johnson's and Dickens's *many* locals. *145 Fleet St., EC4, tel. 0171/353-6170.*

# 7 Lodging

Make no mistake, London hotels are expensive. The city has a peculiar dearth of the pleasant medium-priced hotels that other European capitals have no difficulty in supplying. Grand hotels London has got (and, at the other end of the scale, seedy lodging houses which you will not find in these pages), but modest, family-run hotels tend to inflate their rates a few notches above what one would expect in, say, Paris or Madrid. There's nothing for it but to resign yourself to spending the greater part of your budget on a bed—or investigate the B&Bs at the end of this chapter.

Our grading system is based simply on price, and does not itself indicate the quality of the hotel, although we have been at pains to select ones whose caliber is tried and tested. Our gradings are based on the average room cost, and you should note that in some establishments, especially those in the $$$$ category, you could pay considerably more—well past the £200 mark in some cases. Like hotels in most other European countries, British hotels are obliged by law to display a tariff at the reception desk. If you have not prebooked, you are strongly advised to study this carefully.

The general custom these days in all but the bottom end of the scale is for rates to be quoted for the room alone; breakfast, whether Continental or "Full English," comes as an extra. VAT is usually included, and service, too, in nearly all cases. All the hotels listed here are graded according to their spring 1994 rates, so check for the latest figures, remembering, of course, that there can be a significant difference off-season.

Be sure to make reservations well in advance, as seasonal events, trade shows, or royal occasions can fill hotel rooms for sudden brief periods. However, if you arrive in the capital without a room, the **London Tourist Board Information Centres** at Heathrow and Victoria Station Forecourt can help; or call the **LTB Accommodation Sales Service** (tel. 0171/824–8844, weekdays 9:30–5:30) for prepaid credit-card bookings (V, MC).

A word of warning: visitors to London have complained of the exorbitant rates exacted by certain accommodations agencies for their "services." So try to deal directly with the hotel.

Highly recommended hotels are indicated by a star ★.

| Category | Cost* |
| --- | --- |
| $$$$ | over £170 |
| $$$ | £120–£170 |
| $$ | £65–£120 |
| $ | under £65 |

*cost of a double room; VAT included; add service*

## Mayfair to Regent's Park

$$$$ **Athenaeum.** Now independently run, this Green Park baby grand is celebrating its 21st birthday with a soup-to-nuts refit, in progress at press time. Standards at the dear old Athenaeum had been slipping under its previous owners, Rank Hotels. ("Rank" was indeed becoming the appropriate epithet, not to mention "dear" and "old.") The new decor retains the distinctive leather-topped mahogany and yew furniture, but the '70s bachelor-pad ambience has been replaced by Regency-esque comfiness in emerald- and ruby- on-cream colors.

# London Lodging *(Boxes Refer to Detail Maps)*

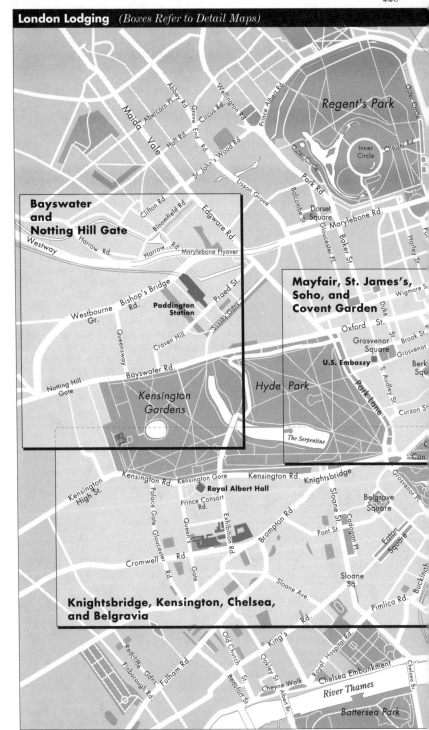

Regent's Park

Outer Circle

Inner Circle

Chester Rd.

Maida Vale

Abbey Rd.

Abercorn Pl.

Hall Rd.

Grove End Rd.

Circus Rd.

Wellington Rd.

Prince Albert Rd.

St. John's Wood Rd.

Lisson Grove

Park Rd.

Outer Circle

Balcombe St.

Dorset Square

Marylebone Rd.

Baker St.

Gloucester Pl.

Harley St.

**Bayswater and Notting Hill Gate**

Clifton Rd.

Bloomfield Rd.

Edgware Rd.

Westway

Harrow Rd.

Harrow Rd.

Marylebone Flyover

Bishop's Bridge Rd.

Praed St.

**Paddington Station**

Sussex Gdns.

**Mayfair, St. James's, Soho, and Covent Garden**

Wigmore S

Westbourne Gr.

Queensway

Craven Hill

Oxford St.

Duke St.

Grosvenor Square

Brook St.

Grosvenor

Notting Hill Gate

Bayswater Rd.

**U.S. Embassy**

S. Audley St.

Berk Squ

*Kensington Gardens*

Hyde Park

Park Lane

Curzon S

*The Serpentine*

Con

Kensington Rd.

Kensington Gore

Kensington Rd.

Knightsbridge

Grosvenor Pl.

Kensington High St.

Palace Gate

Gloucester Rd.

Prince Consort Rd.

**Royal Albert Hall**

Queen's Gate

Exhibition Rd.

Brompton Rd.

Sloane St.

Cadogan Pl.

Pont St.

Belgrave Square

Eaton Square

Buckingh

Cromwell Rd.

Sloane Ave.

Sloane Sq.

**Knightsbridge, Kensington, Chelsea, and Belgravia**

Pimlico Rd.

Redcliffe Gdns.

Fulham Rd.

Old Church St.

King's Rd.

Oakley St.

Cheyne Walk

Royal Hospital Rd.

Chelsea Embankment

Chelsea Br.

Finborough Rd.

Beaufort St.

Albert Br.

*River Thames*

*Battersea Park*

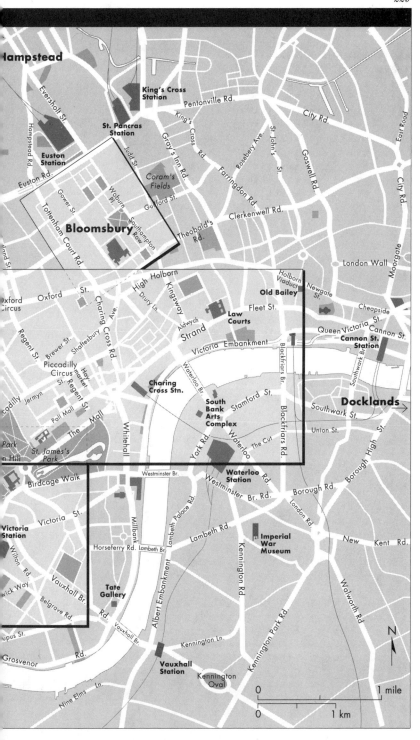

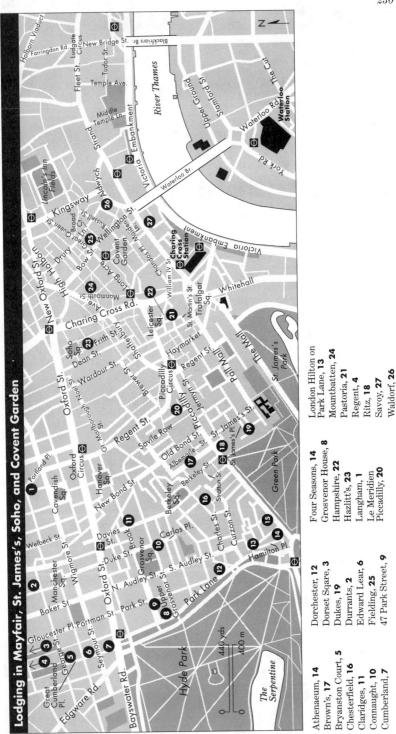

# Lodging in Mayfair, St. James's, Soho, and Covent Garden

Athenaeum, **14**
Brown's, **17**
Bryanston Court, **5**
Chesterfield, **16**
Claridges, **11**
Connaught, **10**
Cumberland, **7**

Dorchester, **12**
Dorset Square, **3**
Dukes, **19**
Durrants, **2**
Edward Lear, **6**
Fielding, **25**
47 Park Street, **9**

Four Seasons, **14**
Grosvenor House, **8**
Hampshire, **22**
Hazlitt's, **23**
Langham, **1**
Le Meridien
Piccadilly, **20**

London Hilton on
Park Lane, **13**
Mountbatten, **24**
Pastoria, **21**
Regent, **4**
Ritz, **18**
Savoy, **27**
Waldorf, **26**

The lobby has polished wood floors, a jazzy Matisse-motif carpet, and super-concierge Donald still in position, and the long, narrow, Edwardian-style Windsor Lounge has been retained, as has the famed 56-malt Whisky Bar. These are now augmented by a conservatory rooftop fitness center and bedrooms with free CD and video loans, bedside air-conditioning control, voltage converters, two-line phones with voice mail/fax/modem capability, and marble bathrooms with power showers. Most rooms overlook quiet Down Street; only Nos. 201–205 boast a Green Park view. The Athenaeum has always been a film biz fave. *116 Piccadilly, W1V OBJ, tel. 0171/499–3464, fax 0171/493–1860. 133 rooms with bath. Facilities: lounge, bar, restaurant, fitness center, in-room VCR and CD players, 24-hour room service. AE, DC, MC, V.*

**Brown's.** Founded in 1837 by Lord Byron's "gentleman's gentleman," James Brown, Forte Hotels' Victorian country house in central Mayfair occupies 11 Georgian houses and is occupied by many Anglophile Americans—a habit that was established by the two Roosevelts (Teddy while on honeymoon). A recent major refurbishment enlarged 100 bedrooms but didn't besmirch the oak-paneled, chintz-laden, grandfather-clock-ticking-in-the-parlor ambience. Bedrooms feature thick carpets, soft armchairs, sweeping drapes, brass chandeliers, and moiré or brocade wallpapers, as well as, in the newly refitted ones, air-conditioning. On the doorstep are the boutiques and art galleries of Bond and Cork streets, while in the lounge, London's favorite afternoon tea is served from 3 to 6. *34 Albemarle St., W1A 4SW, tel. 0171/493–6020, fax 0171/493–9381. 132 rooms with bath. Facilities: restaurant, lounge, writing room, cocktail bar. AE, DC, MC, V.*

★ **Claridges.** A hotel legend, with one of the world's classiest guest lists. The liveried staff are friendly and not in the least condescending, and the rooms are never less than luxurious. It was founded in 1812, but present decor is either 1930s Art Decor country-house traditional. Have a drink in the Foyer lounge (24 hours a day) with its Hungarian mini-orchestra, or retreat to the reading room for perfect quiet, interrupted only by the sound of pages turning. The bedrooms are spacious, as are the bathrooms, with their enormous shower heads and bells (which still work) to summon either "maid" or "valet" from their station on each floor. Beds are handmade and supremely comfortable—the King of Morocco once brought his own, couldn't sleep, and ended up ordering 30 from Claridges to take home. The grand staircase and magnificent elevator are equally impressive. *Brook St., W1A 2JQ, tel. 0171/629–8860 or 800/223–6800, fax 0171/499–2210. 200 rooms with bath. Facilities: 2 restaurants, lounge (with orchestra), hairdressing, valeting. AE, DC, MC, V.*

★ **Connaught.** Make reservations well in advance for this *very* exclusive, small hotel just off Grosvenor Square. The bar and lounges have the air of an ambassadorial residence, an impression reinforced by the imposing oak staircase and dignified staff. Each bedroom has a foyer, antique furniture (if you don't like the desk, they'll change it), and fresh flowers, and the management is above such vulgarities as brochure and tariff—which would be extraneous for guests who inherited the Connaught from their great-grandfathers, anyway. If you value privacy, discretion, and the kind of luxury that eschews labels, then you have met your match here. For a preview of the hotel's style, lunch at its famous Grill or Restaurant (booking well ahead), where waiters speak only when spoken to (*see* Chapter 6, Dining). *Carlos Pl., W1Y 6AL, tel. 0171/499–7070, fax 0171/495–3262. 90 rooms with bath. Facilities: restaurant, lounge, cocktail bar, air-conditioning, disabled access in some rooms. MC.*

★ **The Dorchester.** A London institution since its 1931 inception (apart from a break in continuity for its recent complete refurbishment), the Dorchester appears on every "World's Best" list. The glamour level is off the scale: 1,500 square meters of gold leaf, 1,100 of marble, and 2,300 of hand-tufted carpet gild this lily, and bedrooms (some not as spacious as you might imagine) feature Irish linen sheets on canopied beds, brocades and velvets, Italian marble and etched glass bathrooms with Floris goodies, individual climate control, dual voltage outlets, and cable TV. There's a beauty spa, run by Elizabeth Arden, a nightclub, the Oriental and Terrace restaurants, plus the well-known power-dining Grill Room. Afternoon tea, drinking, lounging, and posing are all accomplished in the catwalk-shaped Promenade lounge, where you may spot one of the film-star types who will stay nowhere else. Probably no other hotel this opulent manages to be this charming. *Park La., W1A 2HJ, tel. 0171/ 629–8888, fax 0171/409–0114. 197 rooms, 55 suites with bath. Facilities: 3 restaurants, bar, lounge, nightclub, health club (no pool), business center, banqueting suites, ballroom, shopping arcade, free in-house movies, CNN, air-conditioning, valeting, theater ticket desk. AE, DC, MC, V.*

★ **47 Park Street.** Secreted back to back with the grand hotels of Park Lane, this dear (in every sense) little all-suite hotel has the best room service in town, with 24-hour food direct from the kitchen of Le Gavroche (*see* Chapter 6, Dining). The hotel shares its bar with that poshest of posh dining establishments, too, which means there's a jacket-and-tie requirement for your quiet nightcap. Bathrooms are on the small side, but no other drawbacks are apparent in this fabulously discreet, exquisitely decorated, quiet, relaxed, and homey haven, as long as you can afford it. One woman who could afford it liked it so much that she's still there—four years later. *47 Park St., W1Y 4EB, tel. 0171/491–7282, fax 0171/491–7281. 52 suites with bath and kitchen. Facilities: lounge, bar (jacket and tie required), private dining room, air-conditioning, satellite TV, fax, VCR on request, shopping, baby-sitting. AE, DC, MC, V.*

**Four Seasons.** The former Inn on the Park is now known simply by the name of its ever-expanding parent company, but apart from an entirely refurbished lobby it remains its lovable old self. Howard Hughes was one of the patrons who appreciated the discretion of this beautifully situated (opposite Hyde Park, off the end of Piccadilly, but tucked away) hotel, which inspires more-than-average loyalty in its guests, most of whom, these days, are business travelers, although it's particularly child-friendly too, supplying a "VIK" (Very Important Kid) package of games, videos, books, and baby-sitting. The bedrooms are extremely comfortable, with gigantic beds; the bathrooms have plenty of extras. One extra nonguests can also enjoy is the Four Seasons restaurant, which has lost one star chef, Bruno Loubet, only to gain another, Jean-Christophe Novelli—even younger, and just as bright (*see* Chapter 6, Dining). There's also a less formal restaurant, Lane's, which is open from early till late. *Hamilton Pl., Park La., W1A 1AZ, tel. 0171/499– 0888 or 800/223–6800, fax 0171/493–6629. 228 rooms with bath. Facilities: air-conditioning, shopping arcade, in-house movies, valeting, garden, fitness center, 2 restaurants. AE, DC, MC, V.*

**Grosvenor House.** "The old lady of Park Lane" has settled happily back into top-dowager position, having thrown off her creeping frumpiness during a complete overhaul. It's not the kind of place that encourages hushed whispers or that frowns on jeans, despite the marble floors and wood-paneled "library," open fires, oils, and fine antiques, all inspired by the Earl of Grosvenor's residence, which occupied the site in the 18th century. The hotel health club is just about the best around. Bedrooms are spacious, and most of the freshly glamorized big marble bathrooms have natural lig^t. *Park La., W1A 3AA, tel. 0171/499–6363, fax 0171/493–3341. 360 rooms, 70 suites with bath. Facilities: 3 restaurants, bar, lounge, health club with pool, banquet suites, ballroom, valeting, satellite TV, theater ticket desk. AE, DC, MC, V.*

**Hampshire.** Leicester Square often seems to be the real center of London. It's the only place with any life after midnight, being next to all the theaters, big movie houses, and clubs—and so, therefore, is the Hampshire. Though built in 1899 to house the Royal Dental Hospital, virtually all that's left of the original structure is the elegant Edwardian facade, but a very reliable small chain called Edwardian Hotels was responsible for fixing the interior, and the place is done out in their trademark "gracious country house" style, with open fires, dark wood, and, in this one, a fair bit of Chinoiserie. There are six rooms and two suites with four-poster beds, and 42 studios with seating areas and huge, magnificently equipped bathrooms. Try for one of the rooms in the front of the hotel, overlooking the square, as they are the largest. This location would suit a shopping spree or theater crawl. *31 Leicester Sq., WC2H 7LH, tel. 0171/ 839–9399, fax 0171/930–8122. 124 rooms with bath. Facilities: restaurant, wine bar, bar, satellite TV. AE, DC, MC, V.*

**Langham.** A historic hotel (*see* Regent and Oxford Streets under St. James's and Mayfair in Chapter 3, Exploring London) reconstructed, renovated, and reopened by Hilton Hotels in 1991, the Langham is certainly an impressive landmark from the outside, especially at night with its fairy-tale floodlighting. Inside, the lobby has varnished white marble floors and sandblasted stone walls, and there are two theme restaurants (one Raj, one Czarist Russia), a Chukka Bar (polo is in this year), and a Palm Court serving tea and piano tinkling. Proportions are grand, but you could be in Disney's London; the only clues to the past are in the punctuation: a preserved ironwork "LH"motif and assembly-line prints of the old city. Standard bedrooms are generic deluxe, medium-size and very pale peach; only the more expensive, larger front ones have the good view over Portland Place to the park, as well as a snazzier decor, wishfully referred to as French provincial. Marble bathroom, robe, trouser press, and hair dryer are standard issue. *1C Portland Pl., W1N 3AA, tel. 0171/636–1000, fax 0171/323–2340. 410 rooms with bath. Facilities: 2 restaurants, bar, ballroom, garden, air-conditioning, Harvey Nichols shop. AE, DC, MC, V.*

**London Hilton on Park Lane.** London's only major high-rise hotel offers fine views over Hyde Park—when you can see through the mist—and an impressive array of facilities, including the Fitness on Five center, with personal trainers at your beck and call. Public areas are glitzy in white marble, topped off by an oblong of crystal chandelier; suites have been recently redecorated to bring them out of *Dynasty* territory and into the '90s. Bedrooms, too—at least, those on floors 14 through 19, 22, and 23—have been renovated. They're a fair size, but you may forget which city they're in, since decor is uniform corporate Hiltonese; any antiques here, one feels, are reproduction. The top-floor Windows Roof Restaurant is known for the view rather than the food, but Trader Vic's Caribbean bar and restaurant on the ground floor does great fancy cocktails. *22 Park La., W1A 2HH, tel. 0171/493–8000, fax 0171/493–4957. 448 rooms with bath. Facilities: restaurant, hairdressing, in-house movies, laundry, shopping arcade, doctor, CNN, florist, health center, theater ticket desk, baby-sitting, airline reservations. AE, DC, MC, V.*

**Le Meridien Piccadilly.** The massive, turn-of-the-century building, run by the French chain of the same name, is *fin de siècle* elegant, if slightly antiseptic in its white marble and plush carpet public areas. The vast Oak Room restaurant, however, is exquisite in limed oak paneling and gilt, and it is (yes, another) one of the best hotel restaurants in London. The hotel's second restaurant, far less formal, is a miniature Kew Gardens of arched glass, ferns and palms. Bedrooms vary ridiculously in size, though most are on the small side; others are very large indeed, and a few seventh-floor ones have balconies overlooking Piccadilly. Decor is Edwardian gent's club with frills. The health club is the most luxurious and exclusive in London and boasts squash courts, saunas, and billiard tables, as well as a swimming pool. You can't be more central than here. *Piccadilly, W1V 0BH, tel. 0171/734–8000, fax 0171/437–3574. 284 rooms with bath. Facilities: 3 restaurants, bar, health club, library, business center, shops. AE, DC, MC, V.*

**The Regent.** A year older than the century, the onetime Great Central Hotel and former BritRail HQ was resuscitated by a three-year injection of £75 million and transformed into London's latest luxury hotel—and a most elegantly understated place it is, too. A palm-filled, eight-story glazed atrium "Winter Garden" forms the core, and odd-numbered rooms—somewhat surreally—overlook this. If size matters to you, note that even standard rooms here are among the largest in London and that this Hong Kong–based hotel group is famous for glamorous bathrooms—these are marble and chrome, complete with robe and hair dryer. Despite appearances, this is the only London grand hotel that doesn't force you to dress up—even jeans are okay. Unsurprisingly, the Regent is very near Regent's Park; the West End is a 15-minute walk away. *222 Marylebone Rd., NW1 6JQ, tel. 0171/631–8000, fax 0171/631–8080. 309 rooms with bath. Facilities: restaurant, 2 bars, Winter Garden, health club with pool, cable TV, VCR and personal fax on request, business center. AE, DC, MC, V.*

**$$$** **Chesterfield.** This former town house of the Earl of Chesterfield is popular with American visitors, many of whom are repeat guests or have links with the English Speaking Union, which has its headquarters next door. It is deep in the heart of Mayfair and has welcoming, wood-and-leather public rooms and spacious bedrooms. The staff is outstandingly pleasant and helpful. *35 Charles St., W1X 8LX, tel. 0171/491–2622, fax 0171/491–4793. 113 rooms with bath. Facilities: restaurant, in-house movies. AE, DC, MC, V.*

**Cumberland.** This huge, busy hotel (built in 1933, with some Art Deco features on the facade and in the public areas) is double-glazed to counter the traffic noise of Oxford Street, and boasts every modern convenience, though it lacks character of any sort. Impersonal bedrooms are comfortable and well-fitted, with adequate bathrooms. The hotel's restaurants—a carvery, a café, a Japanese restaurant, and a fourth, Austen's—serve plastic food, but there's little need to eat here when you're this centrally based. Although there are no fitness facilities in the hotel, there are a pool and a health club nearby. *Marble Arch, W1A 4RF, tel. 0171/262–1234, fax 0171/724–4621. 905 rooms with bath. Facilities: 4 restaurants, lounge, 3 bars, hairdressing, in-house movies, coffee shop. AE, DC, MC, V.*

**★** **Dorset Square Hotel.** Just over a decade old, this special small hotel off Baker Street was the first of three London addresses for husband and wife Tim and Kit Kemp, an architect and an interior designer. What they did was decant the English country look into a fine pair of Regency town houses, then turn up the volume. Everywhere you look are covetable antiques, edibly rich colors, and ideas *House Beautiful* subscribers will steal. Naturally, every room is different, with the first-floor balconied "Coronet" ones the largest (two have grand pianos), and a virtue made of the smallness of the small ones. The marble and mahogany bathrooms have power showers; glossy magazines, a half-bottle of claret, and boxes of vitamin C are complimentary. Instead of minibars guests will find an "honesty bar" in the small front parlor. There's a reason for the ubiquitous cricket memorabilia: Dorset Square was the first Lord's ground. (Nowadays you can have your drinks served in the garden that still remains.) The basement bar/restaurant has cheerful frescoes, chess, and backgammon boards. *39–40 Dorset Sq., NW1 6QN, tel. 0171/723–7874, fax 0171/724–3328. 37 rooms with bath. Facilities: bar/restaurant, garden, vintage Bentley limousine, 24-hour room service, air-conditioning. AE, MC, V.*

**$$ Bryanston Court.** Three Georgian houses have been converted into a hotel in a historic conservation area, a couple of blocks north of Hyde Park and Park Lane. The style is traditional English—open fireplaces, comfortable leather armchairs, oil portraits—though the bedrooms are small and modern, with pink furnishings, creaky floors, and minute bathrooms. Rooms at the back are quieter and face east, so they're bright in the mornings; room 77 is as big as a suite, but being on the lower ground floor typical of London houses, it's dark. This family-run hotel is excellent value for the area. *56–60 Great Cumberland Pl., W1H 7FD, tel. 0171/262–3141, fax 0171/ 262–7248. 56 rooms with bath. Facilities: bar, lounge, restaurant. AE, DC, MC, V.*

**Durrants.** A hotel since the late 18th century, Durrants occupies a quiet corner almost next to the Wallace Collection, a stone's throw from Oxford Street and the smaller, posher shops of Marylebone High Street. It's good value for the area, and if you like Ye woodpaneled, leather-armchaired, dark-red-patterned-carpeted style of olde Englishness, this will suit you. Bedrooms, by way of contrast, are wan and motel-like but perfectly adequate—a few have no bathrooms, though this disadvantage has the advantage of saving you £10 a night. Each landing harbors a communal minibar (a maxibar?) and ice machine. Best give the baron of beef–type restaurant a miss. *George St., W1H 6BH, tel. 0171/935–8131, fax 0171/487–3510. 96 rooms, 85 with bath. Facilities: restaurant, bar, private dining rooms, lounges. AE, MC, V.*

**$ Edward Lear.** One-time home of writer/artist Edward Lear (famous for his nonsense verse), this good-value hotel has an inviting entranceway leading to a black-and-white tiled hall. Rooms vary enormously in size, with some family rooms very spacious indeed and others barely big enough to get out of bed (avoid Room 14); rooms at the back are quieter. It's a friendly place with a lot of repeat customers, but there are no hotel-type facilities (although if you want a jacket pressed you're welcome to borrow the iron), except for a lounge and the light and pleasant brick-walled breakfast room. The management is very proud of the English breakfasts—they use the same butcher as the queen. *28–30Seymour St., W1H 5WD, tel. 0171/ 402–5401, fax 0171/706–3766.31 rooms, 15 with shower (no WC), 4 with full bath. MC, V.*

## St. James's

**$$$$ Dukes.** This small, exclusive, Edwardian-style hotel, with its lantern-lit entrance, is situated in a quiet cul-de-sac behind the Ritz, and is now run by the same upmarket management that operates the Franklin (*see* Knightsbridge, Chelsea, and Belgravia, *below*). Portraits of notable dukes hang on the walls, in a successful bid for a stately-home ambience, which is continued in the bedrooms, with their marble bathrooms equipped with imperial-size towels. Ask for a top-floor bedroom; they're the most spacious. *35 St. James's Pl., SW1A 1NY, tel. 0171/491–4840, fax 0171/493–1264. 62 rooms with bath. Facilities: restaurant, valeting, private dining. AE, DC, MC, V.*

**The Ritz.** The Ritz has sumptuous Louis XVI decor, near-faultless service, and a pleasing air of bustle, from the Reuters ticker-tape printout by reception to the Palm Court (cranberry velvet chairs, gilt statues, fluted columns, cascades of greenery), which is famous for its touristy tea. The dining room, with its frescoed ceiling and Italian garden, is famous, too, for being the nonpareil of opulence, and the bedrooms are—as you'd expect—ritzy: antique furniture and mirrors, heavy brocades,and linen embroidered with "R." They come in one of four sherbet colors, all with much gilding, and some have splendid bathrooms to match, although, sadly, most of the original marble baths were ripped out in the '70s. *Piccadilly, W1V 9DG, tel. 0171/493–8181, fax 0171/493–2687. 128 rooms with bath. Facilities: restaurant, cocktail bar, valeting, in-house movies, baby-sitting. AE, DC, MC, V.*

## Soho and Covent Garden

$$$$ **The Savoy.** This historic, grand, late-Victorian hotel is beloved by
★ the international influential, now as ever. Like the other Savoy Group hotels, it boasts handmade beds and staff who are often graduates of its exclusive training school. Its celebrated Grill (*see* Chapter 6, Dining) has the premier power lunch tables; it hosted Elizabeth Taylor's first honeymoon in one of its famous river-view rooms; and it poured the world's first martini in its equally famous American Bar—haunted by Hemingway, Fitzgerald, Gershwin, *et al.* And does it measure up to this high profile? Absolutely. The impeccably maintained, spacious, elegant, bright, and comfortable rooms are furnished with antiques and serviced by valets. A room facing the Thames costs an arm and a leg and requires an early booking, but there are few better views in London. Bathrooms have original fittings, with the same sunflower-size shower heads as at Claridges, and there's a compact new "Fitness Gallery" (with pool) secreted above the entrance. Though the Savoy is as grand as they come, the air is tinged with a certain naughtiness, which goes down well with Hollywood types. *Strand, WC2R 0EU, tel. 0171/836–4343, fax 0171/240–6040. 202 rooms with bath. Facilities: hairdressing, florist, theater ticket desk, 3 restaurants, 2 bars, valeting, fitness center, free in-house movies. AE, DC, MC, V.*

**Waldorf.** Close to the Aldwych theaters and Covent Garden,the Waldorf emerged from a total refit a couple of years ago, gleaming in luscious Edwardiana, and very pretty it is, with polished marble floors, chandeliers, and cozily comfortable period bedrooms. This place now lives up to its flagship status as the first hotel in the £1.5 billion worldwide Forte empire, providing a booking challenge for the wealthy theater goer (Waldorf or Savoy?) and a suitably glamorous setting for the famous Palm Court tea dances, still going strong every weekend after 87 years. *Aldwych, WC2B 4DD, tel. 0171/836–2400, fax 0171/836–7244. 292 rooms with bath. Facilities: air-conditioning, brasserie, lounge, hairdressing, valeting, restaurant. AE, DC, MC, V.*

$$$ **Hazlitt's.** The solo Soho hotel is in three connected early 18th-centu-
★ ry houses, one of which was the essayist William Hazlitt's (1778–1830) last home. It's a disarmingly friendly place, full of personality,

but devoid of such hotel features as elevators, room service (though if the staff aren't too busy, you can get ad-hoc take-outs), and porterage. Robust antiques are everywhere, assorted prints crowd every wall, plants and stone sculptures (by one of the owners' fathers-in-law) appear in odd corners, and every room has a Victorian claw-foot bath in its bathroom. There are a tiny sittingroom, wooden staircases, and more restaurants within strolling distance than you could patronize in a year. Book way ahead—this is the London address of media people, literary types, and antiques dealers everywhere. *6 Frith St., W1V 5TZ, tel. 0171/434–1771, fax 0171/439–1524. 23 rooms with bath. AE, DC, MC, V.*

**Mountbatten.** It may seem rather odd for one of London's newer hotels to be named after the late Lord Mountbatten, last viceroy of India and favorite uncle of Prince Charles. But the name is probably just an excuse to go overboard with the old British Raj theme, since the decor reflects Mountbatten's life—photos of the estate where he lived, Indian furnishings, silks, inlaid tables, and screens. It is another Edwardian Hotels property, with a good standard of service, bedrooms in various shades of red, with chintz drapes, and bathrooms of Italian marble. A pianist plays in the comfortable bar, but you may not have time for the "French cuisine" at L'Amiral when you could fall out of bed into a dozen excellent restaurants. A minute's walk brings you to the Royal Opera House or the Covent Garden Piazza. Rates drop £20, and include breakfast, on weekends. *Seven Dials, Covent Garden. WC2H 9HD, tel. 0171/836–4300, fax 0171/340–3540. 127 rooms with bath. Facilities: cocktail bar (with pianist), lounge (with harpist), CNN, free in-house videos, restaurant. AE, DC, MC, V.*

**$$ Fielding.** Tucked away in a quiet alley by the world's first police station (now Bow St. Magistrates' Court), and feeling far from the madding crowds of Covent Garden, this very small and pretty hotel is so adored by its regulars that you'd be wise to book well ahead. Cameron Mackintosh, the Broadway musical producer (who could no doubt afford Claridges), stays here—presumably for the homey atmosphere; the old London Town character; the continuity of a loyal, friendly staff who maintain the place as the two founders, now retired, have kept it for over two decades; and, of course, for the convenience of having the Royal Opera House, every theater, and half of London's restaurants within spitting distance. It is not uneccentric. The bedrooms are all different, shabby-homey rather than chic, and cozy rather than spacious, though you can have a suite here for the price of a chain-hotel double. There's no elevator; only one room comes with bath (most have showers); and only breakfast is served in the restaurant. Cute. *4 Broad Ct., Bow St., WC2B 5QZ, tel. 0171/836–8305, fax 0171/497–0064. 26 rooms, 1 with bath, 23 with shower. Facilities: bar, breakfast room. AE, DC, MC, V.*

**Pastoria.** A less exorbitant choice for the theatergoer than the Waldorf, handily situated just off Leicester Square. The building is about 70 years old, with a suitably modern decor, the bedrooms done in limed oak with light pink walls and navy blue carpets. There's a brasserie-style restaurant to dine in, but Soho, which is restaurant central, is only a few hundred yards away. *3–6 St. Martin's St., WC2H 7HL, tel. 0171/930–8641, fax 0171/925–0551. 58 rooms with bath. Facilities: air-conditioning, restaurant, bar, coffee shop. AE, DC, MC, V.*

## Kensington

**$$$$ Blakes.** Blakes is another world—some would say a time-warp. It
★ was designed by owner Anouska Hempel (aka Lady Weinberg), and
each room is a fantasy packed with precious Biedermeier, Murano
glass, and modern pieces inside walls of red lacquer and black, or
dove-gray, or perhaps—like 007, the movie stars' favorite suite—
pink. Moody lighting, including recessed spotlights, compounds the
impression that you, too, are a movie star living in a big-budget
biopic. The foyer sets the tone with its piles of cushions, Phileas
Fogg valises and trunks, black walls, rattan and bamboo, and a noisy
parakeet under a gigantic Asian parasol. Downstairs, an equally
dramatic black-and-white restaurant displays Thai warriors' costumes in glass cases. Stay away if you don't like Hollywood or the
music biz. *33 Roland Gardens, SW7 3PF, tel. 0171/370-6701, fax
0171/373-0442. 52 rooms with bath. Facilities: restaurant, satellite
TV. AE, DC, MC, V.*

**$$$ The Cranley.** The pedigree of this small young Georgian townhouse
hotel is Ann Arbor, Michigan (where the owners hail from) out of
South Ken (where it stands, near the big museums), and it looks the
part. Anglo antiques, oils, and etchings are mixed with a lot of U.S.-
style swagged drapery in assorted florals and vivid color schemes.
Bedrooms have kitchenettes, and many are high-ceilinged and
huge-windowed, while two of the apartments have Jacuzzis and cute
patio gardens. The cheaper rooms here and at the nearby 10-room
**One Cranley Place** (SW7 3AB, tel. 0171/589-7944, fax 0171/225-
3931), which operates March to October, belong in the $$ category.
*10-12 Bina Gardens, SW5 0LA, tel. 0171/373-0123, fax 0171/373-
9497. 26 rooms with bath, 10 apartments. Facilities: breakfast
room, room service. AE, DC, MC, V.*

★ **The Gore.** Just down the road from the Albert Hall, this small, very
friendly hotel is run by the same people who run Hazlitt's (*see* Soho
and Covent Garden, *above*) and features a similar eclectic selection
of prints, etchings, and antiques. Here, though, are spectacular fol-
ly-like rooms—Room 101 is a Tudor fantasy with minstrel gallery,
stained glass, and four-poster bed, and Room 211, done in over-the-
top Hollywood style, has a tiled mural of Greek goddesses in the
bathroom. Despite all that, the Gore manages to remain most elegant. Bistrot 190 and Downstairs at 190 (*see* Chapter 6, Dining)
serve as dining rooms and bar. *189 Queen's Gate, SW7 5EX, tel.
0171/584-6601, fax 0171/589-8127. 54 rooms with bath. Facilities:
brasserie restaurant, lounge. AE, DC, MC, V.*

**Number Sixteen.** A luxury bed-and-breakfast close to South Kensington tube and three blocks or so from the great museums, Number Sixteen stands in a white-porticoed row of Victorian houses,
many of which are fellow B&Bs, with not a sign outside to indicate it.
There's no uniformity to the bedrooms except for their spaciousness
and recently refitted bathrooms, but the decor overall is not so much
interior-designed as understated, with new furniture and antiques,
yellowed oils and modern prints juxtaposed. There's an elevator,
and an enticing garden complete with conservatory and fountain-
ette. *16 Sumner Pl., SW7 3EG, tel. 0171/589-5232, fax 0171/584-
8615. 36 rooms with bath. Facilities: bar, 2 lounges, conservatory,
garden. AE, DC, MC, V.*

**$$ Kensington Close.** This large, fairly utilitarian hotel feels like a
smaller one and boasts a few extras you wouldn't expect for the rea-
sonable rate and convenient location (in a quiet lane off Kensington
High Street). The main attraction is the health club, with an 18-me-
ter pool, two squash courts, a steam room, and a beauty salon;

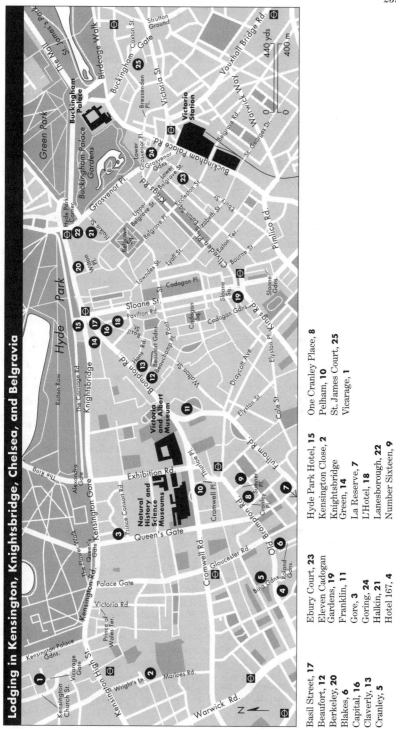

# Lodging in Kensington, Knightsbridge, Chelsea, and Belgravia

Basil Street, **17**
Beaufort, **12**
Berkeley, **20**
Blakes, **6**
Capital, **16**
Claverly, **13**
Cranley, **5**

Ebury Court, **23**
Eleven Cadogan
 Gardens, **19**
Franklin, **11**
Gore, **3**
Goring, **24**
Halkin, **21**
Hotel 167, **4**

Hyde Park Hotel, **15**
Kensington Close, **2**
Knightsbridge
 Green, **14**
La Reserve, **7**
L'Hotel, **18**
Lanesborough, **22**
Number Sixteen, **9**

One Cranley Place, **8**
Pelham, **10**
St. James Court, **25**
Vicarage, **1**

there's also a secluded little water garden. Standard rooms are on the small side, with plain chain-hotel (this one has belonged to the British Forte Hotels for 50 years) built-in furniture. Some Executive rooms are twice the size. Good value. *Wrights La., W8 5SP, tel. 0171/937–8170, fax 0171/937–8289. 530 rooms with bath. Facilities: 2 restaurants, 2 bars, lounge, garden, health club with indoor pool, satellite TV, baby-sitting. AE, DC, MC, V.*

**Hotel 167.** This friendly little bed-and-breakfast is a two-minute walk from the V&A, in a grand white-stucco Victorian corner house. The lobby is immediately cheering, with its round marble tables, wrought-iron chairs, palms, and modern paintings; it also does duty as lounge and breakfast room. Bedrooms have a hybrid antiquey/Ikea style, with Venetian blinds over double-glazed windows (which you need on this noisy road), plus cable TV and minibars. *167 Old Brompton Rd., SW5 OAN, tel. 0171/373–0672, fax 0171/373–3360. 19 rooms with bath/shower. Facilities: lounge/breakfast room. AE, DC, MC, V.*

**$ ★ Vicarage.** A great deal of care goes into the running of this family-owned hotel in a leaf-shaded big white Victorian house just off Kensington Church Street (spend the cash you save here in its antiques shops). The decor is sweetly anachronistic, full of heavy, dark-stained wood furniture, patterned carpets, and brass pendant lights, and there's a little conservatory. Six of the spotless bedrooms have just been redecorated, and many now have TVs. *10 Vicarage Gate, W8 4AG, tel. 0171/229–4030. 19 rooms without bath. Facilities: lounge. No credit cards.*

## Knightsbridge, Chelsea, and Belgravia

**$$$$ ★ Berkeley.** The Berkeley is a remarkably successful mixture of the old and the new. It is a luxurious, air-conditioned, double-glazed modern building with a splendid penthouse swimming pool that opens to the sky when the weather's good. The bedrooms are decorated by various designers, but tend to be serious and opulent, some with swags of William Morris prints, others plain and masculine with little balconies overlooking the street. All have sitting areas and big, tiled bathrooms with bidets. For the ridiculously rich, there are spectacular suites, one with its own conservatory terrace, another with a sauna, but—such is the elegance of this place—you'd feel almost as spoiled in a normal room. There's a rather good French restaurant (simply called the Berkeley Restaurant), as well as the Buttery, which serves light Mediterranean food, and the Oriental, tiered Perroquet bar, offering 52 cocktails until the early morning. The hotel is conveniently placed for Knightsbridge shopping. *Wilton Pl., SW1X 7RL, tel. 0171/235–6000, fax 0171/235–4330. 160 rooms with bath. Facilities: rooftop heated indoor and outdoor pool, gymnasium, massage, sauna, hairdressing, movie theater, florist, 2 restaurants. AE, DC, MC,V.*

**Capital.** Reserve well ahead if you want a room here—as you must for a table in the hotel's superb restaurant (*see* Chapter 6, Dining). This grand hotel decanted into a private house is the work of David and Margaret Levin, who also own L'Hôtel (*see below*), and it exudes their irreproachable taste, with French floral fabrics, fine-grained woods, sober prints, and shelves of books. The 10 rooms of the Edwardian Wing, with its carved wooden staircase, enjoyed the attentions of superstar designer Nina Campbell (who did some of Claridges' suites), and were already the height of fashion in the 1920s, when this was the Squires Hotel. *22–24 Basil St., SW3 1AT,* *tel. 0171/589–5171, fax 0171/225–0011. 48 rooms with bath. Facilities: air-conditioning, bar, lounge. AE, DC, MC, V.*

**Goring.** Useful if you have to drop in at Buckingham Palace, just around the corner. In fact, visiting VIPs use it regularly as a conveniently close, and suitably dignified, base for royal occasions. The hotel was built by Mr. Goring in 1910 and is now run by third-generation Gorings. The atmosphere remains Edwardian: Bathrooms are marble-fitted, and some of the bedrooms have brass bedsteads and the original built-in closets; many have been opulently redecorated. The bar/lounge looks onto a well-tended garden. *15 Beeston Pl., Grosvenor Gardens, SW1W 0JW, tel. 0171/834–8211, fax 0171/834–8211. 87 rooms with bath. Facilities: bar, restaurant, lounge. AE, DC, MC, V.*

★ **The Halkin.** If you can't take any more Regency stripes, English-country florals, or Louis XV chaises, this luxurious little place is the antidote. You could say its slickness doesn't belong in the '90s, or you could just enjoy the Milanese design: the clean-cut white marble lobby with its royal-blue leather bucket chairs, the arresting curved charcoal-gray corridors, the "diseased mahogany" veneers that darken as you climb, and the gray-on-gray bedrooms that light up when you insert your electronic key. Wealthy business and media types frequent the Halkin, and they can't breathe easy without a fax, Reuters, and two phone lines with conference-call. These are provided, along with two touch-control pads for all the gadgets, cable TV and video (library downstairs), room safe, and minibar. The bathrooms are palaces of shiny chrome, anti-mist mirrors, and marble that changes color according to which floor you're on. It might be like living in the Design Museum, except that this place employs some of the friendliest staff around—and they look pretty good in their white Armani uniforms, too. *Halkin St., SW1X 7DJ, tel. 0171/333–1000, fax 0171/333–1100. 41 rooms with bath. Facilities: restaurant, cable TV, video library, personal faxes on request, Reuters news service. AE, DC, MC, V.*

★ **Hyde Park Hotel.** For just over 100 years, the Hyde Park has entertained lavishly, its banqueting rooms and ballroom regularly hosting royalty—including the current batch, who still have a designated Royal Entrance—its bedrooms assorted stars from Rudolph Valentino to Winston Churchill. Forte Hotels owns it now, and has done a grand job restoring its eight-kinds-of-marble halls and strewing fine antiques and paintings throughout. Bedrooms are large and hushed. Some have gentle windowfuls of treetop; from others, you can preview your Harvey Nichols purchases, since the building stands on the cusp of Knightsbridge shops and Hyde Park itself. The 1993 opening of Marco Pierre White: The Restaurant (*see* Chapter 6, Dining) did no harm to the Hyde Park's image—they've now got the chef with the biggest attitude, and one of the biggest talents, in London. The blinding white basement gym isn't bad, either. *66 Knightsbridge, SW1Y 7LA, tel. 0171/235–2000, fax 0171/235–2000. 160 rooms with bath. Facilities: lounge, hairdresser, bar, 2 restaurants, fitness center, theater ticket desk. AE, DC, MC, V.*

**The Lanesborough.** This very grand hotel acts for all the world as though the Prince Regent took a ride through time and is about to resume residence. Royally proportioned public rooms (not lounges but "The Library" and "The Withdrawing Room") lead one off the other like an exquisite giant Chinese box in this multimillion-pound conversion of the old St. George's Hospital opposite Wellington's house. Everything undulates with richness—brocades and Regency stripes, moiré silks and fleurs-de-lys in the colors of precious stones, magnificent antiques and oil paintings, reproductions of more gilded splendor than the originals, handwoven £250-per-square-yard carpet, as if Liberace and Laura Ashley had collaborated on the design. All you do to register is sign the visitors book, then retire to your room, where you are waited on by a personal butler. Full-size Lanesborough toiletries, umbrellas (take them home), robes (don't), a drinks tray (pay by the inch), and even business cards with your temporary fax (in every room) and phone numbers (two lines) are waiting. If you yearn for a bygone age and are very rich, this is certainly for you. Nonresidents can have lunch in the heavily handsome restaurant or the slightly self-conscious conservatory. *1 Lanesborough Pl., SW1X 7TA, tel. 0171/259–5599, fax 0171/259–5606. 95 rooms with bath. Facilities: 2 restaurants, bar, satellite TV, video and CD library, personal direct-dial telephone, fax, business cards. AE, DC, MC, V.*

**St. James Court.** You enter this Edwardian pile through a pair of enormous wrought-iron gates, which used to admit carriages into what is now the towering Reception. From here, you pass ranks of green leather sofas to reach the *pièce de résistance*, the landscaped courtyard with its fountain and ceramic frieze of scenes from Shakespeare. Some bedrooms are disproportionately large but cost the same as standards, and all are plainly decorated in pallid shades with a smattering of antiques and the odd (and some *are* very odd) painting. There's a health club, well-equipped except for the lack of a pool, and an extensive business center. The two restaurants aren't at all bad, especially the Mediterranean Auberge de Provence. *Buckingham Gate, SW1E 6AF, tel. 0171/834–6655, fax 0171/630–7587. 400 rooms with bath. Facilities: 2 restaurants, coffee shop, sauna, solarium, gym, business center. AE, DC, MC, V.*

**$$$** **Beaufort.** You can practically hear the jingle of Harrods's cash registers from a room at the Beaufort, the brainchild of ex–TV announcer
★ Diana Wallis, who employs an all-woman team to run the hotel. Actually, "hotel" is a misnomer for this elegant pair of Victorian houses. There's a sitting room instead of Reception; guests have a front door key and the run of the drinks cabinet, and even their own phone number, with the customary astronomical hotel surcharges waived. The high-ceilinged, generously proportioned rooms are decorated in muted, sophisticated shades to suit the muted, sophisticated atmosphere—but don't worry, you're encouraged by the incredibly sweet staff to feel at home. The rates are higher than the top range for this category but include unlimited drinks, breakfast, plus membership at a local health club. *33 Beaufort Gardens, SW3 1PP, tel. 0171/584–5252, fax 0171/589–2834. 29 rooms with bath. Facilities: 24-hr complimentary bar in the sitting room, air-conditioning, video library, access to nearby health club with pool. AE, DC, MC, V.*

★ **Eleven Cadogan Gardens.** This aristocratic, late-Victorian gabled town house is the perfect spot for a pampered honeymoon, but very difficult to get into—and we're not referring to the lack of a sign or a reception desk. Fine period furniture and antiques, books, and magazines on the tables, landscape paintings and portraits, coupled with some of that solid, no-nonsense furniture that *real* English country houses have in unaesthetic abundance make for a family-home ambience; you might be borrowing the house and servants of some wealthy friends while they're away. Take the elevator or walk up the fine oak staircase to your room, which will have mahogany furniture, a restful color scheme, and pretty bedspreads and drapes. The best rooms are at the back. There's a private garden for summertime. *11 Cadogan Gardens, Sloane Sq., SW3 2RJ, tel. 0171/730–3426, fax 0171/730–5217. 62 rooms with bath. Facilities: garden, chauffeur-driven car. AE, MC, V.*

**The Franklin.** It's hard to imagine, while taking tea in this pretty hotel overlooking a quiet, grassy square, that you're a hop, skip, and a jump away from busy Brompton and Cromwell roads and the splendors of the V&A. A few of the rooms are small, but the marble bathrooms—in which Floris cosmetics and heated towel racks are standard issue—are not; the large garden rooms and suites (which fall into the $$$$ category) are romantic indeed. Tea is served daily in the lounge, and there's also a self-service bar. The staff is friendly and accommodating. If the Franklin is booked up, then consider its slightly older (1990) sister hotel, the **Egerton House** (tel. 0171/589–2412, fax 0171/584–6540), just around the corner on Egerton Terrace. *28 Egerton Gardens, SW3 2DB, tel. 0171/584–5533 or 800/473–9487, fax 0171/584–5449 or 800/473–9489. 40 rooms with bath. Facilities: lounge, bar, air-conditioning, 24-hour room service, satellite TV, valet parking. AE, DC, MC, V.*

★ **L'Hotel.** An upscale bed-and-breakfast run by the same Levins who own the Capital next door. This is a plainer alternative—less pampering, unfussy decor. There's an air of provincial France around, with the white wrought-iron bedsteads, pine furniture, and delicious breakfast croissants and baguettes (included in the room rate) served on that chunky dark green and gold Parisian café china in Le Metro cellar wine bar (also open to nonresidents). This really is like a house—you're given your own front door key, there's no elevator, and the staff leaves in the evening. Reserve ahead—it's very popular. *28 Basil St., SW3 1AT, tel. 0171/589–6286, fax 0171/225–0011. 12 rooms with bath. Facilities: wine bar, restaurant. AE, V.*

**The Pelham.** The second of Tim and Kit Kemp's gorgeous hotels; they opened it in 1989 and run it along exactly the same lines as the Dorset Square (*see* Mayfair to Regent's Park, *above*), except that this one looks more the country house. There's 18th-century pine paneling in the drawing room, flowers galore, quite a bit of glazed chintz and antique lace bed linen, and the odd four-poster and bedroom fireplace. Everything is exquisite, including the nearby garden with its heated pool. The Pelham stands opposite the South Kensington tube stop, by the big museums, and close to the shops of Brompton Cross and Knightsbridge, with Kemps restaurant supplying an on-site trendy menu. Lauren Bacall deserted the Athenaeum for this hotel. *15 Cromwell Pl., SW7 2LA, tel. 0171/589–8288, fax 0171/584–8444. 37 rooms with bath. Facilities: restaurant, air-conditioning, access to garden with outdoor pool, valet. AE, MC, V.*

$$ **Basil Street.** A gracious Edwardian hotel on a quiet street behind
★ busy Brompton Road and off (rich) shoppers heaven, Sloane Street. It's been family-run for three quarters of a century, and has always been popular with lone woman travelers, who get automatic membership at the Parrot Club—an enormous lounge, with copies of *The Lady* and *Country Life* among the coffee cups. All the bedrooms are different; many are like grandma's guest room, with overstuffed counterpanes and a random selection of furniture—some good pieces, some utilitarian. You can write letters home in the peaceful gallery, which has polished wooden floors and fine Turkish carpets underneath a higgledy-piggledy wealth of antiques. Americans with a taste for period charm like this place; some come back often enough to merit the title "Basilite"—a privileged regular offered a 15% discount. *Basil St., SW3 1AH, tel. 0171/581–3311, fax 0171/581–3693. 92 rooms, 72 with bath. Facilities: wine bar, lounge, ladies' club, restaurant. AE, DC, MC, V.*

**Claverley.** Can't afford the Beaufort, but like the area? This B&B is on the same quiet street a moment from Harrods and makes a good alternative. The less expensive rooms have either bath or shower (not both); as you go up the scale, rooms get larger, decor (homey florals, either Victorian- or Edwardian-style) newer, and bathrooms better equipped; some top-rate rooms have four-poster beds. The service is friendly, everything's spotless, and breakfast is included. *13–14 Beaufort Gardens, SW3 1PS, tel. 0171/589–8541, fax 0171/ 584–3410. 36 rooms with bath. AE, V.*

**Ebury Court.** Here five 19th-century houses have been converted into an old-fashioned, family-run hotel close to Victoria Station. The rooms are smallish, with antique furniture to give them extra character—one of them has a grandfather clock and a Hepplewhite four-poster bed. The reception area, lounge, and restaurant were renovated fairly recently, as were many of the bedrooms, although some of them still have no bathroom. Be warned: Since the rates went up, these are the only rooms in the $$ category. *26 Ebury St., SW1W 0LU, tel. 0171/730–8147, fax 0171/823–5966. 45 rooms, 36 with bath. Facilities: bar, restaurant. MC, V.*

**Knightsbridge Green.** There are more suites than bedrooms at this Georgian hotel that's a two-minute walk from Harrods. One floor is French-style, with white furniture, another English, in beech. Costing only £15 more than a double room, the suites are not overpriced, and all the rooms have trouser presses and tea- and coffee-making facilities installed. There's no restaurant, but there are plenty in the area; or if you ask they'll send the porter out to find you a sandwich. There's also coffee and cake left out in the lounge—a detail that exemplifies the friendliness of this place. *159 Knightsbridge, SW1X 7PD, tel. 0171/584–6274, fax 0171/225–1635. 24 rooms/suites with bath. Facilities: lounge, free tea and coffee. AE, MC, V. Closed 5 days over Christmas.*

**La Reserve.** You'll find this unique small hotel in the lively, classy residential neighborhood of Fulham. The varnished floorboards, black Venetian blinds, works of art (for sale), and primary-colored upholstery in the public areas are contemporary and sophisticated. Bedrooms are cluttered only with the minibars, hair dryers, trouser presses, and tea/coffee makers of more expensive places. It's a two-minute walk from Fulham Broadway tube, near Chelsea Football (soccer) Grounds and plenty of restaurants; there's also a brasserie in-house. *422–428 Fulham Rd., SW6 1DU, tel. 0171/385–8561, fax 0171/385–7662. 37 rooms with bath. Facilities: restaurant, bar, lounge, satellite TV. AE, DC, MC, V.*

## Bayswater and Notting Hill Gate

$$$$ **Halcyon.** It certainly is expensive, but you're paying for one of London's best small hotels. The Halcyon was converted from two enormous wedding cake town houses just off Holland Park Avenue, which looks like a Parisian boulevard lined with mansions and plane trees and runs through this very upscale and leafy residential neighborhood. Elegance, space, and taste are unavoidable once you're through the doors here and the uniformed staff starts catering to your every whim. Each room has been designed separately; some have four-poster beds, others Jacuzzis. There's a stunning patio garden and a not-too-formal restaurant, The Room at the Halcyon. *81 Holland Park, W11 3RZ, tel. 0171/727–7288, fax 0171/229–8516. 44 rooms with bath. Facilities: restaurant, patio. AE, DC, MC, V.*

**Whites.** A cream-facaded Victorian "country mansion" with a delightful white wrought-iron portico and a view of Kensington Gardens. Thick carpets, gilded glass, marble balustrades, swagged silk drapes, and Louis XV–style furniture all make this the most luxurious hotel in the area. Some of the bedrooms have balconies (one also

245

Abbey Court, **3**
Camelot, **7**
The Gate, **2**
Halcyon, **4**
Lancaster Hall
Hotel, **6**
Pembridge
Court, **3**
Portobello, **1**
Whites, **5**

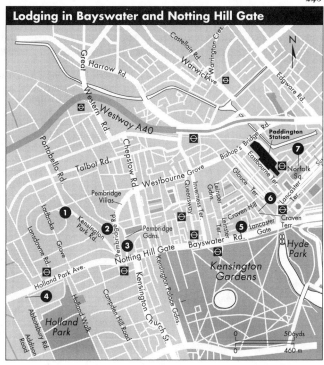

**Lodging in Bayswater and Notting Hill Gate**

has a four-poster bed), and the colors are muted—powder blue, old rose, and lemon yellow—and prettiest when softly illuminated by the crystal wall-lights. The bathrooms are splendid. *Lancaster Gate, W2 3NR, tel. 0171/262–2711, fax 0171/262–2147. 55 rooms with bath. Facilities: lounge, in-house movies, air-conditioning, restaurant. AE, DC, MC, V.*

**$$$** **Abbey Court.** Another very elegant little hotel that is more like a pri-
**★** vate home—albeit one with a resident designer. It's in a gracious white Victorian mansion in a quiet streetlet off Notting Hill Gate, which gives easy access to most of London. Inside, the era of Victoria is reflected in deep-red wallpapers (downstairs), Murano glass and gilt-framed mirrors, framed prints, mahogany, and plenty of antiques. Bathrooms look the part but are entirely modern in gray Italian marble, with brass fittings and whirlpool baths. There's 24-hour room service instead of a restaurant (there are plenty around here, though), and guests can relax in the lounge or the pretty conservatory. *20 Pembridge Gardens, W2 4DU, tel. 0171/221–7518, fax 0171/792–0858. 22 rooms with bath. Facilities: Jacuzzis, conservatory, drawing room. AE, DC, MC, V.*

**$$** **Pembridge Court.** A few doors down from the Abbey Court, in a simi-
**★** lar colonnaded white-stucco Victorian row house, is Paul and Merete Capra's sweet home-away-from-home of a hotel, cozy with scatter cushions and books, quirky Victoriana, and framed fans from the neighboring Portobello Market. Bedrooms have a great deal of swagged floral drapery, direct-dial phones, and satellite TV, and there's an elevator to the upper floors. Unusually for a small hotel, there's a restaurant, Caps, serving a French-bistro menu, plus the English breakfast that rates include (brought to your room if you

prefer)—take that into account when doing your sums, since only the half-size small twin rooms fall into the $$ category; larger ones are £10–£30 more. *34 Pembridge Gardens, W2 4DX, tel. 0171/229–9977, fax 0171/727–4982. 25 rooms with bath. Facilities: lounge, restaurant. AE, DC, MC, V.*

★ **Portobello.** This small, eccentric hotel consists of two adjoining Victorian houses which (as is common around here) back onto a beautiful large garden that is shared with the neighbors. It has long been the favorite of the arty end of the music biz and other media types. Some rooms are minute, others huge—you mustbook well ahead or depend on luck. Big mirrors, palms, and ferns are everywhere, as befits the fantasy Victorian decor. The naughty round-bedded suite is popular, though it falls in the top end of our $$$ category; only the small (some are *very* small) doubles are $$, but all rates include breakfast. The 24-hour basement bar/restaurant is one of many hangouts for locals in this very happening area. *22 Stanley Gardens, W11 2NG, tel. 0171/727–2777, fax 0171/792–9641. 25 rooms with bath. Facilities: bar, restaurant. AE, DC, MC, V. Closed 10 days over Christmas.*

$ **Camelot.** Top marks go to this affordable hotel, with its freshly deco-
★ rated bedrooms (featuring utility pine furniture, TVs, and tea/coffee makers) and attractive bathrooms, just around the corner from Paddington Station. There's a lounge, and a very pretty breakfast room complete with exposed brick wall, large open fireplace, wooden farmhouse tables and floorboards, and a gallery of child guests' works of art. Everyone here is friendly beyond the call of duty. The few bathless single rooms are great bargains; the normal rate just busts the top of this category, but includes a breakfast of anything you want—full English or organic muesli, fruit, and herb tea. *45–47 Norfolk Sq., W2 1RX, tel. 0171/723–9118, fax 0171/402–3412. 44 rooms, 36 with bath. Facilities: lounge with VCR. MC, V.*

**The Gate.** It's absolutely teeny, the Gate, just a normal house at the very top of Portobello Road, off Notting Hill Gate. The plain bedrooms have fridges, TVs, direct-dial phones, and tea/coffee facilities, plus bath (unless you opt for a smaller, £10 cheaper, shower-only room), and you can have the inclusive Continental breakfast brought up to them, or take it in the first-floor lounge. *6 Portobello Rd, W11 3DG, tel. 0171/221–2403, fax 0171/221–9128. 6 rooms with bath/shower. Facilities: lounge. AE, MC, V.*

**Lancaster Hall Hotel.** This modest hotel is owned by the German YMCA, which guarantees efficiency and spotlessness. There's a bargain 20-room "youth annex" offering basic rooms with shared baths. *35 Craven Terr., W2 3EL, tel. 0171/723–9276, fax 0171/224–8343. 100 rooms, 80 with bath or shower. Facilities: restaurant, bar. MC, V.*

## Bloomsbury

$$$ **Grafton Hotel.** This is the lone hotel at the north end of the area as you head toward Camden Town; it sits on the unaesthetic Tottenham Court Road, which some rooms overlook. Yet another in the Edwardian chain, this well-run property has had an executive Plaza Wing added recently; rooms here cost an extra £40 per night but, unlike the standard model, they feature air-conditioning and marble bathrooms with power showers. The style, needless to say, is Edwardian, with lots of dark wood, reds and deep pinks, palms, and paintings. There's a restaurant and a noisy basement wine bar, but the fun restaurants of Charlotte Street are close by, too. It's a good bet if you're planning to travel on to the north of England or Scot-

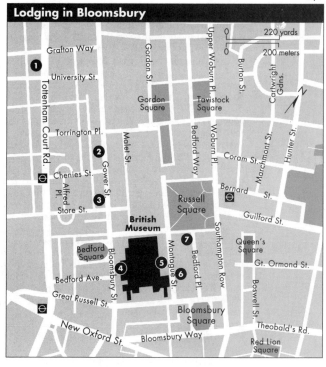

**Lodging in Bloomsbury**

land from nearby Euston or King's Cross station. *130 Tottenham Court Rd., W1P 9HP, tel. 0171/388–4131, fax 0171/387–7394. 324 rooms with bath. Facilities: bar, lounge, restaurant, in-house movies. AE, DC, MC, V.*

**\$\$ Academy.** These three joined-up Georgian houses, boasting a little patio garden and a fashion-conscious wood-floored, mirrored basement bar/brasserie, supply the most sophisticated and hotel-like facilities in the Gower Street "hotel row." The comfortable bedrooms have TV (with no extra channels), direct-dial phones, and tea/coffee makers, and the two without ensuite bathrooms are an entire £30/night cheaper. Like all the hotels in this section except the Grafton, the Academy neighbors the British Museum and University of London, a circumstance that appeals to culture vultures on a budget and the more affluent students. *17–21 Gower St., WC1E 6HG, tel. 0171/ 631–4115, fax 0171/636–3442. 33 rooms, 25 with bath/shower. Facilities: patio garden, restaurant/bar, lounge. AE, DC, MC, V.*

**Whitehall.** An imposing entrance promises good things, which the interior more than lives up to. There's an elegant lobby with arched windows, and a garden bar leading onto a patio and not-too-manicured garden. It's worth paying the extra £8/night for an ensuite shower room, but all rooms come with English or Continental breakfast included in the (very moderate) rate. *2–5 Montague St., WC1B 5BU, tel. 0171/580–5871, fax 0171/323–0409. 74 rooms, 20 with shower/WC. Facilities: breakfast room, lounge. AE, DC, MC, V.*

**\$ ★ Morgan.** A Georgian row-house hotel, family-run with charm and panache. Rooms are small and functionally furnished, yet friendly and cheerful overall, with phones and TVs. The five newish apartments are particularly pleasing: three times the size of normal rooms (and an extra £15/night, placing them in the $$ category), complete with eat-in kitchens (gourmet cooking sessions are discouraged) and private phone lines. The tiny, paneled breakfast room (rates include the meal) is straight out of a doll's house. The back rooms overlook the British Museum. *24 Bloomsbury St., WC1B 3QJ, tel. 0171/636–3735. 15 rooms with bath or shower, 5 apartments. Facilities: breakfast room. No credit cards.*

★ **Ridgemount.** The kindly owners, Mr. and Mrs. Rees, make you feel at home. The public areas, especially the family-style breakfast room, have a friendly, cluttered Victorian feel. Some rooms overlook a leafy garden, and two now have an ensuite bathroom, for an extra £9/night. *65 Gower St., WC1E 6HJ, tel. 0171/636–1141. 34 rooms, 2 with bath. Facilities: lounge. No credit cards.*

**Ruskin.** Immediately opposite the British Museum, the family-owned Ruskin is both pleasant and quiet—all front windows are double-glazed. The bedrooms are clean, though nondescript; the back ones overlook a pretty garden. Note the bucolic mural (c. 1808) in the lounge. Well-run and very popular. *23–24 Montague St., WC1B 5BN, tel. 0171/636–7388, fax 0171/323–1662. 35 rooms, 7 with shower. Facilities: lounge. AE, DC, MC, V.*

**St. Margaret's.** This guest house on a tree-lined Georgian street has been run for many years by a friendly Italian family. You'llfind spacious rooms and towering ceilings, and a wonderful location close to Russell Square. The back rooms have a garden view. *24 Bedford Pl., WC1B 5JL, tel. 0171/636–4277. 64 rooms, 10 with bath. Facilities: 2 lounges. No credit cards.*

## Docklands

**$$ Scandic Crown.** This Swedish-owned place is Scandic by name and by nature, with efficiency and blond wood everywhere. It has its peculiarities, since it's split in two. Block 2 comprises a modern apartment building, while Block 1, containing all the bars and fun stuff, is a converted warehouse. Bedrooms in the latter (prefixed by a "1") are 10 times nicer than the new ones, with rich exposed-brick walls, recessed spotlights, and big windows, some overlooking the Thames. All have the "Most Comfortable Beds In Town," on which you're offered a free night if you fail to sleep soundly (improbably, nobody's taken them up on it). A separate building houses a fine health club with pool, and the dining options (you need them out here—the courtesy bus into town stops early) include the lower deck of a dry-docked three-masted bark, a smörgåsbord buffet, and summertime terrace barbecues. *265 Rotherhithe St., SE16 1EJ, tel. 0171/231–1001, fax 0171/231–0599. 386 rooms with bath. Facilities: 2 restaurants, 2 bars, riverside terrace, lounges, health club with pool, in-room movies. AE, DC, MC, V.*

## Hampstead

**$$ Swiss Cottage Hotel.** It's a little out of the way on a peaceful street behind Swiss Cottage tube stop, but this charming, family-run hotel will suit those who like to stay in a residential district, save a little on the check, and still have their home comforts. The lounge, bar, and reception area are stuffed with antiques and reproductions, cheerfully lit, and smilingly staffed. In summer, French windows open from the bar and the downstairs restaurant—which serves an old-fashioned Anglo-French menu—onto the garden. Bedrooms off the creaky, labyrinthine corridors are freshly decorated in Victorian style, and most are good-sized. (Note that the elevator doesn't reach the 4th floor.) Executive rooms have bathrooms with pretty painted ceramic sinks and brass fittings. *4 Adamson Rd., NW3 3HP, tel. 0171/722–2281, fax 0171/483–4588. 80 rooms with bath. Facilities: lounge, bar, restaurant. AE, DC, MC, V.*

$ **La Gaffe.** Another find, a short walk from the Hampstead tube stop. Italian Bernardo Stella has been welcoming the same guests back to these early 18th-century shepherds' cottages for over a decade. Make no mistake, rooms are tiny, and the predominantly pink and beige decor isn't luxurious, but the popular wine bar and restaurant, which (naturally) serve Italian food, are yours to lounge around in at all hours—there's a shelf of assorted books to borrow. Between the two "wings" is a raised patio for summer, and each room has TV and phone. You'll love the place if you're a fan of quaint. *107–111 Heath St., NW3 6SS, tel. 0171/435–8965, fax 0171/794–7592. 14 rooms with shower. Facilities: restaurant, wine bar/café. AE, MC, V.*

### Bed-and-Breakfast Agencies

$$ **Bulldog Club.** You must join Amanda St. George's *very* exclusive B&B club before being eligible to book a stay with some of London's grandest families. Many have converted their now grown-up children's rooms; others have newly built guest annexes; all offer total comfort, with breakfast included and TV and tea/coffee facilities in your room. Most houses revolve around a Knightsbridge/Belgravia axis, though other areas are covered, too. *Further details from: 35 The Chase, SW4 0NP, tel. 0171/622–6935, fax 0171/491–1328. Facilities vary. Most rooms have private bath/shower. AE, MC, V.*

**Uptown Reservations.** As the name implies, this B&B booking service accepts only the tonier addresses, and specializes in finding hosted apartments and homes for Americans, often executives of small corporations. Nearly all the 50 or so homes on their register are in Knightsbridge, Belgravia, Kensington, and Chelsea, with a few lying farther west in Holland Park and Maida Vale. The private homes vary, of course, but all are good-looking and have private ensuite bathrooms for guests. *50 Christchurch St., SW3 4AR, tel. 0171/351–3445, fax 0171/351–9383. Facilities vary. Payment by bank transfer or US$ check; 20% deposit required. No credit cards.*

$ **Central London Accommodations.** From their personally inspected pool of private-home B&Bs, Peter and Vera Forrest will select one within your budget, and in the area you prefer, and handle the booking. The Forrests bring years of experience, and fluency in five languages, to bear on what amounts to a two-person total travel bureau—they can also procure hotels, guest houses, theater tickets, and sightseeing tours in and out of London. Calling to discuss your requirements is a good idea. Their own B&B, Forrest House, is perennially full of repeat guests who have become virtual family. *83 Addison Gardens, W14 0DT, tel. 0171/602–9668, fax 0171/602–5609. B&Bs in most neighborhoods. Facilities vary. AE, MC, V.*

**Primrose Hill B&B.** A small, friendly bed-and-breakfast agency that's genuinely "committed to the idea traveling shouldn't be a rip-off." Expatriate American Gail O'Farrell has family homes (to which guests get their own latchkeys) in or near villagey Hampstead on her books, and all are comfortable or more than comfortable. So far this has been one of those word-of-mouth secrets, but now that everyone knows, book well ahead. *14 Edis St., NW1 8LG, tel. 0171/722–6869. 15 rooms with varying facilities. No credit cards.*

# 8 The Arts and Nightlife

# The Arts

There isn't a "London arts scene"—there are lots of them. As long as there are audiences for Feydeau revivals, drag queens, obscure teenaged rock bands, hit musicals, body-painted Parisian dancers, and improvised stand-up comedy, someone will stage them in London. Commercial sponsorship of the arts is in its infancy here compared to what it is in the United States, and most major arts companies, as well as those smaller ones lucky enough to be grant-aided, are dependent, to some extent, on (inadequate) government subsidy. This ought to mean low ticket prices, but it doesn't necessarily work that way. Even so, when you consider how much a London hotel room costs, the city's arts are a bargain.

We've attempted a representative selection in the following listings, but to find out what's showing now, the weekly magazine *Time Out* (it comes out every Wednesday—Tuesday in central London) is invaluable. The *Evening Standard* also carries listings, especially the Friday edition, as do the "quality" Sunday papers and the Friday and Saturday *Independent*, *Guardian*, and *Times*. You'll find racks overflowing with leaflets and flyers in most cinema and theater foyers, too, and you can pick up the free fortnightly *London Theatre Guide* leaflet from hotels and tourist information centers.

**Theater** Although the price of a seat rarely falls below a tenner, London's West End theaters still pull in enough punters to cause a mini traffic jam each night before the house lights dim and the curtain rises. From Shakespeare to the umpteenth year of *Les Misérables* (or *The Glums*, as it's affectionately known), the West End has what visitors think of as London's theater. But there's more to see in London than the offerings of Theaterland and the national companies.

Of the 100 or so legitimate theaters in the capital, 50 are officially "West End," while the remainder go under the blanket title of "Fringe." Much like New York's Off- and Off-Off-Broadway, Fringe Theater encompasses everything from off-the-wall "physical theater" pieces to first runs of new plays and revivals of old ones. At press time, in West End and Fringe together, you could catch big new productions of those British giants Pinter, Stoppard, and Wesker (and two Ortons); two Strindbergs, a Gogol, and a Chekhov; Cocteau, Genet, Camus, and Sartre from the French corner; and every other American playwright, from Mamet to Albee. And that's leaving out Sophocles and Euripides, half a dozen concurrent Shakespeares (including an all-black *Lear*), musicals (including a Rodgers and Hammerstein and a Sondheim alongside *Cabaret* and all the Lloyd-Webber you could stomach), and oddities from Victorian music-hall to a one-woman Samuel Beckett recital.

Most theaters have matinees twice a week (Wednesday or Thursday and Saturday) and evening performances that begin at 7:30 or 8; performances on Sunday are rare, but not unknown. Prices vary, but in the West End you should expect to pay from £6 for a seat in the upper balcony to at least £20 for a good one in the stalls (orchestra) or dress circle (mezzanine). Tickets may be booked at the individual theater box offices or over the phone by credit card (some box offices or agents have special numbers for these marked "cc" in the phone book); most theaters still charge no booking fee for the latter. You can also book through ticket agents, such as **First Call** (tel. 0171/497–9977) or **Ticketmaster** (tel. 0171/344–0055), though these usually do charge a booking fee. If you're coming from the United States and wish to book seats in advance, **Keith Prowse** has a New York of-

# Theaters and Concert Halls

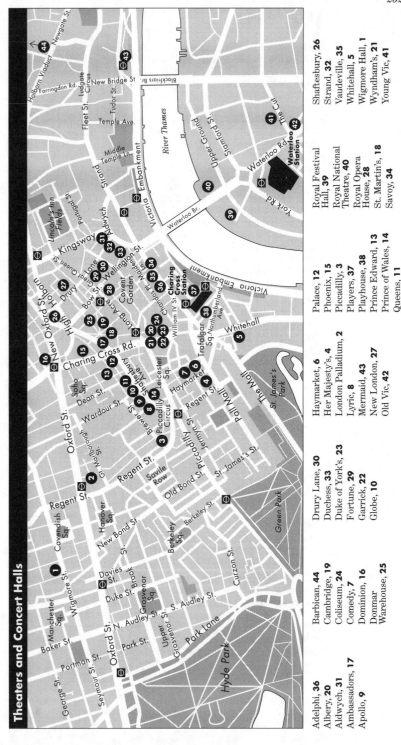

Adelphi, **36**
Albery, **20**
Aldwych, **31**
Ambassadors, **17**
Apollo, **9**

Barbican, **44**
Cambridge, **19**
Coliseum, **24**
Comedy, **7**
Dominion, **16**
Donmar
Warehouse, **25**

Drury Lane, **30**
Duchess, **33**
Duke of York's, **23**
Fortune, **29**
Garrick, **22**
Globe, **10**

Haymarket, **6**
Her Majesty's, **4**
London Palladium, **2**
Lyric, **8**
Mermaid, **43**
New London, **27**
Old Vic, **42**

Palace, **12**
Phoenix, **15**
Piccadilly, **3**
Players, **37**
Playhouse, **38**
Prince Edward, **13**
Prince of Wales, **14**
Queens, **11**

Royal Festival
Hall, **39**
Royal National
Theatre, **40**
Royal Opera
House, **28**
St. Martin's, **18**
Savoy, **34**

Shaftesbury, **26**
Strand, **32**
Vaudeville, **35**
Whitehall, **5**
Wigmore Hall, **1**
Wyndham's, **21**
Young Vic, **41**

fice (234 W. 44th St., Suite 1000, New York, NY 10036, tel. 212/398–1430 or 800/669–8687). Alternatively, the Half Price Ticket Booth (no phone) on the southwest corner of Leicester Square sells half-price tickets on the day of performance for approximately 25 theaters (subject to availability). It's open Monday–Saturday from noon for matinees and 2:30–6:30 for evening performances; there is a £1.50 service charge, and only cash is accepted. All the larger hotels offer theater bookings, but as they tack on a hefty service charge, you would do better visiting the box offices yourself. You might, however, consider using one particular booking line that doubles the price of tickets: **West End Cares** (tel. 0171/867–1111) donates half of what it charges to AIDS charities.

**Warning:** Be *very* careful of scalpers outside theaters; they have been known to charge £200 or more for a sought-after ticket. In recent years, there has been another problem: unscrupulous ticket agents, who sell tickets at four or five times their price from the ticket box offices. While a service charge is legitimate, this type of scalping certainly isn't, especially since the vast majority of theaters have some tickets (returns and "house seats") available on the night of performance. If you have a bad experience with a scalper, contact the Development Officer at the Society of London Theatre (Bedford Chambers, The Piazza, Covent Garden, WC2E 8HQ, tel. 0171/836–3193). They probably can't get you a refund, but your letter will help stamp out scalpers in the future.

*West End*   The **Royal Shakespeare Company** and the **Royal National Theatre Company** perform at London's two main arts complexes, the **Barbican Centre** and **The Royal National Theatre** respectively. Both companies mount consistently excellent productions and are usually a safe option for anyone having trouble choosing which play to see.

The following is a list of West End theaters:

**Adelphi,** Strand, WC2E 7NA, tel. 0171/379–8884
**Albery,** St. Martin's La., WC2N 4AH, tel. 0171/867–1115
**Aldwych,** Aldwych, WC2B 4DF, tel. 0171/836–6404
**Ambassadors,** West St., WC2H 9ND, tel. 0171/836–6111
**Apollo,** Shaftesbury Ave., W1V 7HD, tel. 0171/494–5070
**Apollo Victoria,** Wilton Rd., SW1V ILL, tel. 0171/416–6042
**Barbican,** Barbican, EC2Y 8DS, tel. 0171/638–8891
**Cambridge,** Earlham St., WC2H 9HU, tel. 0171/379–5299
**Comedy,** Panton St., SW1Y 4DN, tel. 0171/494–5080
**Dominion,** Tottenham Court Rd., W1 0AG, tel. 0171/416–6060
**Donmar Warehouse,** 41 Earlham St., WC2H 9LD, tel. 0171/867–1150
**Drury Lane (Theatre Royal),** Catherine St., WC2B 5JF, tel. 0171/494–5001
**Duchess,** Catherine St., WC2B 5LA, tel. 0171/494–5075
**Duke of York's,** St. Martin's La., WC2N 4BG, tel. 0171/836–5122
**Fortune,** Russell St., WC2B 5HH, tel. 0171/836–2238
**Garrick,** Charing Cross Rd., WC2H 0HH, tel. 0171/494–5085
**Globe,** Shaftesbury Ave., W1V 8AR, tel. 0171/494–5067
**Haymarket,** Haymarket, SW1Y 4HT, tel. 0171/930–8800
**Her Majesty's,** Haymarket, SW1Y 4QR, tel. 0171/494–5400
**London Palladium,** 8 Argyll St., W1V 1AD, tel. 0171/494–5020
**Lyric,** Shaftesbury Ave., W1V 7HA, tel. 0171/494–5045
**Lyric Hammersmith,** King St., W6 0QL, tel. 0181/741–2311
**Mermaid,** Puddle Dock, EC4 3DB, tel. 0171/410–0000
**New London,** Drury La., WC2B 5PW, tel. 0171/405–0072
**Old Vic,** Waterloo Rd., SE1 8NB, tel. 0171/928–7616

**Open-Air Theatre,** Inner Circle, Regent's Park, NW1 4NP, tel. 0171/935–5884

**Palace,** Shaftesbury Ave., W1V 8AY, tel. 0171/434–0909

**Phoenix,** Charing Cross Rd., WC2H 0JP, tel. 0171/867–1044

**Piccadilly,** Denman St., W1V 8DY, tel. 0171/867–1118

**Players,** The Arches, Villiers St., WC2N 6NQ, tel. 0171/839–1134

**Playhouse,** Northumberland Ave., WC2N 6NN, tel. 0171/839–4401

**Prince Edward,** Old Compton St., W1V 8AH, tel. 0171/734–8951

**Prince of Wales,** 31 Coventry St., W1V 8AS, tel. 0171/839–5972

**Queens,** 51 Shaftesbury Ave., W1V 8BA, tel. 0171/494–5041

**Royal Court,** Sloane Sq., SW1W 8AS, tel. 0171/730–1745 (*see also* Theatre Upstairs under Fringe, *below*)

**Royal National Theatre** (Cottesloe, Lyttelton, and Olivier), South Bank Arts Complex, SE1 9PX, tel. 0171/928–2252

**St. Martin's,** West St., WC2H 9NH, tel. 0171/836–1443

**Savoy,** Strand, WC2R 0ET, tel. 0171/836–8888

**Shaftesbury,** Shaftesbury Ave., WC2H 8DP, tel. 0171/379–5399

**Strand,** Aldwych, WC2B 5LD, tel. 0171/930–8800

**Vaudeville,** Strand, WC2R 0NH, tel. 0171/836–9987

**Victoria Palace,** Victoria St., SW1E 5EA, tel. 0171/834–1317

**Westminster,** 12 Palace St., SW1E 5JA, tel. 0171/834–0283

**Whitehall,** 14 Whitehall, SW1A 2DY, tel. 0171/867–1119

**Wyndham's,** Charing Cross Rd., WC2H 0DA, tel. 0171/867–1116

*Fringe* Shows can be straight plays, circus, comedy, musicals, readings, or productions every bit as polished and impressive as those in the West End—except for their location and the price of the seat. Fringe tickets are always considerably less expensive than tickets for West End productions. The following theaters are among the better-known fringe venues:

**Almeida,** Almeida St., N1 1AT, tel. 0171/359–4404

**Arts Theatre,** 6–7 Great Newport St., WC2H 7JB, tel. 0171/836–2132

**Battersea Arts Centre,** Old Town Hall, Lavender Hill, SW1 1JX, tel. 0171/223–2223

**Bloomsbury Theatre,** Gordon St., WC1H 0AH, tel. 0171/387–9629

**Bush,** Shepherds Bush Green, W12 8QD, tel. 0181/743–3388

**Chats Palace,** 42–4 Brooksby's Walk, E9 6DF, tel. 0181/986–6714

**Drill Hall,** 16 Chenies St., WC1E 7EX, tel. 0171/637–8270

**The Finborough,** Finborough Arms, Finborough Rd., SW10 9ED, tel. 0171/373–3842

**The Gate,** The Prince Albert, 11 Pembridge Rd., W11 3HQ, tel. 0171/229–0706

**Hackney Empire,** 291 Mare St., E8 1EJ, tel. 0181/985–2424

**Hampstead,** Swiss Cottage, NW3 3EX, tel. 0171/722–9301

**ICA Theatre,** The Mall, SW1Y 5AH, tel. 0171/930–3647

**Kings Head,** 115 Upper St., N1 1QN, tel. 0171/226–1916

**Latchmere,** 503 Battersea Park Rd., SW11 3BW, tel. 0171/228–2620

**Lyric Studio,** Lyric Theatre, King St., W6 9JT, tel. 0181/741–2311

**Man in the Moon,** 392 Kings Rd., SW3 5UZ, tel. 0171/351–2876

**New End Theatre,** 27 New End, NW3 1JD, tel. 0171/794–0022

**Orange Tree,** 1 Clarence St., Richmond, TW9 1SA, tel. 0181/940–3633

**Riverside Studios,** Crisp Rd., W6 9RL, tel. 0181/748–3354

**Theatre Royal,** Stratford East, E15 1BN, tel. 0181/534–0310

**Theatre Upstairs,** Royal Court, Sloane Sq., SW1W 8AS, tel. 0171/730–2254

**Tricycle Theatre,** 269 Kilburn High Rd., NW6 7JR, tel. 0171/328–1000

**Watermans Arts Centre,** 40 High St., Brentford, TW8 0DS, tel. 0181/
568–1176
**Young Vic,** 66 The Cut, SE1 8LZ, tel. 0171/928–6363

**Concerts**   The ticket prices to symphony-size orchestral concerts are fortu-
nately still relatively moderate, usually ranging from £5 to £15. If
you can't book in advance, then arrive at the hall an hour before the
performance for a chance at returns.

The London Symphony Orchestra is in residence at the **Barbican
Centre,** although other top orchestras—including the Philharmonia
and the Royal Philharmonic—also perform here. The **South Bank
Arts Complex,** which includes the **Royal Festival Hall,** the **Queen
Elizabeth Hall,** and the small **Purcell Room,** forms another major
venue; the Royal Festival Hall is one of the finest concert halls in Europe. Between the Barbican and South Bank, there are concert performances almost every night of the year. The Barbican also
features chamber music concerts with such celebrated orchestras as
the City of London Sinfonia.

For a different concert-going experience, as well as the chance to
take part in a great British tradition, try the **Royal Albert Hall** during the Promenade Concert season: eight weeks lasting from July to
September. Special "promenade" (standing) tickets usually cost half
the price of normal tickets and are available at the hall on the night
of the concert. Another summer pleasure is the outdoor concert series by the lake at **Kenwood** (Hampstead Heath; tel. 0181/348–6684).
Concerts are also part of the program at the open-air theater in **Holland Park** (no phone). Check the listings for details.

You should also look for the lunchtime concerts that take place all
over the city in smaller concert halls, the big arts center foyers, and
churches; they usually cost under £5 or are free and will feature
string quartets, singers, jazz ensembles, or gospel choirs. **St.
John's, Smith Square** and **St. Martin-in-the-Fields** are two of the
more popular locations. Performances usually begin about 1 PM and
last an hour.

*Concert Hall*   **Barbican Centre,** Barbican, EC2Y 8DS, tel. 0171/638–8891 (res-
*Box Office*   ervations); 0171/638–4141 (information)
*Information*   **Royal Albert Hall,** Kensington Gore, SW7 2AP, tel. 0171/589–8212
**St. John's, Smith Square,** SW1P 3HA, tel. 0171/222–1061
**St. Martin-in-the-Fields,** Trafalgar Sq., WC2N 4JJ, tel. 0171/839–
1930
**South Bank Arts Complex,** South Bank, SE1 8XX, tel. 0171/928–
8800 (reservations); 0171/928–3002 (information)
**Wigmore Hall,** 36 Wigmore St., W1H 9DF, tel. 0171/935–2141

**Opera**   The main venue for opera in London is the **Royal Opera House** (Covent Garden), which ranks with the Metropolitan Opera House in
New York—particularly where expense is concerned. Prices range
from £5 in the upper slips (whether the stage is visible is anyone's
guess) to more than £100 for the best seats, and even more when
great and famous singers appear. Performances are divided into
booking periods and sell out early, although returns and standing
spaces are sold on the day. (Conditions of purchase vary—call the
box office for information.)

English-language productions are staged at the **Coliseum** in St.
Martin's Lane, home of the **English National Opera Company.** Prices
here are generally lower than at the Royal Opera House, ranging
from £8 to £43, and productions are often innovative and exciting.

The occasional megaproduction with international stars (plus live elephants and herds of horses) is staged at the **Wembley Arena.**

Ballet
The Royal Opera House is also the home of the world-famous **Royal Ballet.** Prices are slightly more reasonable for the ballet than they are for the opera, but bookings should be made well in advance, as tickets sell out fast. The **English National Ballet** and visiting international companies perform at the Coliseum and the Royal Festival Hall from time to time. **Sadler's Wells Theatre** also hosts various other ballet companies and regional and international modern dance troupes. Prices here are much cheaper than at Covent Garden.

*Opera and*  **Coliseum,** St. Martin's La., WC2N 4ES, tel. 0171/836–3161
*Ballet Box*  **Royal Opera House,** Covent Garden, WC2E 9DD, tel. 0171/240–1066
*Office*  **Sadler's Wells,** Rosebery Ave., EC1R 4TN, tel. 0171/278–8916
*Information*  **Wembley Arena,** HA9 0DW, tel. 0181/900–1234

Modern Dance
Contemporary dance thrives in London, with innovative young choreographers and companies constantly emerging (and then, it often seems, moving to New York). Michael Clark was one of the first of the new wave; Yolanda Snaith and choreographer Lea Anderson's troupe, the Cholmondeleys (pronounced "Chumleys"), are two more examples of home-grown talent. In addition to the many Fringe theaters that mount the odd dance performance, the following theaters showcase contemporary dance:

**The Place,** 17 Duke's Rd., WC1, tel. 0171/387–0031
**Riverside Studios** (*see* Fringe Theater, *above*)
**Sadler's Wells** (*see* Opera and Ballet, *above*)

Movies
Despite the video invasion, West End movies continue to do good business. Most of the major houses (Odeon, MGM, etc.) congregate in the Leicester Square/Piccadilly Circus area, where tickets average £4–£7, sometimes even more. Mondays and matinees are sometimes better buys at £2–£4, and there are also fewer crowds. Prices drop to around £5 as you get out of the West End, and are even lower in the suburbs, but unless you're staying there, any savings could be eaten up by transportation costs.

Movie clubs and repertory cinemas screen a wider range of movies, including classic, Continental, and underground, as well as rare or underestimated masterpieces. Some charge a membership fee of under £1. One of the best is the **National Film Theatre** (in the South Bank Arts Complex; tel. 0171/928–3232), where the London Film Festival is based in the fall; there are also lectures and presentations. Daily memberships cost 40p. Other notable rep cinemas include the **Everyman** (Hollybush Vale, Hampstead, tel. 0171/435–1525; membership 50p/year), the **Electric** (191 Portobello Rd., W11, tel. 0171/792–2020), and the **Riverside** (*see* Fringe Theater, *above*).

The **Institute of Contemporary Arts** (the Mall, tel. 0171/930–3647) contains two cinemas (one is tiny), while the **French Institute** (17 Queensbury Pl., SW7, tel. 0171/589–6211) and the **Goethe Institute** (Princes Gate, SW7, tel. 0171/411–3400) show French and German films respectively. Films are also shown irregularly at many of the national museums.

# Nightlife

**Jazz** **Bass Clef.** Owned by the delightful Peter Ind (himself a bass player), this bohemian backstreet club offers some of the best live jazz in London, along with fried chicken and burgers on weekends, snacks the rest of the time. It can get very smoky and packed in here, when the best view of the stage is from the closed-circuit screen at the bar, but there is no problem with the acoustics. Music also at the adjoining **Tenor Clef** (1 Hoxton Sq.). *35 Coronet St., N1, tel. 0171/729–2440/2476. Admission: £3.50–£7, depending on the band. Open Mon., Wed.–Sat. 7:30 PM–2 AM. AE, DC, MC, V.*

**100 Club.** The best for blues, trad, and Dixie, plus the occasional straight rock-and-roll, this Oxford Street subterranean has the correct paint-peeling, smoke-choked, dance-inducing atmosphere. There's a food counter most nights. *100 Oxford St., W1, tel. 0171/636–0933. Admission: £4–£10, depending on the night. Open 7:30–11:30, later on weekends. No credit cards.*

**Jazz Café.** This palace of high-tech cool in a converted bank in bohemian Camden has its problems—you often have to stand in line, and there never seems to be enough seating—but still it remains an essential hangout for fans of the mainstream end of the repertoire and younger crossover performers. It's way north, but steps from Camden Town tube. *5–7 Pkwy., NW1, tel. 0171/916–6000. Admission: £6–£12, depending on the band. Open Mon.–Sat. 7 PM–late (time varies). Reservations advised for balcony restaurant. AE, DC, MC, V.*

**Pizza Express.** It may seem strange, since Pizza Express is the capital's best-loved chain of pizza houses, but this is one of London's principal jazz venues, with music every night except Monday in the basement restaurant. The subterranean interior is darkly lit, the line-ups (often featuring visiting U.S. performers) are interesting, and the Italian-style thin-crust pizzas are great! *10 Dean St., W1, tel. 0171/437–9595. Admission: £6–£9, depending on band. Open from noon for food; music from 9:30 PM to 1 AM Tues.–Sun. Reservations advised; essential some nights. AE, DC, MC, V.*

**Pizza on the Park.** Situated in the heart of Knightsbridge, this is another branch of the same Pizza Express chain, offering the same good food with your jazz in the downstairs restaurant. Dinner for two, including drink, shouldn't come to more than £30, but don't forget to add the cover charge. *11–13 Knightsbridge, SW1, tel. 0171/235–5273. Admission: £8–£12, depending on band. Open daily; jazz Tues–Sat. 8 PM–2 AM. Reservations advised; essential some nights. AE, DC, MC, V.*

**Ronnie Scott's.** The legendary Soho jazz club which, since its opening in the early '60s, has been attracting all the big names. It's usually packed and hot, the food isn't great, service is slow—because the staff can't move through the crowds, either—but the atmosphere can't be beat, and it's probably still London's best. *47 Frith St., W1, tel. 0171/439–0747. Admission £10–£12 non-members. Open Mon.–Sat. 8:30 PM–3 AM, Sun. 8 PM–11:30 PM. Reservations advised; essential some nights. AE, DC, MC, V.*

**Rock** **The Forum.** The former Town & Country, this ex-ballroom with balcony and dance floor packs in the customers and consistently attracts the best medium-to-big-name performers, too. Get the tube to Kentish Town, then follow the hordes. *9–17 Highgate Rd., NW5, tel. 0171/284–2200. Admission: around £8–£12. Open most nights 7–11.*

**The Roadhouse.** True to its name, this cavernous place beneath the Jubilee Market pays homage to the American dream of the open road, with a Harley behind the bar and much memorabilia. The bands tend to fit into the feel-good, tuneful, middle-of-the-road end of the R&B/blues/rock/soul spectrum. Great fajitas, happy hours, and U.S.-style Sunday Blues Club brunch (free admission). *Jubilee Hall, Covent Garden, WC2, tel. 0171/240–6001. Admission: £3–£6. Open Mon.–Wed. 5:30 PM–1 AM; Thurs.–Sat. 5:30 PM–3 AM, Sun. 12:30 PM–5:30 PM. AE, MC, V.*

**The Rock Garden.** Famous for the setting and for encouraging young talent to move on to bigger and better things. Talking Heads, U2, and The Smiths are just a few who made their debuts here. Music is in the basement, where there is standing room only, so eat first. *6–7 The Piazza, Covent Garden, WC2, tel. 0171/240–3961. Admission: £4–£7 depending on band. Open Mon.–Sat. 7:30 PM–late (times vary); Sun. 8 PM–midnight. AE, DC, MC, V.*

**Shepherd's Bush Empire.** London's newest major venue was converted from the BBC TV theater, where Terry Wogan, the United Kingdom's Johnny Carson, recorded his show for years and years. Now it hosts the same kind of medium-big names as the north London Forum. *Shepherd's Bush Green, W12, tel. 0181/740–7474. Admission: £8–£12. Open 7:30–11. AE, MC, V.*

**Subterania.** Home of Notting Hillbillies everywhere—that is, the hip and cool bohemians of the neighborhood—this large, medium-tech balconied club never welcomes mainstream bands but books the top musicians in any alternative genre from all over the world. *12 Acklam Rd., W10, tel. 0181/960–4590. Admission: £6–£8. Call for hours; bands play Tues.–Thurs. MC, V.*

**Clubs** Always call ahead, especially to the dance and youth-oriented places, because the club scene changes constantly.

**Café de Paris.** This former gilt and red velveteen ballroom still looks like a disreputable tea-dance hall but hosts hot, hip nights for twenty-to-thirty-somethings who dress the part. At press time, Wednesday was "Ego," and probably the best night—but ring for current details. (*See* The Gay Scene, *below*). *3 Coventry St., W1, tel. 0171/287–3602. Admission: £5–£12. Open Wed. 10 PM–4 AM, Thurs.–Sat. 11 PM–6 AM. No credit cards.*

**Camden Palace.** This is the student tourist's first stop, though some nights are hipper than others. Still, it would be difficult to find a facial wrinkle, even if you could see through the laser lights and find your way around the three floors of bars. There's often a live band. *1A Camden High St., NW1, tel. 0171/387–0428. Admission: £3–£9. Open Tues.–Sat. 9 PM–3 AM. No credit cards.*

**Gardening Club.** Next door to the Rock Garden (*see* Rock, *above*), this club has different music, ambience, and groovers on different nights, but is consistently the place to be, especially if you're not yet 30. (*See* The Gay Scene, *below*.) *4 The Piazza, WC2, tel. 0171/497–3154. Admission: £4–£12. Open Mon.–Wed. 10 PM–3 AM, Fri. and Sat. 11 PM–6 AM. AE, MC, DC, V.*

**Heaven.** London's premier (mainly) gay club is the best place for dancing wildly for hours. A state-of-the-art laser show and a large, throbbing dance floor complement a labyrinth of quieter bars and lounges and a snack bar. (*See* The Gay Scene, *below*.) *Under the Arches, Villiers St., WC2, tel. 0171/839–2520. Admission: £4–£8 depending on night. Call for opening times (Tues.–Sat. approx. 10 PM–3:30 AM). AE, DC, MC, V.*

**Hippodrome.** A neon horseman marks Peter Stringfellow's second-string club. Much like his first-string one (*see below*), this one has lots of sparkly black and silver, several tiers of expensive bars, a restaurant, and lots of enthusiastic lighting around a large dance floor. Very middle-of-the-road. *Hippodrome Corner, Cranbourn St.,*

*WC2, tel. 0171/437–4311. Admission: Mon.–Thurs. £8, Fri. £10,*
*Sat. £12 (half price before 10:30). Open Mon.–Sat. 9 PM–3:30 AM.*
*AE, DC, MC, V.*

**Palookaville.** Conveniently close to Covent Garden tube, this basement restaurant/bar charges a cover only on Friday and Saturday.
It's popular with office people for after-hours drinks. You won't
write home about the food or the undemanding music—usually
there's a jazz trio or similar live band—but you might about the
friendly, mellow ambience. *13A James St., WC2, tel. 0171/240–*
*5857. Admission: £3 Fri., Sat. Open Mon.–Thurs., 8:30–midnight;*
*Fri. and Sat. 8:30–1. AE, DC, MC, V.*

**Stringfellows.** Peter Stringfellow's first London nightclub is not at
all hip, but *is* glitzy, with mirrored walls, the requisite dance-floor
light show, and an expensive art deco–style restaurant. Suburban-
ites and middle-aged swingers frequent it. *16–19 Upper St. Mar-*
*tin's La., WC2, tel. 0171/240–5534. Admission: Mon.–Wed. £8;*
*Thurs. £10; Fri.–Sat. before 10, £10, after 10, £15. Open Mon.–Sat.*
*8 PM–3:30 AM. AE, DC, MC, V.*

**Velvet Underground.** A DJ-dominated house/hip-hop/Balearic dance
floor of a club, which is as young as it sounds, sauna-like, and louche.
Different sounds pull in slightly different crowds, of course, but you
have to be a regular London clubber to tell the difference. *143 Char-*
*ing Cross Rd., WC2, tel. 0171/439–4655. Admission: £5–£10. Open*
*Wed., Thurs. 10 PM–3 AM, Fri., Sat. 10 PM–4 AM, Sun. 7 PM–mid-*
*night. No credit cards.*

**The Wag.** This tenacious representative of Soho's club circuit takes
on a different character according to which night it is and which DJ
is spinning. One extremely loud, sweaty floor houses bars and dance
spaces, and a quieter, cooler one a restaurant serving dinner and
breakfast. *33–35 Wardour St., W1, tel. 0171/437–5534. Admission:*
*£4–£9, depending on the night. Open Mon.–Thurs. 10:30 PM–3 AM;*
*Fri. and Sat. 10:30 PM–6 AM. No credit cards.*

**Cabaret**  **Comedy Café.** Talent nights, jazz, and video karaoke, but mostly
stand-up comedy, take place at this popular dive in the City. Admission charges are occasionally waived. There's food available in the
evening and usually a late license (for alcohol). *66 Rivington St.,*
*EC2, tel. 0171/256–1242. Admission free or £3–£5. Open Mon.–Sat.*
*5:30 PM–midnight; show at 9 PM. MC, V.*

**Comedy Store.** This is the improv factory where the United Kingdom's funniest standups cut their teeth, now relocated to a bigger
and better place. The name performers and new talent you'll see
may be strangers to you, but you're guaranteed to laugh. *Haymar-*
*ket House, Oxendon St., SW1, tel. 0171/344–4444, or 01426/914433*
*for information. Admission: £8–£9. Shows Tues.–Thurs., Sun. at*
*8, Fri.–Sat. at 8 and midnight.*

**Casinos**  The 1968 Gaming Act states that any person wishing to gamble *must*
make a declaration of intent to gamble at the gaming house in question and *must* apply for membership in person. Membership usually
takes about two days. In many cases, clubs prefer for the applicant's
membership to be proposed by an existing member. Personal guests
of existing members are, however, allowed to participate.

**Charlie Chester Casino.** The drawing cards here are an international
restaurant and a modern casino with blackjack, roulette, craps, and
Punto Banco. *12 Archer St., W1, tel. 0171/734–0255. Membership £5*
*for life. Open daily 2 PM–4 AM. Jacket and tie required.*

**Crockford's.** This is a civilized club, established 150 years ago, with
none of the jostling for tables that mars many of the flashier clubs. It
has attracted a large international clientele since its move from St.

James's to Mayfair. The club offers American roulette, Punto Banco, and blackjack. *30 Curzon St., W1, tel. 0171/493–7771. Membership £150 a year. Open daily 2 PM–4 AM. Jacket and tie required.*

**The Golden Nugget.** This large casino just off Piccadilly has blackjack, roulette, and Punto Banco. *22 Shaftesbury Ave., W1, tel. 0171/439–0099. Membership £3.50 for life. Open daily 2 PM–4 AM. Jacket required (tie optional).*

**Palm Beach Casino.** Situated in what used to be the old ballroom of the Mayfair Hotel, this is a fast-moving and exciting club attracting a large international membership. It has a red-and-gold interior, with a plush restaurant and bar. You can choose from American roulette, blackjack, and Punto Banco. *30 Berkeley St., W1, tel. 0171/493–6585. Membership £10. Open daily 2 PM–4 AM. Jacket and tie required.*

**Sportsman Club.** One of the few casinos in London to have a dice table as well as Punto Banco, American roulette, and blackjack. *3 Tottenham Court Rd., W1, tel. 0171/637–5464. Membership £3.45 a year. Open daily 2 PM–4 AM. Jacket and tie required.*

## The Gay Scene

Since February 1994, with the long-overdue lowering of the age of consent from 21, 18-year-old gay men in Britain have had the blessing of the law in doing together what they've always done together. (Westminster mooted 16, the boys-and-girls age, but British MPs could not quite deal with that). The change did not extend to lesbians, nor did it need to, since there has never been any legislation that so much as mentions gay women—a circumstance that, believe it or not, dates from Queen Victoria's point-blank refusal to believe that women did it with women. AIDS is, of course, a large issue, but the epidemic hasn't yet had quite as devastating an impact as it has on San Francisco and New York.

There are signs of a gay renewal in London. Soho, especially Old Compton Street, is acquiring a pre-AIDS Christopher Street atmosphere, with gay shops, bars, restaurants, and even beauty salons (get your chest waxed here) jostling for space. The lavender pound is a desirable pound. Though lesbians are included in the "Compton" scene (as are anyone's straight friends), it's predominantly men-for-men. The dyke scene certainly exists, and lesbian chic is as trendy in London as it is in New York or Los Angeles, but it has a lower profile, generally, than the male equivalent, and also tends to be more politically strident. Any women-only event in London attracts a large proportion of gay women.

Check the listings in *Time Out*, the weekly *MetroXtra (MX)*, and the monthly *Gay Times* for events.

**Bars, Cafés, Pubs**

**Comptons.** This pub, which has been here forever, is run by Bass Charrington, one of the big U.K. breweries. It's a useful rendezvous for the Soho strip. *53 Old Compton St., W1, tel. 0171/437–4445.*

**Crews Bar.** As it sounds: a big West End pub with a swanky, New Yorky look, and testosterone on tap. *14 Upper St. Martin's La., W1, tel. 0171/379–4880.*

**Drill Hall.** A woman-centric arts center with a great program of theater/dance/art events and classes, plus a popular bar, which is women-only Monday. *16 Chenies St., WC1, tel. 0171/631–1353.*

**The Edge.** Poseurs welcome at this newish, hip Soho hangout, where straight groovers mix in, and there are sidewalk tables in summer. Great for breakfast. *11 Soho Sq., W1, tel. 0171/439–1223.*

**Fanny's.** It's mainly women who frequent this popular West London place, though Friday night and Sunday lunch are the only times men are not admitted. Thursday is transvestite/transsexual night. *305A North End Rd., W14, tel. 0171/385–9359. Admission charged for some events.*

**First Out.** A relaxed, fairly long-established café/bar in the shadow of Centrepoint. Fridays are women-only. *52 St. Giles High St., WC2, tel. 0171/240–8042.*

**Village Soho.** A cavern of a fashionable three-floored bar/restaurant/café/disco, whose name makes explicit the similarities between New York a decade back and London now. *81 Wardour St., W1, tel. 0171/434–2124.*

**The Yard.** Just opened at press time, this is Soho's best-looking, hippest, and biggest bar/café, centered around the stunning Courtyard restaurant. *57 Rupert St., W1, tel. 0171/437–2652.*

**Cabaret**    **Madame Jo Jos.** By no means devoid of straight spectators, this place has long been one of the most fun drag cabarets in town—civilized of atmosphere, with barechested bar boys. *8 Brewer St., tel. 0171/287–1414. Admission: Mon.–Thurs. £6, Fri. and Sat. £8. Doors open at 10 PM; shows at 12:15 and 1:15.*

**Royal Vauxhall Tavern.** This venerable, curved pub had a drag cabaret before the Lady Bunny was born. Sometimes it's full of gay mafia, other times local media folk having a different night out, and Thursday is the night for the lesbian cabaret, Vixens. *372 Kennington La., SE11, tel. 0171/582–0833. Admission free. Open Mon. 8 PM–1 AM, Tues., Thurs.–Sat. 8 PM–2 AM, Wed. 8 PM–midnight, Sun. 7 PM–10:30 PM.*

**Clubs**    **The Bell.** This downtown King's Cross pub/club has been popular for years for its friendly, mixed lesbian/gay dance nights. Jo's Original Tea Dance on Sunday (5 PM–midnight; dance lessons 1 PM–4 PM) is a fave. *257–259 Pentonville Rd., N1, tel. 0171/837–5617. Admission: free–£3.*

**Heaven.** Aptly named, it has by far the best light show on any London dance floor, is unpretentious, *loud,* and huge, with a labyrinth of quiet rooms, bars, and live-music parlors. If you go to just one club, this is the one to choose. Thursday is straight night. *The Arches, Villiers St., WC2, tel. 0171/839–2520. Admission: £4–£8. Open Tues.–Sat. 10:30 PM–3:30 AM.*

**One-nighters**    Some of the best gay dance clubs are held once a week in mixed clubs. The following are well-established, and likely still to be going, but it's best to call first.

**Love Muscle.** A steaming mixed gender Saturday-night party, with eight hours of dance classics at a big Brixton club. On Friday, **M** (for "Music, Muscle, and Meat") alternates with **Venus Rising** (guess which gender goes where). *Town Hall Parade, Brixton Hill, SW2, tel. 0171/326–5100. Admission: £6 before midnight, £8 midnight–5 AM, £5 after 5. Open 10 PM–6 AM.*

**Queer Nation.** This Sunday club is adorable for its laid-back, high-fashion friendliness, with hordes of gay and straight men and women recovering from the weekend together. *The Gardening Club, 4 The Piazza, Covent Garden, WC2, tel. 0171/497–3153. Admission: £6. Open 9 PM–2 AM.*

**Red Hot.** London fixture Yvette invites muscular go-go boys to the campiest Tuesday dance night at this 500-capacity ex-ballroom; even the bouncers are gay. *Café de Paris, 3–4 Coventry St., W1, tel. 0171/287–3602. Admission: free before 11:30, then £5. Open 10:30 PM–3 AM.*

**Village Youth.** Monday is Limelight night, for mixed lesbian and gay garage and deep house dancing, in this converted church related to the New York club of the same name. *136 Shaftsbury Ave., WC2, tel. 0171/436–2468. Admission: £6. Open 10 PM–4 AM.*

# 9 Excursions from London

Here are five ideas for day visits to some of Britain's major sights outside London. Even the most chauvinistic Londoner will admit—eventually—that, however absorbing the capital is, life does go on outside. Indeed, regional Britain has its own definite characteristics and values, often sharply contrasted with those of London.

All the places listed in this chapter can be reached in a relatively short journey from London, usually either by train or by coach. It would be wise to check all train and coach times before the day of travel; weekend timetables vary, and journey times are often longer on weekends.

# Bath

**Getting There**  By **train** from Paddington station to Bath Spa: journey time 1 hour 25 minutes: trains about once an hour. By **National Express coach** (tel. 0171/730–0202) from Victoria Coach Station: journey time 3 hours: coaches about every 2 hours.

**Tourist Information**  **Bath Tourist Information Centre** is on Bath Street in the Colonnades (tel. 01225/462–831).

**Exploring**  Bath is the most perfect 18th-century city in all Britain. It is a compact place, easy to explore on foot: The museums, elegant shops, and terraces of magnificent town houses are all close to one another. But far from being merely a museum piece, Bath today is a lively and vibrant place with a thriving cultural life.

It was the Romans who first took the waters at Bath, building a temple in honor of their goddess Minerva and a sophisticated series of baths to make full use of the curative hot springs. To this day these gush from the earth at a constant temperature of 46.5°C (116°F). In the **Roman Baths Museum,** underneath the 18th-century Pump Room, you can see the excavated remains of almost the entire baths complex. *Abbey Churchyard, tel. 01225/461–111. Admission: £5 adults, £3 children. Combined ticket with Museum of Costume: £6.60 adults, £3.50 children, £16 family. Open daily 9–6.*

Next to the Pump Room is the **Abbey,** built in the 15th century. There are superb fan-vaulted ceilings in the nave.

In the 18th century, Bath became the fashionable center for taking the waters. The architect John Wood (1704–54) created a harmonious city from the mellow local stone, building elegantly executed terraces, crescents, and villas. The heart of Georgian Bath is the perfectly proportioned **Circus** and the **Royal Crescent.** On the corner, **Number 1 Royal Crescent** is furnished as it might have been when Beau Nash, the master of ceremonies at the Assembly Rooms (*see below*) and arbiter of 18th-century Bath society, lived in Bath. *Royal Crescent, tel. 01225/428–126. Admission: £3 adults, £2.50 students, children, and senior citizens. Open Mar.–Oct., Tues.–Sun. 10:30–5; Nov.–mid-Dec., Tues.–Sun. 10:30–4.*

Also near the Circus are the **Assembly Rooms,** frequently mentioned by Jane Austen in her novels of early 19th-century life. This classical villa now houses a **Museum of Costume,** where some of the fashions of Bath's heyday are featured. *Bennett St., tel. 01225/461–111. Admission: £3.20 adults, £2 children 8–18, £9 family (2 adults and 4 children). Open Mon.–Sat. 10–5, Sun. 11–5.*

The city's main shopping areas are in Stall Street and Union Street: Explore the numerous narrow alleyways and passages leading off, all full of fascinating shops. Take one of these—say, Northumberland Passage—and head toward **Pulteney Bridge,** an 18th-century bridge over the river Avon lined with little shops. Then walk along Upper Borough Walls to the **Theatre Royal,** one of the finest surviving Georgian theaters in England.

**Time Out**  Bath has a good selection of coffee and lunch spots. Try the **Pump Room** (in Abbey Churchyard on Stall St.) for morning coffee, lunch, or afternoon tea in elegant surroundings, perhaps listening to the music of a string quartet. Or in nearby North Parade Passage, try **Sally Lunns,** where the famous Bath bun is still baked. **The Theatre Vaults** in Saw Close is a good place for a pre- or post-theater drink or meal.

# Cambridge

**Getting There**  By **train** from Liverpool Street or King's Cross station; journey time 1 hour; trains hourly. By **National Express coach** (tel. 0171/730–0202) from Victoria Coach Station; journey time 2 hours; coaches hourly.

**Tourist Information**  **Cambridge Tourist Information Centre** is in Wheeler Street, an extension of Benet Street, off King's Parade, tel. 01223/322–640.

**Exploring**  Cambridge is one of the most beautiful cities in Britain, and the celebrated Cambridge University sits right at its heart. Students have been coming to Cambridge since the end of the 13th century, and even in a short visit you will see fine buildings from virtually every generation since then, often designed by the most distinguished architects of their day. The city center is lively and compact—one of the special pleasures of Cambridge is that in just a few yards one can pass from the bustle of the shopping streets to the cloistered seclusion of one of the colleges.

As at Oxford, the university is based on colleges, each of which is an autonomous institution with its own distinct character and traditions. Students join an individual college and receive their education from the dons attached to it, who are known as "fellows." Each college is built around a series of "courts," or quadrangles. As students and fellows live in these courts, access is often restricted (especially during examination weeks in early summer). Visitors are not normally allowed into college buildings other than chapels and halls (dining rooms).

**King's College** is possibly the best known of all the colleges. Its chapel is a masterpiece of late Gothic architecture (1446), with a great fan-vaulted roof supported only by a tracery of soaring side columns. Behind the altar hangs Rubens's painting *The Adoration of the Magi.* Every Christmas Eve the college choir sings the Festival of Nine Lessons and Carols, which is broadcast all over the world.

Behind King's are the famous "Backs," the gardens that run down to the River Cam, onto which many of the colleges back. From King's, make your way along the river and through the narrow lanes past **Clare College** and **Trinity Hall** to **Trinity,** the largest college, straddling the river. It has a handsome 17th-century Great Court and a library by Christopher Wren. The massive gatehouse houses "Great Tom," a large clock that strikes each hour with high and low notes. Prince Charles was an undergraduate here in the late 1960s. Beyond Trinity lies **St. John's,** the second largest college.

Going in the other direction along the Backs from King's, you come to **Queen's College,** where Isaac Newton's **Mathematical Bridge** crosses the river. This arched wooden structure was originally held together by gravitational force; when they took it apart to see how Newton did it, they could not reconstruct it without using nails. In from the river, on Trumpington Street, stands **Pembroke College,** with some 14th-century buildings and a chapel by Wren, and **Peterhouse,** the oldest college. Beyond this is the **Fitzwilliam Museum,** which contains outstanding collections of art (including paintings by Constable) and antiquities (especially from ancient Egypt). *Trumpington St., tel. 01223/332–900. Admission free. Open Tues.– Fri., Lower galleries 10–2, Upper galleries 2–5, Sat. both galleries 10–5, Sun. both galleries 2:15–5; closed Good Friday and Christmas–Jan. 1.*

If you've time, hire a punt at **Silver Street Bridge** or at **Mill Lane.** You can go along the Backs past St. John's or upstream to **Grantchester,** the pretty village made famous by the poet Rupert Brooke. On a sunny day, there's no better way of absorbing Cambridge's unique atmosphere—somehow you will seem to have all the time in the world.

**Time Out** The coffee shop in the **Fitzwilliam Museum** is an excellent place for a pastry or a light lunch, as is **Henry's Café Bar** in Quayside. **The Pickerel** (30 Magdalene St., by the bridge) is a pleasant pub with a small courtyard.

# Oxford

**Getting There** By **train** from Paddington station; journey time 55 minutes; trains run hourly. By **coach** from Victoria Coach Station (several companies operate services); journey time 1 hour 40 minutes; buses every 20 minutes.

**Tourist Information** **Oxford Information Centre** is in St. Aldate's, opposite the Town Hall, tel. 01865/726–871.

**Exploring** Oxford is a place for strollers. The surest way of absorbing its unique blend of history and scholarliness is to wander around the tiny alleyways that link the honey-colored stone buildings topped by "dreaming" spires, exploring the colleges where the undergraduates live and work. Like Cambridge, Oxford University is not a single body but a collection of 35 independent colleges; most are open to visitors, including many magnificent chapels and dining halls, though the times, displayed at the entrance lodges, vary. **Magdalen College** (pronounced "Maudlin") is one of the most impressive, with 500-year-old cloisters and lawns leading down to the River Cherwell. **St. Edmund Hall** has one of the smallest and most picturesque quadrangles, with an old well in the center. **Christ Church** has the largest, known as Tom Quad; portraits of former pupils, including John Wesley, William Penn, and no less than 14 prime ministers, hang in the impressive dining hall. The doors between the inner and outer quadrangles of **Balliol College** still bear the scorch marks from the flames that burned Archbishop Cranmer and Bishops Latimer and Ridley at the stake in 1555 for their Protestant beliefs.

The **Oxford Story** is a multimedia presentation of the university's 800-year history, in which visitors travel through depictions of college life. *6 Broad St., tel. 01865/728–822. Admission: £4.50 adults, £3.95 senior citizens and students, £3.25 children. Open Apr.–June,*

*Sept., and Oct., daily 9:30–5; July and Aug., daily 9–6:30; Nov.–Mar., daily 10–4.*

Two other places not to be missed are the **Sheldonian Theatre** and the **Ashmolean Museum.** The Sheldonian was Christopher Wren's first building, which he designed like a semi-circular Roman amphitheater; graduation ceremonies are held here. The Ashmolean, Britain's oldest public museum, holds priceless collections of Egyptian, Greek, and Roman artifacts, Michelangelo drawings, and European silverware. *Sheldonian Theatre, Broad St., tel. 01865/277–299. Small admission charge. Open Mon.–Sat. 10–12:45, 2–4:45; closes at 3:45 Dec.–Feb. Ashmolean, Beaumont St., tel. 01865/278–000. Admission free. Open Tues.–Sat. 10–4, Sun. 2–4, bank holiday Mons. 2–5; closed Mon. and some holidays.*

For a relaxing walk, make for the banks of the Cherwell, either through the University Parks area or through Magdalen College to Addison's Walk, and watch the undergraduates idly punting a summer's afternoon away. Or hire a punt yourself—but be prepared, it's more difficult than it looks!

**Time Out** The **Queen's Lane Coffee House** on High Street prepares inexpensive snacks and is popular with undergraduates. The **Eagle and Child** is a historic pub in St. Giles; a group of writers called the Inklings, including C. S. Lewis and J. R. R. Tolkien, used to meet here.

# Stratford-upon-Avon

**Getting There** The **train service** from Paddington Station (tel. 0171/262–6767 for times) is poor and usually involves at least one change, at Leamington Spa. But there is a direct train from London each morning and two direct trains back from Stratford each afternoon; journey time is 2 hours 20 minutes. Or you can go by **National Express coach** (tel. 0171/730–0202) from Victoria Coach Station; journey time is 2 hours 20 minutes, and there are three coaches daily. The fastest way to get there is a **combined train-bus ticket:** Take the train from Euston Station and switch to a Guide Friday bus at Coventry. The trip takes 2 hours, and there are four departures daily (tel. 0171/387–7070 for information).

**Tourist Information** **Stratford Tourist Information Centre** is at Bridge Foot, by the bridge, tel. 01789/293–127.

**Exploring** It goes without saying that Stratford is a must for Shakespeare enthusiasts. But even without its most famous son, the town would be worth visiting. Its timbered buildings show how prosperous it was in the 16th century, when it was a thriving craft and trading center. There are also attractive 18th-century buildings.

There are four main Shakespearean places of interest. The **Shakespeare Centre** and **Shakespeare's Birthplace** on Henley Street contain the costumes used in the BBC's dramatization of the plays and an exhibition of his life and work. **Anne Hathaway's Cottage** is the early home of the playwright's wife, in Shottery, on the edge of town; and in **Holy Trinity Church** Shakespeare, his wife, and several of their family are buried. *Shakespeare's Birthplace, Henry St., tel. 01789/204–016. Combined admission for all 5 Shakespeare Birthplace Trust properties: £7.50 adults, £7 senior citizens and students, £3.50 children, or individual tickets £2.60 adults, £1.20 children. Open Mar.–Oct., Mon.–Sat. 9–5:30, Sun. 10–5:30; Nov.–*

*Feb., Mon.–Sat. 9:30–4, Sun. 10:30–4; closed Dec. 24–26, New Year and Good Friday mornings.*

Two very different attractions reveal something of the times in which Shakespeare lived. ***World of Shakespeare*** is a lavish spectacle using modern multimedia techniques to describe Queen Elizabeth's royal progress from London to Kenilworth Castle in 1575. A complete contrast is **Hall's Croft,** a fine Tudor town house that was the home of Shakespeare's daughter Susanna and her doctor husband. It has contemporary furniture, and the doctor's dispensary and consulting room can also be seen. *World of Shakespeare, 13 Waterside, tel. 01789/269–190. Admission: £3.50 adults, £2.50 students, children, and senior citizens, £8 family (2 adults and 2 children). Open daily 9:30–5; closed Dec. 25. Hall's Croft, Old Town, tel. 01789/292–107. Admission: £1.80 adults, 80p children. Open Mar.–Oct., Mon.–Sat. 9:30–5, Sun. 10:30–5; Nov.–Feb., Mon.–Sat. 10:30–4, Sun. 1:30–4.*

The **Royal Shakespeare Theatre** (Stratford-upon-Avon, CV37 6BB, tel. 01789/295–623) occupies a perfect position on the banks of the Avon. Try to take in a performance if you can. The company (always referred to as the RSC) gives several Shakespeare plays each season, between March and January. Apart from its main auditorium, the RSC has an exciting small theater, the **Swan,** based on the original Elizabethan Globe. Its construction was funded by an Anglophile American millionaire, Frederick Koch. It's best to book well in advance, but day-of-performance tickets are always available, and it is also worth asking if there are any returns. Programs are available in February from the Royal Shakespeare Theatre.

**Time Out**  **Mistress Quickly** in Henley Street serves light refreshments and meals throughout the day; an unusual feature is the jigsaw tree sculpture. **The Black Swan**—better known locally as the Dirty Duck—is a riverside pub serving good ales and bar meals. The **Theatre Cafeteria** is open all day and provides a good snack immediately after a performance. The **Vintner Wine Bar** on Sheep Street serves large portions of excellent hot dishes, and a selection of wines you can wash them down with.

# Windsor

**Getting There**  By **train** either from Waterloo direct to Windsor and Eton Riverside or from Paddington Station to Windsor Central, changing at Reading. Journey time 45 minutes from Paddington, 50 minutes from Waterloo Station; 2 trains per hour on each route. By **Green Line bus** (tel. 01737/242–411) from Eccleston Bridge, behind Victoria train station, *not* from Victoria Coach Station. Make sure you catch the fast direct service, which takes 45 minutes and runs hourly; the stopping services take up to 1 hour 15 minutes.

**Tourist**  The **Windsor Tourist Information Centre** is in Central Station, tel.
**Information**  01753/852–010.

**Exploring**  Windsor has been a royal citadel since the days of William the Conqueror, who built a timber stockade here on a mound overlooking the River Thames soon after his victory in 1066. Later kings added stone towers, but it was Edward III in the 1300s who transformed the old castle, building the Norman gateway, the great round tower, and new state apartments. Thereafter the castle gradually grew in complexity and grandeur, as subsequent monarchs added new buildings or improved existing ones according to their tastes and their finances. Charles II restored the state apartments in the 1600s, and in the 1820s George IV, that most extravagant of kings with a mania for building, converted what was still essentially a medieval castle into the royal palace the visitor sees today.

Windsor remains a favorite spot of the royal family. The queen and Prince Philip spend most weekends here, often joined by family and friends. The state apartments are also used from time to time to entertain visiting heads of state. The entire castle is closed when the queen is in residence, but a large part—though not the royal family's private apartments—is open the rest of the time.

These are some of the highlights of the castle: **St. George's Chapel,** more than 230 feet long with two tiers of great windows and hundreds of gargoyles, buttresses, and pinnacles, is one of the noblest buildings in England. Inside, above the choir stalls, hang the banners, swords, and helmets of the Knights of the Order of the Garter, the senior order of chivalry. The many monarchs buried in the Chapel include Henry VIII and George VI, father of the present queen. The **State Apartments** indicate the magnificence of the queen's art collection; here hang paintings by Rubens, Van Dyck, and Holbein; drawings by da Vinci; and Gobelin tapestries, among many other treasures. There are magnificent views across to Windsor Great Park, the remains of a former royal hunting forest. Make time to view **Queen Mary's Dolls' House,** complete with electricity, running water, and miniature books on the library shelves. The dollhouse was designed by Sir Edward Lutyens, who planned New Delhi and many gardens (with the well-known gardener Gertrude Jekyll).

The terrible fire of November 1992, which started in the queen's private chapel, totally gutted some of the State Apartments. A swift rescue effort meant that, miraculously, hardly any works of art were lost. However, parts of the castle will remain closed while repairs and rebuilding are in progress—probably at least until the year 2000. Admission charges have recently been standardized, with one charge now for all areas of the castle—a reform that saves the visitor about £1. *Windsor Castle, tel. 01753/868–286. Admission: £8 adults, £5.50 senior citizens, £4 children under 17. Call 01753/831–118 for opening times.*

A short walk over the river brings you to **Eton,** Windsor's equally historic neighbor, and home of the famous public school. (In Britain, so-called "public" schools are private and charge for tuition.) Classes still take place in the distinctive redbrick Tudor-style buildings; the oldest buildings are grouped around a quadrangle called School Yard. The **Museum of Eton Life** has displays on the school's history, and a guided tour is also available. *Brewhouse Yard, tel. 01753/671–177. Admission: £2.20 adults, £1.50 children under 16. Open daily during term 2–4:30, 10:30–4:30 on school vacations; closed 1st Sun. in Oct.–Apr. 1. Guided tours daily at 2:15 and 3:15; charge £3.20 adults, £2.70 children under 16, including admission to museum.*

# Index

*The only guide to explore a
Disney World® you've never seen before:*

# The one for grown-ups.

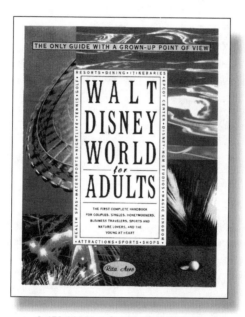

0-679-02490-5 $14.00 ($18.50 Can)

This is the only guide written specifically for the millions of adults who visit Walt Disney World® each year <u>without</u> kids. Upscale, sophisticated, packed full of facts and maps, *Walt Disney World® for Adults* provides up-to-date information on hotels, restaurants, sports facilities, and health clubs, as well as unique itineraries for adults. With *Walt Disney World® for Adults* in hand, you'll get the most out of one of the world's most fascinating, most complex playgrounds.

At bookstores everywhere, or call **1-800-533-6478**.

# Fodor's Travel Guides

*Available at bookstores everywhere, or call 1–800–533–6478, 24 hours a day.*

## U.S. Guides

Alaska

Arizona

Boston

California

Cape Cod, Martha's Vineyard, Nantucket

The Carolinas & the Georgia Coast

Chicago

Colorado

Florida

Hawaii

Las Vegas, Reno, Tahoe

Los Angeles

Maine, Vermont, New Hampshire

Maui

Miami & the Keys

New England

New Orleans

New York City

Pacific North Coast

Philadelphia & the Pennsylvania Dutch Country

The Rockies

San Diego

San Francisco

Santa Fe, Taos, Albuquerque

Seattle & Vancouver

The South

The U.S. & British Virgin Islands

USA

The Upper Great Lakes Region

Virginia & Maryland

Waikiki

Walt Disney World and the Orlando Area

Washington, D.C.

## Foreign Guides

Acapulco, Ixtapa, Zihuatanejo

Australia & New Zealand

Austria

The Bahamas

Baja & Mexico's Pacific Coast Resorts

Barbados

Berlin

Bermuda

Brittany & Normandy

Budapest

Canada

Cancún, Cozumel, Yucatán Peninsula

Caribbean

China

Costa Rica, Belize, Guatemala

The Czech Republic & Slovakia

Eastern Europe

Egypt

Euro Disney

Europe

Florence, Tuscany & Umbria

France

Germany

Great Britain

Greece

Hong Kong

India

Ireland

Israel

Italy

Japan

Kenya & Tanzania

Korea

London

Madrid & Barcelona

Mexico

Montréal & Québec City

Morocco

Moscow & St. Petersburg

The Netherlands, Belgium & Luxembourg

New Zealand

Norway

Nova Scotia, Prince Edward Island & New Brunswick

Paris

Portugal

Provence & the Riviera

Rome

Russia & the Baltic Countries

Scandinavia

Scotland

Singapore

South America

Southeast Asia

Spain

Sweden

Switzerland

Thailand

Tokyo

Toronto

Turkey

Vienna & the Danube Valley

## Special Series

**Fodor's Affordables**

Caribbean

Europe

Florida

France

Germany

Great Britain

Italy

London

Paris

**Fodor's Bed & Breakfast and Country Inns Guides**

America's Best B&Bs

California

Canada's Great Country Inns

Cottages, B&Bs and Country Inns of England and Wales

Mid-Atlantic Region

New England

The Pacific Northwest

The South

The Southwest

The Upper Great Lakes Region

**The Berkeley Guides**

California

Central America

Eastern Europe

Europe

France

Germany & Austria

Great Britain & Ireland

Italy

London

Mexico

Pacific Northwest & Alaska

Paris

San Francisco

**Fodor's Exploring Guides**

Australia

Boston & New England

Britain

California

The Caribbean

Florence & Tuscany

Florida

France

Germany

Ireland

Italy

London

Mexico

New York City

Paris

Prague

Rome

Scotland

Singapore & Malaysia

Spain

Thailand

Turkey

**Fodor's Flashmaps**

Boston

New York

Washington, D.C.

**Fodor's Pocket Guides**

Acapulco

Bahamas

Barbados

Jamaica

London

New York City

Paris

Puerto Rico

San Francisco

Washington, D.C.

**Fodor's Sports**

Cycling

Golf Digest's Best Places to Play

Hiking

The Insider's Guide to the Best Canadian Skiing

Running

Sailing

Skiing in the USA & Canada

USA Today's Complete Four Sports Stadium Guide

**Fodor's Three-In-Ones (guidebook, language cassette, and phrase book)**

France

Germany

Italy

Mexico

Spain

**Fodor's Special-Interest Guides**

Complete Guide to America's National Parks

Condé Nast Traveler Caribbean Resort and Cruise Ship Finder

Cruises and Ports of Call

Euro Disney

France by Train

Halliday's New England Food Explorer

Healthy Escapes

Italy by Train

London Companion

Shadow Traffic's New York Shortcuts and Traffic Tips

Sunday in New York

Sunday in San Francisco

Touring Europe

Touring USA: Eastern Edition

Walt Disney World and the Orlando Area

Walt Disney World for Adults

**Fodor's Vacation Planners**

Great American Learning Vacations

Great American Sports & Adventure Vacations

Great American Vacations

Great American Vacations for Travelers with Disabilities

National Parks and Seashores of the East

National Parks of the West

**The Wall Street Journal Guides to Business Travel**

# At last — a guide for Americans with disabilities that makes traveling a delight

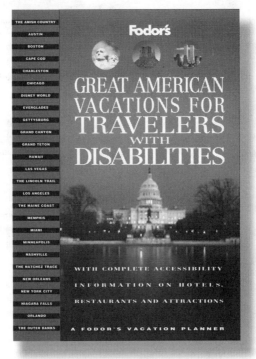

0-679-02591-X $18.00 ($24.00 Can)

This is the first and only complete guide to great American vacations for the 35 million North Americans with disabilities, as well as for those who care for them or for aging parents and relatives. Provides:

- Essential trip-planning information for travelers with mobility, vision, and hearing impairments
- Specific details on a huge array of facilities, along with solid descriptions of attractions, hotels, restaurants, and other destinations
- Up-to-date information on ISA-designated parking, level entranceways, and accessibility to pools, lounges, and bathrooms

 At bookstores everywhere, or call **1-800-533-6478**

# AT LAST

YOUR OWN PERSONALIZED LIST
OF WHAT'S GOING ON IN THE
CITIES YOU'RE VISITING.

KEYED TO THE DAYS WHEN
YOU'LL BE THERE, CUSTOMIZED
FOR YOUR INTERESTS,
AND SENT TO YOU BEFORE YOU
LEAVE HOME.

## GET THE INSIDER'S
## PERSPECTIVE. . .

UP-TO-THE-MINUTE
ACCURATE
EASY TO ORDER
DELIVERED WHEN YOU NEED IT

# Fodor's WORLDVIEW
## TRAVEL UPDATE

## Now there is a revolutionary way to get customized, time-sensitive travel information just before your trip.

Now you can obtain detailed information about what's going on in each city you'll be visiting <u>before</u> you leave home—up-to-the-minute, objective information about the events and activities that interest you most.

**Your Itinerary:**
Customized reports available for 160 destinations

Travel Updates contain the kind of time-sensitive insider information you can get only from local contacts – or from city magazines and newspapers once you arrive. But now you can have the same information before you leave for your trip.

The choice is yours: current art exhibits, theater, music festivals and special concerts, sporting events, antiques and flower shows, shopping, fitness, and more.

The information comes from hundreds of correspondents and thousands of sources worldwide. Updated continuously, it's like having your own personal concierge or friend in the city.

You specify the cities and when you'll be there. We'll do the rest — personalizing the information for you the way no guidebook can.

It's the perfect extension to your Fodor's guide and the best way to make the most of your valuable travel time.

**Use Order Form on back or call 1-800-799-9609**

to
99
**Regen**
The ar
in this
domain o
tion as Joe
worthwhile.
the performan
Tickets are usu
venue.    Alternat
mances are cancel
given.  For more info
Open-Air Theatre, Inn
NW1 4NP Open Air T
Tel: 935-5756. Ends: 9-11
**International Air Tattoo**
Held biennially, the world
military air display :
d e m o s t r a -
tions, mili
band

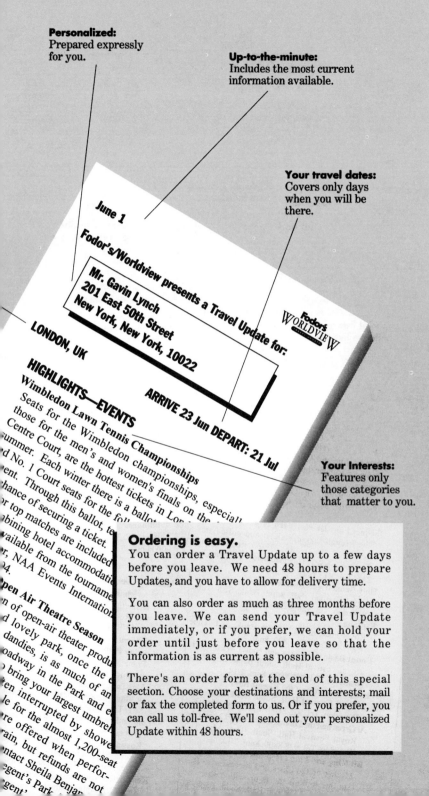

**Personalized:**
Prepared expressly
for you.

**Up-to-the-minute:**
Includes the most current
information available.

**Your travel dates:**
Covers only days
when you will be
there.

June 1

Fodor's/Worldview presents a Travel Update for:

Mr. Gavin Lynch
201 East 50th Street
New York, New York, 10022

Fodor's
WORLDVIEW

LONDON, UK

ARRIVE 23 Jun DEPART: 21 Jul

**HIGHLIGHTS—EVENTS**

**Wimbledon Lawn Tennis Championships**
Seats for the Wimbledon championships, especiall
those for the men's and women's finals on the
Centre Court, are the hottest tickets in Lon
summer. Each winter there is a ballo
d No. 1 Court seats for the fol
ent. Through this ballot, t
hance of securing a ticket.
or top matches are included
bining hotel accommodatio
vailable from the tourname
r, NAA Events Internation
4.

**pen Air Theatre Season**
n of open-air theater produ
d lovely park, once the
dandies, is as much of an
oadway in the Park and e
o bring your largest umbre
en interrupted by showe
le for the almost 1,200-seat
re offered when perfor-
ain, but refunds are not
ntact Sheila Benja
egent's Park
gent'

**Your Interests:**
Features only
those categories
that matter to you.

### Ordering is easy.
You can order a Travel Update up to a few days
before you leave. We need 48 hours to prepare
Updates, and you have to allow for delivery time.

You can also order as much as three months before
you leave. We can send your Travel Update
immediately, or if you prefer, we can hold your
order until just before you leave so that the
information is as current as possible.

There's an order form at the end of this special
section. Choose your destinations and interests; mail
or fax the completed form to us. Or if you prefer, you
can call us toll-free. We'll send out your personalized
Update within 48 hours.

**Special concerts—
who's performing
what and where**

**One-of-a-kind,
one-time-only events**

**Special interest,
in-depth listings**

## Children — Events

**Angel Canal Festival**

The festivities include a children's funfa
entertainers, a boat rally and displays on th
water. Regent's Canal. Islington. N1. Tub
Angel. Tel: 267 9100. 11:30am-5:30pm. 7/04

**Blackheath Summer Kite Festival**

Stunt kite displays with parachuting tedd
bears and trade stands. Free admission. SE
BR: Blackheath. 10am. 6/27.

**Megabugs**

Children will delight in this infestation o
giant robotic insects, including a prayin
mantis 60 times life size. Mon-Sat 10am
6pm; Sun 11am-6pm. Admission 4.5
pounds. Natural History Museum, Cromwe
Road. SW7. Tube: South Kensington. Te
938 9123. Ends 10/01.

**Childminders**

This establishment employs only women
providing nurses and qualified nannies to

## Music — Jazz & Blues

**Tito Puente's Golden Men of Latin Jazz**

The father of mambo and Cuban rumba king
comes to town. Royal Festival Hall. South Bank.
SE1. Tube: Waterloo. Tel: 928 8800. 8pm. 7/15.

**Georgie Fame and The New York Band**

Riding a popular tide with his latest album, the
smoky-voiced Fame and his keyboard are on a
tour yet again. The Grand. Clapham Junction.
SW11. BR: Clapham Junction. Tel: 738 9000.
7:30pm. 7/07.

**Jacques Loussier Play Bach Trio**

The French jazz classicist and colleagues.
Kenwood Lakeside. Hampstead Lane.
Kenwood. NW3. Tube: Golders Green, then bus
210. Tel: 413 1443. 7pm. 7/10.

**Tony Bennett and Ronnie Scott**

Royal Festival Hall. South Bank. SE1. Tube:
Waterloo. Tel: 928 8800. 8pm. 7/11.

**Santana**

Royal Festival Hall. South Bank. SE1. Tube
Waterloo. Tel: 928 8800. 8pm. 7/12.

**Count Basie Orchestra and Nancy Wilson Trio**

Royal Festival Hall. South Bank. SE1. Tube
Waterloo. Tel: 928 8800. 8pm. 7/14.

**King Pleasure and the Biscuit Boys**

Royal Festival Hall. South Bank. SE1. Tube
Waterloo. Tel: 928 8800. 6:30 and 9pm. 7/16.

**Al Green and the London Community Gospel Choir**

Royal Festival Hall. South Bank. SE1. Tube
Waterloo. Tel: 928 8800. 8pm. 7/13.

**BB King and Linda Hopkins**

Mother of the blues and successor to Bessi
Smith, Hopkins meets up with "Blues Boy
al Festival Hall. South Bank. SE

## Music — Classical

**Marylebone Sinfonia**

Kenneth Gowen conducts music by P
and Rossini. Queen Elizabeth Hall.
Bank. SE1. Tube: Waterloo. Tel: 928
7:45pm. 7/16.

**London Philharmonic**

Franz Welser-Moest and George Be
conduct selections by Alexander
Messiaen, and some of Benjamin's ow
positions. Queen Elizabeth Hall. Sout
SE1. Tube: Waterloo. Tel: 928 8800.

**London Pro Arte Orchestra and Fores**

Murray Stewart conducts select
Rossini, Haydn and Jonathan Willcoc
Queen Elizabeth Hall. South Bar
Tube: Waterloo. Tel: 928 8800. 7:45p

**Kensington Symphony Orchestra**

Russell Keable conducts Dvorak'

# Here's what you get . . .

## Detailed information about what's going on — precisely when you'll be there.

**Show openings during your visit**

**Handy pocket-size booklet**

**Reviews by local critics**

**Fodor's WORLDVIEW**
TRAVEL UPDATE

London, England
Arriving: June 23
Departing: July 21

# Interest Categories

For <u>your</u> personalized Travel Update, choose the categories you're most interested in from this list. Every Travel Update automatically provides you with *Event Highlights* - the best of what's happening during the dates of your trip.

| | | |
|---|---|---|
| 1. | **Business Services** | Fax & Overnight Mail, Computer Rentals, Photocopying, Protocol, Secretarial, Messenger, Translation Services |

**Dining**

| | | |
|---|---|---|
| 2. | **All Day Dining** | Breakfast & Brunch, Cafes & Tea Rooms, Late-Night Dining |
| 3. | **Local Cuisine** | In Every Price Range—from Budget Restaurants to the Special Splurge |
| 4. | **European Cuisine** | Continental, French, Italian |
| 5. | **Asian Cuisine** | Chinese, Far Eastern, Japanese, Other |
| 6. | **Americas Cuisine** | American, Mexican & Latin |
| 7. | **Nightlife** | Bars, Dance Clubs, Casinos, Comedy Clubs, Ethnic, Pubs & Beer Halls |
| 8. | **Entertainment** | Theater—Comedy, Drama, English Language, Musicals, Dance, Ticket Agencies |
| 9. | **Music** | Country/Western/Folk, Classical, Traditional & Ethnic, Opera, Jazz & Blues, Pop, Rock |
| 10. | **Children's Activities** | Events, Attractions |
| 11. | **Tours** | Local Tours, Day Trips, Overnight Excursions, Cruises |
| 12. | **Exhibitions, Festivals & Shows** | Antiques & Flower, History & Cultural, Art Exhibitions, Fairs & Craft Shows, Music & Art Festivals |
| 13. | **Shopping** | Districts & Malls, Markets, Regional Specialities |
| 14. | **Fitness** | Bicycling, Health Clubs, Hiking, Jogging |
| 15. | **Recreational Sports** | Boating/Sailing, Fishing, Golf, Ice Skating, Skiing, Snorkeling/Scuba, Swimming, Tennis & Racquet |
| 16. | **Spectator Sports** | Auto Racing, Baseball, Basketball, Boating & Sailing, Football, Golf, Horse Racing, Ice Hockey, Rugby, Soccer, Tennis, Track & Field, Other Sports |

Please note that interest category content will vary by season, destination, and length of stay.

# Destinations

The Fodor's/Worldview Travel Update covers more than 160 destinations worldwide. Choose the destinations that match your itinerary from this list. (Choose bulleted destinations only.)

## Europe
- Amsterdam
- Athens
- Barcelona
- Berlin
- Brussels
- Budapest
- Copenhagen
- Dublin
- Edinburgh
- Florence
- Frankfurt
- French Riviera
- Geneva
- Glasgow
- Istanbul
- Lausanne
- Lisbon
- London
- Madrid
- Milan
- Moscow
- Munich
- Oslo
- Paris
- Prague
- Provence
- Rome
- Salzburg
* Seville
- St. Petersburg
- Stockholm
- Venice
- Vienna
- Zurich

## United States (Mainland)
- Albuquerque
- Atlanta
- Atlantic City
- Baltimore
- Boston
* Branson, MO
* Charleston, SC
- Chicago
- Cincinnati
- Cleveland
- Dallas/Ft. Worth
- Denver
- Detroit
- Houston
* Indianapolis
- Kansas City
- Las Vegas
- Los Angeles
- Memphis

- Miami
- Milwaukee
- Minneapolis/ St. Paul
* Nashville
- New Orleans
- New York City
- Orlando
- Palm Springs
- Philadelphia
- Phoenix
- Pittsburgh
- Portland
* Reno/ Lake Tahoe
- St. Louis
- Salt Lake City
- San Antonio
- San Diego
- San Francisco
* Santa Fe
- Seattle
- Tampa
- Washington, DC

## Alaska
- Alaskan Destinations

## Hawaii
- Honolulu
- Island of Hawaii
- Kauai
- Maui

## Canada
- Quebec City
- Montreal
- Ottawa
- Toronto
- Vancouver

## Bahamas
- Abaco
- Eleuthera/ Harbour Island
- Exuma
- Freeport
- Nassau & Paradise Island

## Bermuda
- Bermuda Countryside
- Hamilton

## British Leeward Islands
- Anguilla

- Antigua & Barbuda
- St. Kitts & Nevis

## British Virgin Islands
- Tortola & Virgin Gorda

## British Windward Islands
- Barbados
- Dominica
- Grenada
- St. Lucia
- St. Vincent
- Trinidad & Tobago

## Cayman Islands
- The Caymans

## Dominican Republic
- Santo Domingo

## Dutch Leeward Islands
- Aruba
- Bonaire
- Curacao

## Dutch Windward Island
- St. Maarten/ St. Martin

## French West Indies
- Guadeloupe
- Martinique
- St. Barthelemy

## Jamaica
- Kingston
- Montego Bay
- Negril
- Ocho Rios

## Puerto Rico
- Ponce
- San Juan

## Turks & Caicos
- Grand Turk/ Providenciales

## U.S. Virgin Islands
- St. Croix
- St. John
- St. Thomas

## Mexico
- Acapulco
- Cancun & Isla Mujeres
- Cozumel
- Guadalajara
- Ixtapa & Zihuatanejo
- Los Cabos
- Mazatlan
- Mexico City
- Monterrey
- Oaxaca
- Puerto Vallarta

## South/Central America
* Buenos Aires
* Caracas
* Rio de Janeiro
* San Jose, Costa Rica
* Sao Paulo

## Middle East
* Jerusalem

## Australia & New Zealand
- Auckland
- Melbourne
* South Island
- Sydney

## China
- Beijing
- Guangzhou
- Shanghai

## Japan
- Kyoto
- Nagoya
- Osaka
- Tokyo
- Yokohama

## Pacific Rim/Other
* Bali
- Bangkok
- Hong Kong & Macau
- Manila
- Seoul
- Singapore
- Taipei

* Destinations available by 1/1/95

## Fodor's WORLDVIEW TRAVEL UPDATE Order Form

**THIS TRAVEL UPDATE IS FOR (Please print):**

Name

Address

| City | State | Country | ZIP |
|------|-------|---------|-----|

Tel # (        )        -              Fax # (        )        -

Title of this Fodor's guide:

Store and location where guide was purchased:

**INDICATE YOUR DESTINATIONS/DATES:** You can order up to three (3) destinations from the previous page. Fill in your arrival and departure dates for each destination. **Your Travel Update itinerary (all destinations selected) cannot exceed 30 days from beginning to end.**

|  |  | | Month | Day | | Month | Day |
|--|--|--|-------|-----|--|-------|-----|
| (Sample) | LONDON | From: | 6 | 21 | To: | 6 | 30 |
| 1 |  | From: | / | | To: | / | |
| 2 |  | From: | / | | To: | / | |
| 3 |  | From: | / | | To: | / | |

**CHOOSE YOUR INTERESTS:** Select up to eight (8) categories from the list of interest categories shown on the previous page and circle the numbers below:

**1   2   3   4   5   6   7   8   9   10   11   12   13   14   15   16**

**CHOOSE WHEN YOU WANT YOUR TRAVEL UPDATE DELIVERED (Check one):**
❑ Please send my Travel Update immediately.
❑ Please hold my order until a few weeks before my trip to include the most up-to-date information.
*Completed orders will be sent within 48 hours. Allow 7-10 days for U.S. mail delivery.*

**ADD UP YOUR ORDER HERE. *SPECIAL OFFER FOR FODOR'S PURCHASERS ONLY!***

|  | Suggested Retail Price | Your Price | This Order |
|--|------------------------|------------|------------|
| First destination ordered | $ 9.95 | $ 7.95 | $ 7.95 |
| Second destination (if applicable) | $ 6.95 | $ 4.95 | + |
| Third destination (if applicable) | $ 6.95 | $ 4.95 | + |

**DELIVERY CHARGE (Check one and enter amount below)**

|  | Within U.S. & Canada | Outside U.S. & Canada |
|--|----------------------|------------------------|
| First Class Mail | ❑ $2.50 | ❑ $5.00 |
| FAX | ❑ $5.00 | ❑ $10.00 |
| Priority Delivery | ❑ $15.00 | ❑ $27.00 |

**ENTER DELIVERY CHARGE FROM ABOVE:** +

**TOTAL: $**

**METHOD OF PAYMENT IN U.S. FUNDS ONLY (Check one):**
❑ AmEx   ❑ MC   ❑ Visa   ❑ Discover   ❑ Personal Check (U. S. & Canada only)
❑ Money Order/ International Money Order
   *Make check or money order payable to: Fodor's Worldview Travel Update*

Credit Card —/—/—/—/—/—/—/—/—/—/—/—/—/—/—/ **Expiration Date:___/___**

**Authorized Signature**

**SEND THIS COMPLETED FORM WITH PAYMENT TO:**
Fodor's Worldview Travel Update, 114 Sansome Street, Suite 700, San Francisco, CA 94104

**OR CALL OR FAX US 24-HOURS A DAY**
Telephone **1-800-799-9609** • Fax **1-800-799-9619** (From within the U.S. & Canada)
(Outside the U.S. & Canada: Telephone 415-616-9988 • Fax 415-616-9989)

(Please have this guide in front of you when you call so we can verify purchase.)
Code: FTG                                                    Offer valid until 12/31/95.